The writings of Lucius Annaeus Seneca, tutor and political advisor to the young emperor Nero, are among our most important sources for Stoic philosophy. This volume offers, in clear and forceful contemporary translations, four of Seneca's most interesting 'Moral Essays': *On Anger, On Mercy, On the Private Life* and the first four books of *On Favours*. They provide an attractive insight into the social and moral outlook of a Stoic thinker at the centre of power in the Roman empire of the mid first century AD. A General Introduction on Seneca's life and work explains the fundamental ideas in the philosophy that informs the essays. Individual introductions place the works in their specific historical and intellectual contexts. Biographical Notes, based on up-to-date scholarship, provide the information necessary for a full understanding of the texts. To assist the student further, section headings have been inserted into the translations to mark the principal transitions in the argument and reveal the organization of these writings.

D1566737

CAMBRIDGE TEXTS IN THE
HISTORY OF POLITICAL THOUGHT

———

SENECA
Moral and Political Essays

CAMBRIDGE TEXTS IN THE
HISTORY OF POLITICAL THOUGHT

Series editors

RAYMOND GEUSS
Reader in Philosophy, University of Cambridge

QUENTIN SKINNER
Regius Professor of Modern History in the University of Cambridge

Cambridge Texts in the History of Political Thought is now firmly established as the major student textbook series in political theory. It aims to make available to students all the most important texts in the history of western political thought, from ancient Greece to the early twentieth century. All the familiar classic texts will be included, but the series seeks at the same time to enlarge the conventional canon by incorporating an extensive range of less well-known works, many of them never before available in a modern English edition. Wherever possible, texts are published in complete and unabridged form, and translations are specially commissioned for the series. Each volume contains a critical introduction together with chronologies, biographical sketches, a guide to further reading and any necessary glossaries and textual apparatus. When completed the series will aim to offer an outline of the entire evolution of western political thought.

For a list of titles published in the series, please see end of book

SENECA

Moral and Political Essays

EDITED AND TRANSLATED BY
JOHN M. COOPER
Professor of Philosophy, Princeton University

AND
J. F. PROCOPÉ

CAMBRIDGE
UNIVERSITY PRESS

CAMBRIDGE UNIVERSITY PRESS
Cambridge, New York, Melbourne, Madrid, Cape Town, Singapore, São Paulo

Cambridge University Press
The Edinburgh Building, Cambridge CB2 8RU, UK

Published in the United States of America by Cambridge University Press, New York

www.cambridge.org
Information on this title: www.cambridge.org/9780521348188

First published 1995
Tenth printing 2007

Printed in the United Kingdom at the University Press, Cambridge

A catalogue record for this publication is available from the British Library

Library of Congress Cataloguing in Publication data
Seneca, Lucius Annaeus, c. 4BC–AD65
[Selections. English. 1995]
Moral and political essays / Seneca: edited and translated by John M. Cooper and
J. F. Procopé.
p. cm. – (Cambridge texts in the history of   political thought)
Includes bibliographical references and index.
Contents: On anger – On mercy – On the private life – On favours.
ISBN 0 521 34291 0. – ISBN 0 521 34818 8 (pbk)
1. Conduct of   life – Early works to 1800. 2. Political ethics – Early works to 1800.
I. Cooper, John M. (John Madison), 1939–   .
II. Procopé, J. F. (John Fredrik), 1941–   . III. Title.   IV. Series.
BJ214.S3E5   1995
188–dc20   94–15708 CIP

ISBN-13 978-0-521-34818-8 paperback

Contents

Editors' Notes

The initial work on this volume was divided as follows. The General Introduction (apart from the pages on 'Style and Composition'), the Special Introductions and the notes to *On the Private Life* and *On Favours* were first drafted by J. M. Cooper. The translations (with the addition of section headings to clarify the course of Seneca's argument), the Biographical Notes and the annotations to *On Anger* and *On Mercy* began as the work of J. F. Procopé. But each author has revised and amplified the work of the other to the point where neither can be held solely responsible, or escape responsibility, for any part of the book.

Numerous debts have to be acknowledged. J. M. Cooper would like to thank Kathleen Much, Alexander Nehamas and J. B. Schneewind. J. F. Procopé would like to thank Robert Coleman, John Crook, Richard Duncan-Jones, Brad Inwood, Caroline Moore, Michael Reeve, Malcolm Schofield and Edward Shils. J. M. Cooper would also like to acknowledge the hospitality of the Center for Advanced Study in the Behavioural Sciences and the financial support, while he was a Fellow there, of the Andrew W. Mellon Foundation.

Note on the text

The manuscript transmission of the works in this volume is varied. For a good summary, see L. D. Reynolds ed., *Texts and Transmission: A Survey of the Latin Classics* (Oxford 1983), pp. 363–9. Our principal manuscript for *On Anger* and the other *Dialogi* is the

Ambrosiana (A), written at Montecassino near Naples between AD 1058 and 1087 and preserved in the Ambrosian Library in Milan; for *On Mercy* and *On Favours* the main text is the *codex Nazarianus* (N) written in north Italy around AD 800 and now in the Vatican Library. The transmission of *On Mercy* has been notably worse than that of the other essays translated here.

Except where stated in the footnotes, our translations of *On Anger* and *On the Private Life* are of the text in *Senecae Dialogi*, ed. L. D. Reynolds (Oxford 1977). Those of *On Mercy* and *On Favours* follow that of C. Hosius' Teubner edition (Leipzig 1914), reprinted by J. W. Basore in his Loeb Classical Library edition of *Seneca: Moral Essays* I (1928) and III (1935), and are indebted further to the Budé editions of F. Préchac (*Sénèque: De la clémence* 3rd edn (Paris 1967), and *Sénèque: Des bienfaits* 3rd edn (Paris 1972)). These modern editions rest on the work of numerous earlier scholars, from Erasmus onwards, some of whose readings and comments are mentioned in our footnotes. For the most part, a variant reading will simply be attributed to its author (e.g. Gronovius, Vahlen, Gertz, Koch, Sonntag, Kronenberg) without further references. Special mention should, however, be made here to three scholars whose work will be cited repeatedly: W. H. Alexander (Seneca's *De Beneficiis Libri VII* (University of California Press, Classical Philology 1950), a monograph which continues the work of two earlier articles, 'Notes on the *De beneficiis* of Seneca' (*Classical Quarterly* 28 (1934) pp. 54 f.) and 'Further Notes on the Text of Seneca's *De beneficiis*' (*Classical Quarterly* 31 (1937) pp. 55–9; J. Calvin ('Calvin's commentary on Seneca's De Clementia', with Introduction, Translation and Notes by F. L. Battles and A. M. Hugo (Leiden 1969)); and J. Lipsius (cited from *L. Annaei Senecae opera quae extant, integris Justi Lipsii, J. Fred. Gronovii, et selectis Variorum Commentariis illustrata* (Amsterdam 1672)).

General introduction

Seneca: life, public career and authorship

Seneca is the principal ancient proponent in Latin of Stoic philosophy. His surviving *Moral Essays*, the more political of which have been selected for this volume, are the most important body of more or less complete Stoic writings to survive from antiquity. He was born Lucius Annaeus Seneca between about 4 and 1 BC in southern Spain, at Corduba (modern Cordoba), a leading provincial centre of Roman culture. His parents had also been born in Spain, though their families were of Italian origin. They belonged to the equestrian order, a section of the Roman upper class that, unlike the senatorial families, had traditionally avoided political careers in favour of commerce and the pursuit of wealth. Seneca's father, likewise named Lucius Annaeus Seneca, had spent much of his adult life in Rome. As a young man he had interested himself in oratory, attending the disputations and rhetorical exercises of the leading declaimers there. Leaving his wife in charge of his estates in Spain, he later returned to Rome to oversee the education and subsequent careers of his three sons. As well as a history of Rome from the civil wars of the mid first century BC down to the 30s AD, which has not survived and may never have been published, the elder Seneca produced reports and commentaries on the performances he had witnessed in the rhetorical schools of Rome as a youth. Written near the end of his life at his sons' request, these have partly survived, as the so-called *Controversiae* and *Suasoriae*.[1]

---

[1] Available in the Loeb Classical Library in translations by M. Winterbottom. For more about the elder Seneca's life, see Griffin, pp. 29–34.

We have little information about the younger Seneca's life until he was well into his thirties. He was brought up and educated in Rome. His father, intending that he, like his older brother Annaeus Novatus, should pursue a political career, put him into contact with the leading practitioners of oratory at Rome. The effects of this training are much in evidence in his *Essays*. Philosophical in subject-matter, they are a product in style and composition of Roman rhetoric. But the younger Seneca also received extensive instruction in philosophy, again at Rome; he never went to Athens to study it. Several times in his *Moral Letters to Lucilius*,[2] written in the last years of his life, he refers with feeling to his early teachers of philosophy and their profound effect upon him: Sotion, a Greek from Alexandria, of uncertain philosophical allegiance; Attalus, a Stoic perhaps from Pergamum in Asia Minor; and Papirius Fabianus, formerly an orator, who had studied in the school of the famous and very Roman philosopher Quintus Sextius.[3] Regrettably, Seneca tells us little about what he heard in their lectures or read under their guidance, but it must have been at this time that he formed his life-long attachment to Stoic philosophy and began to acquire the extensive knowledge of Stoic writings that he was to display in his own works.

Seneca speaks often in the *Letters* of his frail health in youth and later on. He seems to have spent some time, in his twenties or early thirties, recuperating from tuberculosis in Egypt, under the care of his mother's sister (her husband was 'prefect' or administrative head of the Roman military government there). Not till some time after his return from Egypt in the year 31 (when he was between thirty-two and thirty-six years old) did he take firm steps towards the political career his father had intended for him. Thanks to his aunt's influence, he was appointed to his first magistracy, that of quaestor or financial officer, and was enrolled in the Senate, probably under the emperor Tiberius (who died in 37). By the end of the decade he was well known and highly regarded at Rome as an orator. Tiberius' successor, Caligula (emperor from 37 to 41), is reported by Suetonius (*Life of Caligula*

---

[2] See especially *Letters* 100 (on Papirius Fabianus) and 108 (on Sotion and Attalus).
[3] Seneca was deeply impressed by Sextius' writings which were in Greek (we know almost nothing about them), describing him as in effect a Stoic, though he says Sextius himself denied it (*Letter* 64. 2).

53) to have been offended by his successes, so much so that, according to a somewhat improbable story told by the third-century historian Dio Cassius, only Seneca's tubercular condition saved him from a death-sentence. (He was going to die soon anyway, it was said.) We have unfortunately no evidence about Seneca's literary or philosophical work before or at this time: with the sole exception of the *Consolation to Marcia*, all the surviving works seem certainly to date from after Seneca's banishment to Corsica in 41.[4]

In January 41, Caligula was murdered. His uncle Claudius ascended the throne. Later that year, probably in the autumn, Seneca was accused of adultery with one of Caligula's sisters, tried before the Senate in the presence of the emperor, convicted and actually sentenced to death. The emperor spared his life, banishing him instead to the dismal island of Corsica,[5] where he languished for eight years. In 49, Claudius married Caligula's only surviving sister, Agrippina, who promptly arranged to have Seneca recalled and even appointed to a praetorship, the office immediately below that of consul. He was then between fifty and fifty-four years old. According to the historian Tacitus (*Annals* XII 8), Agrippina thought that Seneca's rehabilitation would have popular appeal, on account of his literary eminence. He was already known as an outstanding orator, poet and writer of philosophical treatises.[6]

But Agrippina had other motives. She hoped to insert her twelve-year-old son, the future emperor Nero, into the line of succession above Claudius' own son, Britannicus, who was several years younger. (Her plans came to fruition when, in the following year, Claudius adopted Nero, making him thus his eldest son.) In return

---

[4] The preceding two paragraphs are based, in the main, on the account in Griffin, pp. 34–59 and 397, which may be consulted for details and documentation.

[5] In his *Consolation to his Mother Helvia* (6. 5, 7. 8–9, 9. 1), written to console his mother in her grief for the disgrace and deprivations of his exile, Seneca describes the island as a 'barren and thorny rock' (7. 9), afflicted by a harsh climate and provided neither with rivers nor harbours by the sea.

[6] He seems to have devoted his exile to literary pursuits. He claims as much in his *Consolation to his Mother Helvia*, (1. 2, 20. 1–2). In Corsica, he also published a third consolation, the *Consolation to Polybius* (a disguised petition to be allowed home), as well as writing much, perhaps all, of *On Anger*. It seems reasonable to suppose that his (lost) *Life* of his father was also written then, and that some of his poetry (epigrams, conceivably some of his tragedies) had appeared by the time of his recall. So Tacitus' account of Agrippina's motives has something to be said for it, though he bulk of Seneca's surviving philosophical writings were written after his return from exile.

for her help in arranging his recall, Seneca accepted overall responsibility for Nero's education. Thus began a long and fateful involvement in the imperial household. Seneca's responsibilities as 'tutor' did not include instruction in philosophy: according to Suetonius (*Life of Nero* 52), Agrippina thought this an unsuitable subject for an intended emperor and forbade its inclusion in the curriculum. Even in later years, when the ban no longer applied, Nero found other instructors in philosophy, and did not turn – at least, not formally – to him for tuition. It was as a teacher of rhetoric that Seneca contributed directly to the prince's formal education. But he was also expected to offer moral instruction and general guidance in practical politics, and here his Stoic outlook would come into prominence. It was in this capacity that, shortly after Nero's accession to the throne in 54, Seneca addressed to him a Stoic 'mirror of princes', his *On Mercy*.

Nero became emperor at the age of not quite seventeen. For a number of years, Seneca was his principal adviser behind the scenes, writing his speeches and exercising influence in imperial appointments.[7] He and his ally Burrus, the able and upright prefect of the Pretorian Guard, are given the credit by Tacitus (*Annals* XIII 2 4–5) for the decent restraint and effectiveness of the imperial government in the early years of Nero's reign. But Seneca's functions were not formal or official, and it is very difficult to give any detailed account of how the official acts of the emperor reflected his policies or advice. With the death of Agrippina in 59 (she was murdered on Nero's orders), his influence and that of Burrus declined sharply ; it soon became clear that Nero had relied on them largely in order to resist his mother's attempts at domination. With Agrippina out of the way, his wilfulness, self-indulgence and murderous inclinations came rapidly to the fore. No one was any longer in a position to check him, or even to moderate his excesses. Already in 55, when the influence of Seneca and Burrus was at its height, he had arranged for the thirteen-year-old Britannicus, whom he feared as a threat to his throne, to be poisoned at a family banquet before his very eyes. By the time Burrus himself died in 62, it was clear to Seneca that he had no further useful

---

[7] Seneca himself was suffect consul (a consul appointed for a couple of months to fill out the term of one of the 'ordinary' consuls) in 55 or 56. His brother Annaeus Novatus had received the same honour in the year before.

role to play, and no effective power. He asked for leave to retire. The emperor refused – it would look bad if Seneca distanced himself. But though appearances were kept up, from that time onwards he no longer functioned as Nero's adviser and agent. He absented himself from the city much of the time. Two years later, he renewed his request. Nero granted it, accepting back from him much of the vast wealth which Seneca had amassed in his service. In the following year, however, in 65, Seneca was denounced for involvement in a widely spread plot – his nephew, the poet Lucan, seems in fact to have been one of the principal co-conspirators. Seneca was questioned, and then given the emperor's order to commit suicide, which he did by opening his veins.[8]

The bulk of Seneca's surviving philosophical writings were written after his return from exile in 49,[9] in the period of his association with the imperial household and in the relatively brief retirement (62–5) that followed it. The 124 so-called *Moral Letters to Lucilius* and the seven books of 'Investigations into Nature' (*Naturales Quaestiones*), also addressed to Lucilius,[10] date from this final retirement. Of the texts translated in this volume, *On Favours* had not been completed by then. Against that, *On Anger*, most of it probably written during or even before Seneca's exile, was finished before 52; *On Mercy* was composed in 55 or 56, early in the reign of Nero to whom it is dedicated; while *On the Private Life*, though its date is uncertain, must be later than 48 and is almost certainly

[8] In Tacitus' extended account of Seneca's accusation and death (*Annals* xv 60–4), his manner of dying was clearly modelled on that of Socrates as portrayed by Plato in the *Phaedo*. Seneca even took a supplementary dose of hemlock, but too late for it to have any effect (64. 3). According to Tacitus, Nero had no proof of Seneca's complicity in the plot, and had already attempted to poison him a year earlier (xv 45). A judicious and complete discussion of this and the other ancient evidence for Seneca's final years can be found in Griffin, pp. 66–128.

[9] Many scholars suppose that his tragedies belong to this same time, having mostly been written during the decade of the 50s. Tacitus (*Annals* xiv 52) connects Seneca's writing of tragedies with Nero's interest in the genre. See discussion and references in M. Schanz and C. Hosius, *Geschichte der Römischen Literatur* (Munich, 1935), pt 2, pp. 456–59. Other scholars maintain that the tragedies were largely composed during the Corsican exile, 41–9; see P. Grimal, *Sénèque* (Paris 1981, in the collection *Que sais-je?*), p. 427.

[10] This Lucilius was an old friend of Seneca's, about the same age, of the equestrian order from Pompeii near Naples. He wrote poetry and philosophical prose, while also working in the imperial government in Sicily and elsewhere. See Griffin, p. 91, for details and references.

earlier than 63, the year in which its presumed dedicatee, Serenus, probably died. Works of Stoic philosophical theory, the four texts presented here reflect in places their author's familiarity at the highest level with the politics of imperial Rome. How far this familiarity affected what he has to say in them, his readers must judge for themselves.

Seneca and Stoic philosophy

The Stoic school of philosophy had been founded in Athens, three centuries before Seneca's birth, by Zeno of Citium (335–263 BC). Zeno's teachings were refined and elaborated by his successors, most notably by Chrysippus of Soli (c. 280–207 BC). Indeed, 'Stoicism' was generally understood as the system bequeathed by Chrysippus. Thoroughly absorbed by Seneca, it lies at the heart of the essays in this volume.

Seneca counts as a late, Roman Stoic. Scholars customarily distinguish three principal periods in the history of the school. To the 'Old Stoa' at Athens belongs the original formation of the doctrines of the school and their organization into a teachable, complete system of philosophy, comprising logic, epistemology, theory of nature, ethics and politics. In the third and second centuries BC, these underwent progressive reformulation and defence – first by Chrysippus, then by Diogenes of Babylon (c. 240–152 BC) and his successor Antipater of Tarsus (died before 137 BC) – against attacks by the Academic sceptics, Arcesilaus (316/5–242/1 BC) and Carneades (214/3–129/8 BC). Next, the 'Middle Stoa' (c. 150–50 BC), under Panaetius (c. 185–109 BC) and his pupils Posidonius (c. 135–51/50 BC) and Hecaton (c. 100 BC), with its centres of activity still in Greece (at Athens and Rhodes), produced various innovations. Finally, with Seneca and then Musonius Rufus (c. AD 30–100), Epictetus (c. AD 55–135) and Marcus Aurelius (AD 121–180) (all three of whom, however, wrote in Greek, not Latin), the 'Roman Stoa', addressing Romans within the ambit of Rome itself, offers a somewhat popularized Stoic 'philosophy of life'.

Scholars have sometimes seen departures from scholastic rigour and orthodoxy in the Middle and Roman periods, but these have been much exaggerated. Seneca and the other later authors have not in fact abandoned any essential point of traditional Stoic ethics, psychology, theology or natural philosophy. But they do take up new topics and introduce new focuses of attention. The original Stoic theorists, for example, had spent much effort describing the state of mind and way of life of the perfect, fully 'virtuous' human being, the 'wise man.' Seneca, following the example of Panaetius, asks instead how people who are not fully virtuous and know they are never going to be, but seriously wish to live as well as they possibly can, should organize their lives. Again, instead of writing technical philosophical treatises, contributions to debate on disputed questions with other philosophical experts, he prefers to expound to the intelligent general reader the theory of Stoicism and its application to his – or her[11] – life. Seneca's philosophical works are all oriented to questions of practical ethics; about logic, physical theory, epistemology and metaphysics he has little to say. Even his *Investigations into Nature* regularly stress, in the Prefaces and elsewhere, the moral edification to be derived from their subject. On all fundamental questions, however, especially those of moral philosophy, his starting-point is a firm commitment to the orthodox positions of Zeno and Chrysippus. He develops his own thought with impressive independence, but always on the basis of their philosophical system.

Here a brief account of that system may prove helpful.[12] Following Plato in the *Timaeus*, the Stoics thought that the world, with the earth at its centre and the 'sphere' of the fixed stars at its circumference, is a single living, rational animal.[13] They identified this 'world-animal' with the god of the universe, that is with Zeus (Roman Jupiter). Its body is Zeus's body; its mind, directing its

---

[11] Two of the *Essays* (the *Consolation to Marcia* and the *Consolation to his Mother Helvia*) are in fact addressed to women. At the same time, Seneca was no more concerned than any other ancient writer with 'gender-neutral' language. He always speaks of the 'wise *man*', meaning nothing more specific than 'wise human-being', and he automatically treats moral agents as masculine.

[12] The following is a brief account of the Stoic world-view and ethical theory, presupposed rather than expounded by Seneca in the works included in this volume. See the passages collected in Long–Sedley, Chapters 46–7, 53–5, 57–63. Cicero's *On Ends* III contains a good general treatment of Stoic ethics, philosophy of action and political theory.

[13] For the Stoics, the universe is limited to this single world. The Epicureans, on the other hand, held that ours is only one of infinitely many worlds situated in an infinity of space (Epicurus, *Letter to Herodotus* 45 = Long–Sedley 1A). See *On Favours* IV 19.

movements from within it and maintaining its internal variety and arrangements, is Zeus's mind, a mind perfectly and completely rational, perfectly fitted to govern that body. Everything that happens in the world of nature is caused by his thought and occurs as it does for a good reason, as a necessary part of the on-going life of the divine animate cosmos[14]. Apart from the gods (that is, apart from Zeus himself in his various distinguishable aspects),[15] the only other rational animals are human beings. We are the only individual things on earth which Zeus (or, equivalently, Nature) governs through an autonomous use of our own individual rational capacities. As such we have a special and specially honoured position in the world-order and in Zeus's plans for it. The reasoning power which we share with Zeus gives us a close solidarity, a sense of common purpose with one another and with him.

This thought lies at the heart of Seneca's social thinking in all four of these essays. Like Zeus himself, we have the ability to cause changes in our bodies and in the world around us through our *own* power of thought and decision. It is entirely up to us how we use this power, how – individually and in cooperation with one

---

[14] Stoic theology here creates a difficulty for anyone translating Seneca's Latin into English. For us it is still conventional, when we are not using the articles 'a' or 'the,' to write 'God' as a proper noun with a capital letter, on the tacit assumption, derived from Christianity, that the deity must be a *person*, named 'God.' But the Stoics saw 'god' as a physical *substance*, a kind of fire. They defined 'god' as 'intelligent, designing fire proceeding methodically towards creation of the world' (Long–Sedley 46A); and they understood 'nature', simply another aspect of 'god', in the same terms (Diogenes Laertius VII 156). Now 'fire' is normally a 'mass-noun', like 'gas' or 'water,' written in lower case with or without an article (e.g. 'the hottest element is fire'). That, strictly, is how 'god' or 'nature' in translations of Stoic texts should be written. Unfortunately, the divine Stoic fire has some decidedly personal characteristics. Identified with Zeus, 'father of gods and men' in the Olympian pantheon, it is intelligent; it acts with a purpose and carries out plans; it is frequently given a gender, 'god' being masculine and 'nature' feminine; and it is sometimes directly addressed as a person. There are passages in Seneca (e.g. *On the Private Life* 4 f.; *On Favours* IV 5–8) where the personification becomes so strong as to make the use of capitals well nigh unavoidable. If the readers of our translation find both 'nature' and 'Nature', 'god' and occasionally 'God', the inconsistency, which also occurs with 'fortune', reflects a certain slide in Seneca's own theology. Our readers may usefully ask themselves whether, at any occurrence of the words, there is some point in our choice there of upper or lower case. They might also recall that confusions of divine 'substance' with divine 'persons' were later to cause untold difficulties to Christian theologians.

[15] See Diogenes Laertius. VII 147. Seneca has an eloquent digression on this theme at *On Favours* IV 7 f.

another – we organize our lives, our societies and our cultures. But we derive this power from our endowment with reason, and it is therefore subject to the rules of reason. When we choose what to think on some question or what to do in some situation, there are always better and worse reasons, more and less rational grounds, on which to rest the choice. We are free to prefer bad reasons for believing things. We are free to live in ways that we could not successfully defend on standards of reason common to all. But if we violate the rules of reason in deciding what to think or do we can legitimately be criticized.

We are privileged in another way, as well. Any living thing, be it plant or animal, can grow or fail to grow to maturity in perfect accordance with what is natural for things of its kind. It can then live out its life in the normal, unhindered exercise of its natural capacities, or it can fail to do so. An animal or plant has thus what we popularly, if incorrectly,[16] call a 'good', which will consist in the perfect growth and unhindered exercise of these capacities throughout its adult lifetime. But because we are rational animals, the perfect development and exercise of *our* natural capacities puts us on a wholly different and vastly higher level. In exercising our rational power to decide what to think and how to act, if we do so in a perfectly rational manner, we experience the very type of activity in which Zeus himself is continuously engaged. Zeus will always know vastly more than any human being; but his ways of reasoning and standards of evaluation can only be identical with what ours would be at our rational best. For Zeus's reason is simply reason in its perfected state. Compared in quality and value with that activity, the most perfect life possible for any non-rational being is something very low indeed. To mark this difference the Stoics reserved the term 'good' to describe the perfectly rational life and actions of Zeus and of human beings who have brought to perfection their own capacity for rational thought and decision.[17] The most ideal life imaginable for any other animal, with all the successful activities and satisfying experiences which make it up, cannot strictly be called 'good', either in itself or from the animal's point of view. Not, of course, that such a life would be a *bad* one.

---

[16] See below, p. xx.
[17] See Seneca *Letter* 124 especially 8–15.

It is just that the lives of other animals, because they cannot think rationally, have to be judged along a range of values altogether separate from those of good and bad. Whether the life of a non-human animal counts as flourishing or not will depend on how far it gets what it needs for an unhindered exercise of its natural capacities throughout its adult lifetime. Even so, its activities and experiences will not count as good or bad. They are only ones 'to be preferred' or 'to be rejected' by it.[18]

Of course, there is much more to human nature than just our power to think and decide. Most of the functions which we have as living things are like those of other animals. They take place without rational thought or decision on our part. Biological growth and functioning, the experience of sensory pleasure and pain, lie outside our rational control – we can at most decide to *use* them in some way. All these aspects of our lives, however, matter to us as human beings, as do the internal and external conditions that are needed if they are to be satisfactory. So also does the way in which we are treated by other human beings in the exercise of *their* capacity for thinking and deciding. But the fact that as rational beings we are on a level with Zeus means that these other aspects of our nature and what happens to them are much less important for the overall quality of our lives than we commonly think. For everything that happens, except our actions and those of other human beings, is controlled directly by Zeus. It is made to happen for reasons known to him. It is a necessary part of his – and hence the world's – on-going, overall life. Our biological development, our physiological state and the material effects on us of events in the world of nature outside us – in short, our physical life – are all controlled in this way by Zeus. So are the effects of voluntary actions by ourselves and others, insofar as these depend upon natural laws maintained by Zeus's decisions. But our own physical lives, and those of all other living things, are themselves parts of that larger unified life of the whole world. Thus in as much as what happens to us is the direct result of decisions by Zeus, we should conclude that it is what our lives – as integral parts of his life – really needed.[19] Hence the first and crucial step if we are

---

[18] See below, p. xxii.

[19] Epictetus quotes Chrysippus as saying that 'if I actually knew that I was fated now' (by Zeus's decision) 'to be ill I would even have an impulse to be ill. For

to perfect our own practical reasoning is to realize, with as much conviction as possible, that whatever happens to us in any way through the operation of natural laws is a positive contribution to the course of our lives. As Seneca puts it, the manifestations of nature advance the purposes of the universe and we, as a part of it, have reason to be grateful for them.[20] So all external states and events that affect us in any way and all states and events internal to our organisms (except the operations of our own power to think and decide) are manifestations of nature. They must never be judged to damage or harm us. When our physical lives are properly understood as integral parts in the life of the whole universe, all such manifestations can be seen instead to enhance them. Hence every disease, every painful or debilitating accident that befalls us or those whom we love, is something to be taken positively and greeted as such.

The quality of our individual lives depends crucially on the active use of our rational capacities in planning for the future and executing our plans. Zeus himself may control the course of nature. But that does not in the least mean that we should face life passively. For we, like Zeus, are endowed with reason in order to *use* it – by taking control of our own lives to the greatest possible extent.[21] From experience and observation of nature itself we can learn what the natural norms are for a human being's growth and subsequent course of life, as we can for any other animal. Whether in any individual case these norms are realized is another question. Often they are not. People are born seriously malformed and defective; they die at an early age from terrible diseases or accidents. Or rebelling against what the Stoics thought an evident fact, that we are formed by nature with a view to living cooperatively, they may choose instead to live selfishly, anti-socially and violently. We have already seen that when such things happen, their occurrence – and that includes the physical effects of selfish, anti-social and violent choices on the agents themselves and on others – is, none the less, a positive contribution to the lives of those immediately or indirectly affected by them. But what happens to us is seldom

my foot too, if it had intelligence, would have an impulse to get muddy' (Long–Sedley, 58J = *SVF* III 191).

[20] *On Favours* VI 23. 3–5. See also *On Anger* II 27. 2 and note 42 there.

[21] See Long–Sedley, 57A(5) = Diogenes Laertius, VII 86.

the effect exclusively of causes operating outside the sphere of our own decisions: our action or inaction – sometimes innocent, sometimes not – contributes to the natural disasters that befall us and to the effects of other people's malevolence The same is true even of our biological growth and the organic functions that lie at the greatest distance from our own decisions and actions. What we decide and do will make a difference to what comes about.

How then should we use our power of decision? What aims should we have? The Stoic answer was: we should aim at what accords most fully with the norms established, as we can see, by nature for human life. These natural norms include continued good health, material resources in plenty to maintain a comfortable existence, a good family life, the completest possible absence of bodily pain, and so forth – as well as the cooperative support owed by each member of the human community to the others. Such things, on the Stoic classification, are 'to be preferred', and their opposites are 'to be rejected', as we decide on our goals of action. They have thus a definite, if subsidiary, value; and the Stoics maintained that they are to be cared about, pursued or avoided, as things *worth* having or doing without, as the case may be.[22] We should do the utmost with our powers of reasoning and decision to achieve the things that are 'to be preferred' and avoid the ones 'to be rejected.' We should care about our health, our physical welfare and comfort, our family and friends, our work, the moral, social and economic well-being of our community; and we should do all that is in our power to protect and advance these interests. In so doing, we control our lives so far as that is possible. If we simply *do our best* to advance these norms, we shall have done our part. The rest is up to other human agents and to Zeus.

A perfected use of our rational capacities would therefore require, firstly, a full understanding of the norms laid down by nature for everything in human life outside the exercise of these rational capacities themselves. All evaluations and decisions would be governed by the informed pursuit of these norms. Secondly, however,

---

[22] This was a central part of the orthodox Stoic view, accepted even by Epictetus, however strongly he may have emphasized the indifference for our happiness of all 'externals'. Chrysippus had argued for it against his fellow-Stoic Ariston of Chios, who held that such 'externals' were not just neither good nor bad, but of no positive or negative value whatsoever. See Long–Sedley, 2G, 58A–G.

it would include a deeply embedded recognition that, once you have done your fullest and best, no matter how things turn out in those 'external' respects, the outcome can only be positive for you. If despite all reasonable efforts you fail to achieve your goal, that is no loss, when viewed after the fact. Evidently Zeus did not intend it to come about. If so, your failure will have advanced the life of the whole world and hence your own life as well, since the physical life of each one of us is just a single small part of the overall life of the world. The same is true also for all other human beings – even if they have *not* done *their* fullest and best. No failure of theirs, no disappointment, diminishes the true quality of their lives. Equally, when your efforts actually meet with success, your life is in no way better than it would otherwise have been. Whatever happens is acceptable, a positive development in your life. As we have seen, the only activities in life that can be described as really good or bad for you are those of rational thought, evaluation and decision. So the perfected use of our rational capacities requires, thirdly and finally, a deep recognition that the only thing good or bad for a human being, the only thing that affects the quality of our lives for better or worse, is simply our development and use of these capacities. The person whose reason is perfected in this way lives a good and happy life, the best life possible for a human being – no matter how things may go in other, 'external' respects. On the other hand, all whose rational capacities are less than fully perfected live bad, failed lives – again, however things go for them otherwise.

This perfected rationality the Stoics identified with the condition of virtue.[23] If you are perfectly rational, you possess human virtue, as a whole and in all its parts. This includes a full knowledge of, and a commitment to, the norms laid down by nature for private and family life – a recognition of what you should to try to achieve and avoid, in your personal life, in your family and among your friends. But it also includes knowledge of and commitment to all the natural norms for life with your fellow-citizens, your business associates and with human beings generally. So it carries with it the kinds of commitments recognized by traditional standards not just of personal prudence and decency in your private life but also

[23] See Diogenes Laertius, VII 94, *sub fin.*

xxiii

of social morality: justice, respect for others, and mutual aid, based in the fellowship and solidarity of all rational beings with one another. It was characteristic of the ancients to group together both sorts of standards as norms simply of virtue, without special distinction. Thus the Stoic theory provides a basis for saying that critically corrected versions of all the traditionally recognized virtues – intelligence, self-discipline and courage in the pursuit of personal aims, as well as justice and respect for others and concern for their welfare – are simply aspects of this single perfected state of our rational powers. Indeed, we can now see that, on the Stoic theory, the whole of what is good or bad for a human being, the whole of what affects for better or worse the quality of our lives, is our standing with respect to the virtues. The virtuous person lives a good and happy life, the best life possible for a human being, the happiest life – no matter how things turn out in other respects. On the other hand, all who are not fully virtuous, who fall short and live faulty lives, are bound – again, whatever happens to them in other respects – to live bad (and that means unhappy) lives.

In his philosophical writings Seneca has no need to expound this fundamental theory. He is concerned with its practical consequences for ordinary people. And these consequences are far-reaching. The solidarity, for instance, of human beings with one another and with Zeus, based in our common rationality, means that it is wrong to be hostile, angry and cruel (the theme of *On Anger*). It is also why princes should be merciful (*On Mercy*), why it is quite possible to be of as much use in retirement as in public life (*On the Private Life*), and why we should be altruistic in doing favours for one another (*On Favours*). Concern for the well-being of other people and of society in general is among the norms laid down by nature, to be understood and followed by us all. A good society and a well governed state are goals which we should do our utmost to achieve. But our success in achieving them is a purely 'external' matter, of secondary importance at most. It is still possible in the vilest society and the worst political conditions, as Socrates and Cato proved, for individuals to live good lives. And the good life lived by the individual is what counts.

Seneca's writing has thus a markedly apolitical character,[24] which it shares with other Stoic literature. The founder of the school, admittedly, does seem to have written on politics. Zeno's notorious *Republic* appears to have been a work of political theory in the tradition of Plato's *Republic*, prescribing an ideal community where the greatest possible concord is achieved by communist institutions and the moral character of its citizens. His somewhat Spartan city of the good and wise was still a recognizable *polis*, a 'community of people living in the same place under the same law'.[25] But it was subsequently reinterpreted by Chrysippus as the cosmic 'city of gods and men', in a theory which now focused on the moral potentialities of human beings – and the high moral demands placed on them – as 'rational animals' rather than citizens, and which treated 'law' no longer as a set of statutes but as the internal voice of prescriptive reason.[26] This conception had its influence on Roman jurists as they reflected on *ius gentium*, 'the sum of rules common to all legal systems',[27] and its relation to *ius naturale* or 'law of nature'. Through them it contributed to a long and important tradition of political thought about 'natural rights'. But that was of little concern to Seneca. The four essays in this volume may indeed touch on questions to do with social and political philosophy.[28] But Seneca is not writing as a 'political theorist' nor as an advocate of any political programme. He has nothing to say about divisions of power, virtually nothing about sources of authority or forms of government,[29] and very little on social regulation. He has no conclusions to draw for institutional reform. He is simply not interested in institutions. A slave, he argues with eloquence, is a fully human being who can do a favour just as much as a free man can (*On Favours* III 18–28). But that does not mean that slavery is a social

---

[24] It was later to have a profound effect on the 'quietist' attitudes of sixteenth and seventeenth century thinkers like Justus Lipsius. See Q. Skinner, *The Foundations of Modern Political Thought* (Cambridge 1978), I pp. 276–8.

[25] *SVF* III 329.

[26] See the important recent monograph by M. Schofield, *The Stoic Idea of the City* (Cambridge 1991), particularly pp. 96 f., 102 f., 138.

[27] P. Stein, *Roman Law* (*The Cambridge History of Medieval Political Thought*, ed. J. H. Burns, Cambridge 1988), p. 44.

[28] Even *On Anger* has its political dimension. See our Introduction to it.

[29] But note *On Mercy* I 1.2 and *On Favours* II 20. 2.

evil which ought to be be abolished. It is simply an external handicap which good people can overcome. Nor are the institutions of a state what determine its well-being. The moral character of its citizens and governors is far more important. Indeed, a reader of these essays might easily get the impression that all would be well with society if only its top people such as Seneca himself and his dedicatees – a future provincial governor, the emperor, a prefect of the Praetorian Guards and a provincial grandee[30] – could train themselves to stay good-tempered, merciful and generous. It can hardly be claimed[31] that a work like *On Favours* was conceived *'comme un instrument de combat politique'* – though much of what Seneca says in this and other essays could provide later political theorists with a moral basis for their own contentions.[32]

In other words, Seneca writes as a moralist – and an inward-looking moralist at that. What matters to him as a Stoic is first of all your own state of mind, your attitudes and moral endeavours; all else is 'external'. So he speaks to his readers individually, as a counsellor, offering them advice above all on how to heal their own minds, how to foster the virtues of mercy, good temper and altruism. He attempts to make them see things from his own Stoic point of view, to deepen their conviction that it does represent the truth about the world and the way to conduct a decent human life within the confines laid down for the exercise of human freedom. And he uses his considerable rhetorical skills to encourage them to do what they can towards eliminating the recurrence of feelings and actions in which they betray and fall away from this true outlook on life.

Style and composition

Seneca was a philosopher with training in oratory, a Stoic who employed his highly developed rhetorical talents to instruct, to

---

[30] See the sections on the 'addressee' in our Introductions to the essays.
[31] With F. Chaumartin, *ANRW* II 36. 3, p. 1703.
[32] E.g. satirical comments on greed and luxury, by Seneca and other Roman writers, could be invoked by a Guicciardini or Machiavelli as proof that luxurious habits and the pursuit of wealth are a threat to political liberty (see Skinner, *Foundations.* I pp. 162 f.). Again, many of the claims made by Seneca in *On Mercy* – that the prince should be kind, generous, affable etc. – became a stock-in-trade of the Renaissance 'mirror of princes' and as such a target for criticism by Machiavelli.

persuade or simply to charm his reader into accepting the truths of Stoicism. He was not the first Stoic to use rhetoric for pedagogical ends. Chrysippus, the greatest head of the school, had done so as well.[33] What is disconcerting about Seneca's writings as a medium for philosophy is their sheer virtuosity.

Seneca's works are acknowledged masterpieces of 'silver' Latin artistry, of the pointed and brilliant style that dominated Latin literature in the century after the death of Augustus. Its hallmark was a certain cleverness, a striving for neatness and wit, for epigrammatic crispness and immediate impact,[34] which Seneca achieves largely through artful contrasts. Where Cicero[35] would use complex periodic structures with subordinate clauses arranged to form grand architectural sentences, his own prose relies principally on the juxtaposition of sharpened phrases. Its sentences are chopped up by a variety of syntactic devices; their components have a compression achieved, if need be, at the cost of imprecision; and the contrast between these components is sharpened by metaphor, word-play and the omission of connecting particles (of 'and', 'but' and 'for'). The vocabulary is enlivened with unexpected poetical words and colloquialisms.

The result is a style[36] in which the brilliance of the parts tends to attract more attention than the argument of the whole, a style which entices, stimulates and entertains, but is less suited for systematic instruction or for rousing the stronger emotions. Its very cleverness can become too much of a good thing. 'There is hardly a sentence which might not be quoted', Macaulay complained,[37] 'but to read him straightforward is like dining on nothing but

See Q. Skinner. *Machiavelli: The Prince* (Cambridge 1988), Introduction, pp. xv, xvii, xxi, xxiii.

[33] *SVF* II 27.

[34] On Seneca's prose, see the Introduction (especially pp. xv–xcv) to W. C. Summers, *Select Letters of Seneca* (London 1910) and R. G. Coleman, 'The Artful Moralist: A Study of Seneca's Epistolary Style,' *Classical Quarterly* 68 (1974), pp. 276–89.

[35] What follows is heavily indebted to Coleman, especially pp. 285–7.

[36] It translates readily into English, largely because of Seneca's popularity among writers of the seventeenth century, a decisive period in the development of English prose. (See G. Williamson, *The Senecan Amble: A Study in Prose from Bacon to Collier* (London 1951)). His lapidary way of writing makes him an ancestor of the modern 'sound-bite'.

[37] G. O. Trevelyan, *Life and Letters of Lord Macaulay* (London 1908), p. 324 (quoted by Coleman, pp. 286 f. n. 6).

anchovy sauce.' Seneca, to be sure, is quite capable of writing in a lower key, of sober exposition as well as of high pathos. A master of the well-told narrative like that of Augustus and Cinna in *On Mercy* (1 9), he can manage all the registers in the orator's repertory.[38] Even so, the choppy epigrams are never far away. The virtuosity remains rather too much in evidence.

A more serious charge which has often been levelled against Seneca's writings is that of incoherence. Seductive and brilliant, the prose of a typical Senecan paragraph has a way of sweeping his readers along from one glittering phrase to the next, ending with a clinching epigram that leaves them impressed though not quite sure how it all hangs together. 'Sand without lime' to bind it – Caligula's famous comment[39] could well apply not only to Seneca's prose but still more to the *composition* of his essays.[40] With their repetitions,[41] apparent inconsistencies and abrupt transitions, they all too often leave the reader in a state of confusion about what is being said where and for precisely what reason. For the structure of Seneca's paragraphs and essays alike is literary, not logical. The movement from one sentence to another tends, in fact, to be by association of ideas, 'a carefully controlled progression in which a particular idea or group of ideas is approached from a number of different angles and reinforced at each new exposition. The technique is not that of the philosopher, developing a systematic argument with a logical beginning, middle and end, but of the preacher.'[42] It is above all in the transition from one group of ideas to another that readers are likely to lose their way.[43]

'Seneca writes as a Boar does pisse . . . by jirkes.'[44] The apparent jerkiness of Seneca's prose style and composition alike reflects the

[38] Note, for instance the effortless switch from a recapitulation of bare Stoic syllogisms to high-flown peroration at *On Favours* III 35–8.
[39] Suetonius, *Life of Gaius Caligula* (53. 2).
[40] On the composition of Seneca's essays see J. R. G. Wright, 'Form and Content in the *Moral Essays*', in *Seneca*, ed. C. D. N. Costa (London 1974), pp. 39–69. Also E. Albertini, *La Composition dans les ouvrages philosophiques de Sénèque* (Paris 1923).
[41] Roundly condemned by Fronto (second century): Marcus Cornelius Fronto, *Epistles*, Loeb edn (1919a), II p. 102.
[42] Coleman, p. 285.
[43] For that reason, we have introduced section-headings of our own into our translation of the essays, to indicate the ordering of topics under discussion there and to mark the major transitions between them.
[44] A witticism attributed to the seventeenth-century scholar Ralph Kettel, president of Trinity College Oxford, in *Aubrey's Brief Lives* (ed. O. Lawson Dick, Harmondsworth 1972, p. 347).

oratory of his time. The first century of the Roman empire was an age of declamations, school exercises in forensic and political eloquence, treated less and less as preparation for real public speaking than as works of art in their own right.[45] The principal aim of the declaimer was simply to win the applause of his fellow practitioners. For that end, instant impact was what counted. Sustained argument mattered rather less. The schools of declamation were forcing grounds for the flashier tricks of rhetoric, above all for the *sententiae*, or pointed epigrams, on which Seneca and his brothers, according to their father,[46] were especially keen. But there was a further factor at work to the same effect on Seneca's style and composition. He was not producing school treatises. He was addressing a general educated public. And the normal way at his time to do so was by the essay or homily, what scholars till recently were pleased to call 'diatribe',[47] a genre which includes the so-called 'Diatribes' of Epictetus and the fragments of the Cynic preacher Teles (third century BC). In contrast to philosophical dialogues, these works were not meant to be a cooperative search for truth; they were combative expositions of truth already known to their authors. Their first objective was to grab the attention of listener or reader, and to hold on to it without making too many demands on his concentration. For that, they needed little more than a vivacious rhetoric; sustained or complex argument was best avoided. They did, however, share one feature of the dialogue, albeit in attenuated form. The unspecified interlocutor ('But, someone will say ...') who raises objections only to have them shot down or jerks the discussion back to the purely ethical questions – which, according to the Cynics, were the only part of philosophy that matters – was an indispensable device for changing the subject and papering over cracks in the argument.[48]

---

[45] See, for a start, Summers, *Select Letters*, pp. xxxi–xxxii.

[46] *Controversiae* 1 Pref. 22.

[47] See H. D. Jocelyn, 'Diatribes and Sermons', *Liverpool Classical Association* 7. 1 (1982), pp. 3–7.

[48] The presence of this interlocutor may account for the title *Dialogi* (or 'Dialogues') given to the twelve essays, including *On Anger* and *On the Private Life*, in the Ambrosian manuscript – and indeed to all Seneca's *Moral Essays*. According to Quintilian (IX 2. 31), the technical term in rhetoric for the imaginary conversation was διάλογος (Latin *sermocinatio*). Seneca's works could have been labelled *Dialogi* for their frequent use of that figure, though the title would also recall the most famous of all philosophical compositions, Plato's *Dialogues*.

None the less, Seneca's moral essays are vastly more ambitious and successful compositions than anything by Epictetus or Teles. What holds them together is, firstly, their author's thorough rhetorical training. There were recognized ways of putting a work together, standard 'parts' of a speech, conventional headings in a conventional order under which to deal with a topic. Seneca has a professional knowledge of them. In all four texts of this volume, for instance, he goes through the rhetorical procedure of 'dividing' the material for discussion into its principal questions.[49] Having proposed a scheme of argument, Seneca broadly observes at least its major divisions, though he is rather less firm when it comes to working out the detailed discussion.[50] Here his structural grip relaxes, and he indulges the temptation to call in the imaginary interlocutor and compose by association of ideas. But the relaxation is artful. The broad framework of argument is generally so fixed in his mind that he can take it for granted. On occasion, he can blur the transition, quite deliberately, from one topic to another[51] – an unexpected change of direction keeps the readers on their toes. He can play about with his material, varying it to suit the immediate context, correcting and apparently contradicting things said earlier, repeating himself in such a way as to bring out the numerous facets of his subject[52] and wear down any resistance.

A second and still more important factor in holding Seneca's moral essays together – and his moral letters too, for that matter – is an underlying vision derived from his Stoic philosophy. His aim in all four essays in this volume is to present this vision, or aspects of it, to a Roman public, to translate the abstract doctrines of his school into the language of real life – of commerce, the law-courts, and so forth – at Rome.[53] His efforts to do so are often brilliantly successful, well up to the high seriousness of their subject. Seneca

---

[49] *On Anger* I 5. 1, II 18. 1, III 5. 2; *On the Private Life* 2.1; *On Favours* I 11. 1; *On Mercy* I 3.1, 20. 1 (on which Calvin commented: 'This division adds much to the clarity of the discourse and would have added still more if it had embraced the work as a whole').

[50] Compare Wright, p. 59.

[51] E.g. at *On Favours* III 17. 4–18. 1.

[52] Hence his multiple definitions of anger and mercy (*On Anger* I 2. 4–3, *On Mercy* II 3.1).

[53] See the fine essay by M. Armisen Marchetti ('La Métaphore et l'abstraction dans la prose de Sénèque', *Entretiens Hardt* 36 (1991), 99–139), particularly pp. 109–14.

can wear his Stoicism lightly enough. But he regularly falls back on its vision of the universe as a community of rational beings, of the gods as our exemplars, of the demands which our rationality makes upon us, of the solidarity which binds all humans together – free, freedman and slave – by virtue of their endowment with reason, a solidarity which itself reflects the cosmic order. This vision – above all, in Book IV of *On Favours* – is what gives strength to his most powerful writing.

The influence of Seneca's philosophical writings

Philosophers writing in Greek – and that includes Epictetus and Marcus Aurelius, both of them Stoics very familiar with things Roman – paid no attention to philosophy written in Latin. Not surprisingly, such writers do not quote Seneca or discuss his views. Only Plutarch (c. 50–120) refers to him – and then only in an anecdote as an adviser to Nero.[54] But the neglect of Seneca on the part of philosophers is also explained by the character of his work. As we have seen, he was not writing technical treatises but essays addressed to the educated public. For Stoic philosophy and its development later writers had other and better sources to consult.[55]

Latin writers of later antiquity, especially Christian ones, appear to have appreciated Seneca more highly, especially in his native Iberia, where he is still regarded as the first great Spanish writer.[56] In the sixth century St Martin, archbishop of Braga in Portugal (580), wrote a short treatise on the cardinal virtues, taken almost entirely from Seneca, which (usually under Seneca's name) was among the most widely circulated works during the middle ages; he also wrote a work *On Anger* based on Seneca's. Collections of Senecan sayings and witticisms – their origins are obscure –

---

[54] *On the Control of Anger*, 461f–462a. Plutarch refers a second time to Seneca in his *Life of Galba* (20. 1. 1).

[55] See, further, G. M. Ross, 'Seneca's Philosophical Influence' (Costa, ed., *Seneca*, pp. 116–165), p. 119 n. 7. The material on Seneca in later pagan and Christian writers is massively assembled by W. Trillitzsch, *Seneca im literarischen Urteil der Antike* I, Amsterdam 1971).

[56] See K. A. Blüher, *Seneca in Spanien* (Munich: 1969) an account of Seneca's reception in Spain from the thirteenth to the seventeenth centuries, with useful and full chapters on the earlier history.

also had a wide popularity in later antiquity and the middle ages.[57]

With the revival of classical learning, from the mid fourteenth century until the mid seventeenth, Seneca was among the most highly admired and widely read of all ancient philosophers. Petrarch (1304–74) called him the greatest of moral teachers and developed a philosophy of life modelled partly on his version of Stoicism. Erasmus (1467–1536) published a first edition of Seneca's complete works in 1516, followed by another (philologically much improved) in 1529. The young Calvin wrote a commentary on *On Mercy* (1532).[58] Seneca's reputation and influence were at their highest in the latter half of the sixteenth century and on into the seventeenth. Montaigne († 1592), despite his engagement with Pyrrhonian scepticism, frequently cites and make extensive use of Seneca's ideas (chiefly from the *Letters*) in his *Essays*. In seeking to establish a comprehensive Neo-Stoic philosophy, both in metaphysics and moral philosophy, to replace the Aristotelianism inherited from the middle ages, the Belgian philosopher and scholar Justus Lipsius (1547–1606) based himself almost entirely on Seneca. Frequently republished in the seventeenth and eighteenth centuries, his commentaries on Seneca remain invaluable. Thereafter Seneca remained the central source for the Neo-Stoic movement. But as modern science and the 'new' philosophy developing under its influence gained their independence from ancient models Seneca's influence declined. The untechnical character of his writings and their rhetorical panache put him increasingly out of court with technical philosophers. His Stoic outlook on life lost much of the appeal it had earlier had. In this century he has been received little attention from academic philosophers, especially in English-speaking countries where his career and style of writing have all too often aroused a puritan disapproval.

However, Seneca remains, for us today no less than for the revivers of Stoicism in the sixteenth century, our best representative of ancient Stoicism. In his case as in few others we have the luxury of reading, with their full contexts, whole works of philosophy by a Stoic. He is still an excellent, indeed indispensable, source for those who may wish to learn about, and learn from, Stoicism and its outlook on life.

[57] See Trillitzsch *Seneca*, I pp. 211–21, II pp. 393–419.
[58] Still highly useful. See the splendid dual-language edition of Battles and Hugo.

Synopsis

General introduction

On anger

Introduction

Book I

On Mercy

Introduction

Book I

On the Private Life

Introduction

On the Private Life

Preface (1. 1–3)

On Favours

Introduction

Synopsis

Book I

Preface
Errors in doing and accepting favours (1–3. 1)
The three Graces (3. 2–4)

What is a favour? (5–9. 1)
Ingratitude, the worst form of human depravity (9. 2–10)

(I) What favours to grant (11–15)

Book II

(II) How to do a favour (1–17)
Be prompt (1–5)
Avoid ungraciousness (6–8)
Do some favours openly, some in secret (9–10)
Avoid reminders, add on new favours (11. 1–6)
Avoid arrogance (11. 6–13)
Take the beneficiary's true interests into account (14)
Avoid doing anything that will cause you shame (15. 1–2)
Consider both your own and your recipient's position (15. 3–17. 2)
The game of ball (17. 3–7)

(III) How to behave in accepting favours (18–35)
Be discriminating about whom you allow to do you a favour, and about what counts as one (18–21)
Accept cheerfully (22–5)
Ingratitude: due principally to self-regard, greed and envy (26–30)
To accept a favour gladly is to have repaid it (31–5)

Book III

Ingratitude (1–17)
Ingratitude: its worst form is forgetfulness (1–5)
Should ingratitude be made subject to legal prosecution? (6–15)
The punishment for ingratitude (17)

Slaves and masters (18–28)
Can a slave do his master a favour? (18–22)

Abbreviations

Certain ancient writings and collections of extracts from ancient writings are regularly cited in the following footnotes.

Aelian, *Varia Historia.*	*Varia Historia* by Claudius Aelianus (c. AD 170–235), a collection of historical anecdotes.
Diogenes Laertius (D.L.)	*Lives of Eminent Philosophers* by Diogenes Laertius (early third century AD), a compilation of information about the lives and opinions of famous philosophers.
Gnomologium Vaticanum	*Gnomologium Vaticanum*, ed L. Sternbach (Berlin 1963).
Long–Sedley	*The Hellenistic Philosophers I, Translations of the Principal Sources with Philosophical Commentary*, by A. A. Long and D. N. Sedley (Cambridge 1987).
Stobaeus (Didymus)	The enormous *Anthology* compiled by John of Stobi (fifth century AD), ed. C. Wachsmuth and O. Hense (Berlin 1884–1912). Book II (pp. 37–152) contains a substantial extract from *On Philosophy: Ethics*, a doxographical work by Arius Didymus, friend of the emperor Augustus.
SVF	*Stoicorum Veterum Fragmenta*, ed. J. von Arnim (3 vol. plus a fourth of indices) (Teubner 1905–24), the standard collection of fragments of the 'Old Stoics,' Zeno and Chrysippus and their pupils.

Valerius Maximus	*IX Books of Memorable Deeds and Sayings*, a compilation for the use of orators, by Seneca's elder contemporary, Valerius Maximus.

Other standard collections of ancient material are cited simply by the name of their editors: e.g.

Baehrens	*Poetae Latini Minores*, ed. E. Baehrens (Leipzig 1878–80).
Diels–Kranz	*Die Fragmente der Vorsokratiker*, ed. H. Diels and W. Kranz (Berlin 1961).
Nauck–Snell	*Tragicorum Graecorum Fragmenta*, ed. A. Nauck and B. Snell (Hildesheim 1964).
Rose	*Aristotelis qui ferebantur librorum fragmenta*, ed. V. Rose (Leipzig 1886)
Sandbach	*Plutarch's Moralia XV – Fragments*, ed. F. Sandbach, (Harvard Loeb 1969).
Usener	*Epicurea*, ed. H. Usener (Stuttgart 1966).
Wehrli	*Die Schules des Aristoteles*, ed. F. Wehrli (Basel 1944–59).

A few modern works also make repeated appearances in the footnotes, notably:

Crook	J. A. Crook *Law and Life of Rome* (London 1967).
Griffin	M. T. Griffin *Seneca: A Philosopher in Politics* (Oxford 1976).
Syme	R. Syme, *The Roman Revolution* (Oxford 1960).
Veyne	P. Veyne, *Bread and Circuses*, English edn, Intr. O. Murray (Harmondsworth 1990).

Three very useful collections of articles are:
Seneca, ed., C.D.N. Costa, London 1974.
Sénèque et la prose latine, Entrétiens Hardt 36, 1992.
ANRW Aufstieg und Niedergang der Römischen Welt II 36.3, a volume devoted to Stoicism in the Roman Empire, with numerous articles on Seneca (pp. 1545–2065).

To Novatus
On Anger

Ad Novatum
De Ira

Introduction

Addressee and date

On Anger is addressed to Lucius Annaeus Novatus, Seneca's elder brother. Subsequently adopted by the orator Iunius Gallio whose name he took, he is best known to posterity as Lucius Iunius Gallio Annaeanus, the proconsul of Achaea who refused to try the case brought against St Paul by the Jews of Corinth (Acts XVIII 12–17). On his brother's downfall, he too had to commit suicide.

Gallio was proconsul from AD 51 to 52, having adopted his new name some time before that. *On Anger* must have been addressed to him before he adopted it, but after the assassination in AD 41 of the emperor Caligula, whom it roundly abuses (I 20. 8, II 33. 3–6, III 18. 3–19. 5).

Organization and purpose

Like other ancient essays on particular emotions or moral failings, Seneca's *On Anger* comes in two parts: a discussion of theoretical *questions* (I–II 17), followed by *remedies* (II 18–III). After a preamble on the horrors of anger (1–2. 3), Book I deals first with definitions of anger (2. 4–4) and then enquires 'is anger natural?' (5 f.), 'can it be moderate?' (7 f.), 'has it any practical use?' (9–19) and 'has it anything to do with greatness of mind?'[1] (20 f.). Book II opens with similar theoreti-

---

[1] A combination of high ambition, high merit and high self-esteem traditionally prized by Greeks and Romans. See below, on I 20.

3

cal questions – 'is anger involuntary?' (II 1–4), 'is it required by the wickedness that we see around us?' (II 6–10), 'does it fend off contempt?' (11 f.), 'can it be excised altogether?' (12–14), 'has it any connection with noble character?' (15 f.) – before broaching the second main topic of the work: how to cure the emotion (18). It then prescribes how children should be educated to be good-tempered (19–21) and how adults can avoid displays of bad temper (22–36). After a further preamble of the horrors of anger (1–5. 1), Book III makes a fresh start (5. 2), offering advice on how to stay in a good mood (5. 3–9), then a long string of precepts on how to forestall or extinguish one's fits of anger (10–38), interrupted with a copious mass of examples to be avoided or imitated (13. 7–23), and finally some tips on how to mollify other people (39 f.), before it concludes with a highly coloured peroration (41–3). The exposition throughout is informal, in places deliberately repetitive and disordered.

Seneca's avowed aim (I 1) in writing *On Anger* is therapeutic: to advise us on how to 'alleviate anger'. But he can only do this if we have some reliable knowledge of what has to be cured as well as a sincere wish to cure ourselves and others of this emotion. So before giving his advice, Seneca must first explain what anger *is*. He must also persuade us that the Stoics are right in thinking that emotions are among the most persistently harmful effects of that unnatural, deranged condition of character and mind that they called 'vice' (Greek κακία, Latin *vitium*), and that anger is the most vicious emotion of all. By 'emotion' (Greek πάθος, Latin *adfectus*), the Stoics – like other philosophers in antiquity – understood an agitated state of mind and feeling, whether of positive elation or of something negative such as anxiety, depression or resentment. Anger itself they regarded – again like other philosophers – as a reaction specifically to something perceived as deliberate injustice or mistreatment, insult or slight; it was never, in their eyes, a mere response to general frustration of desires or hopes.[2] For Seneca, it is the 'most hideous and frenzied of all

[2] In I 2. 5 Seneca classifies the 'anger' of small children when they fall and hurt themselves, which one might think of as just that kind of response to frustration, as only 'quasi-anger'. Even then he emphasizes that their screams count as

4

the emotions' (I I), the one in which we are the most violently and unattractively *moved*, and the most important for us to avoid or at least to control. His discussion, in the first half of *On Anger*, of theoretical questions is designed to give his readers the same conviction and to leave them receptive to the therapy that follows. Indeed, as we shall see, a conviction that anger should at all costs be avoided is itself, for Seneca, our principal remedy against succumbing to anger.

The Stoic theory of the emotions

Why did Seneca and his fellow Stoics have such a low opinion of emotions in general and anger in particular? Why did they not think, as most of us today surely do, that, even if *extremes* of emotion are to be avoided most of the time, it is often natural and right to become angry, depressed, or resentful – indeed, that a person who does not respond to *some* circumstances in that way is less than human? Seneca himself replies to such questions in the first half of *On Anger*; and it may be useful to summarize here, in systematic terms, the Stoic analysis of the emotions on which he draws in his more informal discussion.

It is no accident that our fundamentally favourable attitude towards the emotions was advanced by Plato in the *Republic* and by Aristotle in his ethical treatises. In later antiquity, Platonism and Aristotelianism triumphed over rival systems; and their view of the emotions, with only temporary challenges during the seventeenth-century revival of Epicureanism and Stoicism, remained standard in medieval and modern philosophy. For Plato and Aristotle an emotion or 'passion' or 'affection' – the three terms all cover the same range of phenomena – is an evaluative response to some significant event in our lives, or to one anticipated in the future: and it derives from a part

expressions of such 'quasi-anger' only to the extent that they somehow childishly *blame* the ground, or their toys, or other inanimate objects, for getting in their way and tripping them up. Similarly, at II 26. I–5, he cites the absurdity of getting angry with animals or inanimate objects that cannot possibly have intended to harm us. On a modern view of anger, there would be nothing illogical in feeling angry if a machine breaks down, if rain spoils a picnic, or a dog disrupts it.

of our psyche separate from the central 'reasoning' capacity in which our identity as persons, as responsible agents, rests. According to this conception, anger is an agitated feeling that arises – indeed, it boils up – when we have a strong sense of having been unjustly treated or slighted in some significant way, quite independently of what we *think* or how we judge at the time about whatever it may be that has occurred. We may think that no injustice or slight really occurred, that it was all a mistake, that no ground for getting upset really exists. Yet, in another 'part' of our psyche, it may strike us, and continue to strike us, that it has. We may go on *feeling* misused even if, as we say, our 'reason tells us' that we were not.

On this view emotions are involuntary forces from which 'we' – the reasoning, responsible agents who have to judge what to do in the light of events and circumstances – stand aside and which we are sometimes unable to control. The result is that we lash out against our better judgment and respond angrily to something that was not, and that we judged at the time was not, worth our anger. It can often happen, of course, that things strike us, and so engage our anger, in a way that conforms quite precisely to 'our' judgments of what has happened, of how we have been treated, and of what sort of counter-action is justified. In that case, anger can be said to aid 'us', reinforcing the possibly inadequate motivation that 'we' feel to vindicate ourselves or punish the wrongdoing done to us.[3] But the challenge that faces us as responsible adults, who wish to live in accordance with our own judgment of what is true and what is best, is to train ourselves to the point where things will not automatically arouse emotions in us, except on those occasions and to the extent that our judgments of what is best, what is justified, may dictate. For Plato and Aristotle, a very large part of ethical self-discipline consists in gradually working upon this other 'part' of the psyche to the point where we are no longer struck so forcibly by events and circumstances as to feel emotions with whose evaluative, normative content 'we' – the reasoning, planning agents – do not agree.

---

[3] Seneca has much to say against this consequence of the Platonic–Aristotelian analysis, that anger often aids us to carry out correct ethical judgments and so, for example, to punish wrongdoers (I 7, 9, 17; II 6–9).

The Stoics rejected this analysis of what an emotion is, of its relation to the central 'reasoning' capacity, of how it comes to affect a person's behaviour, and of the task that, in consequence, faces a responsible, rational adult.[4] They believed – as indeed did Plato and Aristotle – that whenever we get carried away by an emotion so as to do something which 'we' (that is, the reasoning, planning, responsible agent in us) would disown, we are none the less responsible for doing what we have done.

For Plato and Aristotle, however, the responsibility would lie in our not having controlled ourselves at the time or, further back, in our not having trained ourselves beforehand to the point of not having such involuntary impulses to be controlled then at all. It was not the reasoning planning agent in us that acted then; rather, that other 'part' of our psyche was the sole source of the psychic energy that expressed itself in the action and so of the action itself. 'We' were responsible only for 'our' *in*action, at the time and previously.

For the Stoics this consequence of the Platonic–Aristotelian view was deeply objectionable, both as psychological analysis and in its implications for moral, if not legal, accountability. It is false, they thought, to insist that when people have acted wrongly under the influence of emotion 'they' (the reasoning, planning, responsible agents) have not positively endorsed the action, but have only failed, as it were, to intervene and prevent it. What is more, to say this encourages people to make excuses in a way very damaging to themselves. What really happens in the case of anger, for instance, is that, before getting carried away and lashing out contrary to their better judgment, 'they' have been divided in 'their own' view of the facts about what has happened to them and what sort of reaction is merited. In feeling angry '*they*' – and not some other 'part' of their psyche, acting on its own – are judging that an insult has occurred and that it requires a response in kind. If at the same time 'they' also judge that that is not so, that is only because 'they' are torn between these two views and cannot make up their minds which view to adopt and hold on to. When finally they get 'carried away', what happens is that the provocative

[4] On the Stoic analysis of emotions, see Long–Sedley, Chapter 65.

7

view of things has got the upper hand with '*them*'; 'they' adopt and stick to it long enough to decide upon action and to lash out in angry retaliation. In fact, the reasoning, planning agent in them is behind the action throughout. Hence no one can be allowed an easy excuse like 'The devil' (i.e. the anger in some other part of the psyche) 'made me do it!'[5] It may have been only a momentary decision, only a momentary view of the circumstances, that caused the outburst. The circumstances may not have been seen in that light a moment earlier, the decision may have been regretted and withdrawn immediately afterwards. But the agent's own decision, the agent's own view of things – and nothing else – was responsible for the action. So the Stoics insisted that emotions are conditions into which the 'reasoning' capacity itself may fall. They are evaluative responses to, or anticipations of, significant events in our lives; and they represent views held at the time by us in our 'reasoning' capacity itself.[6]

But the Stoics went further. On the Platonic–Aristotelian view the ultimate goal of moral self-discipline was to train the alleged other 'part' of one's psyche to the point where it would not be stirred up by events and circumstances into emotions *except* when, or to the extent that, a correct judgment by the 'reasoning' capacity would itself confirm that emotional view of things. But, as Seneca rightly notes (I 9. 2), this means that there are times when an emotion does correctly represent things, when the 'reasoning' capacity will approve of it and indeed make use of it in giving rise to an action that responds, with appropriate force and feeling, to the circumstances, as viewed jointly by itself and the other 'part'. To this, too, the Stoics strenuously objected. On their analysis,[7] the only things that are good or bad for a human being, and so merit what

---

[5] Later on, Christian monastic writers were to go the whole way in externalizing the causes of moral inadequacy, blaming it on personified 'spirits of wickedness' (of gluttony, fornication, sloth, anger and the other cardinal sins), rather than on something in the lower part of the psyche. The evasion, however, is essentially the same in both cases.

[6] Of course, that does not mean that the emotional view of things is the sole view that a person's 'reasoning' capacity may be holding; he may quite well hold other views of them – at any rate intermittently or indecisively – at the same time.

[7] See General Introduction p. xxiii.

one might call ultimate concern, are certain features of one's own mind. Things external to it are of only secondary concern; what primarily matters is how one deals with them – how one approaches them or distances oneself from them. In other words, what matters is how, in one's own mind, one regards them. But emotions are characteristically directed at just such external things, at the things that befall one:[8] one becomes angry when someone acts dismissively or arrogantly towards oneself or towards someone or something one cares about; one grieves at the death of a parent or a friend; one feels elated at coming first in some competition; one glories in the accomplishments or success of one's children; one feels depressed or anxious at not seeing one's way through some difficulty or finding oneself in some other respect seriously incompetent. Moreover, emotions (even phenomenologically, since they are by definition elevated or depressed – but in any event *agitated* – states of mind) betray the fact that they represent all these matters as being of really grave importance. When grieving for someone who is gone, one feels that life is no longer worth living, that one cannot go on in any satisfactory way, without the presence and assistance of that person. Glory at being successful and recognized, or resentment at lack of success and recognition, can leave one with a sense of one's whole life as transfigured or blighted. But all such reactions are in fact exaggerated, if the Stoics are right that the only things of ultimate concern are certain features of one's own mind. In reacting in these ways to external events one is showing that in one's own mind one has a wrong – an excessive – regard for them.

In the very act of responding emotionally to significant events and circumstances in life, then, one displays for all to see the fact that one's own state of mind lacks some of those very features which, on the Stoic analysis, it is of ultimate concern to any human being to possess. Hence it is vital to rid oneself of emotions altogether. For they systematically misrepresent the actual value to oneself of the 'external' things in one's life,

---

[8] The standard word in Greek for 'emotion' – πάθος – had in fact originally meant 'something which happens' to a person, something which he or she suffers.

and so the effects of such things on its quality and character. Responsible adults who wish to live in accordance with their own judgment of what is true and what is best must learn never to view things in an emotional – that is to say, in a *distorted* – way. Thus the standard picture of the Stoics, as recommending the total eradication of the emotions, is entirely accurate, though one should bear in mind that it applies only to such feelings, desires and other responses as are 'emotional' – that is, agitated and excessive. Calm, rational desires, feelings of rational wariness in the face of threats to one's life, rational determination to punish ill-treatment, are all perfectly acceptable, indeed they are positively recommended by the theory.[9] From this point of view, it is not difficult to see how anger could rank for Seneca as the worst of the emotions. It is the most agitated and violent of them, as well as the most likely to make people act against their rational, 'better judgment'.

The cure of anger

As we have seen, the Stoics regarded anger and the other emotions as aberrations, indeed perversions, of one's central reasoning capacity, not as impulses from some other part of the psyche. Accordingly, their cure was to strengthen and correct that reasoning capacity. They did not go in for 'non-rational' therapy – that is, for remedies which require no thought from the patient, such as music to soothe the furious soul. Nor does Seneca as a Stoic make use, in the way that Plutarch (a Platonist) can do, of exercises designed to habituate the non-rational part of the psyche to the point where its reactions conform to the correct judgments of the reasoning capacity. For the Stoics identified emotions themselves with 'judgments' – or, rather, misjudgments – 'of the reasoning capacity'. Their therapy was to replace the misjudgments with true judgments, and to instil these as deeply as possible, by reshaping and strengthening that very capacity.

On the Stoic view, any emotion entails in fact a double misjudgment. A response to significant events in the past or

---

[9] See Diogenes Laertius, VII 116.

future, it contains an evaluative judgment about the good or bad in the event – for instance, that the death of your child is something really and terribly bad. But Chrysippus maintained that a further judgment is required: to succumb to an emotion like grief, you must further judge that it is right and proper, indeed your rational duty, to lament and tear your hair. So the Stoic therapy for any emotion comes down to two kinds of argument. The sufferer must be shown, firstly, that whatever has befallen him or is about to befall him is not the good or bad that he supposes it to be; and that, secondly, even if it were, an emotional reaction on his part would be seriously wrong. For Chrysippus, the second kind of argument was far the most useful, since it could work on people whose judgments of good and bad were not those of a Stoic.[10] Similarly, in Seneca's *On Anger*, the most prominent therapy is simply to persuade us as forcefully as possible of how undesirable, of how hideous and dangerous, anger is. The theme of the extended purple passages at the start of Books I and III and the end of Book II, this is also the moral to be drawn from the entire theoretical discussion of anger in the first half of the work.

It is when Seneca turns explicitly to offering therapeutic advice that the two lines of argument appear side by side.[11] The central chapters in the second half of Book II (Chapters 26–34) are based on a definition of anger, ascribed to Posidonius at 1 2, as 'a burning desire to punish him by whom you think yourself to have been unfairly harmed'. Seneca systematically offers a set of reflections showing that you have not really been 'harmed' (26 f., 29 f.), that anyhow you have not suffered 'unfairly' (28, 31. 1–5) and that 'a burning desire to punish' offences is small-minded, inhuman and and inexpedient, ugly and dangerous, in no case one that you should entertain.[12]

---

[10] See *SVF* III 474.

[11] What follows is heavily indebted to the acute analyses of P. Rabbow, *Antike Schriften zur Seelenheilung und Seelenleitung* I, (Leipzig and Berlin 1914).

[12] II 31. 6–36. Much of what these chapters contain (e.g. the pronouncements on 'greatness of mind') is a reworking of material from earlier 'theoretical' parts of *On Anger* (see 31. 6, n. 48). It appears yet again, still further reworked and disguised, towards the end of Book III (24–38).

It will be noticed that these reflections apply specifically to one stage in a complex psychological process. They are at their most useful in the relatively short period in which you are under provocation and deciding what to do about it. But there are earlier and later stages in the process of losing your temper, as well. Seneca has help to offer for both. There is quite a lot, firstly, that you can do in advance to discourage the tendency to anger. There are remedies for 'irascibility' as well as for outbreaks of rage. Seneca offers two kinds of prophylaxis. You can bring up children to be good-tempered;[13] and you can also do a certain amount to see that you yourself, as an adult with no special upbringing, are less likely to lose your temper. For instance, 'don't believe all that people say' (II 22–5), 'don't be self-indulgent and oversensitive' (25), 'don't exhaust yourself by overdoing things' (III 6. 3–7. 2), 'choose the right easy-going friends' (III 8). But there is also a stage where you have been provoked, where you feel yourself getting angry, but have not yet lashed out. Here Seneca has a repeated bit of advice: 'Don't do anything for the moment – don't even show that you are angry.'[14] The advice serves two purposes. For a start, it is a precaution against your doing anything dreadful under the influence of anger. (Seneca has numerous examples of just how dreadful such deeds can be.) But it is also therapy for the emotion itself. By stifling its expression, you stifle your anger as well. You 'break its circuit', to use a modern metaphor.[15]

Seneca's application of this material is a good deal less systematic than our account of it has attempted to be. Anger may be a state of the 'reasoning' capacity, through which a person decides what to believe and how to act. But it would be extremely naive to think (and Seneca and the other Stoics did not think) that you could either cure a person of the

---

[13] This is the theme of II 19–21, a rather Posidonian passage.
[14] See particularly III 10–13.
[15] This non-rational mechanical remedy, so unlike the others in *On Anger*, was older than the Stoics. We find something like it attributed to the followers of Pythagoras, a generation before Zeno (see below on III 10). Its value to Seneca at this stage of the proceedings is easily explained. Anger distorts your judgment more than any other passion. Once you are under its influence, you can no longer think straight; and rational therapy is no longer possible. The only remedy left is to put everything 'on hold'.

general tendency to become angry or make him desist from
anger once aroused, simply by argument. People can refuse to
accept the conclusions of arguments that they cannot give any
good reason to reject. The person prone to anger may simply
not listen to reason on the subject of insults, or if he does
listen beforehand he may none the less not listen when insulted.
He needs to *train* his 'reasoning' capacity – to strengthen, to
deepen it – so that he learns to accept, instinctively and
automatically, as the truth what his own, or someone else's,
reason reveals to him to be true. Seneca's *On Anger* provides
a demonstration of the moral and intellectual training that is
needed. Its lengthy and rhetorically elaborate exposition, its
heaping up of of historical examples,[16] its constant interweaving
of themes, its endless repetitions which muddy the argument
but refresh the memory, are all intended to educate the reader.
Their aim is not simply to give him an understanding of what
Seneca has to say, but to embed this understanding so deeply
in his mind that he will never fall victim to anger again.

The literary context

Much was written in Hellenistic and Roman times about anger.
We know of essays *On Anger* by the Cynic preacher Bion
(c. 325–255 BC), by the Stoics Antipater and Posidonius, by
Seneca's teacher Sotion, by the Epicurean Philodemus of
Gadara (c. 110–c. 40–35 BC), by Plutarch, and by Seneca
himself. (The last three of these survive.) There were also
numerous works *On Emotions*, the most famous of them that
by Chrysippus. It contained three books of 'theoretical' questions about the emotions, followed by a fourth book[17] on their
therapy. This was to be the standard format – theory leading
to practical advice – of works like Seneca's *On Anger.*[18] It

---

[16] On which see now R. G. Mayer, 'Roman Historical Exempla in Seneca', *Entrétiens Hardt* 36 (1991), pp. 139–71
[17] Or perhaps it was a separate work: Galen, our principal source of information about Chrysippus' work on the emotions, is confusing on this score. (Cf. *On the Doctrines of Hippocrates and Plato* V 6. 44–5 and 7. 52 with IV 1. 14, 4. 23, 5. 10–13 and 5. 20.).
[18] Cicero used the same format in Books III and IV of his *Tusculan Disputations.*

seems safe to assume that in writing it Seneca consulted Chrysippus' *On Emotions* as well as the work by Posidonius of the
same title.[19] He will also have referred to a treatise *On Anger*
by his teacher Sotion, which he appears to be quoting in one
passage;[20] and he mentions the Roman philosopher Sextius
(first century BC) in two passages,[21] the first of which seems
to be recalling some text specifically on anger.

So much for the sources.[22] Seneca's is the only treatment
of anger (or the emotions generally) by a Stoic to survive
substantially complete from antiquity. Its rhetorical presentation,
extended use of historical examples and avoidance of technical-
ities were all meant to enhance its appeal to the general
educated reader. Philosophers may be put off by these features,
as well as by Seneca's repetitions and his tendency to run on
too long. But the essay presents an admirably sensitive and
careful exposition, with extended helpful applications, of the
Old and Middle Stoic analysis of anger and the other emotions.
We may regret that writings in Greek of Chrysippus and
Posidonius, and other professional Stoic teachers from the third
to first centuries BC, have not survived. But Seneca's *On Anger*,
for all its lack of technicality, remains an excellent example of
Stoic philosophizing on ethics and moral psychology.

The political context

Why was so much written on anger? Why should a person like
Seneca's brother Novatus have felt the need for a work on

[19] He does not in fact mention Chrysippus, and only names Posidonius in a lost
part of Book I preserved by Lactantius. (See below on I 2. 3.) He may also have
looked at a work by Posidonius specifically *On Anger*, of which we know nothing
apart from its title, which is cited from a papyrus from Memphis (third century
AD) as Fragment F36 in L. Edelstein and I. Kidd, *Posidonius I: The Fragments*
(Cambridge 1972). See Kidd's comments, *Posidonius II. The Commentary*
(Cambridge 1988), I pp. 178–9.
[20] At II 10. 6 he reworks a remark from Sotion's *On Anger* preserved in Stobaeus
(III 20. 53).
[21] II 36 and III 36.
[22] The quest for sources, pursued on the assumption that a writer like like Seneca
could only be copying and contaminating the work of earlier and better authors,
was a regular enterprise in nineteenth- and early twentieth-century scholarship.
For a recent example of this aproach to Seneca see J. Fillion-Lahille, *ANRW* II
36. 3, pp. 1619–38.

this subject? We do not have to suppose that Romans and Hellenistic Greeks had filthier tempers than we have. But it does seem that the scope for some individuals to wreak havoc was much greater in antiquity than it would be in a modern society where violence is supposed to be the monopoly of the bureaucratic state. People in positions of power could cause enormous damage by losing their tempers – this had been obvious since the wrath of Achilles had 'brought countless woes to the Achaeans' in the Trojan War. But the disastrous consequences of anger were most obvious where power was absolute. The outrages of monarchs – Persian, Greek and Roman – were the supreme example of the cruelty to which anger could lead. That is why Seneca reels off so many stories about Cambyses, Darius, Xerxes, Alexander the Great, and the local monster, Caligula.[23] (Here *On Anger* reinforces by anticipation the panegyric to mercifulness, the opposite of cruelty, in the somewhat later *On Mercy*.) But lesser personages were also in a position to do great harm, especially if, like Novatus, they belonged to the Roman ruling class. During his term of office, a provincial governor[24] would have the powers – and the military strength – of a king. Even in private life, a person of that class could find himself with virtually monarchical power over a large household of dependants and slaves whom it was easy, if sometimes dangerous, to abuse.[25] An outburst of anger on his part could thus have wide and disruptive social consequences, though Seneca, typically for a moralist of his time and for a Stoic, is more overtly concerned with its brutalizing effect on the person himself.

Novatus may have seemed a suitable addressee for an essay *On Anger* simply as a representative of this class.[26] In any event,

---

[23] See especially II 33. 3–6, III 16–20.
[24] Like the irascible Gnaeus Piso (*On Anger* I 18. 3–6). Another notable case of a provincial governor with a vile temper was Cicero's Brother Quintus. See Cicero's *Letters to his brother Quintus* I 1. 27–9, 2. 5–7.
[25] See III 5.4 and the story of Vedius Pollio at III 40. 2–5.
[26] He does not seem to have had any problems with anger (cf. Seneca, *Investigations into Nature* 4 Praef. II. Fillion-Lahille (*ANRW* II 36. 3, pp. 1616–19) supposes that *On Anger* was really written for the benefit of the newly ascended emperor Claudius who was some given to cruelty and who procaimed on his accession that his anger would be 'brief and blameless', his irascibility 'not unjust' (Suetonius, *Life of Claudius* 38.1).

Seneca's advice appears to have been highly successful – or
perhaps it was never really needed. As governor of Achaea,
Novatus showed commendable restraint and finesse in adjudi-
cating the quarrel between members of the Jewish community
at Corinth and the apostle Paul (Acts XVIII 12–17).[27] He was
to be remembered for his 'sweetness'.[28]

[27] See Griffin, p. 83 and n. 5.
[28] Seneca, *Investigations into Nature* 4 Praef. II; Statius, *Silvae* II 7. 31 f.

Book I

Preface*

The horrors of anger

1 (1) You have demanded, Novatus, that I write on how anger can be alleviated. I think that you were right to have a particular dread of this the most hideous and frenzied of all the emotions. The others have something quiet and placid in them, whereas anger is all excitement and impulse. Raving with a desire that is utterly inhuman for instruments of pain and reparations in blood, careless of itself so long as it harms the other, it rushes onto the very spear-points, greedy for vengeance that draws down the avenger with it.

(2) Some of the wise, accordingly, have described anger as 'brief insanity'[1] – it is just as uncontrolled. Oblivious of decency, heedless of personal bonds, obstinate and intent on anything once started, closed to reasoning or advice, agitated on pretexts without foundation, incapable of discerning fairness or truth, it most resembles those ruins which crash in pieces over what they have crushed. (3) You can see that men possessed by anger are insane, if you look at their expression. The sure signs of raving madness are a bold

---

* The subheadings in these translations have been inserted by the editors.
[1] Compare Horace, *Epistles* I 2. 62; Cato the Censor, as reported by Plutarch (*Sayings of Kings and Generals* 199a); Philodemus, *On Anger* XVI 36–20. The association of anger with madness, brief or otherwise, was a commonplace. See Seneca, *On Anger* I 1. 3, II 25. 1, 35. 5, III 1. 5, 34. 2; Cicero, *Tusculan Disputations* IV 77; Plato, *Laws* 934d; Aristotle, *Nicomachean Ethics* 1147a 15–17; Epicurus, Fragment 484 Usener, etc. We still make the association in modern English when we speak of being 'mad' at someone.

and threatening look, a gloomy countenance, a grim visage, a rapid pace, restless hands, change of colour, heavy and frequent sighing. The marks of anger are the same: (4) eyes ablaze and glittering, a deep flush over all the face as blood boils up from the vitals, quivering lips, teeth pressed together, bristling hair standing on end, breath drawn in and hissing, the crackle of writhing limbs, groans and bellowing, speech broken off with the words barely uttered, hands struck together too often, feet stamping the ground, the whole body in violent motion 'menacing mighty wrath in mien',[2] the hideous horrifying face of swollen self-degradation – you would hardly know whether to call the vice hateful or ugly.

(5) Other passions can be concealed and nourished in secret. Anger parades itself; it shows on the face; the greater it is, the more obviously it seethes out. You can see how any animal, the moment it rears itself to do harm, shows some preliminary sign; the entire body forsakes its normal state of repose as it whets its savagery. (6) Boars foam at the mouth, grinding and sharpening their teeth; bulls toss their horns about, stamping and scattering the sand; lions growl; serpents swell at the neck when roused; rabid dogs are a grim spectacle – no animal has a nature so horrendous, so pernicious that it does not reveal, at the onset of anger, a fresh access of ferocity.[3] (7) I know that other emotions, too, can scarce be concealed. Lust, fear and overconfidence have their indications, and can be told in advance. None, in fact, of the more violent disturbances makes its entry without causing some change to the face. What, then, is the difference? The other affections make themselves seen. Anger sticks right out.

2 (1) Now look at its consequences and the losses which it occasions. No plague has cost the human race more. You will see slaughter, poisoning, charge and sordid counter-charge in the

---

[2] The Latin appears to be a fragment of an iambic verse, not otherwise known.

[3] On the Stoic view, animals cannot experience anger, strictly speaking (see below, I 3. 4–8). Since they cannot think rationally, they cannot hold beliefs, so that any aroused state of ferocious feeling in them is essentially a different thing from human anger. According to the Stoics, the latter is based upon the belief that one has been unjustly mistreated (see 'Definitions of anger' below, I 2). There is nothing illegitimate, however, in Seneca's applying the term here to the corresponding psychological state in an animal. As he argues in *On Favours* II 34. 1–5, such extended uses, guided by analogy and resemblance, are both a practical necessity and entirely appropriate.

law-courts, devastation of cities, the ruin of whole nations, persons of princely rank for sale at public auction, buildings set alight and the fire spreading beyond the city walls, huge tracts of territory glowing in flames that the enemy kindled. (2) Look and you will see cities of greatest renown, their very foundations now scarcely discernible – anger cast them down; deserts, mile after mile without inhabitant – anger emptied them. Look at all those leaders remembered as examples of ill fortune – anger stabbed one in bed, smote down another amid the solemnities of the banquet,[4] tore a third to pieces in sight of the law-courts and crowded forum;[5] anger made one the bleeding victim of his parricide son, told another to expose his royal throat to the hand of a slave and ordered a third to stretch spreadeagled in crucifixion.[6] (3) So far, I have told only of single executions. What if you cared to leave aside the individuals consumed in the flame of anger? Then look upon gathered throngs put to the sword, on the military sent in to butcher the populace *en masse*, on whole peoples condemned to death in an indiscriminate devastation . . .[7]

<Anger changes all things from their best and justest condition into the opposite. Whoever falls into its power, forgets all obligation. Allow it, and a father turns into an enemy, a son into a parricide, a mother into a stepmother, a citizen into an enemy, a king into a tyrant.>

Questions

What counts as anger

<Anger is 'a burning desire to avenge a wrong' or, according to Posidonius, 'a burning desire to punish him by whom you think yourself to have been unfairly harmed.' Some define it thus: 'anger

---

[4] Perhaps a reference to the fate of Alexander the Great's friend Clitus (see III 17. 1).
[5] Perhaps a reference, as Lipsius suggests, to the lynching of the praetor Asellio in 89 BC at the end of the Social War (Appian, *The Civil Wars* I 54; Valerius Maximus, IX 7. 4).
[6] Perhaps a reference to Aristotle's patron, Hermias tyrant of Atarneus, crucified in 341 BC by Darius III for intrigues with Macedonia.
[7] There is a gap in the text as transmitted at this point. We insert here two passages from later authors apparently quoting from the lost section. The first is from Martin of Braga (sixth century), *On Anger* II.

is an incitement of the mind to damage him who has done damage or wished to do damage'.[8]>

(4) ... as though escaping from our care or despising our authority.[9] Tell me, you might ask, why is the populace angry with gladiators – and so unfairly[10] as to think it an injury that they object to dying? It judges itself to be despised. In look, gesture and violence, it changes from spectator into opponent. (5) Whatever this is, it is not anger. It is a *quasi*-anger, like that of children who fall and then wish to thrash the ground. They often have no idea why they are angry – they just *are* angry, without cause and without being wronged, but not without some impression[11] of being wronged and not without some desire to punish. So they dupe themselves with pretended punches, placating themselves by imagining tears and pleas for mercy, dispelling spurious grief with spurious vengeance.

3 (1) 'We are often angry', it may be said, 'not with those who have harmed us, but with those who are about to harm us; which shows you that anger is not generated by being wronged.'[12] It is true that we are angry with those who are about to harm us. But

---

[8] These three definitions come from Lactantius (early fourth century), *On the Anger of God* 17. 13. Lactantius in fact cites four definitions of anger from Seneca, since he goes on to quote 3. 3: 'Aristotle's definition is not far from ours: he says that "anger is a burning desire to pay back pain".' Of these, the first definition is a commonplace of Hellenistic philosophy, the second a refinement by the innovative Stoic Posidonius (first century BC), the third is probably Epicurean (compare Philodemus, *On Anger* XLI 29 f.), while the fourth is quoted from Aristotle's *On the Soul* (403a 30 f.). Seneca's inclusiveness is significant. He is less concerned to distinguish between the definitions than to point out what they all have in common, namely revenge. At *On Mercy* II 3, he applies the same inclusive method to defining mercy.

[9] As our text resumes, Seneca is considering objections to the definitions just presented, e.g. that people roar 'angrily' at one gladiator as another attacks him, whereas under the definitions this will apparently not count as anger, since they have not been wronged.

[10] An ironical echo of the Posidonian definition.

[11] A technical term. On the Stoic account of the emotions, an 'impression' (Greek φαντασία) is received by the mind and given 'assent' (Greek συγκατάθεσις), thus triggering off the 'impulse' (Greek ὁρμή) or emotional reaction. See further II 1–4. On Stoic theory small children cannot yet think and decide rationally, so that their irrational outbursts at best resemble (adult) anger, but are not the same thing.

[12] This looks like an objection from opponents who have adopted the third (Epicurean) definition of anger. The objection that comes after it may have the same provenance.

the very intention is what does the harm. Anyone on the point of doing a wrong is already doing one. (2) 'You can see that anger is not a desire for punishment', it may be said, 'from the fact that the weakest are often angry with the most powerful, without desiring a punishment which they cannot hope to exact.' In the first place, we said that it is a *desire* – not a capacity – to inflict punishment; people may desire even what is beyond their power. Secondly, no one is in so low a state that he cannot *hope* for the punishment of even the highest. When it comes to doing damage, we are all of us powerful.

(3) Aristotle's definition is not far from ours:[13] he says that 'anger is a burning desire to pay back pain.' To explain the difference between this definition and ours would take long. Against both it may be said that wild animals are angered without being provoked by wrong and without aiming to inflict punishment or pain on others. That may be what they succeed in doing; it is not what they are seeking. (4) To this we must reply that wild animals are incapable of anger, as is everything, apart from man. Anger may be the enemy of reason. It cannot, all the same, come into being except where there is a place for reason. Wild animals are subject to impulse, to fits of frenzy, ferocity and aggression. But not to anger, any more than to self-indulgence – even if, in some pleasures, they are more intemperate than man. (5) There is no reason to believe the poet when he says:

> Anger the boar forgets, the deer its trust
> In speed, the bear its raids on sturdy kine.[14]

By 'anger' he means 'arousal', 'onrush'; boars have no more idea of being angry than of pardoning. (6) Without speech, animals are without human emotions, though they have certain impulses that are similar to them. Otherwise, if they were capable of love and hatred, they would also be capable of friendship and feud, disagreement and concord. Of these, too, there is some trace in animals. But they belong properly to the good and evil in human breasts. (7) No creature save man has been granted prudence, foresight, scrupulousness, deliberation. Nor is it only from the virtues of

[13] Seneca speaks as a Stoic. 'Ours' here, as at I 6. 5 and elsewhere, means 'that of the Stoics'.
[14] Ovid, *Metamorphoses* VII 545 f.

man, but from his vices as well, that animals have been debarred.[15] Their entire form, external and internal alike, is different from that of men; their 'ruling principle'[16] is differently moulded. An animal has a voice certainly, but a voice unsuitable for articulate utterance, confused and incapable of forming words. They have a tongue, but one that is trammelled and inhibited from varied movements. In the same way, the ruling principle itself of the animal soul is not refined or precise enough. It can receive images and impressions of objects sufficient to evoke impulses, but these are disordered and confused. (8) The onset of those impulses and their turmoil may, hence, be violent. They do not, however, amount to fear or anxiety, sorrow or anger, but only to something like these affections. That is why they quickly subside and change into their contraries. From the fiercest raging and terror, animals turn to feeding. Bellowing and crazy running around are followed at once by peace and slumber.

4 (1) I have said enough about what anger is. Its difference from irascibility will be apparent. It is the difference between the drunk and the drunkard, the frightened and the timid. An angry man need not be irascible; the irascible can sometimes not be angry. (2) Other specific varieties of anger, marked off from one another by numerous nouns in Greek, I shall pass over.[17] Our language lacks the equivalent terms, though we can speak of someone as 'acrimonious' and 'acerbic,' not to say 'testy', 'frantic', 'brawling', 'difficult', 'exasperated' – all of these are kinds of anger. (In their number you may include the 'pernickety' – a pampered form of irascibility.) (3) Some forms of anger die down amid shouts; some are as persistent as they are common; some are savage in action but short on words; some discharge themselves in a bitter flood of words and curses; some go no further than complaints and expressions of disgust; some are deep, serious and turned inwards – and there are a thousand other forms of the multifarious malady.

---

[15] Compare Socrates in Plato's *Laches* 196e–197b, who anticipates the Stoics in denying that animals can have virtues or vices, because they have no knowledge or understanding of anything.

[16] Another Stoic technical term: the *principale* (Greek ἡγεμονικόν), in Stoic psychology, was the 'command centre' of the soul, seat of perception, of impulse and (in human beings) of thought.

[17] Andronicus of Rhodes (first century BC) in his *On Passions* distinguished at least five sub-varieties of anger (*SVF* III 397). See also Cicero, *Tusculan Disputations* IV 21. The Greek Stoics were renowned for their attention to such details.

Is anger natural?

5 (1) We have asked what anger is, whether it occurs in any animal other than man, how it differs from irascibility, how many species of it there are. We must now ask whether anger accords with nature and whether it is useful and, in part, worth retaining. (2) Is anger in accordance with nature? The answer will be clear, if we turn our eyes upon man. What is milder than man, when he is in his right mind? But what is crueller than anger? What is more loving of others than man is? What more adverse than anger? Man was begotten for mutual assistance, anger for mutual destruction. The one would flock together with his fellows, the other would break away. The one seeks to help, the other to harm; the one would succour even those unknown to him, the other would fly at even those who are dearest. Man will go so far as to sacrifice himself for the good of another; anger will plunge into danger, if it can draw the other down. (3) What greater ignorance of nature could there be than to credit its finest, most flawless work with this savage, ruinous fault? Anger, as I said, is greedy for punishment. That such a desire should reside in that most peaceful of dwellings, the breast of man, is utterly out of accord with his nature. Human life rests upon kindnesses and concord; bound together, not by terror but by love reciprocated, it becomes a bond of mutual assistance.[18]

6 (1) 'Tell me then, is not chastisement sometimes necessary?' Of course! But chastisement without anger, chastisement aided by reason. It is not a matter of doing harm, but of curing in the guise of doing harm. To straighten shafts that are bent, we apply heat; we drive wedges in and use pressure, not to break them but to flatten them out. We make the same use of physical or mental pain to straighten out characters that are warped and faulty. (2) A doctor, you see, will first, where nothing much is the matter, try a slight modification of daily routine. Imposing a regimen of food, drink and exercise, he attempts to secure the patient's health by a mere change in his way of life. His immediate recourse is to moderation. If moderation and order do no good, he takes away

---

[18] On Stoic theory humans are made by nature to be socially cooperative animals, devoted to the common good of all. This theme also appears towards the beginning of both *On Mercy* (1 3. 2) and *On the Private Life* (1. 4), as well as being central to *On Favours*.

or cuts back on some parts of the diet. If the patient still makes no response, he takes him off food altogether and relieves the body by starving it. If these gentler methods fail, he opens a vein and applies force to limbs which would harm and infect the body by remaining on it – no treatment is seen as harsh if its effects are wholesome. (3) Similarly, the proper course for a guardian of the law and governor of the state is, so long as he can, to cure people's character by words, and by gentle words at that – to urge their duties upon them, to win their minds over to desiring what is honourable and fair, to make them hate their faults and value their virtues. Next he should proceed to grimmer speech, though still for admonishment and reproach. Finally he should turn to punishments, but these too should still be light punishments, easily revoked – ultimate penalties are for ultimate crimes; no one should be put to death save he whose death will benefit even himself. (4) He differs from doctors in this one respect. When they cannot bestow life, they provide an easy end; whereas those whom he has condemned he puts to death with disgrace and public humiliation, not because he enjoys punishing anyone – far be the wise man[19] from such inhuman savagery! – but to make them an example for all. They were no good alive – they had no wish to be. At least by their death they can serve the public good![20]

The nature of man, therefore, is not eager to punish; nor, then, can anger be in accordance with the nature of man; for anger is eager to punish.

(5) I will also bring in some evidence from Plato – what harm is there in using other people's ideas on points where they coincide with ours? 'A good man', he says, 'does no damage.'[21] Punishment does do damage: therefore punishment does not go with being a good man. Nor, for that reason, does anger, since punishment does go with anger. If a good man does not delight in punishment,

[19] By this term Seneca refers, as often, to the ideal, fully perfected person, who possesses a deep-seated and unshakeable knowledge of how to act in all possible circumstances, and of why he should do so. This knowledge, on the Stoic theory, counts as 'wisdom' and is the foundation for all the human virtues.

[20] Compare the similar line of thought at 16. 2–3 and 19. 5–7. Humane, rational, medicinal punishment, as Seneca understands it, can in fact go to the length of infanticide and wholesale exterminations. See 15. 2 and 19. 2.

[21] Plato, *Republic* 335d.

neither will he delight in that affection which sees punishment as a pleasure; therefore anger is not natural.

Can anger be useful, or controlled?

7 (1) Can it really be that anger, although it is not natural, should be adopted because it has often proved useful? 'It rouses and spurs on the mind. Without it, courage can achieve nothing magnificent in war – without the flame of anger beneath, to goad men on to meet danger with boldness.' Some, accordingly, think it best to moderate anger, not to remove it. They would confine it to a wholesome limit by drawing off any excess, while retaining what is essential for unenfeebled action, for unsapped force and vigour of spirit.[22] (2) <Well>, in the first place, it is easier to exclude the forces of ruin than to govern them, to deny them admission than to moderate them afterwards. For once they have established possession, they prove to be more powerful than their governor, refusing to be cut back or reduced. (3) Moreover, reason itself, entrusted with the reins,[23] is only powerful so long as it remains isolated from the affections. Mixed and contaminated with them, it cannot contain what it could previously have dislodged. Once the intellect has been stirred up and shaken out, it becomes the servant of the force which impels it. (4) Some things at the start are in our power; thereafter they sweep us on with a force of their own and allow no turning back. Bodies in free fall have no control over themselves. They cannot delay or resist the downward course.

---

[22] Seneca is attacking the view of Aristotle and his followers that moral virtue in general is a fixed disposition to feel a 'mean' or intermediate amount of various desires or emotions (see *Nicmachean Ethics* II 5–7), and that the specific virtue of 'good temper' consists of a fixed disposition to feel intermediate amounts of anger, as suits the circumstances (*ibid.*, IV 5). Seneca's principal target – the claim that anger is needed to give power and vigour to the intellect and to the intellect's own virtues – is not, however, a central contention of Aristotle's, but at best an implication of his theory. (Even that is disputable.) Seneca was not the only writer to attack the Aristotelians in this way. See Cicero, *Tusculan Disputations* IV 43–7; Philodemus, *On Anger* xxxi 24–xxxiv 6.

[23] The concept of reason with the passions as its horses, a concept much invoked in favour of the Peripatetic position, goes back to Plato (*Phaedrus* 253c–256b). The Stoics, as Seneca makes clear, treated reason and emotion not as separate agencies but as permutations of one and the same mind. (See Introduction, p. 7f.)

Any deliberation and second thoughts are cut short by the peremptory force of gravity. They cannot help completing a trajectory which they need not have begun. In the same way, the mind, if it throws itself into anger, love and other affections, is not allowed to restrain the impulse. It is bound to be swept along and driven to the bottom by its own weight and by the natural downward tendency of any failing.

8 (1) It is best to beat back at once the first irritations, to resist the very germs of anger and take care not to succumb. Once it has begun to carry us off course, the return to safety is difficult. Reason amounts to nothing, once the affection has been installed and we have voluntarily given it some legal standing. From then on, it will do what it wants, not what you allow it. (2) The enemy, I say, must be stopped at the very frontier; when he has invaded and rushed on the city gates, there is no 'limit' which his captives can make him accept. It is not the case that the mind stands apart, spying out its affections from without, to prevent their going too far – the mind itself turns into affection. It cannot, accordingly, reinstate that useful and wholesome force which it has betrayed and weakened. (3) As I said, it is not the case that they dwell apart, in isolation from one another. Reason and affection are the mind's transformations for better or for worse. How then can reason, under the oppressive domination of its failings, rise again, if it has already given way to anger? How can it free itself from the chaos, if the admixture of baser ingredients has prevailed? (4) 'But some people', it may be said, 'control their anger.' So as to do nothing that anger dictates – or some of it? If nothing, there is clearly no need, when it comes to doing things, of the anger which you recommend as somehow more forceful than reason. (5) Now my next question: is anger stronger than reason – or weaker? If stronger, how can reason put a limit on it? It is only the feebler, normally, who submit. If anger is weaker, reason can do without it. It is sufficient by itself for getting things done and has no need for a weaker ally. (6) 'But some people stay true to themselves and control themselves in their anger.' When? As their anger evaporates and departs of its own accord, not at its boiling-point – it is too strong then. (7) 'Well, is it not sometimes true that, even in anger, people release the objects of their hatred unharmed and untouched? Do they not refrain from harming them?' They do. But when?

When affection has driven back affection, when fear or lust has obtained its demand. Quiet has ensued, thanks not to reason, but to an evil, untrustworthy armistice between the affections.

The use of anger in war and in peacetime

9 (1) Again, there is nothing useful in anger. It does not whet the mind for deeds of war. Virtue needs no vice to assist it; it suffices for itself. Whenever impetus is necessary, it does not break out in anger; it rises to action aroused and relaxed to the extent that it thinks necessary, in just the same way that the range of a missile shot from a catapult is under the control of the operator. (2) 'Anger', says Aristotle, 'is needful; no fight can be won without it, without its filling the mind and kindling enthusiasm there; it must be treated, however, not as a commander but as one of the rank and file.'[24] That is false. If it listens to reason and follows where led, it is no longer anger, the hallmark of which is wilful disobedience. But if it rebels against orders to stay still and follows its own ferocious fancy, it is as useless a subordinate in the soul as a soldier who ignores the signal for retreat. (3) So if it accepts a limit, it needs some other name, having ceased to be anger, which I understand to be something unbridled and ungoverned. If it does not, it is ruinous and not to be counted as an assistant. Either it is not anger at all, or it is useless. (4) Anyone who exacts punishment not through greed for the punishment itself, but because he should, does not count as angry. A good soldier is one who knows how to obey orders and carry out decisions. The affections are no less evil as subordinates than they are as commanders.

10 (1) So reason will never enlist the aid of reckless unbridled impulses over which it has no authority, which it can only contain

---

[24] This is not a quotation from any of Aristotle's surviving works. Seneca may be quoting from one of his lost dialogues, or he may be mistaking for a quotation some statement of Aristotle's view by a later Peripatetic author, such as Theophrastus or Hieronymus of Rhodes. But he may simply, for vividness' sake, be putting the words into Aristotle's mouth. (In any event, he probably derived the military language from some later Peripatetic writer, as Philodemus, *On Anger* XXXIII 22–8, may also have done.) In fact, it is difficult even to trace the sentiment here to anything in Aristotle. The nearest thing to it in the *Nicomachean Ethics* is perhaps the view expounded and then criticized at 1116b23–1117a9.

by confronting them with matching and similar impulses – anger with fear, indolence with anger, fear with greed. (2) May virtue be spared the horror of reason's seeking refuge in vices! Trustworthy peace is impossible, turmoil and vacillation inevitable, for the mind that would find safety in its own evils. Incapable of bravery without anger, of industry without greed, of quietude without fear, it is doomed to live under a tyranny, once it has entered the service of an affection. Are you not ashamed to demote the virtues to dependency on vices? (3) Moreover, reason will cease to have any power at all, if it is powerless without affection. It will start to match and resemble it. For how will they differ? After all, affection without reason will be as unwise as reason without affection is unavailing. Each matches the other, where neither can exist without the other. But who would have the gall to make affection the equal of reason?

(4) 'Emotion does have some use,' it may be said, 'if it is moderate.' No. Only if its nature is to be useful. But if it will not submit to the command of reason, the sole consequence of moderation is that the less the affection the less its harm. Moderate affection means simply moderate evil.

11   (1) 'But against enemies,' it may be said, there is need for anger.' Nowhere less. The requirement there is not for impulses to be poured out, but to remain well tuned and responsive. What else leaves the barbarian shattered, for all his greater strength of body and powers of endurance? What else, if not his anger, its own worst enemy? Gladiators, too, are protected by skill but left defenceless by anger. (2) Again, what is the need for anger when reason serves as well? Do you suppose the hunter to be angry with the prey? He catches it as it comes, pursues it as it flees – and all this is done, without anger, by reason. What of the Cimbri and Teutons, pouring over the Alps in their thousands? What carried off so many of them that the magnitude of their disaster needed no messenger – rumour was enough – to bring the news of it home?[25] What else, if not that anger served them in place of courage? Driving down and flattening whatever stands in its way,

---

[25] Seneca is recalling the defeat by Gaius Marius of the Teutons at Aquae Sextiae (modern Aix-en-Provence) (102 BC) and of the Cimbri at Vercellae (101 BC), after they and other Germanic tribes had invaded Roman Gaul and northern Italy.

28

it results still more often in its own ruin. (3) Is there anything more spirited than a German? Or fiercer in the attack? Or keener for arms? Born and reared among arms, they care about nothing else. Is anything better hardened for every form of endurance? They are unprovided, most of them, with clothing or shelter against the unabated rigour of their climate. (4) Yet these Germans are slaughtered by Spaniards and Gauls, by soft unwarlike men of Asia and Syria, before the real army comes into sight,[26] easy victims for no other reason than their readiness to anger. Take them, body and soul, unfamiliar as they are with comfort, luxury and wealth; add reason and discipline. To say nothing more, we would certainly have to revive our old Roman ways! (5) What enabled Fabius to rebuild the stricken power of our state? He knew how to hold back, postpone, delay – a skill which entirely escapes the angry. The state would have perished – it stood at the last extremity – had Fabius run all the risks which anger urged on him. He took thought for the fate of the nation, calculating its resources – a single loss would have meant the loss of everything. Discarding all thought of grief and vengeance, he concentrated simply on expediency and the available opportunities. He overcame anger before overcoming Hannibal.[27] (6) What of Scipio? Abandoning Hannibal, the Carthaginian army and all the obvious objects of anger, he carried the war to Africa, so slowly as to give the ill-disposed an impression of self-indulgent sloth. (7) What of the other Scipio? Hard and long he sat before Numantia, calmly bearing his distress, which he shared with the nation, that Numantia was taking longer than Carthage to be conquered. Surrounding and enclosing the enemy with siegeworks, he brought them to the point of falling on their own swords.[28] (8) Anger is useless, even in battle or in war. With its wish to bring others into danger, it lowers its own guard. The surest courage is to look around long and hard, to govern oneself, to move slowly and deliberately forward.

---

[26] It was normal for foreign auxiliaries to open the battle while the legions of the main Roman army itself came up behind them.

[27] After the shattering defeat by the Carthaginians under Hannibal at Cannae (216 BC), Roman military fortunes recovered under Fabius Maximus Verrucosus Cunctator (the 'Delayer').

[28] Seneca is recalling the invasion of Africa by Scipio Africanus Major (204–202 BC), and the capture of Numantia in Spain (134–133 BC) by Scipio Africanus Minor, who had long since destroyed Carthage (146 BC).

12 (1) 'Tell me then, is the good man not angry if he sees his father slain and his mother ravished?' No, he will not be angry. He will punish and protect. Why should not filial devotion, even without anger, be enough of a stimulus? You could argue in the same way: 'Tell me then, if he sees his father or son undergoing surgery, will the good man not weep or faint?' We see this happening to women whenever they are struck by the slightest suggestion of danger. (2) The good man will do his duty, undismayed and undaunted; and he will do what is worthy of a good man without doing anything unworthy of a *man*. 'My father is about to be killed – I will defend him; he has been killed – I will avenge him; not because I am pained, but because I should.' (3) 'Good men are angry at wrongs done to their friends.' When you say this, Theophrastus,[29] you cast odium on braver teachings. You turn from the judge to the gallery. Since everyone is angry when something like that happens to his friends, you think that men will judge what they do to be what ought to be done. Nearly everyone holds emotions to be justified which he acknowledges in himself. (4) But they behave in the same way if the hot drinks are not served properly, if a piece of glassware is broken, if a shoe has mud on it. The motive for such anger is not devotion, but weakness, just as it is with children who bewail the loss of their parents – exactly as they bewail the loss of their toys. (5) Anger for one's friends is the mark of a weak mind, not a devoted one. What is fine and honourable is to go forth in defence of parents, children, friends and fellow-citizens, under the guidance of duty itself, in the exercise of will, judgment and foresight – and not through some raving impulse. No affection is keener to punish than anger is. For that very reason, it is ill fitted for punishing. Headlong and mindless like almost every burning desire, it gets in the way of what it rushes to do. So neither in peace nor in war has it ever been any good. In fact it makes peace resemble war. Under arms, it forgets that 'Mars is impartial' and falls into the power of others, having no power over itself.

(6) Again, failings should not be pressed into service on the grounds that they sometimes achieve something. Fevers, too, alleviate

---

[29] Theophrastus of Eresos (c. 370–288/5 BC) succeeded Aristotle as head of the Peripatetic school. The remarks which Seneca here and in 14. 1 below attributes to him are not elsewhere attested, and may be a reformulation of his views rather than strict citations from any of his writings. See William W. Fortenbaugh, *Quellen zur Ethik Theophrasts* (Amsterdam 1984), Fragment 110.

some kinds of ill health. But that does not mean that it would not be better to be without them altogether – it is a hateful sort of remedy that leaves one owing one's health to disease. In the same way, anger may sometimes have proved unexpectedly beneficial – like poison, a fall, or a shipwreck. But that does not make it wholesome. Lives, after all, have often been saved by deadly objects.

13 (1) Again, things worth having are the better and more desirable the more of them there is. If justice is a good thing, no one will say that it is better with a bit taken off. If courage is a good, no one will want it partly diminished. (2) Therefore, in the case of anger too, the more, the better. Who would refuse an addition of anything that is good? But the augmentation of anger is not of positive use. Nor, therefore, is its existence.[30] There is no good that becomes bad by increment.

(3) 'Anger is of use', it may be said, 'because it makes men keener to fight.' On that principle, drunkenness too would be useful – it makes men reckless and bold; many have proved better at arms when worse for drink. On the same principle, you could say that lunacy and madness are necessary for strength – frenzy often makes men stronger. (4) Tell me, have there not been times when fear has, paradoxically, made for boldness and dread of death has aroused even the most indolent to battle? But anger, drunkenness, fear and other such conditions are vile, unsteady incitements. What they provide is not the equipment for courage – virtue has no need for vices – but merely a slight uplift for souls otherwise slothful or cowardly. (5) No one is braver for being angry, save he who would not have been brave without anger. It comes not as an aid to courage, but as a replacement for it.

And what about this? If anger were a good, it would go with the highest degree of moral perfection. But those most prone to anger are children, the old and the sick. Anything weak is naturally inclined to complain.

Anger and punishment

14 (1) 'A good man', says Theophrastus, 'cannot help being angry at bad people.'[31] On that principle, the better a man is, the more

---

[30] Alternatively, 'But it is harmful for anger to be increased. So also, for anger to exist.'

[31] See 12. 3 above and n. 29.

prone he will be to anger. Are you sure that he will not, on the contrary, be the calmer and free from affections, someone who hates no one? (2) What has he, in truth, to hate about wrongdoers? Error is what has driven them to their sort of misdeeds. But there is no reason for a man of understanding to hate those who have gone astray. If there were, he would hate himself. He should consider how often he himself has not behaved well, how often his own actions have required forgiveness[32] – his anger will extend to himself. No fair judge will reach a different verdict on his own case than on another's. (3) No one, I say, will be found who can acquit himself; anyone who declares himself innocent has his eyes on the witness-box, not on his own conscience. How much humaner it is to show a mild, paternal spirit, not harrying those who do wrong, but calling them back! Those who stray in the fields, through ignorance of the way, are better brought back to the right path than chased out altogether.

15 (1) The wrongdoer should thus be corrected, by admonition and also by force, gently and also roughly; he needs to be improved for his own benefit no less than that of others. That may call for chastisement, but not for anger. For when is the patient an object of anger? 'But they are incapable of correction! There is nothing tractable in them, no grounds for hope.' Remove them then from human society – whatever they touch they will only make worse! In the one way that they can, let them cease to be bad! But that does not call for hatred. (2) Why should I hate him whom I most help when I rescue him from himself? No one, surely, hates his limb as he amputates it. His action is not one of anger, just a painful cure. We put down mad dogs; we kill the wild, untamed ox; we use the knife on sick sheep to stop their infecting the flock; we destroy abnormal offspring at birth; children, too, if they are born weak or deformed, we drown. Yet this is not the work of anger, but of reason – to separate the sound from the worthless. (3) Nothing is less proper in punishment than anger, since punishment serves the more to improve if it is imposed with considered judgment. Hence the remark of Socrates to the slave: 'I would hit

---

[32] The reflection 'I too have erred' will in fact be prescribed more than once as a remedy for anger. See II 28. 6, III 12. 1, 25. 2.

you, if I were not angry.'[33] Rebukes to his slave he postponed to
a saner moment; at the time, he rebuked himself. Who, I ask you,
will keep his affections moderate, when even Socrates dared not
entrust himself to anger?

16 (1) There is no need, therefore, to chastise in anger if error
and crime are to be repressed. Anger is a misdemeanour of the
soul, and one ought not to correct wrong-doing while doing wrong
oneself.[34] 'Tell me then, should I not be angry with a robber? Or
with a poisoner?' No. For neither am I angry with myself when I
let my own blood. (2) I can employ every kind of punishment as
a remedy. *You* are still in the first stages of error; your lapses are
light but frequent: reprimands, first in private, then made public,
will attempt your reform. *You*, however, have gone too far to be
curable by mere words: your constraint shall be official disgrace.
You again, for your part, need branding with something stronger,
something to feel: you shall be sent into exile and unfamiliar
surroundings. In *you*, though, the wickedness has already hardened,
requiring sterner remedies: recourse will be had to public fetters
and prison. (3) *Your* soul, on the other hand, is incurable as it
weaves its mesh of crimes. You need no pretext – and pretexts
for the wicked are never wanting – to drive you on; you find cause
enough for doing wrong in wrong-doing itself. You have drained
the cup of wickedness and so mingled it with your entrails that it
can only be discharged along with them. Long since, in your misery,
you have sought to die. We shall serve you well; we shall take
away this madness by which you cause and are caused vexation;
after the torment to yourself and others in which you have long
wallowed, we shall present you with the one good which remains
to you – death. Why should I be angry with him whom most I

---

[33] At III 12. 5–6, Seneca tells the same story about Plato. So do Plutarch (*Against
Colotes* 1108a) and Diogenes Laertius (III 26). Cicero (*Tusculan Disputations* IV 78
and *Republic* I 59) and others tell it about Plato's friend the Pythagorean philosopher Archytas (fourth century BC), who may well have been the original hero
of the story (see below on III 10). Seneca here is alone in assigning it to Socrates.
The principle that 'punishment should be administered without anger' has already
appeared at I 6. 1. Turned into the the prescription 'Don't punish in anger', it
will reappear several times as a precaution against punishing wrongly (II 22. 4,
III 32. 2) and even as a technique for stifling your anger (II 29. 1, III 12. 4).
[34] Compare Plutarch, *On the Control of Anger* 459c: 'I came to realize that it was
better to make my slaves worse by indulging them than to pervert my self with
bitterness and rage for the improvement of others.'

benefit? Killing is sometimes the best form of compassion.[35] (4) If I entered a hospital or a rich man's household as a trained expert,[36] I would not prescribe the same thing for everyone, given the diversity of ailments. In the minds about me, I see as great a variety of failings. Called in to cure the state, I must find for each man's illness the proper remedy – one person may be cured by a sense of shame, another by exile, a third by pain, another by poverty, another by the sword. (5) Hence, even if I have to wear my garb of office reversed and summon the assembly by trumpet,[37] I shall mount the tribunal not in fury or hatred, but with the aspect of law; I shall pronounce those solemn words in a gentle and grave, not a raging, tone of voice; I shall command, not in anger but sternly, that the law be carried out; when I order the guilty to be beheaded, when I have the parricide sown in the sack,[38] when I send the soldier to execution, when I have the traitor or public enemy placed upon the Tarpeian rock,[39] I shall be without anger, with the same look on my face and the same spirit, as when I crush a serpent or poisonous insect. (6) 'A readiness to anger is needed for punishment.' Tell me, does the law seem angry with men whom it has never known, whom it has never seen, whom it hoped would never exist? That is the spirit to be adopted, a spirit not of anger but of resolution. For if anger at bad deeds befits a good man, so too will resentment at the prosperity of bad men. What is more scandalous than the fact that some should flourish and abuse the kindness of fortune, when no fortune could be bad enough for them? Yet he will view their gains without resentment and their crimes without anger. A good judge condemns what is damnable; he does not hate it.

(7) 'Tell me then. When the wise man has to deal with something of this sort, will his mind not be touched by some unwonted

---

[35] With this passage and I 6. 3 f., compare the theory of punishment (also based on a medical analogy) at Plato, *Gorgias*, 477e–481b. The whole paragraph is quite notably for the benefit of those who, like the addressee Novatus, are going to hold magistracies with the power of life and death.

[36] Reading, with the MSS, *exercitatus et sciens*. A rich man's household containing hundreds of slaves might well need the services of a full-time doctor.

[37] In order to indicate that the trial is on a capital charge.

[38] See *On Mercy* I 15. 7 and notes.

[39] And hurled down from it. This traditional mode of execution for murder or treason was still occasionally used in Seneca's lifetime. See Tacitus, *Annals* II 32. 5.

excitement?' It will, I admit. He will feel a slight, tiny throb. As Zeno says, the soul of the wise man too, even when the wound is healed, shows the scar.[40] He will feel a hint or shadow of them, but will be without the affections themselves.

17 (1) Aristotle says that some emotions, if well used, serve as arms.[41] That would be true if, like weapons of war, they could be picked up and put down at will. But these arms which Aristotle would give to virtue go to war by themselves, without awaiting the hand of the warrior. They possess us; they are not our possessions. (2) We have no need for other weapons; it is enough that nature has equipped us with reason. What she has given us is firm, enduring, accommodating, with no double edge to be turned on its owner. Reason by itself is enough not merely for foresight but for action. Indeed, what could be stupider than for reason to seek protection in bad temper, for something that is stable, trustworthy and sound to seek protection in something unsteady, untrustworthy and sick? (3) And what of the fact that for action too, the one area with some apparent need for the services of bad temper, reason by itself is far stronger? Having judged that something should be done, it sticks to its judgment. It will find nothing better than itself into which it might change. So it stands by its decisions once they are made. (4) Anger is often driven back by pity. For it has no solid strength. An empty swelling with a violent onset, like winds which rise from the earth and, begotten in river and marsh, are strong without staying-power, (5) it begins with a mighty impulse, and then fails exhausted before its time. Having pondered nothing save cruelty and new kinds of punishment, it shows itself, when the time has come to punish, broken and weak. Affections collapse quickly; reason remains constant. (6) Moreover, even where anger has persisted, we sometimes find that, if there are several who deserve to die, it stops the killing after the first two or three. Its first blows are the fierce ones. In the same way, it is when the serpent first crawls out of its den that its venom is harmful; drained by repeated use, its fangs are innocuous. (7) Hence equal crimes receive unequal punishment, and one who has committed less often receives more, being exposed to fresher wrath. Anger is altogether

---

[40] Seneca is our sole authority for this remark of Zeno's (*SVF* 1 215).
[41] See 9. 2 above.

inconsistent. Sometimes it goes further than it should, sometimes it stops short. It indulges itself, judges capriciously, refuses to listen, leaves no room for defence, clings to what it has seized and will not have its judgment, even a wrong judgment, taken from it.

18 (1) Reason gives time to either side, and then demands a further adjournment to give itself room to tease out the truth: anger is in a hurry. Reason wishes to pass a fair judgment: anger wishes the judgment which it has already passed to seem fair. (2) Reason considers nothing save the matter at issue; anger is roused by irrelevant trifles. An overconfident look, a voice too loud, speech too bold, a manner too refined, a rather too ostentatious show of support, popularity with the public – all serve to exasperate it. For hatred of the lawyer it often damns the accused. Even if the truth is put before its eyes, it fondly defends its error. Refusing to be proved wrong, it sees obstinacy, even in what is ill begun, as more honourable than a change of mind.

(3) I can remember Gnaeus Piso,[42] a man free of many faults, but wrong-headed in taking obduracy for firmness. In a fit of anger, he had ordered the execution of a soldier who had returned from leave without his companion, on the grounds that, if he could not produce him, he must have killed him. The man requested time for an enquiry to be made. His request was refused. Condemned and led outside the rampart, he was already stretching out his neck for execution, when suddenly there appeared the very companion who was thought to have been murdered. (4) The centurion in charge of the execution told his subordinate to sheathe his sword, and led the condemned man back to Piso, intending to exonerate Piso of guilt – for Fortune had already exonerated the soldier. A huge crowd accompanied the two soldiers locked in each other's embrace amid great rejoicing in the camp. In a fury Piso mounted the tribunal and ordered them both to be executed, the soldier who had not committed murder and the one who had not been

---

[42] Gnaeus Calpurnius Piso, consul in 7 BC, was appointed governor of Syria by Tiberius in AD 17, to assist and control Germanicus Caesar, with whom he quarrelled and for whose death (AD 19) he was put on trial. He committed suicide before the trial was over. Tacitus (*Annals* II 43. 2) describes him as a 'violent and insubordinate character, with an intractability inherited from his father', an opponent of Caesar and caesarism who remained unreconciled to the new order long after Augustus' supremacy was an established fact.

murdered. (5) What could be more scandalous? The vindication of the one meant the death of the two. And Piso added a third. He ordered the centurion who had brought the condemned man back to be himself executed. On the self-same spot, three were consigned to execution, all for the innocence of one! (6) How skilful bad temper can be at devising pretexts for rage! 'You,' it says, 'I command to be executed, because you have been condemned; you, because you have been the cause of your companion's condemnation; and you, because you have disobeyed orders from your general to kill.' It invented three charges, having discovered grounds for none.

19 (1) Anger, I say, has this evil: it refuses to be governed. It rages at truth itself, if truth appears to conflict with its wishes. With shouting, turmoil and a shaking of the entire body, it makes for those whom it has earmarked, showering them with abuse and curses. (2) Reason does none of this. Silently and serenely, if the need arises, it obliterates entire households; families that are a plague to the commonwealth it destroys, wives, children and all; it tears down their roofs and levels them to the ground;[43] the very names of foes to liberty it extirpates.[44] But it does this without gnashing its teeth or shaking its head or acting in any way improperly for a judge whose countenance should be at its calmest and most composed as he pronounces on matters of importance. (3) 'When you wish to hit some one,' says Hieronymus, 'what need is there to bite your lips first?'[45] What if he had seen a proconsul leaping off the tribunal, grabbing the fasces from the lictor,[46] and tearing his own garments, because others were too

---

[43] Seneca could be recalling the punishment of Spurius Maelius, a rich plebeian suspected of aiming to make himself tyrant and killed in 439 BC (Livy IV 15. 8).

[44] After Marcus Manlius Capitolinus had been thrown off the Tarpeian rock as a traitor (see above, 16. 5), no one of the Manlian family was permitted to have the name 'Marcus' (Livy VI 20. 13).

[45] I.e. ... to conceal and control your feelings, as against expressing and inflaming them further by gnashing your teeth, tearing your clothes, etc. (Hieronymus Fragment 21 Wehrli). Hieronymus of Rhodes, a Peripatetic philosopher and historian of literature, lived and worked in Athens c. 290–230 BC None of his works survive.

[46] The fasces, bundles of rods originally with an axe in the middle, were a mark of office carried by attendant lictors before all Roman officials who held active power of command. In modern times the emblem was adopted by Mussolini and his *Fascisti*.

slow in tearing theirs?[47] (4) What need is there to kick the table over? to smash the goblets? to bang yourself against columns? to tear your hair? to strike your thigh? beat your breast? Surely you see the sheer madness of anger? Since it cannot erupt against others as quickly as it would like, it turns on itself. They have to be held down by their next of kin and begged to make peace with themselves!

(5) None of this would be done by a person who is free of anger when imposing a deserved punishment. He often releases a miscreant of proven guilt, if the man's repentance gives good grounds for hope. If he sees that the wickedness is not deep-seated but on the 'surface', as they say, of the soul, he will grant him a remission that can be accepted and granted without harm. (6) Sometimes he curbs a major crime less severely than a minor one, if the one is merely a lapse and not an expression of ingrained cruelty,[48] while the other conceals a secret, hidden and hardened craftiness. Two men guilty of the same crime will not be visited with the same penalty, if the one committed it through carelessness, whereas the other took positive care to do harm. (7) In all punishment at any time, his rule will be that it serves either to reform or to eliminate the wicked. In either case, he will look not to the past but to the future. (As Plato says,[49] a man of sense punishes not because a crime has been – but to prevent its being – committed; the past, that is, cannot be revoked, but the future is being forestalled.) And those whom he wishes to become an example of wickedness meeting a bad end he will kill openly, not just so that they may themselves die, but so that their death may deter others. (8) You see how anyone with responsibility for weighing and considering these things must be free from all disturbing emotions as he comes to grips with a matter requiring the utmost care – the power of life and death. Anger is the wrong trustee for the sword.

Anger and greatness of mind

20 (1) Nor should you think even this, that anger contributes

---

[47] It was conventional for a person to rend his garments as an expression of grief, particularly on being sentenced, but altogether outrageous for a magistrate to do so out of rage at failing to impose a death-sentence.

[48] Cf. II 5. 3

[49] *Laws* 934a–b.

something to greatness of mind.[50] It is not a matter of greatness, but of morbid enlargement. Disease in bodies which bulge with a mass of tainted fluid is not 'growth' but pestilential excess. (2) All whose thoughts have been raised by derangement to superhuman heights, credit themselves with a spirit of lofty sublimity. But there is nothing solid beneath. Ruin awaits what has risen without foundation. Anger has no footing, no firm, lasting base on which to rise. Windy and void, it is as remote from greatness of mind as rash confidence is from courage, as cheek is from assurance or cruelty from sternness.[51] (3) There is a great difference, I tell you, between a lofty and an arrogant mind. Bad temper achieves nothing imposing or handsome. On the contrary, I think it the mark of a morbid unhappy mind, aware of its own weakness, to be constantly aching, like sore sick bodies which groan at the slightest touch. Anger is thus a particularly feminine and childish failing. 'But men, too, get it.' Yes. For men, too, can have feminine and childish characters.

(4) 'Tell me, then. Might not some utterances poured out in anger seem to be outpourings of a great mind?' You mean outpourings of ignorance about true greatness, like that dire, detestable saying: 'let them hate, provided that they fear.'[52] A sentence, as you can see, from the time of Sulla![53] I am not sure which wish was worse –

---

[50] For most of antiquity there were two rival concepts of *magnitudo animi,* μεγαλοψυχία, 'greatness of mind'. Aristotle, in his *Posterior Analytics* (97b15–26) had cited it as a prize example of an equivocal term, since it could mean either 'refusal to put up with insult', the attitude of a hero like Achilles whose greatness demands recognition from his peers, or 'imperviousness to fortune', the mark of a person like Socrates who is too great to be affected by anything external. 'Greatness of mind' was ordinarily understood in the former sense. But the Stoics identified it with superiority to circumstances (*SVF* III 264, 265, 269, 270), exemplified by Socrates and Cato. As ordinarily understood, 'greatness of mind' would allow and sometimes even demand anger. For Seneca it is thus crucial to establish his Stoic idea of the virtue. As we shall see, the thought that greatness of mind lies precisely in *not* reacting angrily will be offered more than once as a remedy for anger (II 32. 3, III 25. 3, 28. 6, 32. 3). (At *On Favours* III 18. 4 a different aspect of the Stoic concept emerges: greatness of mind is not the prerogative of aristocratic heroes like Achilles; it can be shown even by a slave.)
[51] See *On Mercy* II 4.
[52] This sentence, also quoted at *On Mercy* I 12. 4 and II 2. 2, comes from the *Atreus,* a tragedy by Lucius Accius (Fragment 168, *Remains of Old Latin* Loeb edn. (London 1936 II, p. 382).
[53] Accius (170–90 BC) in fact died about a decade before Sulla's worst atrocities. Lucius Cornelius Sulla Felix (138–78 BC), reactionary statesman, was best remem-

39

to be hated or to be feared. 'Let them hate.' It occurred to him that he would be the object of curses, intrigues and crushing attack. So what did he add? He hit on a worthy remedy for hatred, confound him! 'Let them hate.' Then what? '. . . provided that they obey?' No. '. . . provided that they approve?' No. What, then? '. . . provided that they fear!' On that condition, I would not wish even to be loved. (5) Is that the utterance of a great spirit, do you think? If you do, you are wrong. That is not greatness but frightfulness. You have no need to trust the words of the angry: their noise is great and threatening, the mind within terror-struck. (6) Nor need you think it true when Livy, a masterly writer, says: 'a man of great rather than good character'.[54] The two cannot be separated. Either it will be good as well, or it will not be great to start with. For 'greatness of mind', as I understand it, is something unshaken, solid within, firm and even from top to bottom – an impossibility in bad characters. (7) They can be terrifying, tumultuous, destructive; but they cannot be great. For the stay and strength of greatness is goodness. (8) Their speech, of course, their exertion and outward appointments may all make for belief in their greatness; they may say something which you might think was the utterance of a great mind, as did Gaius Caesar:[55] angry with heaven for drowning the noise of his clowns, whom he was keener to imitate than to watch, and for frightening his revels with thunderbolts (not, unfortunately, on target), he summoned Jove to combat – and mortal combat at that – with the line from Homer:

'Or let me lift thee, chief, or lift thou me.'[56]

What madness! He thought that he could receive no harm from Jove himself or that he might even inflict harm on Jove. That utterance of his, I think, added quite some force to the motivation

bered for the cruelty with which, after his final victory over the followers of Gaius Marius, he treated his vanquished opponents. See Biographical Notes and our Introduction to *On Mercy*.

[54] Livy Fragment 66 Weissenborn–Müller.

[55] Better known as the emperor Caligula (37–41); safely dead and unlamented by the time Seneca wrote *On Anger*.

[56] *Iliad* XXIII. 724 (Pope's translation).

of the conspirators.[57] Having to put up with a man who would not put up with Jove was the last straw.

21 (1) So there is nothing about anger, not even in the apparent extravagance of its disdain for gods and men, that is great or noble. If anyone does think that anger makes a great mind manifest, he might think the same about self-indulgence – with its wish to be borne on ivory, dressed in purple, roofed with gold, to transfer whole plots of land, enclose whole stretches of sea, turn rivers into cascades and woodland into hanging gardens. (2) Avarice, too, might betoken a great mind – watching, as it does, over stacks of gold and silver, cultivating estates on a par with provinces, delegating to single bailiffs lands with boundaries wider than those that used to be allotted to consuls. (3) So, too, might lust – it swims across the straits, castrates whole flocks of boys and braves the husband's sword in contempt of death. So, too, ambition – not content with yearly honours, it would, if possible, fill the consul list with one man's name alone,[58] distributing his memorials all over the world. (4) But all these, no matter what lengths they go to or how wide they spread, are narrow, wretched, mean. Virtue alone is exalted and lofty. Nor is anything great which is not at the same time calm.

[57] After a four-year reign beset by conspiracies, Caligula was murdered in his palace at Rome.

[58] Consuls were elected for one year only, though it was possible for emperors to have themselves re-elected for several years in succession. Augustus was consul every year between 31 and 23 BC.

On Anger

Questions

Is anger voluntary?

1. (1) Our first book, Novatus, had abundant material – the downward path into vice is easy. Now we come to barer ground. Our question is whether anger starts with a decision or with an impulse, that is, whether it is set in motion of its own accord – or in the same way as most inner events which occur with our full knowledge. (2) Our discussion must plunge into these topics so that it can rise again to loftier ones. In the organization of our bodies too, the bones, muscles and joints, which underpin the whole and give it vitality, though not at all attractive, come first. They are followed by the components on which beauty in appearance and looks depends. After all this, comes what most seizes the eye; when the body is at last complete, the complexion is finally applied.

(3) Anger is undoubtedly set in motion by an impression received of a wrong. But does it follow immediately on the impression itself and break out without any involvement of the mind? Or is some assent by the mind required for it to be set in motion? (4) Our view is that it undertakes nothing on its own, but only with the mind's approval. To receive an impression of wrong done to one, to lust for retribution, to put together the two propositions that the damage ought not to have been done and that punishment ought to be inflicted, is not the work of a mere involuntary impulse. That would be a simple process. What we have here is a complex

42

with several constituents – realization, indignation, condemnation, retribution. These cannot occur without assent by the mind to whatever has struck it.

2 (1) 'What is the point', you ask, 'of this question?' That we may know what anger is, since it will never, if it comes to birth against our will, yield to reason. Involuntary movements can be neither overcome nor avoided. Take the way that we shiver when cold water is sprinkled on us, or recoil at the touch of some things. take the way that bad news makes our hair stand on end and indecent language brings on a blush. Take the vertigo that follows the sight of a precipice. None of these is in our power; no amount of reasoning can induce them not to happen. (2) But anger *is* put to flight by precept. For it is a voluntary fault of the mind, and not one of those which occur through some quirk of the human condition and can therefore happen to the very wisest of men, even though they include that first mental jolt which affects us when we think ourselves wronged. (3) This steals upon us even while we are watching a performance on stage or reading of things that happened long ago. We have often a sense of being angry with Clodius as he drives Cicero into exile or with Antony as he kills him. Who remains unprovoked by the arms which Marius took up or by Sulla's proscriptions? Who would not feel furious with Theodotus and Achillas or with the boy himself who undertook such an unboyish crime?[1] (4) We are sometimes incited by singing, by a quickened tempo, by the martial sound of trumpets. Our minds are moved by a gruesome painting, by the grim sight of the justest punishment. (5) That is why we join in laughing with those who laugh, why a crowd of mourners depresses us, why we boil over at conflicts which have nothing to do with us. But these are not cases of anger, any more than it is grief which makes us frown

---

[1] In this section Seneca is recalling sensational events from the last decades of the Republic: (1) Cicero's banishment at the instigation of P. Clodius in 58 BC and murder at the hands of Mark Antony's soldiers in 43 BC (see Plutarch's *Life of Cicero* 30–3 and 46–8); (2) Gaius Marius' capture of Rome in 88 BC and the dictator Sulla's 'proscriptions' (publications of citizens' names declaring them outlaws and subjecting their property to confiscation) during and after 84 BC; (3) the murder of Pompey the Great on his arrival in Egypt after being defeated by Julius Caesar in the battle of Pharsalus in 48 BC (On the advice of his tutor Theodotus, the boy king Ptolemy XIII had him murdered by his general Achillas. See Plutarch's *Life of Pompey* 77–80.)

at the sight of a shipwreck on stage or fear that runs through the reader's mind as Hannibal blockades the walls after the battle of Cannae.[2] No, all these are motions of minds with no positive wish to be in motion. They are not affections, but the preliminaries, the prelude to affections. (6) So it is that in time of peace a military man in civilian clothes pricks up his ears at the sound of a trumpet, that camp horses rear at the clattering of arms. Alexander, they say, at Xenophantus' playing[3] reached for his weapons.

3 (1) None of these fortuitous mental impulses deserves to be called an 'emotion.' They are something suffered, so to speak, not something done by the mind. Emotion is not a matter of being moved by impressions received, but of surrendering oneself to them and following up the chance movement. (2) If anyone thinks that pallor, falling tears, sexual excitement or deep sighing, a sudden glint in the eyes or something similar are an indication of emotion or evidence for a mental state, he is wrong; he fails to see that these are just bodily agitations. (3) Thus it is that even the bravest man often turns pale as he puts on his armour, that the knees of even the fiercest soldier tremble a little as the signal is given for battle, that a great general's heart is in his mouth before the lines have charged against one another, that the most eloquent orator goes numb at the fingers as he prepares to speak. (4) Anger, however, must not only be set in motion: it has to break out, since it is an impulse. But impulse never occurs without the mind's assent, nor is it possible to act for retribution and punishment unbeknown to the mind. Suppose that someone thinks himself harmed and wishes to exact retribution, that something dissuades him and he promptly calms down – this I do not call 'anger', since it is a motion of the mind obedient to reason. Anger is a motion which outleaps reason and drags it along. (5) So the first mental agitation induced by the impression of wrong done is no more anger than is the impression itself. The impulse that follows, which

---

[2] A rhetorical exaggeration. Hannibal did not in fact march on Rome till 211 BC, five years after his victory at Cannae (216 BC), and then only in an attempt to divert the Roman army from its siege of Capua. See Livy, XXVI 7–11.

[3] On the aulos (a reed instrument, like an oboe), traditionally used in military contexts. However, Dio Chrysostom (*Oration* I 1–2) and others attribute this effect to the playing of another noted aulos-player, Timotheus. Since Xenophantus was active as late as 283/2 BC, he is unlikely to have played for Alexander, who died in 323.

not only registers but confirms the impression, is what counts as anger, the agitation of a mind proceeding by its own deliberate decision to exact retribution. Nor can there be any doubt that, as fear implies flight, anger implies attack. Do you really think, then, that anything can be sought or shunned without the mind's assent?

4 (1) If you want to know how the emotions begin, grow or get carried away, the first movement is involuntary, a preparation, as it were, for emotion, a kind of threat. The next is voluntary but not insistent – I may, for example, think it right for me to wreak vengeance because I have been harmed or for him to be punished because he has committed a crime. The third really is out of control; wanting retribution not just 'if it is right' but at all costs, it has completely overcome the reason. (2) The first is a mental jolt which we cannot escape through reason, just as we cannot escape those physical reactions which I mentioned – the urge to yawn when some one else yawns, or blinking when fingers are flicked at the eye. These cannot be overcome by reason, though habituation and constant attention may perhaps lessen them. The other sort of movement, generated by decision, can be eliminated by decision.[4]

Anger and savagery

5 (1) We have still to deal with the question of men habitually ferocious, who rejoice in human blood. Are they angry with those whom they kill, neither having received injury at their hands nor supposing themselves to have done so? (Apollodorus or Phalaris would be examples).[5] (2) That is not anger but savagery, not an

[4] Seneca's account here of how of an emotion starts is more articulated than anything to be found in our sources for early Greek Stoics. Usually these speak simply of an 'impression' to which the mind 'assents', thus giving rise to the emotion. They make no reference, as Seneca does here, to an 'involuntary movement, a preparation for an emotion' or 'first mental agitation' that 'registers' the impression before it is assented to and anger proper (or another emotion) infects the mind. These other sources could be abbreviating, and Seneca may be giving us the full, standard Stoic theory. Or he could be incorporating later refinements (of Posidonius, for example) that do not, however, alter the theory in any fundamental way. See also *Letter* 113. 18; and Aulus Gellius, *Attic Nights* xix 1. 14–20.

[5] Phalaris, tyrant of Acragas in Sicily c. 570 B.C (with his well-known penchant for roasting his victims alive in a hollow bronze bull), and Apollodorus, tyrant of Cassandria in Macedonia 279–276 bc (who secured the loyalty of the fellow-

infliction of harm for injury received, but a positive readiness to receive injury so long as harm can be inflicted, an urge to lash and to lacerate, not for retribution, but for pleasure. (3) The source of this evil is indeed anger. Constantly indulged and sated, it comes to forget mercy and casts out all sense of human solidarity from the mind, turning at the last into cruelty. So people like that laugh and enjoy themselves and derive much pleasure, with a look very far from anger on their faces, ferociously at ease. (4) Hannibal, they say, when he saw a trench full of human blood, exclaimed 'O beautiful sight!'[6] How much more beautiful it would have been for him had the blood filled a river or a lake! No wonder that you were seized above all by this sight! You were born for bloodshed, from your infancy you were drawn to slaughter. Fortune's favour will follow your cruelty for twenty years, your eyes will be granted everywhere the spectacle that they love. You will see it at Trasimene and Cannae – and finally at your native Carthage![7] (5) Not long ago Volesus,[8] Proconsul of Asia under our deified Augustus, had three hundred beheaded in a day. Stepping among the corpses with a look of pride on his face, as though he had done something splendid and remarkable, he exclaimed in Greek 'O kingly deed!' What would he have done if he *had* been king? This was not anger, but a greater, incurable evil.

Is it virtuous to be angry at wickedness?

6 (1) 'Virtue that looks with favour upon things that are honourable ought likewise to look with anger upon things shameful.' Do you mean to say that virtue should be both base and great? But that is what is being said by one who would have it exalted and abased,

conspirators with whose help he became tyrant by butchering a youth named Chaenomeles and serving the body to them), were bywords for savagery.

[6] Hannibal's savagery was a commonplace among Roman writers and orators. See e.g. Livy XXI 4. 9, XXIII 5. 12. Seneca's particular barb appears nowhere else (but compare Valerius Maximus, 9. 2, Ext. 2).

[7] Large numbers of Roman soldiers lost their lives in Hannibal's great victories at lake Trasimene in Tuscany (217 BC) and again in the following year at Cannae in Apulia. Seneca's reference to Carthage is rhetorical indulgence: the Romans, under Scipio Africanus, finally defeated Hannibal at Zama, in North Africa, but not at Carthage itself.

[8] Lucius Valerius Messalla Volesus, proconsul of Asia c. 12 AD His cruelty led to his indictment by Augustus before the Senate.

in as much as joy at right action is glorious and splendid, while anger at another's transgression is sordid and narrow-minded. (2) Nor will virtue ever allow itself to imitate vice in the act of suppressing it. Anger itself it holds to deserve chastisement,[9] being not one bit better, and often still worse, than the misdeeds which arouse it. Rejoicing and joy are the natural property of virtue; to be angry accords no more with the dignity of virtue than does grief. Sorrow is the companion of irascibility; all anger reverts to it, either remorseful or rebuffed. (3) Again, if the wise man's nature is to be angry at transgressions, he will be angrier the greater they are, and he will be angry often. It follows that the wise man will not only lose his temper on occasion; he will be habitually bad-tempered. But if we believe that there is no room in his mind for great or frequent anger, why should we not make him free of this affection altogether? (4) For there can be no limit to his anger, if it is to tally with each man's action. Either he will be unfair, if he is equally angry at unequal misdeeds, or he will be very irascible indeed, if he flares up as often as crimes are committed that merit his anger.

7 (1) It would be scandalous – could anything be more so? – for the wise man's state of mind to depend on the wickedness of others. Is Socrates to lose his power to come home with the same expression on his face as when he left it?[10] Yet, if the wise man has a duty to be angry at shameful deeds, to be provoked and depressed by crime, nothing will be more troubled than the wise man. His entire life will be spent in bad temper and grief. (2) At every moment he will see something to disapprove of. Every time that he leaves his house, he will have to step through criminals, grasping, spendthrift, shameless – and prospering as a result. Everywhere that his eyes turn they will find some ground for indignation. His powers will fail him if he forces himself to anger as often as anger is due. (3) All those thousands rushing to the forum at day-break – how vile their law-suits are, how much viler their advocates! One brings an action against the verdicts of his father – he would have done better not to deserve them. Another proceeds

---

[9] See the story about Plato at III 12. 5.

[10] Socrates was proverbial for always wearing the same composed look. See Cicero, *Tusculan Disputations* III 31, *On Duties* I 90 and the material assembled in *Gnomologium Vaticanum*, 573.

against his mother. A third arrives to denounce a crime of which he is the more obvious culprit. A judge is selected to condemn what he himself has committed; and the gallery, corrupted by good pleading, sides with the bad.

8 (1) Why go into details? When you see the forum crammed, the enclosures thronged with an entire population, when you see the Circus with the mass of the people on show,[11] you can be sure of this, that there are as many vices here as men. (2) You will see people here out of military dress but still at war with each other. One man is brought for a paltry gain to ruin someone else; no one makes a profit except by wronging another; they hate the prosperous, they despise the unfortunate; they feel oppressed by their betters, and are themselves oppressive to their inferiors. Goaded by diverse appetites, they would sacrifice everything for some trivial pleasure or plunder. Life is the same here as in a school of gladiators – living together means fighting together. (3) A gathering of wild animals is what you have here, were it not that animals are calm among themselves and refrain from biting their own kind, while these people glut themselves with tearing one another apart. Nor is this their only difference from dumb beasts. Animals grow tame to those who nurture them; human frenzy feeds on those who feed it.[12]

9 (1) The wise man will never cease to be angry, if once he starts. All is crime and vice, with more crimes committed than could be cured by summary punishment. A positive contest in wickedness is being fought out on a huge scale. Every day sees an increase of the appetite to do wrong, a lessening of shame. Regard for what might be better or fairer is banished; lust forces itself in wherever it sees fit. Nor are crimes any longer concealed – they parade in front of you. Wickedness has 'come out', gathering strength in every heart, to the point where innocence is not merely uncommon but unheard of. (2) It is not mere individuals or small groups who break the law, you may be sure of that. From all quarters, as though at a signal, there is a rush to confuse the boundaries of right and wrong:

[11] A 'circus' was an enclosure for chariot-racing.
[12] Reading, after a suggestion of Reynolds, *nec hoc uno ... differunt: [quod].*

The guest by him who harbours him is slain
Kindness 'twixt brothers too is sought in vain
The son-in-law pursues the father's life,
The wife her husband murders, he the wife:
The step-dame poison for the son prepares;
The son enquires into his father's years.[13]

(3) And what a tiny fraction of the crimes this is! There is no description here of opposing armies drawn from one side, of fathers and sons swearing different allegiance, of the fatherland put to the flame by hand of the citizen,[14] of hostile cavalry spreading out in squadrons to hunt down the hiding-places of the proscribed,[15] of wells poisoned[16] and plague artificially manufactured, of trenches dug in front of besieged parents, of prisons full and whole cities ablaze, of murderous tyrannies, of secret plans for monarchies and the ruin of the state, of glory taken in what, so long as it can be suppressed, counts as crime – rape and sexual delinquency, with even the mouth brought into play. (4) Add to all this international perjuries and broken treaties, looting by the stronger of anything that offers no resistance, frauds, thefts, swindles, repudiations of debt – three forums would not be enough to deal with them! If you wish the wise man to be as angry with crimes as their heinousness requires, he must lose not his temper, but his sanity.

10　(1) You will do better to hold, instead, that no one should be angry at error. Surely no one would be angry with people who stumble in the dark or whose deafness stops them from hearing an order. Or with children who fail to see what they should be doing and turn their attention to games and the silly jokes of those their own age. Or with the sick, the old, the weary. This too is one of the misfortunes of our mortal condition: darkness of mind, the inevitability of error – and, still more, the love of error. (2) To avoid anger with individuals, you must forgive the whole group, you must pardon the human race. If you are angry with young and old for their wrongdoing, be angry with infants, too: they are going to do wrong. No one is angry with children who are too young to

---

[13] Ovid, *Metamorphoses* I 444–8 (Dryden's translation, adapted).
[14] Like Rome on its capture by Sulla in 88 BC See Plutarch, *Life of Sulla* 9. 6.
[15] See above, on II 2. 3.
[16] An atrocity first perpetrated, according to Florus (*Epitome* I 35. 7), in Asia by Manius Aquilius (consul 129 BC) in his war against the allies of Aristonicus.

know the difference between things. But being human is more of an excuse, and a juster excuse, than being a child. (3) For this was what we were born to be – animals prone to ailments of the mind no less than of the body, not exactly stupid or slow, but given to misusing our shrewdness, each an example of vice to the other. Anyone who has followed his predecessors down the wrong path has surely the excuse of having gone astray on a public highway. (4) A general applies severity to individuals: when the whole army has deserted, he can only show clemency. What rids the wise man of anger? The sheer multitude of wrongdoers. He knows that it is unfair and unsafe to be angry at failings shared by all.

(5) Heraclitus wept, whenever he went out and saw so many lives wretchedly lived – or, rather, wretchedly lost – around him. He pitied all those whom he met that were happy and prosperous. That was kind of him, but rather too weak; he himself was among those to be lamented. By contrast, they say, Democritus was never seen in public without a smile on his face, so utterly unserious did anything that was taken seriously seem to him.[17] What room is there here for anger, if everything calls either for laughter or tears?

(6) The wise man will not be angry with wrongdoers. Why? He knows that no one is born wise but at best can become so, that the wise are the fewest in any age. For he has surveyed the human condition. No one in his right mind is angry with nature. One might as well be amazed that there are no apples hanging on woodland briars, that thorns and thickets are not full of fruit. No

---

[17] The legend of Heraclitus weeping and Democritus laughing, which Seneca treats again and more fully at *On Peace of Mind* 15. 2–5, had been employed to the same effect as here by his teacher Sotion, author of the saying: 'Among the wise, instead of anger, Heraclitus was overtaken by tears, Democritus by laughter' (Stobaeus, III 20. 53). This is the first attested pairing of the two figures in this way It was a product of Hellenistic fiction, the laughing Democritus being the earlier of the two to be attested (Cicero, *On Oratory* II 235). Their relation to the historical Heraclitus and Democritus is problematic. Heraclitus was associated as early as Theophrastus with 'melancholia' or 'atrabiliousness' (Diogenes Laertius IX 6), but this meant simply an excess of 'black bile' (μέλαινα χολή), and implied emotional instability rather than sadness (cf. Heraclitus' doctrine that 'all is motion'). Again, Democritus had indeed written on how to attain 'good spirits' (εὐθυμίη) and a joyous existence; but nothing in his surviving fragments suggests that he was given, as the legend presents him, to laughing *at* people or their misfortunes.

one is angry at faults where nature is the defence. (7) So the wise man will be calm and fair to the errors which confront him; a reformer of wrongdoers, not their enemy, he will start each day with the thought: 'Many will meet me who are given to drunkenness, lust, ingratitude, avarice, many who are disturbed by raving ambition.'[18] All this he will view with the kindly gaze of a doctor viewing the sick. (8) Surely a man whose ship has timbers loose and is leaking badly will not be angry with the sailors or with the ship itself? No, he will hurry to deal with it, shutting out water, scooping it up, blocking up the obvious gaps, working ceaselessly against hidden, invisible leaks, without ever pausing, since anything drawn off trickles in again. Prolonged help is needed against evils that are ceaseless and fertile – not to stop them, but to stop them winning.

Will anger fend off contempt?

11 (1) 'But anger is useful', someone may say. 'It enables you to escape contempt and it frightens the wicked.' In the first place, if anger is as strong as its threats, the very fact that it is frightening makes it hated as well; but it is more dangerous to be feared than despised. If, however, it lacks the power, it finds itself *more* exposed to contempt and cannot escape derision; nothing falls flatter than an empty show of temper. (2) In the second place, it is not true that the more frightening, the better. I would not wish it said to the wise man: 'the wild animal's weapon is also the wise man's – to be feared'. After all, fever, gout, malignant sores are feared, but that does not mean that there is anything good in them. On the contrary, they are all of them abject, foul, low conditions – that is just why they are feared. In the same way, anger in itself is hideous and not at all to be dreaded; but it strikes fear in most people in the way that a hideous mask strikes fear in children.

(3) And what of the fact that fear always recoils on those who inspire it? No one can be dreaded without dreading something himself. Here you may recall that verse of Laberius – spoken on

---

[18] Such *praemeditatio* or 'meditation in advance' on the vexations that might befall one was a standard exercise in Stoic psychotherapy. Seneca returns to the theme at II 31. 2–5. See also *On Favours* IV 34. 4.

stage at the height of the civil war, it attracted the entire people as an expression of public feeling:

He needs must many fear whom many fear.[19]

(4) Nature has decreed that whatever is great through another's dread shall not be without its own. How the lion's heart shudders at the slightest of sounds! The fiercest animal starts up at a shadow, a sound, a scent that is unfamiliar. Whatever strikes terror must also tremble. There is no reason, therefore, why the wise man should desire to be feared or think that anger is something great because it scares; the most contemptible things – poisons, infectious bones,[20] bites – are also feared. (5) No wonder that huge herds of wild beasts are held in and driven into traps by a line hung with feathers – called the 'scare' after the feeling which it inspires in them. Silly creatures are terrified of silly things. The movement of a chariot and the look of its turning wheels drive the lion back into its cage; the squeal of a pig strikes terror into an elephant.

So anger is a source of fear, in just the same way as a shadow is to children or a red feather to animals. In itself, there is nothing firm or strong about it; it simply impresses little minds.

Can you be rid of anger completely?

12 (1) 'You must first rid the world of wickedness, if you would be rid of anger. But neither can be done.' In the first place, it is possible not to feel cold even in winter and not to feel heat even in the hot months. One can find a favourable spot for protection against the inclemency of the season; or sheer physical endurance can master the feeling of heat or cold. (2) (Then again, consider the reverse of this: you must rid the mind of virtue before you take on bad temper, since virtue and vice cannot coexist. A good man simultaneously in a bad temper is no more possible than a healthy invalid.)

---

[19] Decimus Laberius (c. 106–43 BC), at work in the last decades of the Republic was a leading practitioner of the literary mime. This line (Mime 126, *Comicorum Romanorum praeter Plauti et Syrri quae feruntur sententiās fragmenta* (Leipzig 1898) ed. O. Ribbeck p. 361, 1) was delivered by Liberius himself, portraying a Syrian slave, in the presence of Julius Caesar, at whom it was aimed.

[20] The reference is apparently to the use of bones in casting spells (see Horace, *Epodes* 5, 17–24).

(3) 'It is impossible for the mind to be rid completely of anger. Human nature will not endure it.' But nothing is so hard or uphill that it cannot be overcome by the human mind and reduced by constant application to easy familiarity. No affections are so fierce and self-willed that they cannot be tamed by training. (4) Anything that the mind commands itself it can do. Some people have managed never to smile;[21] some have kept off wine, others off sex, some off liquid of any kind. Another, making do with little sleep, stretches out his waking hours without any sign of tiredness.[22] People have learned to run along thin, sloping ropes, to carry huge, almost superhuman loads, to plunge to a vast depth and endure the water without any pause for breath. There are a thousand other cases where dogged determination has overcome every obstacle and shown that nothing is difficult if the mind itself has resolved to endure it. (5) In the examples which I have just given, the reward for such determination was nil or trifling. Training oneself to walk on a tight-rope or to put a huge load on one's shoulders, to keep one's eyes from closing in sleep or to reach the bottom of the sea, is hardly a splendid achievement. Yet the task, however slight the remuneration for it, came to completion through sheer effort. (6) Are we, then, not to summon up endurance, seeing what a prize awaits us – the unshaken calm of a happy mind? Think what it means to escape the greatest of evils, anger, and with it frenzy, savagery, cruelty, fury and the other affections that accompany it!

13 (1) It is not for us to find a defence, to excuse our indulgence with the claim that anger is useful or unavoidable; was any vice, I ask you, ever without its advocate? You cannot claim that it cannot be cut out. The ills which ail us are curable; we were born to be upright, and nature itself, should we wish to be improved, will help us. Nor is it true, as some have supposed, that the road to the virtues is uphill and rough;[23] no, you approach them on the

---

[21] The poet Lucilius claimed that Marcus Crassus the orator had only laughed once in his life (Cicero, *On Ends* v 92).

[22] According to Pliny (*Natural History* VII 172), Maecenas, the friend of Augustus and patron of Vergil, Horace and other poets, did not have an hour's sleep for the last three years of his life, though this would probably have been due to neurasthenia rather than moral endeavour.

[23] The theme of the 'two ways' – of the easy path to vice and the long, rough and uphill path to virtue – had been a commonplace since Hesiod (*Works and Days* 287 ff.). The fifth century BC Greek sophist Prodicus wrote a famous exhibition

level. (2) I have not come to you in support of an idle cause. The way to blessedness is easy; just embark on it with good auspices and with the good offices of the gods themselves. Doing what *you* do is much more difficult. Nothing is more leisurely than calmness of mind, nothing more toilsome than anger; nothing is more relaxed than mercy, nothing more occupied than cruelty. Chastity comes with time to spare, lechery has never a moment. Every virtue, in short, is easy to guard, whereas vice costs a lot to cultivate. (3) Anger must go – that is agreed in part even by those who say it should just be reduced. It should be dismissed altogether – it will never do any good. Without it, easier and more direct ways can be found to be rid of crime, to punish and transform the wicked. Everything that the wise man has to do he will accomplish without the help of anything evil, without mixing in anything which he must anxiously seek to moderate.

14 (1) So anger can never be permitted, though it may sometimes be simulated if the sluggish minds of the audience are to be aroused, in the same way that we use spurs and brands on horses that are slow to bestir themselves. Sometimes it is necessary to strike fear into those on whom reason has no effect. But of course that does not make being angry any more useful than sorrowing or feeling fear.

(2) 'But are there not situations which might arouse anger?' That is when it should most be resisted. Nor is it difficult to subdue the mind, if even athletes, engaged as they are in the most trivial area of human activity, none the less put up with blows and pain to exhaust the strength of the assailant, striking back not when anger but when the occasion prompts them. (3) They say that Pyrrhus,[24] the greatest instructor in gymnastic contests, would advise those whom he was training to avoid anger, since it interferes with art and only looks for a chance to do harm. Thus it often happens that reason calls for endurance, anger for vengeance, and that, having been able to cope with our first misfortunes, we fall into greater ones. (4) Failure to bear with equanimity a single insulting

---

piece on the choice offered to Heracles between these two ways (see Xenophon, *Memorabilia* II 1. 21–34). With what Seneca says here, contrast *On Favours* II 18. 2.

[24] Otherwise unknown. The same advice was given to gladiators by their trainers, prompting the Stoic philosopher Antipater to wonder whether they had any use for anger in the arena at all (Philodemus, *On Anger* XXXIII 34–40).

word has led to exile; unwillingness to bear a trivial injury in silence has resulted in overwhelming misfortune; indignation at the slightest infringement of liberty has brought on the yoke of servitude.

Anger and noble character

15 (1) 'You can see that anger has something noble about it by looking at free nations, like the Germans and the Scythians, who are very prone to anger.' This happens because characters that are naturally brave and sturdy, before they are softened by discipline, have a tendency to anger. Some tendencies are only innate in the better sort of character, in the same way that strong shrubs are produced by ground that is fertile even though neglected, and tall woodland is a sign of rich soil. (2) Characters that are naturally brave will likewise have a growth of irascibility; fiery and hot, they have no room for anything faint and weak. But their vigour is deficient, as it is in anything that grows up without cultivation purely through the bounty of nature. Unless they are swiftly tamed, their tendencies to courage will turn into habitual overconfidence and rashness. (3) Are not gentler minds, I ask you, joined to milder failings – pity, love, shame? I can often demonstrate a good disposition from the very things that are bad about it; but the fact that they are signs of a better nature does not mean that they are not failings. (4) Again, all those nations that are free because ferocious are like lions and wolves: they cannot obey, but neither can they command. The force of their character is not humane, but intractably wild; and no one can govern if he cannot be governed. (5) Empires generally are in the hands of peoples with a milder climate. Those who lie towards the chilly North, have characters in the words of the poet,

'untamed and all too like their native clime.'[25]

16 (1) 'The noblest animals are reckoned to be those with a lot of anger in them.' It is a mistake to find an example for man in creatures that have impulse in place of reason: man has reason in place of impulse. But not even in their case is the same impulse

---

[25] Author unknown; the verse is printed in Baehrens, p. 359. 25.

of use to all. Temper aids the lion, fear the stag, aggression the hawk, flight the dove. (2) Anyway, it is not even true that the best animals are those most prone to anger. I may very well think that wild beasts, that get their food by seizing their prey, are the better the angrier they are: but the endurance of the ox and the obedience of the horse to the bridle, are what I would praise. Why, moreover, direct man to such miserable exemplars, when you have at your disposal the divine cosmos which man, alone of all animals, can understand in order alone to imitate it?[26]

(3) 'Men prone to anger are reckoned to be the most straightforward of all.' Compared with the deceitful and shifty, they do seem straightforward because they are frank. I would not, however, call them straightforward, but careless. That is the word which we apply to the stupid, the self-indulgent, the spendthrift and to all the less intelligent vices.

Anger and oratory

17 (1) 'An orator is sometimes better for being angry.' No – for pretending to be angry. Actors, too, when they speak their lines, stir the populace not by feeling anger but by putting on a good act. Similarly, before a jury, at a public meeting or wherever we have to work the minds of others to our own will, we ourselves will make a show of anger or fear or pity so as to instil them into others; and it often happens that what would never have been achieved by genuine emotion is achieved by its imitation.[27]

Is anger a spur to virtue?

(2) 'Sluggish is the mind that lacks anger.' True – if it has nothing stronger than anger. But one should not be the robber any more than the prey; one should neither be pitying nor cruel. The one state of mind is too soft, the other too hard. The wise man ought to strike a mean, approaching whatever calls for firm action, not with anger, but strength.

---

[26] See further *On the Private Life* 4, *On Favours* IV 4 ff.
[27] Cicero cites the same argument at *Tusculan Disputations* IV 43 and 55 to support the same Stoic view of anger. But in *On Oratory*, a work on rhetoric, he argues that a speaker who wishes to rouse a jury must first be roused himself (II 189 f.).

Therapy

Division of the subject

18 (1) Having dealt with the questions that arise concerning anger, let us go on to its remedies. In my opinion, they come in two parts: not to fall into anger[28] and not to go wrong in a state of anger. For the care of the body, some precepts are about maintaining our health, others about restoring it. Similarly, we have one set of rules for keeping anger at bay and another for restraining it.[29]

How to avoid getting angry[30]

For avoiding anger, there are some precepts which apply to our life as a whole. These can be distinguished under the headings of 'education' and 'later periods.' (2) Education calls for very great – and very rewarding – attention. For it is easy to shape a mind that is still tender, hard to cut back the faults which have grown up with us.

Education of children

19 (1) The likeliest to be irascible is, by its nature, a hot mind. There are four elements – fire, water, air and earth – and each has its corresponding property – hot, cold, dry, wet. Variations

---

[28] Here and in what follows, Seneca ignores an important distinction, which he had in fact drawn at I 4. 1, between 'irascibility' or bad temper and the actual outburst of anger. Advice on 'how not to fall into anger' could either be on how to cease being irascible or how, though remaining so, not to give way to an outburst of anger. The prescriptions for education (19–21) and some of the therapy for adults, such as the warnings against credulity and self-indulgence (22–4), are precautions against bad temper in general, whereas the reflections offered at 26–34 are designed to counter the onset of anger on particular occasions.

[29] The analogy with medicine is confusing, since the contrast between maintaining health and restoring it, i.e. between avoiding and curing an illness, should be strictly matched by one between avoiding anger and curing it, whereas Seneca speaks not of 'curing' but of 'restraining' it and 'not going wrong' under its influence. He makes little distinction between avoiding blunders in anger and actually curing or ridding the mind of it. In fact some remedies, notably the oft-repeated maxim 'Wait a bit. Don't punish in anger' (22. 4, 29. 1: III 12. 4–7, 29. 2, 32. 2), were designed to serve both ends – therapy and damage-limitation – alike.

[30] The rest of Book II is limited to advice on how to avoid getting angry. Questions of what to do once you have begun to feel angry are left to Book III.

\ces, living creatures, bodies and characters are produced
\ure of elements; and the tendencies of a given tempera-
¦ the predominance of a given element in it. Hence we
\ɯɯ some regions 'wet' and some 'dry', some 'cold' and some 'hot';
(2) and the same distinctions apply to animals and to men. It makes
a difference how much moisture or heat anyone contains, since
the preponderance of any one element will determine his character.
A natural endowment of *heat* in the mind makes men irascible,
fire being active and stubborn, while an admixture of *cold* – something inert and congealed – makes them timid. (3) (Some of our
school,[31] accordingly, maintain that anger is roused when the blood
boils around the heart, their reason for locating anger in this
particular area being simply that the breast is the warmest part of
the whole body.) (4) Those with more *moisture* in them, grow angry
little by little, since heat is not already present, but has to be
acquired by motion – which is why the anger of children and
women is sharp rather than oppressive, and lighter at the beginning.
In the *dry* stages of life, anger is fierce and strong but without
growth, without much increase since heat is on the point of decline
and cold follows upon it. Old men are cross and querulous, like
the sick, the convalescent and those whose heat has been drained
by exhaustion or blood-letting. (5) The case is the same with
people wasting through thirst or hunger and with those suffering
from physical anaemia, malnutrition or decay. Wine inflames anger,
because it increases heat. Depending on their natural endowment,
some men have to be inebriated before they boil over, some just
tipsy. For this very reason, those most prone to anger are fair-haired
people of ruddy complexion, whose natural colouring is like that
which others normally have in a state of anger. Their blood, you
see, is unstable and agitated.

20 (1) But while their nature makes some people inclined to
anger, there are many circumstances which can have the same

---

[31] Perhaps Posidonius (early first century BC): the famous medical writer Galen (c.
129–99 AD) reports him as holding at any rate that 'broader-chested and hotter
animals as well as human beings are more spirited, the wide-hipped and colder
ones more cowardly' (*On the Doctrines of Hippocrates and Plato*, v 5. 22 = Fragment
169. 85–8 Edelstein–Kidd); and it was standard Stoic doctrine to place the
emotions, along with all other mental activities, in the heart. That anger involves
the boiling of blood round the heart is a view which goes back to Aristotle (*On
the Soul* 403a31).

effect as nature. Some are led to this state by disease or physical injury, some by exertion or prolonged lack of sleep, by nights full of worry, by yearning and pangs of love.[32] Anything, too, that damages body or mind makes for an unhealthy, querulous disposition. (2) But all these are just the initial causes. The most powerful factor is habit; if oppressive, it feeds the failing.

It is hard, of course, to change a person's nature; once the elements have been mixed at birth, to alter them is out of the question. All the same, it will help to know about them, so as to deprive hot temperaments of wine – something which Plato would have banned to children, forbidding fire to be fanned with fire.[33] Nor should they even be stuffed with food, which expands the body, swelling the mind along with it. (3) They should go in for exercise and exertion without actually tiring themselves, so as to reduce rather than to use up their heat, allowing that excessive fervour to boil down. Games, too, will help; pleasure in moderation relaxes and balances the mind. (4) Those of a moister, drier or cold nature are not in danger from anger; they have more sluggish failings to fear – nervousness, intractability, hopelessness, suspicion. Such characters need to be mollified, coddled and roused to feel joy. And because different remedies have to be used against anger and gloom, and because these call for cures that are not just dissimilar but downright contrary to each other, we shall have to counter whichever failing has come to predominate.

21 (1) The greatest help, I maintain, will be to give children from the start a sound upbringing. Guidance, however, is difficult, since we must take care to avoid either fostering the anger in them or blunting their natural endowment. (2) The matter needs careful consideration. Qualities to be encouraged and qualities to be repressed are fostered by similar things, and even an attentive observer is easily misled by similarities. (3) The spirit grows through freedom to act, subjection crushes it. It rises when praised and given confidence in itself; but these very factors generate arrogance and irascibility. Our pupil has to be guided between the two extremes, sometimes reined in, sometimes spurred on. (4) He should not undergo anything demeaning or servile. He should never

---

[32] Compare Aristotle, *Rhetoric* II 2. 1379a10–29.
[33] Plato, *Laws* 666a.

59

need to make a grovelling request, nor should he benefit from so doing. Anything granted to him should, rather, be for merit, for past achievement or future promise. (5) In contests with others of his age, we should allow him neither to be defeated nor to grow angry, taking care to make him a close friend of his regular opponents, so as to give him the habit, in a contest, of wanting not to hurt, but to win. At any victory or praiseworthy action, we should allow him to hold himself high, but not to swagger. Joy leads to exultation, but exultation to a swollen head and undue self-esteem. (6) We shall give him some free time without, however, letting him slip into idleness and inactivity. And we shall keep him far from any contact with luxury. Nothing does more to make people bad-tempered than a soft, comfortable education. That is why, the more an only child is indulged and the more a ward is given his freedom, the greater the corruption. He will never be able to stand up to the shocks in life, if he has never been denied anything, if he always had an anxious mother to wipe his tears away, if he has always been backed up against his tutor. (7) Surely you have seen how anger increases with every increase in fortune? It shows up especially in the rich, in the noble, in high officials – anything irresponsible or foolish in their minds has a favorable breeze to raise it aloft. Prosperity fosters bad temper, as the crowd of flatterers clusters round a pair of conceited ears: 'you mean, *he* is to answer *you* back?', 'you misjudge your high position', 'you are throwing yourself away' – and all the other things which even a sound mind, well grounded from the start, can scarcely resist. (8) Children should be kept clear of flattery; they should be told the truth. They should even feel fear sometimes – and respect always. They should rise for their elders. They should never get their way through bad temper; once they have calmed down, they can be offered what they could not get through crying. They should have their parents' wealth before their eyes, but not at their disposal. Their mistakes should be brought up against them. (9) Here it will help for them to have kindly teachers and tutors. Anything of a tender nature will attach itself to what is nearest and will grow like it. Soon the adolescent will reflect the character of his nurses and tutors. (10) A boy from Plato's school came home, saw his father shouting and said 'I never saw this at Plato's.'[34] He would

[34] We do not know whence Seneca picked up this story. It is not found elsewhere.

have copied his father sooner than Plato, no doubt about t]
Above all, the boy's diet should be simple, his clothing ine\
his style of life like that of his peers. He will not be angry
someone compared with him, if from the start you have put him
on the same level as a lot of people.

Advice for adults (i) Preliminaries

Don't believe the worst

22 (1) The foregoing applies to our children. In our own case,
luck at birth and education are irrelevant to the fault and to advice
for dealing with it. It is what has resulted from them that has to
be set in order. (2) Well then, the prime causes are what we should
fight against; and the cause of bad temper is the opinion that we
have been wronged.[35] It should not be readily trusted. We should
not accede at once even to things that are open and clear; falsehoods
sometimes have the look of truths. (3) We should always give
ourselves time: its passing reveals the truth. We should not lend
a ready ear to accusations, but recognize and mistrust our natural
human failing of gladly believing what we would rather not be told
and of losing our tempers before we can come to a judgment about
it. (4) Besides, we are incited not just by accusations but by
suspicions, giving the worst interpretation to someone else's look
or smile and thus losing our tempers with the innocent. So we
must plead the other person's case in his absence, against ourselves,
and suspend the sentence of anger. Punishment delayed can still
be exacted; once exacted, it cannot be cancelled.

23 (1) You know of the famous tyrannicide who was caught
before his task was completed and tortured by Hippias to make
him reveal his accomplices. He named the tyrant's friends who
were standing around and those whom he knew to care most about
the tyrant's safety. One by one they were named and their execution
ordered. The tyrant asked whether any remained. 'You alone,'
came the answer, 'I have left no one else who cares about you.'[36]

---

[35] See the definitions of anger in I 2.

[36] Hippias was tyrant of Athens 527–510 BC This much-repeated story is more
commonly set in Sicily or southern Italy with the philosopher Zeno of Elea as
the defiant tyrannicide (it is noteworthy that Herodotus does not include any
such occurrence in his account of Hippias). See Diogenes Laertius, IX 26; Valerius
Maximus, III 3 Ext. 2.

The effect of anger was to make the tyrant an accomplice of the tyrannicide, slaughtering his own guard with his own sword. (2) Alexander was much more spirited. Reading a letter from his mother which warned him to beware of poisoning by Philip his doctor, he took the potion and drank it undeterred, putting more trust in his own judgment of his own friend.[37] (3) He deserved to discover – indeed to inspire – his friend's innocence. I find this all the more praiseworthy in Alexander, since no one was so given as he was to anger. The rarer that moderation is in kings, the more it deserves praise. (4) This was also true of the great Julius Caesar and the supreme clemency with which he exploited his victory in the civil war. Having come upon folders of letters to Gnaeus Pompey from men who appeared to be either on the opposite side or neutral, he burned them. Although his anger was normally moderate, he preferred to avoid the very possibility of it, believing ignorance of a person's misdeeds to be the most gracious form of pardon.[38]

24 (1) The greatest harm comes from readiness to believe things. Frequently, you should not even listen, since it is better in some cases to be deceived than to distrust. You should rid your mind of suspicion and surmise – their influence is very deceptive: 'His greeting was uncivil.' 'He turned away from my kiss.' 'He was quick to break off the conversation which we had started.' 'He did not invite me to dinnner.' 'His face looked rather unfriendly.' (2) Nor will there be a shortage of evidence to support your suspicion. What you need is to be straightforward and kind in your judgment. We should only believe what is under our eyes and obvious. Whenever our suspicions prove to be false, we should reproach our readiness to believe. Such castigation will put us into the habit of not readily believing things.

Don't be soft and oversensitive
25 (1) Next in order comes this: do not be irritated by vulgar trivialities. A clumsy slave or luke-warm water to drink, the couch

---

[37] This anecdote is told by many other authors, but with Alexander's second-in-command Parmenion as the letterwriter (e.g. Plutarch *Life of Alexander* 19. 3).

[38] The same story is told by Pliny (*Natural History* VII 94). Caesar's clemency and 'magnanimity' towards his vanquished enemies were acknowledged even by opponents like Cicero (*Letters to His Friends* IV 4. 4; *In defence of Marcellus* 19).

in a mess or the table carelessly laid – to be provoked by such things is lunacy. It takes a sickly invalid to get goose-pimples at a light breeze. Eyes must have something wrong with them to be dazzled by a white garment. Only the dissolute debauchee will get a stitch in his side at the sight of someone else at work. (2) Mindyrides we are told, was a citizen of Sybaris[39] who saw a man digging and swinging his mattock too high. He complained that it was tiring him and forbade the man do the work in his sight. The same person complained of feeling worse because there were folds in the rose petals on which he had slept. (3) When mind and body have been corrupted by pleasure, nothing seems bearable – not because things which you suffer are hard, but because you are soft. Why else should someone's coughing or sneezing drive you into a fury? Why should a fly infuriate you which no one has taken enough trouble to drive off, or a dog which gets in your way, or a key dropped by a careless servant? (4) Can you expect a man to put up calmly with abuse from his fellow citizens, with slanders heaped upon him in the Assembly or Senate House, if his ears are hurt by the grating of a dragged bench? Will he endure the hunger and thirst of an expedition in summer, if he loses his temper at the incompetence of a slave melting the snow[40]? Nothing, then, fosters bad temper more than immoderate, impatient self-indulgence. The mind must be treated sternly, so as to feel none but a heavy blow.

Advice for adults (ii) Reflections to counter the onset of anger[41]

'They cannot have wronged you or cannot have meant to'
26 (1) We lose our tempers either with what cannot possibly have done us wrong, or with what can. (2) The former includes objects

---

[39] A Greek city in southern Italy. The archetypal 'Sybarite' (Mindyrides was notorious even in the time of Herodotus (VI 127. 2) as the man who had gone furthest of all in the luxuriousness of his habits. The story of the workman is told by several other ancient writers; that of the rose petals is told also by Aelian (*Varia Historia* 9, 24).

[40] Drinks were regularly cooled with melted snow (cf. *Letter* 78. 23; and Xenophon, *Memorabilia* II 1. 30). In his essay *On the Control of Anger* 461b, Plutarch uses the same example in the same context as Seneca does here.

[41] Underlying the therapy here are the definitions of anger cited in I 2. 3, especially that ascribed to Posidonius: 'a burning desire to punish him by whom you think yourself to have been unfairly harmed'. The reflections now put forward are

without sensation, like the book which we throw away because its script is too small or tear up for its mistakes, or the clothes which we rip to pieces because they displease us. How stupid it is to be angry with them! They have not deserved our anger, nor can they feel it. (3) 'We are offended, don't you see, with the people who made them.' In the first place, we often lose our tempers before making this distinction. Secondly, the craftsmen themselves may have reasonable excuses to offer: one of them could not have done better than he did – his lack of skill was not intended to insult you; the other was not trying to offend you. Finally, what is crazier than to save up your spleen for people and then take it out on things?

(4) But, if it is crazy to be angry with inanimate obects, it is just as crazy to be angry with animals who cannot do us wrong because they cannot will to do so. There can be no wrong, you see, which is not deliberate. So they can do us harm, as can iron or a stone; but they cannot do us wrong. (5) And yet some think themselves despised when the same horse obeys one rider and acts up with another, as though their own decision, rather than familiarity or the art of management, were what made some animals more submissive to some people than to others. (6) And yet, if it is stupid to be angry with these, it is likewise stupid to be angry with children and people who are not much more sensible than children. In all these transgressions, after all, if the judge is reasonable, a lack of good sense amounts to innocence.

27 (1) There are things which cannot do harm, having no power that is not beneficent and wholesome. The immortal gods, for instance, neither wish to cause trouble, nor can they. Their nature is gentle and kindly, as averse to wronging others as to wronging themselves. (2) It shows a crazy ignorance of the truth to charge them with the violence of the sea, with excessive rainfall, with the persistence of winter, whereas all the while none of those things that harm or help us is aimed strictly at us. We are not the world's reason for bringing back winter and summer. These follow laws of their own, which govern things divine. We think too well of ourselves, if we see ourselves as the worthy objects of such

designed to convince you that (1) you have not really been wronged (26–7, 29–30), that (2) you have not suffered 'unfairly' (28, 31. 1–5) and that (3) retaliation is anyway a bad thing (31.6–4).

mighty motions. None of them is there to wrong us. Indeed, none occurs except to our benefit.[42]

(3) I have said that there are things which have not the power to harm us and things which have not the wish to do so. Among the latter are good magistrates, parents, teachers and judges. Their chastisement should be accepted in the same spirit as the surgeon's knife, a starvation diet or whatever else offers present torment for future good. (4) Suppose that we have been subjected to punishment; we should think not only of what we are suffering, but of what we have done, taking our whole life into consideration. If we would only tell ourselves the truth, we would set the damages in our case higher.

'We are none of us blameless'

28 (1) If we wish our judgment to be fair in all things, we must start from the conviction that no one of us is faultless. For here is where indignation most arises – 'I haven't done anything wrong!', 'I haven't done a thing!' On the contrary, you won't *admit* anything! We grow indignant at any rebuke or punishment, while at that very moment doing the wrong of adding insolence and obstinacy to our misdeeds. (2) Who can claim himself innocent in the eyes of every law? Suppose he can – to be good in the sense of being law-abiding is a very narrow form of innocence. So much wider are the principles of moral duty than those of law, so many the demands of piety, humanity, justice and good faith, none of them things in the statute-book. (3) But even under that very restricted definition we cannot establish our innocence. We have done some things; others we have planned, or wanted or felt inclined to do. In some cases, our innocence has simply been through lack of success.

(4) This thought should make us more reasonable towards wrong-doers, ready to accept reproach, free of anger, at any rate, towards good men – who would not arouse our anger, if even good people can? – and above all towards the gods. It is not by any fault of

---

[42] The change of the seasons and other manifestations of nature have not come about directly for our personal benefit or discomfort, but rather to meet the needs of the universe, of which we are a part. They are thus indirectly for our benefit, and we have reason to be grateful for them. See further *On Favours* IV 23, VI 20. 1, 23. 3–5. This important Stoic doctrine goes back to Plato (*Laws* 903b–d).

theirs, but through the law of our mortal condition, that anything untoward happens to us. 'But disease and pain intrude upon us!' Some things just have to be endured[43] if your lot is live in a crumbling house. (5) Suppose, then, that someone speaks ill of you – think whether you did not do so to him, think of how many people *you* speak ill of. We should think, I maintain, of some not as doing us wrong but as paying us back, of others as acting on our behalf, or as acting under compulsion, or in ignorance; we should think that even those who wrong us knowingly and deliberately are not out for the wrong itself when they wrong us. A person may have slipped into it through delight in his own wit; or he may have done something, not to disoblige us, but because he could not get what he wanted without first having rebuffed us. Besides, flattery is often offensive in its fawning. (6) Anyone who calls to mind how often he himself has come under false suspicion, how many services on his part have chanced to look like injustice, how many people he has hated and then begun to love, can avoid immediate anger, especially if he says quietly to himself at every vexation 'I too have done this myself.'

(7) But where can you find such a reasonable judge? The very same man who fancies everyone's wife, and finds justification enough for an affair in the mere fact that she belongs to another, will not have his own wife looked at; the keenest to insist on trust will be given to breaking it; the persecutor of lies is himself a perjuror; the vexatious litigant cannot bear to have a case brought against himself; and the chastity of servants is guarded from temptation by a master with no regard for his own. (8) Other people's faults are before our eyes, our own lie over our shoulders. That is why the ungodly hour of a son's dinner-party is berated by a father who is worse than the son, why no allowance is made for other people's self-indulgence by a man with no restraint on his own, why a murderer meets with wrath from a tyrant and theft with punishment from a temple-robber. Many of mankind, indeed, are angry not with the sin, but the sinner. A look at ourselves will make us more forbearing, if we start to consider: 'Surely we too have done something like this? Surely we have made this sort of mistake. Is it in our interest to damn it?'

---

[43] Reading, with Gronovius, *utique aliqua fungendum.*

Book II

'They should get the benefit of the doubt'

29 (1) The greatest remedy for anger is delay. A
for one at the start. You are not asking it to pard
make a judgment. The first attacks are the heavy o
leave off, if it has to wait. And do not try to be ... __
once; you will overcome it entirely, if you attack it piecemeal.

(2) Some of the things that upset us have been reported to us,
some we have heard or seen ourselves. What we are told should
not be believed in a hurry. Many people tell untruths, some to
deceive, some because they have been deceived. One may be
currying favour, inventing some injury so as to put on a show of
sympathy. Another may have a malevolent wish to break up a solid
friendship. And there is the person who[44] just wants sport and
watches from a safe distance the people whom he has brought into
collision. (3) Were a tiny sum of money to come up for judgment
before you,[45] the case would not be proved without a witness, the
witness would carry no weight without an oath, you would allow
both parties to plead, you would allow them time and more than
one hearing, since truth comes to light the more you busy yourself
with it. Is your *friend* to be condemned on the spot? Are you going
to lose your temper, before you have heard him or interrogated
him, before letting him know who the accuser or what the accusation
is? Have you already, I mean, heard both sides of the story? (4)
The man who reported him to you will stop talking if he has to
prove it: 'Don't drag me into it! If you put me in the witness box,
I will deny it all. Do as I say or I won't ever tell you anything
again!' At the very same moment, he eggs you on and withdraws
from the dispute and the fray himself. Anyone who will only speak
to you in secret is hardly speaking at all. Secret credence and open
wrath – what could be unfairer?

30 (1) Some things we ourselves have witnessed. Here we
should go through the character and intentions of their perpetrators.
It might be a child that has upset us – make allowance for his
age, he does not know if he is doing wrong. Or a father – perhaps
he has done so much for us that he has a right to wrong us,

---

[44] Omitting *suspicax* with Haase.

[45] It is perhaps worth recalling that Novatus, Seneca's addressee, as a public servant
would have been called on to discharge various judicial functions, as in fact he
did at Corinth (Acts XVIII 12–17).

67

perhaps the very act that offends us was a service on his part. Or a mother – she may just be making a mistake. It may have been someone under orders – indignation with what was compelled is simply unfair. Or someone whom you have hurt – there is nothing wrong in having to suffer what you did first. Or a judge – you should trust his verdict more than your own. Or a king – if you were guilty, accept his justice; if innocent, accept your fate. (2) It might be a dumb beast or something similar – you will be copying it if you lose your temper. A disease or disaster – it will pass over you more lightly if you put up with it. Or God – you are wasting your time if you are angry with him, as you are when you pray for his anger against another. The injury was done by a good man – then don't you believe it! By a bad man – then don't be surprised! Others will exact the punishment owed to you. Indeed, the wrongdoer has already punished himself.

'Was it "unfair" or merely unexpected?'
31 (1) There are two things, as I said,[46] which arouse bad temper: firstly, a sense of wrong done to us – I have said enough about that; secondly, a sense of its 'unfairness.' Something needs to be said about this. (2) People judge things to be 'unfair' either because they ought not to have suffered them or else because they did not expect to do so. Things unforeseen are, we think, undeserved; and we are most aroused by occurrences that are contrary to hope and expectation, which is the very reason why we are annoyed by trivialities in our domestic life and speak of negligence by our friends as a 'wrong'. (3) 'How is it, then, that wrongs by enemies provoke us?' Because we did not anticipate them, or certainly not on that scale. This is a result of excessive self-love. We consider that we ought not to be harmed, even by enemies. Each of us has within him the mentality of a monarch; he would like *carte blanche* for himself, but not for any opposition. (4) So it is either arrogance or ignorance of the facts that makes us prone to anger. Is it surprising that the wicked should do wicked deeds, or unprecedented that your enemy should harm or your friend annoy you, that your son should fall into error or your servant misbehave? 'I

---

[46] In fact Seneca has not previously said precisely this (unless he said it in the lacuna after I 2. 3). But it is perhaps implicit in the definitions cited there. See n. 41 on section heading at II 26, above.

never reckoned . . .', according to Fabius,[47] is the worst excuse for a general; I myself reckon it the worst excuse for a human being altogether. Reckon on everything, expect every thing! Even in good characters there will be something rather rough. (5) Human nature spawns a mind that is treacherous, ungrateful, greedy, impious. In judging any one man's character, reflect on that of mankind in general. Where most you rejoice, you will most feel fear. Where all seems calm, there is no lack of things to harm you; they are merely resting. You should always think that there will be something to annoy you. No helmsman was ever so confident as to unfurl his entire sail, without arranging the rigging for swiftly pulling it in again.

Anger is inhuman, small-minded and useless

(6) Reflect above all on this.[48] The power to hurt is foul and detestable, utterly foreign to man, thanks to whom even the wild grow tame. Behold the elephant bowing its neck to the yoke, the bull with its back safely trodden by prancing acrobats, child and woman alike, the serpent sliding, harmlessly slithering between the cups and over our laps, the placid visage of bear or lion within the home as people stroke them, the fierce animal fawning on its master – you will feel shame at having swapped natures with animals! (7) It is sacrilege to harm your country; it is therefore sacrilege to harm a citizen, too (for he is a part of your country – and its parts will be sacred, if the whole commands veneration); and therefore it will be sacrilege to harm even a human being, since he is a citizen in that greater city of yours.[49] What if the hands wished to harm the feet or the eyes the hands? The members of the body all accord with each other,[50] since it is in the interest

---

[47] Fabius the 'Delayer': see I 11. 5.

[48] The reflections which follow – that anger is 'inhuman' (31. 6–8), small minded (32) and less useful than forbearance (33) – are largely a restatement of material from Book I where it was argued that anger is contrary to human nature (5–6), useless (9–19) and far removed from true greatness of mind (20–1). (The theoretical arguments there have thus themselves provided a kind of preliminary therapy.) The material is now reworked, rather more briefly, and enlivened with further examples.

[49] On the Stoic theory of the 'two commonwealths', each human being belongs by virtue of his rationality to the universal commonwealth of the cosmos, as well as to his local city. See *On the Private Life* 4.

[50] This popular analogy with parts of the body – it also appears in Livy (I 32.9–11) and St. Paul (I Corinthians 12. 14–26) – is likewise Stoic in origin. Compare Marcus Aurelius, VII 13.

69

hat the parts be preserved. Men, likewise, will spare
, since they were born for fellowship, and the safety
y is only possible through the safe-keeping and love
8) We would not even kill vipers or water-snakes or
with a poisonous bite or sting, if we could tame them
or see to it that henceforward they were of no danger to us or to
others. Neither should we harm a human being for having done
wrong, but to prevent his doing it. Punishment should never be
directed towards the past but towards the future, being as it is an
expression not of anger but of caution.[51] If everyone with a corrupt,
malign character is to be punished, no one will escape.

32 (1) 'But there is a pleasure in anger – paying back pain is
sweet.' Not in the slightest! The case is not like that of favours,
where it is honourable to reward service with service. Not so with
wrongs. In the one case, it is shameful to be outdone; in the other,
to outdo. 'Retribution' – an inhuman word and, what is more,
accepted as right – is not very different from wrongdoing, except
in the order of events. He who pays back pain with pain is doing
wrong; it is only that he is more readily excused for it.[52] (2) Marcus
Cato was once struck in the public baths by some fool who did
not know who he was – would anyone have ill treated that man
if he had known? Afterwards the man apologized and Cato said 'I
don't remember being struck', thinking it better to ignore than to
punish.[53] (3) 'You mean, after such effrontery, he escaped scot-free?'
More than that, he gained a lot – he came to know Cato. The
mark of a great mind is to look down on injuries received. The
most humiliating kind of retribution is to be seen as not worth
inflicting it on. Many, in avenging trivial wrongs, make them all
the more deeply felt. A great and noble person, like a great beast
of the wild, calmly hears out the yapping of tiny dogs.

33 (1) 'We arouse less contempt, if we avenge the wrong done
to us.'[54] If we approach it as a remedy, we should do so without
anger, treating vengeance as something useful rather than something

---

[51] Seneca is repeating what he said at I 19. 7.

[52] Punctuating, with earlier editions, *non multum differt nisi ordine: qui dolorem regerit tantum excusatius peccat.*

[53] Seneca repeats the story in *On the Wise Man's Constancy* 14. 3 to illustrate the theme that the wise man is impervious to insult. On Cato, see Biographical Notes.

[54] Cf. II 11.1.

sweet. Often, however, it is better to dissimulate than to seek retribution. Wrongs done by the powerful should be borne with a cheerful look, not just patiently – they will do them again, if they think that they have managed to do them once. The worst thing about the minds of people insolent through prosperity is that they hate those whom they have harmed. (2) There is a very well-known saying by a man who had grown old in royal service.[55] Asked how he had achieved that rarest of distinctions at court, old age, he answered: 'By suffering wrongs and saying "Thank-you." '

So far is vengeance from paying that it can sometimes pay you not even to mention the wrong. (3) Gaius Caesar[56] had placed the son of Pastor, an illustrious Roman knight, under arrest, annoyed by his elegance and foppish haircut. The father begged that he grant him his son's life. As though that were a reminder to punish him, Caesar promptly ordered his execution. But so as not to be totally impolite towards the father, he invited him to dinner that day. (4) Pastor arrived without a look of reproach on his face. Caesar gave him a huge toast to drink, setting a guard over him. The poor man went through with it, as though he were drinking his son's blood. Ointment and garlands were sent for, and orders given to see if he would put them on. He put them on. On the very day that he had carried his son off to burial – or, rather, had failed to carry him off to safety - he reclined with ninety-nine other guests, downing the sort of drinks that would hardly have been decent even at a birthday party for his children, an old man with the gout. Not a tear did he shed the while, not a sign of grief did he allow to escape him. He dined as though his plea for his son had succeeded. Why?, you may ask. He had another. (5) And was he not just like Priam, who surely concealed his anger? Embracing the king by the knees, taking to his lips that murderous hand besprinkled with the blood of his son, he too dined.[57] But that was without the ointment and the garlands, and his foe for all his savagery had urged him with numerous words of consolation to take food – not to drain enormous goblets with a guard stationed

---

[55] I.e. in one of the monarchies of the Eastern Mediterranean.

[56] I.e. the emperor Caligula. Similar cruelties are told of him by Suetonius (*Life of Gaius Caligula* 27. 4).

[57] See *Iliad* XXIV 477–9. After Achilles has slain Hector, he receives Priam in his tent, a suppliant seeking to ransom his son's body.

at his head! (6) I would despise the Roman father, if his fear had been just for himself. As it was, his anger was restrained by sense of duty. He deserved to be given permission to leave the dinner-party and gather up the bones of his son. Our young monarch, kindly and considerate all the while, did not allow him even this. He harassed the old man with repeated toasts, advising him to lighten his sorrows. But he, on the contrary, showed a blithe oblivion of what had been done that day. The other son would have perished, had the butcher been displeased with his guest.

34 (1) So you should abstain from anger, whether it is an equal who is to be attacked, or a superior or an inferior. It is hazardous to struggle with an equal, crazy to do so with a superior, and mean with an inferior. To bite back is the mark of a wretched little man; mice and ants, if you put your hand near them, turn their jaws towards you; anything weak thinks itself hurt, if touched.

(2) It will make us milder if we think of the help which we may have had from the person with whom we are angry, and allow the good turns to make up for the bad. We should also think of what a recommendation it may be to have a reputation for mercy, of how many valuable friends we have made through forgiveness. (3) We should never be angry with the children of enemies, private or public. A prize example of Sulla's cruelty was his disenfranchise-ment of the children of those whom he had proscribed. Nothing could be unfairer than to make someone heir to hatred incurred by his father.[58] (4) We should consider, whenever we make diffi-culties about pardoning, whether it pays us for everyone to be inexorable. So often one has had to seek pardon, having denied it, so often one has fallen at the feet of the person whose pleas one spurned! Is anything more glorious than to exchange anger for friendship? Where has the Roman people truer allies than those who were once its most obstinate enemies? Where would its empire be today, if a salutary foresight had not united victor and vanquished?

(5) Suppose someone has lost his temper – don't you do so! Challenge him with good turns. If one side goes, the quarrel will promptly collapse. To fight, you have to be matched. Suppose,

---

[58] This is Stoic moralizing. Hereditary vendettas were normal in classical Greece and Rome.

however, that there is anger on both sides, that it comes to a clash – the better man is he who steps back first, the winner loses. Suppose he has hit you – draw back. By hitting back you will merely give him the chance and the excuse to hit more often. You will not be able to pull yourself out, when you want to do so. 35 (1) No one, surely, would want to hit the enemy so hard as to leave his own hand in the wound and find himself unable to draw back from the blow. But anger is that sort of weapon – it can hardly be withdrawn. We keep an eye out for arms that we can easily use, for the handy, manoeuvrable sword. Should we not likewise avoid those mental impulses that are heavy, burdensome, and cannot be drawn back? (2) The only speed that we want is one which stops when told and goes no further than it is meant to, which can change direction and slow down from running to a walk. We know that there is something wrong with muscles when they move against our will. It is only an old man or one with a weak constitution who runs when he wants to walk. We reckon the strongest, healthiest impulses to be those that proceed as we – not as they – see fit.[59]

Advice for adults (iii) Consider the ugliness and the dangers of anger

(3) Nothing, however, may help so much as to examine, firstly, the ugliness of the thing and then its danger. No emotion has a more turbulent look. It mars the loveliest face, turns the calmest countenance into something grim. The angry lose all their grace. Their dress was fastened correctly – they drag it around and waste all the trouble taken over themselves. The line of the hair, naturally or by art, was by no means ugly – it stands on end as their mental hackles rise. The veins swell. The breast heaves with rapid panting; the voice bursts out in fury and the neck strains. Then the limbs tremble, the hands cannot keep still, the whole body tosses. (4) What can the mind be within, do you think, if the outward image is so foul? How much more dreadful the countenance within the breast, how much harsher the breathing, how much fiercer the onrush, ready to break if it cannot break out! (5) Imagine the look of enemies or wild animals dripping with slaughter or making their

---

[59] Seneca is recalling the argument of I 7. 4.

way to the kill; imagine the monsters of hell, as the poets picture them, wreathed in serpents and breathing fire; imagine the ghastliest goddesses of the underworld riding out to raise war, to sow discord and shatter the peace between peoples – that is the likeness which we should form of anger. With its eyes aflame, with a loud noise of hissing, bellowing, groaning, grating and yet more dreadful sound if any there be, brandishing spears in either hand (it has no thought of protecting itself), grim, gory, scarred, black and blue from its own lashes, it lurches crazily, wrapped in thick darkness, attacking, laying waste, putting to flight, consumed with hatred of all, especially of itself, if it can find no other way to do harm, ready to confound earth, sea and sky, loathing and loathed. (6) Or, if you will, let it be like Bellona in our poets,

> her right hand brandishing the blood-stained whip,

or

> Discord, her mantle torn, strides forth in joy,[60]

or in any shape more dire, if you can think of one for this dire emotion.

36 (1) Some people, as Sextius says,[61] have been helped in their anger by looking at a mirror. The extent of their transformation shocked them. They were put on the spot, so to speak, and could not recognize themselves. And yet what a tiny fraction of its true ugliness was reflected in the mirror-image! (2) If the mind could be revealed shimmering through some material, it would astound us to look at it, black and mottled as it would be, boiling, twisted and swollen. So great is its ugliness even now, oozing out through bones, flesh and so many other barriers – what if it were revealed naked?

(3) You may think, however, that a mirror would not be enough to frighten anyone away from anger. After all, anyone coming to a mirror in order to change himself has already changed, whereas the angry would find no image lovelier than one of savagery and frightfulness. They wish to look as they are. (4) More worth

---

[60] The first of these verses is probably by Vergil (it resembles *Aeneid* VIII 703, but also Lucan, Pharsalia VII 568). The second is definitely by him (*Aeneid* VIII 702).

[61] Roman philosopher in the reign of Augustus, much admired by Seneca, who also mentions him at III 36.

considering is how many people anger itself has harmed. Some have burst a blood-vessel in an excess of passion, overtaxed their strength by shouting and suffered a haemorrhage, or drowned their power of vision in a gush of tears to the eyes. The sick have relapsed. (5) There is no swifter way to insanity. Many have continued in the madness of their anger and never recovered the reason they had cast out. Ajax was driven to his death by madness, to madness by anger.[62] They call down death on their children, poverty on themselves, ruin on their home, denying that they are angry just as the mad deny their insanity. Enemies to their closest friends, shunned by those dearest to them, heedless of law save where it can do harm, jumping up at the slightest provocation, impervious to word or act of kindness, they do everything by force, ready to fight with or fall on the sword. (6) The greatest of ills has seized them, one that surpasses all other vices. These come on gradually; but the force of anger is sudden and total. Moreover, it subjects all the other emotions. It overcomes the most ardent love – leading men on to stab the bodies that they love and to lie in the embrace of those whom they have killed. Avarice, hardest and most inflexible of evils, it tramples underfoot, forcing it to scatter its wealth, to set fire to house and assembled property. Have you not seen the man of ambition casting off his treasured badges of office and spurning the honours conferred on him? There is no emotion which anger cannot master.

[62] Ajax, son of Telamon, was one of the leading Greek warriors at Troy. When the arms of the fallen Achilles were awarded to Odysseus, he went mad with anger and disappointment and finally committed suicide.

Book III

Preface

Why anger simply has to be cured

1 (1) What you most wanted, Novatus, I shall now try to do –
to cut out anger from our minds altogether or at any rate to bridle
it and restrain its onrush.[1] This should sometimes be done openly
and without concealment, when the force of the evil is relatively
slight and allows this; sometimes on the sly, when it burns too
strongly, and anything put in its way just exacerbates and increases
it. Its strength and freshness are what determine whether it should
be beaten back and forced into retreat or whether we should give
way before it till the first storm is over, in case it sweeps our
remedies along with it. (2) Each person's character must be taken

---

[1] Novatus had asked how anger 'can be alleviated' (I 1.1). So far, Seneca has simply
prescribed some ways to avoid it. He now anounces what II 18 has led us to
expect, a cure for anger – which must mean, in the first instance, *our own* anger.
He goes on, however, in the next two sentences to treat anger as almost a
personified opponent; and in (2), a recommendation that the therapy be tailored
to the particular character of each sufferer, he gives the impression of also
prescribing ways to deal with anger *in other people*. He does, in fact, in a new
division of the subject (5. 2 below), include the cure of other people's anger as
the third and last of his proposed topics; but he only gets round to discussing it
at c. 39. Most of Book III (like II 22–36) is on the treatment, prophylactic and
therapeutic, of *one's own* anger, beginning (1. 3–5. 1) with a general denunciation
of the emotion, which Seneca justifies with the claim (3. 1) that such denunciation
is necessary, since Aristotle defends the passion. Philodemus' *On Anger* had likewise
backed up a sermon on the evils of anger (VIII–XXXI) by citing and attacking the
Peripatetic doctrines (XXXI 24–XXXIV 6).

into consideration. Some yield to entreaty, some will mock and attack if shown submission, some will have to be terrified into tranquillity. Some may be deflected from their course by reproaches, some by admissions, some by shame, some by delay – a slow cure for an impetuous evil, only to be used as a last resort.

(3) Other affections, you see, allow for postponement and can be cured more slowly; but the violence of anger, excited and hurrying, has no gradual development – it begins at full strength. Unlike other failings, it does not disturb the mind so much as take it by force; harrying it on out of control and eager even for universal disaster, it rages not just at its objects but at anything that it meets on its way. (4) Other failings set the mind in motion; anger drives it headlong. Even if you cannot resist your affections, they themselves at least can come to a standstill. Anger, like gales or lightning or anything else that cannot be called back because its motion is purely one of falling, grows exponentially. (5) Other failings are a departure from reason; their approach is gentle, they grow without your noticing them. Anger is a departure from sanity; the mind is thrown into it. And so nothing is a more powerful motive. Lunatic and ever resorting to its own force, arrogant in success, crazy when frustrated – not even failure can weary it. If the adversary has the luck to escape, it turns its teeth on itself. The gravity of the occasion is irrelevant. From the slightest beginnings it ends as something enormous.

2 (1) It passes over no time of life, makes exception for no race of men. Some nations, thanks to poverty, have no experience of self-indulgence. Others, ever in action and on the move, have avoided idleness. Others, uncouth in character and rural in their way of life, are unfamiliar with fraud, cheating or any of the evils that come to birth in the forum. But there is not a nation which is not goaded by anger. As powerful among Greeks as among barbarians, it is no less a danger to people with respect for law than to those who think that law begins where their own strength ends.

(2) Again, other failings seize hold of individuals; anger is the one emotion that is sometimes caught by a whole community. Never has an entire people burned with love for a woman, nor has a whole state set its hope on money or gain; ambition grabs

individuals one by one. Uncontrollable rage alone is an evil of the public.[2] Often the move to anger is that of a single throng. (3) Men and women, old men and children, leading citizens and the common people join in. Roused by a very few words, the entire crowd races ahead of the rabble-rouser himself. Straight away they run off for weapons and fire, declaring war on their neighbours, or waging it with their fellow-citizens. (4) Entire houses are burnt down with the whole family inside. Held in great honour a moment ago for the appeal of his eloquence, the speaker has the anger of his own assembly turned on him. The legion hurls its spears at its very own general.[3] People and senators are at loggerheads. The council of state, the Senate, without waiting for levies or naming a general, selects on the spot the agents of its wrath, hunting down aristocrats from house to house and taking their punishment into its own hands. (5) Embassies are violated, the law of nations broken. An unspeakable madness seizes the state. No time is given for the public inflammation to sink down. Fleets immediately put to sea, loaded with riotous soldiery. With no regard for auspices or good order, the people march out under the leadership of their anger, grabbing as a weapon whatever happens to be at hand, only to pay with some great disaster for the rashness of their overconfident anger. (6) This has been the fate of barbarians as they rush haphazardly to war. Their excitable minds are struck by an impression of wrong done to them; they promptly move into action, carried along by their resentment, and fall upon our legions like a collapsing ruin. Without any formation, without any fear, without any precaution, with a positive appetite for danger, they rejoice to be struck down, to press upon the sword, to attack the javelin with their own bodies and die from wounds of their own infliction.

3 (1) 'There is no doubt', you may say, 'that this is a powerful, pestilential force. Just show us how to cure it!' But, as I said in the earlier books,[4] Aristotle stands up for anger, telling us not to cut it out. He describes it as the spur to virtue; its removal would leave the mind unarmed, sluggish and useless for any serious endeavour. (2) So there really is a need to prove its foulness and

---

[2] Reading *una* with Vahlen.
[3] As happened to Quintus Pompeius and Gaius Carbo. See Valerius Maximus, IX
7 Mil. 2 f.
[4] I 9. 2, 17. 1.

savagery, to place before your eyes the sheer monstrousness of man raging at man, the sheer brute force that rushes him on, ruinous not least to himself in his effort to sink what cannot be drowned unless he himself drowns with it. (3) I ask you, would anyone call such a person sane? As if caught in a storm, he does not go forward – he is carried along, enslaved by a raging malady. Instead of just ordering retribution, he exacts it himself, savage alike in mind and action, butcher of those dearest to him – whose loss he will shortly lament. (4) No one, surely, will assign this affection to virtue as its assistant and companion – it stirs up confusion in the deliberation without which virtue can do nothing. Frail and baneful, a force for its own undoing, is the strength aroused in the invalid by an onset of fever.

(5) You need not, therefore, think that I am spending time on something superfluous in decrying anger, 'as though there were any doubt in people's minds about it'. You see, there is someone – and one of the famous philosophers at that – who does give it a function, who summons it, as though it had its uses and supplied us with enthusiasm, to battle, to public action, to anything that needs doing with a certain fervour. (6) In case anyone should get the wrong idea that there are times or places where it might be of use, we must display its unbridled, lunatic frenzy; we must give it back its equipment – the 'pony',[5] the cords, the prison, the cross, the rings of fire round half-buried, living bodies,[6] the hook tugging even the dead bodies,[7] the varieties of fetters and punishment, the lacerated limbs and branded foreheads, the cages of savage animals. Let these implements be the setting for anger with its dire and hideous shrieking – anger, ghastlier than all the instruments of its fury.

---

[5] An instrument of torture, apparently a sort of rack. See *On Mercy* I 13. 2.

[6] This variation on burning at the stake is attested in Cicero's *Letters to His Friends* (X 32. 3); and Aulus Gellius' *Attic Nights* (III 14. 19).

[7] For their greater ignominy, the corpses of executed convicts were dragged by a hook (*uncus*), fastened under the chin, from the prison where they had been strangled to the 'Gemonian steps' and down to the Tiber. The best-known recipient of the treatment was probably Tiberius' favourite, Sejanus (Juvenal, X 66), along with his family (Tacitus, *Annals* VI 4). Novatus himself capped his brother's satire on *The Pumpification of Claudius* by joking that the deceased emperor had been hauled ignominiously up to heaven on a hook (Dio Cassius, LX 35. 3).

ıtever doubt you may have in other respects, there is
ffection with an uglier countenance. I have described
er books – rough and harsh, sometimes pale as the
ff and disperses, sometimes reddish and gory as heat
and vitality return to the face, with veins swelling and eyes now
trembling and popping out, now fastened motionlessly in a single
fixed gaze. (2) Add to this the noise of teeth chattering against
one another, as though set on devouring someone – like the noise
of a boar grinding and sharpening its tusks. Add the crackling of
joints as the hands are wrung, the repeated beating of the breast,
the continual panting and deep-drawn sighs, the tottering body, the
sudden outbursts of incomprehensible language, the lips a-quiver,
compressed now and then to hiss out something sinister. (3) Wild
beasts, I swear, goaded on by hunger or a weapon in their entrails,
look less horrible – even when, half-dead, they attack in a final
effort to bite the hunter – than a human being aflame with anger.
And if you could catch the cries and threats – good heavens, what
words of a soul in torment!

(4) Surely anyone would wish to be restored to calm, once he
realizes that anger begins with harm to himself first of all? Surely
you would wish me to remind those who give rein to anger when
in supreme power, who see it as evidence of strength and count
ease of retribution among the great blessings of high estate, of
how little power, indeed how little freedom belongs to any one
caught by his own anger. (5) Surely you would wish me to make
everyone more careful and circumspect by reminding them that,
unlike other evils of the mind which affect the worst sort of people,
bad temper creeps in even upon men of education and sanity in
other respects – so much so that some describe it a mark of
straightforwardness, while it is commonly believed that the most
affable will also be the most prone to it.

5 (1) 'What is the point of this?' you ask. To stop anyone's
thinking himself safe from anger, when it provokes even the naturally gentle and peaceful to savagery and violence. Bodily strength
and careful regard for health are no use against pestilence – it
attacks weak and strong without distinction. In the same way, anger
is a danger to restless characters and, every bit as much, to the
well-ordered and relaxed, for whom it is the more shameful and
dangerous since the change in them is the greater.

Therapy

Division of the subject

(2) Our first need is not to become angry, our second to stop being angry, our third to cure anger in others. So I shall speak, firstly, on how not to fall into anger, then on how to free ourselves from anger, and finally on how the angry should be restrained, pacified and brought back to sanity.[8]

(I) How to avoid the onset of anger[9]

(3) We shall guarantee that we do not become angry if repeatedly we put all the faults of anger on show and appraise it rightly. It must be arraigned at our court and condemned, its evils investigated and brought into the open, its quality revealed by a comparison with all that is worst. (4) Avarice acquires and amasses wealth for a better person to use; anger spends it – few are angry at no cost. How many slaves have been driven to flight, or to their death, by a bad-tempered master! His loss of temper has lost him far more than whatever caused him to lose it! Anger has brought mourning on the father, divorce on the husband, odium on the official, electoral defeat to the candidate. (5) Worse than self-indulgence which revels in its own pleasure, anger revels in the pain of others. It outdoes bad will and envy. They want a man to be made miserable; anger wishes to make him so itself. They rejoice at his bad luck; anger cannot wait for his luck to turn. Its wish is not

---

[8] Seneca deals with the first of these topics (already handled at II 18. 2–36) from 5. 3–9; Chapters 10–39 are broadly on how to free *oneself* from anger; while 39–40 are concerned with pacifying the anger of *others*.

[9] The prophylaxis recommended in this section comes in two parts: (1) further reflections on the odiousness of anger (5. 3–6) and on how a truly great mind would react to provocation (5. 7–6. 2; cf. II 32. 2 f., 34. 1), followed by (2) general advice on how to maintain your good mood or 'good spirits' – what in Greek was called εὐθυμίη, a term translated into Latin as *tranquillitas animi*. This had been the subject of a book by Democritus, the opening words of which are quoted at 6. 3. Seneca and Plutarch also wrote on the theme. The advice here – don't take on too much (6. 3–7, 9), 'avoid temperamental and difficult friends' (8) – derives from the literature on good spirits and being content. But its connection with the avoidance of anger is straightforward. As Aristotle had pointed out (*Rhetoric* 1379a16–18), people who are distressed or frustrated are likelier to lose their tempers.

just for harm to befall the person hated, but to inflict the harm itself. (6) Nothing is worse than quarrels; anger set them up. Nothing is deadlier than war; that is what the anger of the mighty bursts into – though, of course, even the anger of common, private individuals is a kind of war without arms or resources. Besides, anger – to leave aside what is shortly going to follow, the losses, the plots, the perpetual worry of mutual conflict – pays a penalty while exacting one: it denies human nature. For nature exhorts us to love, anger to hatred; nature tells us to help, anger to harm.[10]

(7) And you should add this to your considerations. While its indignation comes from undue self-regard, which gives it a look of spiritedness, anger is petty and mean, since no one can help being inferior to the man who he feels has despised him. A mighty mind with its true self-awareness will not avenge, since it has not noticed the wrong done to it. (8) Weapons rebound from a hard surface; a blow to a solid object hurts only the man who delivers it. In the same way, no wrong done to a great mind will make itself felt, being weaker than its object. How much better it looks, as though impervious to any weapon, to brush off wrongs and insults! Retribution is an admission of pain. A mind bowed by wrong done to it is not a great mind. Whoever harmed you was either stronger or weaker than you. If he was weaker, spare him; if he was stronger, spare yourself. 6 (1) There is no surer proof of greatness than to be unprovoked by anything that can possibly happen. The higher and better ordered part of the world, the part near the stars, is neither compressed into cloud nor thrust into storm nor turned in the whirlwind, free as it is of all turbulence; the lower parts get the lightning. In the same way, a lofty mind, ever at rest in its calm anchorage, stifling anything which might induce anger, maintains its modesty, its claim to respect, its orderliness – none of which you will find in the angry. (2) Where a person is prey to pain and fury, his sense of shame is the first thing to be cast off. In making a violent, impulsive rush at someone, he throws away whatever there was to respect in him. His idea of what to do and the order in which to do it can hardly stay unshaken in his excited state. Can he hold his tongue, or control any part of his body? Has he any command of himself, once he is launched?

---

[10] Cf. 1 5. 2 f.

(3) We may find help in that sound advice of Democritus which points to tranquillity 'if we refrain from doing many things, either in private or in public, or anything beyond our powers'.[11] If one run's off on many different activities, one will never have the luck to spend a day without some annoyance arising, from someone or something, to dispose the mind to anger. (4) If one hurries through the crowded parts of the city, one cannot help knocking into many people; one is bound to slip, to be held back, to be splashed. In the same way, if one's course of life is fragmented and always taking a different direction, many things will get in the way and there will be much to complain about – one man has disappointed us, another put us off, a third cut us short; our plans did not take the course that we intended. (5) No one has fortune so much on his side as always to answer to his wishes, if he attempts many things. As a result, should he do so, he finds his plans thwarted and becomes impatient with people and things. At the slightest provocation he loses his temper with the person involved, with the matter in hand, with his position, with his luck, with himself. (6) So if the mind is to have the possibility of being calm, it must not be tossed about nor, as I said, exhausted by doing many things or anything too ambitious for its powers. It is easy to fit a light load to our shoulders, to shift it here and there without falling. But burdens imposed on us by others we find hard to carry; they have us beaten and we drop them immediately. Even as we stand with the load on top of us, we totter. We just are not up to it.

7 (1) The same thing happens in public as in private, you can be sure of that. Straightforward and manageable tasks follow your directions, unlike the huge tasks that are out of proportion to your capacity. The latter do not yield easily. If you take them on, they weigh you down; they distract you as you carry them out. Just when you think that you have them in your grasp, they fall and bring you down with them. That is why frustration is frequently the fate of one who, instead of undertaking what is easy, finds himself wishing that what he *has* undertaken were easier! (2) Every time that you attempt something, you should make a reckoning of

---

[11] Democritus, Fragment 3 Diels–Kranz. The whole of the following paragraph is an expanded meditation on this text.

yourself, of what you are preparing to do and what has prepared you yourself to do it, since a change of heart at failure to get the job done will make you peevish. (It makes a difference whether your character is hot, or cold and submissive – rebuffs drive the noble to anger, the faint and inert to sorrow.) So our actions should neither be petty nor overconfident and unprincipled. Our hopes should not stray far. We should attempt nothing which leaves us, even at the moment of success, wondering how we did it.

8 (1) We must take care to avoid being wronged, since we do not know how to endure it. We should choose the most indulgent and easy-going people, the least tense and pernickety, to live with. Traits of character are picked up from associates. Just as certain physical disorders are transmitted by contact, so the mind passes on its evils to those nearest at hand. The drunkard draws his companions into a love of alcohol; shameless company softens even a man of natural flinty strength; avarice infects those closest to it. (2) The same principle works in reverse. The virtues civilize all that comes into contact with them. Never was health so improved by a good locality and a superior climate as an unsteady mind by the company of its betters. (3) You can grasp how powerfully this works, if you see how even wild beasts grow tame by living with us; even a savage animal loses its ferocity when subjected to prolonged human company. All its roughness is smoothed down, slowly unlearned in a peaceful environment.

Consider this, too. A person who lives with tranquil people is not improved just by their example, but by the fact that he has no occasion to lose his temper and cannot indulge his failing. So he should avoid all who he knows will provoke his bad temper. (4) 'Who are they?' you may ask. Many people in various ways have the same effect. You may be annoyed by the disdain of the arrogant, the slander of a sharp tongue, the affronts of the self-assertive, the malice of the spiteful, the competitiveness of the aggressive, the lack of substance in a mendacious windbag. You may find it unbearable to be feared by the mistrustful, outdone by the stubborn, looked down on by the choosy. (5) Pick companions who are straightforward, easy-going, restrained, not the sort to arouse your anger, but who can bear it. Still better are those who are submissive, polite and gracious, though not to the point of obsequiousness; too much agreement annoys the bad-tempered. I certainly used to have a friend, a good man but rather too given to anger, who just as dangerous to flatter as to slander.[12] (6) It is well that the orator Caelius[13] was very bad-tempered indeed. I having dinner, the story goes, in his apartment with a client a person of unusual forbearance who, even so, found it difficult, once thrust into contact, to avoid a quarrel with the man at his side. He thought it best to agree with whatever was said and to play second fiddle. Caelius could not stand the way that he kept agreeing and exclaimed 'Say something against me, to show that there are two of us here!' But even he, angry as he was at not being angered, soon stopped when he had no one with whom to argue. (7) So if we are aware of being prone to anger, we should pick out people who adapt themselves to our looks and words. That, of course, will make us spoiled, and give us the bad habit of not listening to anything that we do not want to hear. But it will be some use to give our failing a break and a bit of peace. Even those of an obdurate, untamed nature can bear to be flattered — nothing is harsh and fierce if you stroke it. (8) Whenever an argument becomes too prolonged or heated, we should call a halt at the start, before it gathers strength. Disagreements have a way of feeding themselves and of holding on to those who have got too deeply involved. It is easier to keep out of a fight than to pull out of it.

9 (1) The heavier intellectual activities should also be avoided by those with a tendency to anger. Certainly they should not be pursued to the point of weariness. The mind should not spend its time on hard subjects, but give itself over to the enjoyable arts. It should be soothed by the reading of poetry, entertained by tales of history; it should be treated gently and delicately. (2) Pythagoras settled the soul's disturbances with his lyre;[14] and everyone knows that cornets and trumpets excite the mind, in the same way that

---

[12] It is not known to whom Seneca might be referring.

[13] Marcus Rufus Caelius (82–48 BC), pupil and correspondent of Cicero, who successfully defended him in 56 BC, was a leading orator of the time, celebrated for his powers of invective. His chequered political career ended when he lost his life in an attempted uprising against Julius Caesar.

[14] This story (see also Cicero, *Tusculan Disputations* IV 2. 3; Plutarch, *On Moral Virtue* 441e) reflects the 'Pythagorean' idea that numbers and harmony are fundamental to the nature of things. Pythagoras, guru and mathematician (he is supposed to have discovered Pythagoras' theorem) lived in the sixth century BC

some singing serves to coax and relax it. Greenery is good for bleary eyes, and weak sight finds itself rested by some colours, while it is dazzled by the brightness of others. In the same way, the ailing mind is soothed by intellectual pursuits that it can enjoy. (3) The forum, pleading and verdicts should all be avoided, as should anything that aggravates the fault. We should take just as much care against physical tiredness, which destroys anything mild and peaceable in us and arouses violence. (4) That is why people who are worried about their stomachs, when faced with action of major importance, take food to allay the bile – something particularly brought on by tiredness, either because it drives heat into the middle of the body, harming the blood, halting its circulation and burdening the veins, or because an exhausted and weakened body weighs down the mind. For the same reason, people worn down by ill-health or old age are more prone to anger. Hunger and thirst should also be avoided – they aggravate and inflame the mind. (5) There is an old saying about quarrels' being sought by the weary. The same goes for the hungry, the thirsty, anyone with something to torment him. Just as a sore hurts at the slightest touch, even at the suspicion of a touch, so an afflicted mind is annoyed by the least provocation, so much so that a greeting, a letter, a speech, a question have led to a quarrel. Anything that ails will always complain if you touch it.

How to check one's anger[15]

Prescriptions

10 (1) The best thing, therefore, is to start curing oneself as soon as one is aware of the ailment, to allow oneself the minimum

---

[15] Unobtrusively, Seneca moves on to therapy. III 10–13. 6 is the first stretch of *On Anger* to deal with checking and curing, as against forestalling, the individual fit of anger. His prime remedy is to suppress any symptoms of the emotion as soon as they appear (10, 13. 1–6), the classic exponent of this exercise in autosuggestion being Socrates (13. 3) (see n. 33 above). In between Chapters 10 and 13, Seneca slips in various other precepts, some of which have already appeared in Book II: 'don't be too inquisitive' (11. 1), 'make light of the provocation' (11. 1–12. 1), 'make allowances' (12. 2 f; cf. II 28) and, above all, 'wait a bit and don't punish in anger' (12. 4–7; cf. II 22. 2, 29. 1). This last recommendation serves a double purpose. A precaution against making mistakes under the influence of anger, it is also itself a form of emotional therapy: by denying your anger an outlet, you extinguish it. The principle of curing anger

freedom of speech and inhibit the impulse. (2) And it
intercept one's affections as they first arise, since il'
preceded by symptoms. In the way that storm and rain ...
that come before them, there are certain heralds of anger, of love
and all those squalls that distress the mind. (3) People who suffer
from epilepsy know that the disease is on its way by the departure
of heat from their extremities, by the flickering in their eyes and
the trembling of their muscles, by a slight loss of memory and a
swimming of the head. They apply the usual remedies to anticipate
the cause at its onset – smells and tastes to drive off whatever it
is that is making them insane, poultices to fight against the cold
and stiffness. If the medicine is no use, they keep out of people's
way and fall down unwitnessed. (4) It helps to know one's illness
and to suppress its power before its spreads. We should consider
what most provokes us. Some are enraged by insulting words, some
by insulting actions. One man demands respect for his rank, another
for his personal appearance. One wants a reputation for supreme
elegance, another for supreme scholarship. Arrogance is unbearable
to one man, obstinacy to another. One man does not think slaves
worth his anger, another is fierce at home but mild outside. One
man thinks it an affront to be asked for something, another finds
it insulting not to be. We are not all of us vulnerable in the same
place. You should know your weakness so as to give it the maximum
protection.

11 (1) No good comes from seeing and hearing everything.
Many offences ought to pass us by. Anyone who did know about
them would not take offence at most of them. If you wish to avoid
bad temper, mind your own business. Anyone who asks what was
said about himself and digs up unkind gossip, even if it came in
a private conversation, is disturbing his own peace of mind.[16] Some
things look like wrongs because of the interpretation placed on
them; you should put off thinking about them, or laugh them off,
or make allowance for them.

(2) Anger can be restricted in many ways; much can be turned
to mirth and merriment. Socrates, they say, once had his ears

by suppressing its symptoms and forbidding it all expression was ascribed to the
Pythagoreans of the fourth century BC by Aristotle's pupil Aristoxenus (Fragment
30 Wehrli).
[16] Contrast the story about Julius Caesar at II 23. 4.

boxed and said nothing more than 'What a nuisance it is that one never knows when to go out with a helmet on!'[17] (3) It is not how the wrong is done that matters, but how it is taken. I cannot see any difficulty in moderation, when even tyrants, their heads swollen with good fortune and power, have managed to repress their familiar savagery. (4) There is a tradition, at least, about Pisistratus, tyrant of Athens.[18] A drunken fellow-guest had inveighed at length against his cruelty; numerous people sprang to his assistance, the flame was fanned on all sides. But he took it quietly, replying to those who were urging him on that he was no more outraged than if someone had bumped into him blindfolded.

12   (1) Many people manufacture their grievances by false suspicions or by exaggerating trivialities. Often anger comes over us. More commonly, we resort to it. But it should never be brought on deliberately. If it does fall upon us, it should be cast back. (2) No one ever says to himself: 'What is making me angry is something which I have sometimes done myself or could have done'; no one assesses the motive of the person who did it, only the deed itself. But the motive is what should be considered: was it intentional or an accident, was he forced or misled, was he acting out of hatred or for reward, was he indulging himself or assisting another? The wrongdoer's age and his position are factors which make it humane or prudent to allow and put up with it. (3) We should put ourselves in the place of the man with whom we are angry. As it is, what makes us angry is unwarranted self-esteem. We are unwilling to put up with what we would ourselves like to do.

(4) No one makes himself wait. Yet the greatest remedy for anger is postponement, which allows its initial heat to abate and the darkness that oppresses the mind to subside or thin out. Sometimes what has sent you headlong will be alleviated not just in a day, but in an hour; sometimes it will vanish altogether. If nothing else, the adjournment that I am seeking will bring your judgment, and not your anger, into prominence. Whenever you want to know what a thing is like, give it time; you will not get a good look while it remains in flux. (5) Plato once could not find

---

[17] Diogenes Laertius assigns this anecdote to Diogenes the Cynic (VI 41; cf. also VI 54), as do other ancient authors. Only Seneca gives it to Socrates.

[18] This story about Pisistratus (ruler of Athens c. 561–56, 54–27 BC), which is not found in Herodotus, is told by Valerius Maximus in a fuller version (5, 1 Ext. 2).

the time. Angry with a slave, he immediately told the man to take off his tunic and bare his shoulders for a whipping, intending to inflict it himself. Then he realized that he was angry. He drew back his hand and held it aloft, standing like someone about to deliver a blow. A friend happened to come in and asked what he was doing. 'Punishing an angry man', said he.[19] (6) As though numbed, he kept up that gesture, so ugly in a wise man, of impending savagery, quite forgetting the slave since he had found a more suitable subject for chastisement. He thus stripped himself of power over his servants. Finding himself too provoked by some misdeed, he once said: 'Will *you*, Speusippus,[20] please give this wretched slave a whipping – I am in a temper.'[21] (7) For the very reason that would have led someone else to strike, he refrained from striking. 'I am angry. I will do more than I should, with more pleasure than I should. This slave should not be in the power of someone with no power over himself.' Can anyone wish to see retribution entrusted to a man in a temper, when Plato himself relinquished this office? Nothing is permissible when you are angry. Why? Because you want everything to be.

13 (1) Fight with yourself. If you wish to conquer anger, it cannot conquer you. The start of the conquest is to conceal it, to allow it no way out. We should suppress its symptoms and keep it, so far as possible, hidden and secret. (2) This will cost us a lot of trouble, since anger longs to leap out, to inflame the eyes and alter the countenance. But if once we allow it to appear outside us, we have it over us. It should be hidden in the most remote corner of the breast and carried along, rather than carrying us along. On the contrary, we should turn all its indications into their opposites: the face should be relaxed, the voice gentler, the pace slower. Little by little, the externals will be matched by an inner formation. (3) In Socrates the signs of anger were a lowering of the voice, a greater reserve in speaking, which made it obvious that he was restraining himself.[22] His friends would catch him

---

[19] At I 15. 3 Seneca told a similar story about Socrates, though only to show that you should not punish in anger. Aristoxenus tells it about Plato's friend, the Pythagorean Archytas (Fragment 30 Wehrli; see above on 10. 1).

[20] Plato's nephew and successor as head of the Academy.

[21] Less elaborately and with variations, this anecdote and the preceding one are told about Plato also in Diogenes Laertius (III 38–9).

[22] Plutarch gives a similar report *(On the Control of Anger* 455 a–b).

at it and accuse him, nor was he displeased at being reproached for concealed anger. He had reason to rejoice that so many could discern his anger, while none had felt it. And they *would* have felt it, had he not given his friends that right to criticize which he had adopted towards them. (4) How much more ought we to do this! We should ask all our best friends to show us the greatest frankness precisely when we can least bear it, and not to concur with our anger. We are faced with a powerful evil, and one most agreeable to us; so long as we are of sound mind and in control of our faculties, we should call upon them for help. (5) People who cannot carry their wine, and are afraid of being rash or boisterous when drunk, tell their servants to take them away from the party. Those who have experienced their own lack of self-control in sickness give orders that they are not to be obeyed when their health is bad. (6) It is best to search out barriers to our known failings and, above all, so to order the mind that, even under the heaviest and most sudden blows, it either will not experience anger at all or, if the feeling does arise through the greatness of the unexpected wrong, it will bury it deeply and not proclaim its distress.

Examples

(i) Anger in subordinates suppressed by fear
(7) That this can be done will be apparent if I produce a few examples from a great many to show (a) the evils of anger when it has the entire might of potentates at its disposal, (b) its ability to control itself when hemmed in by a greater fear.
   14 (1) King Cambyses was too fond of wine. Prexaspes, one of his dearest friends, advised him to drink less, declaring drunkenness in a king with the eyes and ears of all upon him to be a disgrace. The king answered: 'To show you that I never lose control of myself, I will now prove to you that the wine leaves my eyes and hands in full working order.' (2) He went on to drink more generously than usual, out of larger cups. Heavily drunk, he ordered his critic's son to go beyond the threshold and stand there with his left hand over his head. Then he drew his bow and shot the boy through the heart – that, he had said, was his aim. He had the breast cut open. He showed the arrow stuck directly in

the heart. He looked at the father, asking whether his hand had been sure enough. 'Not even Apollo', the father replied, 'could have aimed better.'[23]

(3) Confound the man, a slave in mind if not station! There he was, praising something which it was too much even to have witnessed, finding occasion for flattery in the dissection of his son's breast and the palpitation of the heart in the wound. He should have disputed the question of glory with him and called for the shot to be repeated, that it might please the king to show a yet surer hand in aiming at the father. (4) O blood thirsty king! He deserved to have everyone's bow turned on him. And yet, execrable as he is to us for ending the banquet with punishment and slaughter, to praise the shot was still more criminal than to make it. But how *should* a father have behaved as he stood over his son's body, witness and cause of his killing? We shall see. The point now at issue is clear, that anger can be suppressed. (5) Not cursing the king, he uttered not a word even of grief, though he felt his heart transfixed no less than his son's. You can say that he was right to choke back his words; expressions of anger would have denied him the role of a father. (6) You can even think that he behaved more wisely in that misfortune than he had when he gave advice on moderation in wine-bibbing to a man who was better employed drinking wine than blood – when his hands were on the wine-cup, at least that meant peace. He joined the ranks of those whose catastrophes have shown what it costs the friends of kings to give good advice.

15 (1) I have no doubt that Harpagus offered some such advice to *his* Persian king.[24] It annoyed him into serving up the man's children at a feast and repeatedly asking him if liked the seasoning. Then, seeing him with a stomach full of woe for himself, he ordered their heads to be brought in and asked him what he thought of the bounty. Words did not fail the poor man, his lips were not sealed. 'Dinner with a king', said he, 'is always delicious.' What did he achieve by this flattery? He was spared the leftovers. I am not saying that a father should not condemn anything that

[23] Cambyses, son of Cyrus the Great, was king of Persia 530–522 BC. Seneca's story derives, directly or indirectly, from Herodotus (III 34 f.).
[24] In Herodotus' account (I 108–19), Harpagus was being punished by Astyages, the *Median* king, for *disobedience*.

his king does, I am not saying that he should not try to punish such monstrous ferocity as it deserves; I am just proving, for the moment, that even anger generated by enormous affliction can be concealed and compelled to use words that express the opposite.[25]

(3) It is necessary to bridle your indignation in this way, especially if your lot is to have this sort of life and be invited to the royal table. That is how you eat there, how you drink there, the sort of answer that you make there – you just have to smile as your family dies. But is the life worth that much? We shall see. That is a different question. We have no consolation to offer for a prison so gloomy. We are not going to advise men to endure the butcher's commands. We shall simply show that in any slavery the way lies open to freedom. One's afflicton is mental, the misery one's own fault, if one can put an end to it, together with oneself. (4) I shall say both to the man with the luck to have a king who shoots arrows at the heart of his friends and to him whose master gorges the father with the entrails of the son: 'Why the groans, madman? Why wait for an enemy to avenge you through the downfall of your nation, or for some mighty monarch to swoop down from afar? Wheresoever you cast your eyes there lies an end to affliction. Look at that precipice – down it runs the way to freedom. Look at the sea there, the river, the well – at its bottom lies freedom. Look at that tree, short and shrivelled and barren – there on it hangs freedom. Look at your throat, your windpipe, your heart – all are ways of escape from slavery. But perhaps the ways out which I have shown are too toilsome for you, too demanding on spirit and strength. Are you asking for the road to freedom? Take any vein you like in your body!'[26]

16 (1) So long, however, as nothing seems so unbearable as to drive us from life, we should rid ourselves of anger, whatever our station in life may be. For subordinates, anger is ruinous, since any indignation contributes to its own torture and orders weigh

---

[25] Had he not already used it at II 33. 3 f., Seneca could have told the story of Pastor and Caligula as a further example, and nearer to home, of anger suppressed by fear.

[26] It was standard Stoic doctrine that under certain special, extreme conditions it was rational and moral to end one's own life (see Cicero, *On Ends* III 60–1; Diogenes Laertius VII 130). It does not appear, however, that any Greek Stoic counted being subject to such royal whims among them, or that Stoic principles when correctly applied would have licensed doing so.

harder the more defiantly they are taken. That is how an animal, struggling against the noose, tightens it; how a bird, nervously shaking off the lime, smears it all over its plumage. There is no yoke so tight that it will not hurt the animal less if it pulls with it than if it fights against it. The one alleviation for overwhelming evils is to endure and bow to necessity.

(ii) Anger in potentates
(2) But prudent as it is for subjects to control their emotions, especially this the most rabid and unbridled of them, it is still more prudent for kings to do so. All is lost where one's position permits whatever anger suggests. Nor can a power long survive that is exercised to the general harm, since danger besets it when those who separately groan under it are joined in a shared fear. Thus the majority have fallen victim to individual assassins or to whole groups whom a common distress has forced to pool their anger. (3) And yet the majority have treated anger as a badge of royalty, as did Darius[27] who was the first, after the dethronement of the Magus, to rule the Persians and a great part of the East. Having declared war upon the Scythians encircling his eastern border, he was asked by Oeobazus, an elderly noble with three sons, to let one stay behind to console his father, while employing the services of the other two. Promising to go beyond what was asked and excuse all three, he killed them in front of their father and threw down the bodies, since it would have been cruel to take them all with him.[28] (4) Xerxes[29] was much more accommodating. When Pythius, a father of five sons, asked for one to be exempted from service, he allowed him to make the choice. He then had the one who had been chosen torn in half and set on either side of the road, using him as a sacrificial victim to purify the army.[30] So he met the fate he deserved. Defeated, scattered far and wide, with his ruin to see all round him, he picked his way through the bodies of his own troops.

17 (1) 'But that was savagery of barbarian kings in their anger, men with no education or tincture of literary culture.' Then I will

[27] Darius I, the third Achaemenid king of Persia (521–486 BC).
[28] See Herodotus, IV 84.
[29] Xeres I (486–465 BC), son and successor of Darius, launched the great expedition against Greece that met with disaster in 480 and 479 BC.
[30] See Herodotus, VII 38 f.

present to you, right from Aristotle's bosom, king Alexander.[31] With his very own hand in the middle of a banquet he stabbed Clitus, his dearest friend who had been brought up with him, for showing too little flattery and for sluggishness in making the transition from Macedonian freedom to Persian slavery.[32] (2) Again, he threw Lysimachus, no less an intimate, to a lion. But do not think that this made Lysimachus, who fortunately escaped from the lion's jaw, any milder when *he* came to be king.[33] (3) He mutilated his friend Telesphorus of Rhodes in every part. Cutting off his ears and nose, he kept him a long time in a cage, like some new and unfamiliar animal – the ugliness of that lopped, disfigured face had lost any look of a human being. Added to this came hunger, dirt, and the filth of a body left in its own excrement. (4) On top of all that, his knees and hands were calloused (he was forced by his cramped surroundings to use them as feet), his sides chafed and erupting in sores. His appearance aroused disgust as much as terror in those who looked at him. Made by his punishment into a monster he had forfeited even pity. Yet, however far the victim was from the likeness of a man, the one who did this to him was further still.

18 (1) Oh that this cruelty could be confined to examples from abroad, that the barbarity of punishments in anger, on top of other imported vices, had not made its way into the Roman character! Marcus Marius[34] to whom the people had set up statues street by street, whose favour it had sought with offerings of incense and

---

[31] Alexander the Great. Aristotle has been his tutor.

[32] Clitus who had saved Alexander's life at the battle of the Granicus (334 BC) was killed in roughly the manner and circumstances related by Seneca in 328 or 327 BC. His murder was regularly cited by moralists as the most serious blot on Alexander's record.

[33] The story of Lysimachus (361–281 BC), companion and bodyguard of Alexander, and the lion was told in several distinct versions, none of which gives the ground for Alexander's anger. (Seneca recalls it again at *On Mercy* I 25. 1.) Having survived his encounter with the lion, Lysimachus established a kingdom in Thrace and north-west Asia Minor after Alexander's death and in 285 BC gained control of Macedonia and Thessaly, before being defeated and killed at Corupedium in 281 BC. As a monarch, he was disliked for his high-handed administration. His treatment of Telesphorus (below) is also mentioned by Plutarch (*On Exile* 606b).

[34] Marcus Marius Gratidianus, nephew of Gaius Marius (see II 2. 3 above), had received heroic honours for announcing a plan to improve the coinage. In 82 BC, on the orders of Sulla, he was put to death by his own brother-in-law, Catiline.

wine, had his ankles broken at the order of Lucius Sulla, his eyes gouged out, his tongue and hands cut off. As though killing him with each wound, Sulla mangled him little by little, limb by limb. (2) And who executed the command? Who else but Catiline?[35] Already trying his hand at every manner of crime, he dismembered him before the tomb of Quintus Catulus[36] – the harshest affront to the ashes of that mildest of men. It was over these that Marius – a bad influence, but popular, with a popularity that was not so much undeserved as excessive – shed his blood drop by drop. Marius deserved to suffer this punishment, Sulla to order it, Catiline to carry it out. But our commonwealth hardly deserved to be pierced by the swords of public enemies and avengers alike.

(3) But why look at ancient history? Just recently Gaius Caesar[37] had Sextus Papinius, the son of an ex-consul, and his quaestor Betilienus Bassus, the son of his procurator, along with others, senators and knights of Rome, whipped and tortured in one day, not to extract information, but because he felt like it. (4) Next, so impatient was he with any postponement of the enormous pleasure which his cruelty demanded without delay that, as he walked up and down the terrace of his mother's garden (it runs between the colonnade and the river bank) in the company of ladies and other senators, he had some of these men beheaded by lamplight. Why the hurry? What danger to state or individual could a single night have posed? It would not have been much trouble, in point of fact, for him to wait for morning and thus avoid killing senators of the Roman people in his slippers.

19 (1) The sheer arrogance of his cruelty is a relevant point here. Some may think that I am digressing and going off on a sidetrack. But you will find that this itself is an element of abnormally savage anger. He had taken the whip to members of the Senate – and he saw to it that such a thing could be called normal. He had already applied all the most gruesome tortures in the world – the rack, the thumb-screws, the 'pony',[38] the flames, his

---

[35] Subsequently notorious for the 'Catilinarian' conspiracy (62 BC), denounced by Cicero, in which he met his end.

[36] There was some point in this. After being prosecuted by Marcus Marius in 87 BC, Quintus Lutatius Catulus had committed suicide.

[37] I.e. the emperor Caligula.

[38] Apparently a sort of rack; see 3.6 above.

own face. (2) Here you may well answer: 'Big deal! Three senators put to the lash and the flame in turn as though they were slaves of no account – by a man who thought of butchering the entire Senate, who wanted the Roman people to have a single neck, so as to assemble his crimes, spread out as they were over so many times and places, into a single blow on a single day!' What is unheard of is the choice of night-time for punishing. Robberies normally are concealed in darkness, but not visitations of punishment. The better known they are, the more they work as corrective examples. (3) And here you may well answer me: 'What so amazes you is daily routine for that brute. That is what he lives for, stays awake for, burns the midnight oil for.' You will find no one else, I grant you, giving orders that all those whom he has commanded to be punished should have sponges put in their mouths, to deny them the power to cry out. Was there ever a doomed man robbed of the chance to groan? He feared that the final agony might send forth too frank a cry and that he might hear what he would rather not. He knew that he had done countless things which no one but a man on the point of death would dare to lay to his charge. (4) When sponges were not to be found, he ordered the clothes of the poor wretches to be torn up and the rags stuffed in their mouths. What savagery is this? Allow a man to draw his last breath, give the soul room to make its exit, let it escape by some other way than the wound!

(5) It would be too long a business to add that he also had the fathers of those whom he killed dispatched that same night by centurions sent round their homes – I mean, that out of human pity he released them from their misery. Our purpose is not to describe Gaius' savagery but that of anger, which not only rages at individuals but tears entire nations to pieces, lashing at cities and rivers and things quite incapable of pain. **20** (1) Thus the Persian king docked the noses of an entire people in Syria – which gave the place its name Rhinocolura or 'Docked-nose'.[39] Was it an act of mercy on his part, do you think, that he did not cut off their heads entirely? No, the novelty of the punishment was what appealed to him. (2) Some such fate was in store for

---

[39] Strabo (16. 2. 31; Chapter 759) tells the same story about an Ethiopian king; Pliny (*Natural History* v 14. 68) also mentions the town, placing it in Palestine. On Cambyses, see III 14. 1 above.

the Ethiopians, called Macrobioe or 'Long-lived' for their very long life-spans. Instead of holding out their hands and accepting the yoke of slavery, they had answered the ambassadors sent to them with a frankness that kings call impertinence. Cambyses roared. Without seeing to provisions or exploring the routes, he dragged his whole fighting force through impassable desert to get to them. On the first stage of the journey, supplies were running out. Nothing was available in the region, barren as it was, uncultivated, untrodden by human foot. (3) At first they kept hunger at bay with the tenderest tips of leaf and young twig, then with skins softened over the fire and whatever food necessity forced on them. When amid the sands even roots and grass had run out, and a vast wilderness appeared before them lacking animals as well, they drew lots for one man in ten to provide a nourishment ghastlier than hunger. (4) Anger still drove the king impetuously onward until, having lost one part of his army and eaten another, he feared that he himself might be summoned to the lottery. Then at last he gave the sign for retreat. All the while, pedigree fowls were being kept for him and his dinner service was transported on camels, as his soldiers cast lots to see who should perish wretchedly or live more wretchedly still.[40]

21 (1) That king's anger was with an unknown people, who did not deserve it but yet could have felt it. Cyrus' wrath was with a river. He was hurrying to attack Babylon and make war, in which opportunity is what most tips the scale. He attempted to ford the river Gyndes in full flood, a dangerous crossing even when summer has made itself felt and the water is at its lowest. (2) There one of the white horses that usually drew the royal chariot was swept away, to the king's intense annoyance. He swore that he would reduce that river which had carried away a king's retinue to the level where even women could cross and trample it underfoot. (3) To this task he then transferred all his army's equipment, remaining at it long enough to cut one hundred and eighty channels into the river on either side,[41] to disperse it into three hundred and sixty rivulets and leave it dry as the waters flowed off in different directions. (4) And so time was lost (a major loss in matters of

---

[40] This story goes back to Herodotus III 20–5.
[41] Reading *octoginta* <*utrimque*> with Gertz.

major importance), as was the morale of his soldiers, broken down
by the useless labour, and also the chance of attacking the enemy
unprepared, while war declared on the foe was waged against a
river.[42]

(5) Such madness – what else would you call it? – has affected
Romans as well. Gaius Caesar destroyed a very beautiful villa at
Herculaneum because his mother had once been under house-arrest
in it, thereby giving publicity to what had befallen her there.[43]
While it stood, we used to sail past it. Now people ask why it was
pulled down.

(iii) Anger admirably controlled

22 (1) You should think of these as examples of what to avoid.
Here, on the other hand, are examples to follow, examples of
moderation and gentleness on the part of people who had both
cause to be angry and power to exact retribution. (2) Nothing could
have been easier for Antigonus[44] than to order the execution of
two ordinary soldiers who were leaning against the royal tent and
doing something very dangerous as well as very tempting – expressing a low opinion of the king. Antigonus heard everything, as you
might expect since there was only a curtain between speakers and
listener. He shook it gently and said: 'Go a bit further away, in
case the king hears you.' (3) This same Antigonus one night heard
some of his soldiers heaping all manner of curses upon the king
for taking them on such a journey and into such inextricable mud.
He went up to those who were having the worst time and pulled
them out of it without their realizing who was helping them. 'Go
ahead', he said, 'and curse Antigonus, whose fault it is that you
are in this trouble. But bless the man who got you out of this

---

[42] Another story from Herodotus (I 189).
[43] Caligula's mother Agrippina had been arrested in AD 29 on the orders of Tiberius
and banished by the Senate to the island of Pandateria, where she died in 33.
[44] Probably Antigonus I Monophthalmus (The 'One-eyed'), a general and successor
of Alexander's, who met his end, after several successful campaigns, at the battle
of Ipsus (301 BC). (Plutarch, in telling the same anecdote in *Sayings of Kings and
Generals* 182c–d, assigns it to this Antigonus; see also *On the Control of Anger*
457d–e.) At III 11. 2 above Seneca recommends dissipating one's anger by turning
it to 'mirth and merriment', as Socrates did when struck in the face – and as
Antigonus does with the soldiers. Seneca reports another tale about him in *On
Favours* II 17. 1.

quagmire!' (4) Antigonus put up with abuse from enemies as calmly as he did from his fellow-countrymen. Some Greeks were under siege in a small fort. Confident of their position, they showed their contempt for the enemy, making many jokes about Antigonus' ugliness, laughing at his shortness and his boxer's nose. 'I am glad and it gives me optimism', he said, 'to have Silenus in the camp.' (5) Having starved out the jeerers, he disposed of his captives by assigning any who were good for military service to his regiments, putting the rest up for auction. He would not have done this, he said, had it not seemed good for people with such a nasty tongue to have a master.[45]

23 (1) This man's grandson was the Alexander[46] who used to brandish his spear at fellow dinner-guests, throwing one of the friends whom I mentioned a short while ago to a wild animal, the other to himself.[47] (Of the two, it was the one thrown to the lion who survived.) (2) He did not inherit this vice from his grandfather, or indeed from his father. If Philip had any virtues at all, they included an ability to put up with insults, a powerful device for maintaining a throne. Demochares, known as Parrhesiastes or 'Outspoken' for his unduly assertive tongue, had come to him along with other Athenian ambassadors.[48] Philip gave the delegation a friendly hearing and said, 'Tell me, what can I do to please the Athenians?' Demochares seized on this and replied 'Hang yourself!' (3) Indignation at the rudeness of the reply broke out among the bystanders. Philip told them to be quiet and to let that Thersites[49] go away safe and sound. 'You other ambassadors', said he, 'are to tell the Athenians that those who say such things are far more arrogant than those who hear what they say and let them off.'

---

[45] Plutarch relates a lamer version of the same story in *On the Control of Anger* 458 f.

[46] A howler, perhaps caused by the fact that Antigonus, a successor of Alexander's, had a son named Philip (see Cicero *On Duties* II 48), which was also the name of Alexander's father. Alexander's grandfather was Amyntas III (c. 393–370 BC).

[47] See 17. 1 f.

[48] See 17 1 f. Chronologically, this seems improbable. Demochares Parrhesiastes, democratic Athenian statesman and nephew of Demosthenes, was active principally between 307 and 280 BC. If he went on an embassy to Philip who died in 336 BC, he must either have been very young when he did so, or very old at the main points of his career.

[49] The one low-class character in Homer's *Iliad* (II 212–77), ugly and foul-mouthed.

(4) Our deified Augustus, too, showed by many memorable deeds and words that anger was not his master. Timagenes the historian had made some remarks against him, against his wife and his entire family. Nor were his words wasted; foolhardy wit circulates all the wider and remains on people's lips. (5) Caesar frequently warned him to restrain his tongue, banning him from his house when he persisted. Timagenes went on to reach old age in the entourage of Asinius Pollio, lionized by the whole town; not a door was closed to him for having been barred from Caesar's house. (6) He gave public readings of the histories which he had subsequently written, consigning to the flames the books that contained the deeds of Caesar Augustus. He kept up his feud with Caesar. But no one was afraid to be friends with him, no one shrank from him as though he had been struck by lightning. However great his fall, there was still someone to take him to his bosom. (7) Caesar, as I said, bore this in patience, unmoved even by the fact that rude hands had been laid on the eulogy and record of his deeds. He never complained to his enemy's host. (8) He merely said to Asinius Pollio '*Tu nourris un monstre*',[50] and stopped him from making his excuse, with the words 'Enjoy it, my dear Pollio, enjoy it.' 'If you so command me, Caesar,' said Pollio, 'I will immediately ban him from my house.' 'Do you think that I would do that,' said he, 'when it is I who reconciled you?' Pollio, in fact, had once had a quarrel with Timagenes. His sole reason for ending it was that Caesar had started one.[51]

Further advice and reflections[52]

Make allowances – no one can help giving provocation

24 (1) And so everyone should say to himself, whenever he comes under provocation: 'Am *I* more powerful than Philip? Yet he let

---

[50] Augustus delivered his retort in Greek.

[51] Timagenes of Egypt had been captured and brought to Rome in 55 BC. Soldier, orator, tragic dramatist, historian and literary critic, Gaius Asinius Pollio (76 BC–AD4), a correspondent of Cicero's, had supported Julius Caesar and then Antony, becoming consul in 40 BC. He retired to devote himself to literature, retaining to the end a certain republican independence of mind, even against Augustus. Seneca mentions him again in *On Mercy* 1 10. 1.

[52] Chapters 24–38 present a deliberately disorganized miscellany of advice and reflections, most of it by now familiar. Its two broad themes (24–9) that 'error is universal' (so you have no reason to be provoked by anything in particular), a

abuse go unpunished. Have *I* really more power in
than our deified Augustus had in the whole world?
merely to part company with the man who abused
should I treat an answer that is too loud or a lo
rebellious on the part of my slave, or his muttering
cannot quite hear, as something to be punished w _____ ....ps and
manacles? Who am I that it should be a sacrilege to offend my
ears? Many have pardoned their enemies – am I not to pardon
the lazy, the careless, the talkative?' (3) A child can be excused by
his age, a woman by her sex, anyone outside the household by his
rights as a free man, anyone inside it by being part of the family.
This is his first offence – we should think of how long we have
been pleased with him. He has often offended on other occasions –
let us bear what we have long borne. He was a friend – he did
not mean it. An enemy – he did what an enemy ought to do. (4)
The intelligent should be given our trust, the stupid our indulgence.
Whoever it may be, we should answer on his behalf that even the
wisest have done many things wrong, that no one is so circumspect
that his diligence may not lapse on occasion, no one so mature
that some accident may not impair his sense of responsibility and
drive him to hot-headed action, no one so afraid of giving offence
as not to stumble into doing so while trying to avoid it.

25 (1) A man of humble station finds solace for his afflictions
in the thought that even the fortune of great men totters. In his
little corner, he bewails the loss of his son with greater composure
when he sees untimely funerals in the royal palace itself. In the
same way, a greater composure in the endurance of harm and
insult results from the thought that there is no power so great that
wrong cannot be done to it. (2) If even the most intelligent go
wrong, is there anyone whose error has not its own good excuse?
We should look back on our own youth, on how often we were
negligent in our duties, unrestrained in our speech, intemperate in
our drinking. Suppose that someone is angry; we should give him
room to see clearly what he has done. He will chastise himself.

---

reworking of material from II 6–10, and (30–35) that your anger rests upon 'false
accounting' are repeatedly interrupted with appeals to 'greatness of mind' that will
not stoop to anger (25. 3, 28. 6, 32. 3, 38. Cf. II 32. 3) and the recommendation to
'bide your time and not do anything hastily' (29. 2, 32. 2. Cf. 12. 4–7). Seneca ends
(36–8) by recommending a standard spiritual exercise, the *examinatio conscientiae*.

Again, he may deserve punishment. But that is no reason for us to settle accounts with him.

The mark of true greatness is to overlook provocations
(3) Beyond any doubt, one raises oneself from the common lot to a higher level by looking down upon those who provoke. The mark of true greatness is not to feel the blow, to be like the mighty beast looking round slowly at the baying of hounds, like the huge rock as the waves dash in vain against it. Not to be angry is to be unshaken by wrong done to one; to succumb to anger is to become agitated. (4) But he whom I have raised above all annoyance has embraced the supreme good and can reply not to man alone but to Fortune herself: 'Do all that you will, you are too insignificant to cloud my serenity. Reason forbids it, and I have entrusted my life to reason's governance. Anger will harm me more than the wrong done. It cannot help doing so. The wrong done has a definite limit, but quite how far anger will take me is uncertain.'

26 (1) 'I cannot endure it. It is hard to submit to wrong.' Untrue. Anyone can put up with wrong done to him, if he can put up with his own anger. Besides, what you are now doing is to put up with them both. Why do you put up with ravings of an invalid, a lunatic's ranting, or cheeky behaviour by children? Because, of course, they patently do not know what they are doing. Does it matter which fault makes a person foolish? The plea of foolishness holds good for them all. (2) 'Well then, is he to get off without punishment?' Suppose that you wanted him to, he still would not. The greatest punishment for a wrong done is to have done it, the heaviest penalty is to be handed over to the pangs of remorse.

Error is universal
(3) Next we should turn our thoughts to the conditions of human life, if we are to be fair judges of whatever happens. It is quite unfair to blame an individual for a failing shared by all. Among his own people, there is nothing distinctive about the colouring of an Ethiopian; nor is red hair tied in a knot unbecoming to a German male. Nothing in an individual is noteworthy or ugly if it is common to his entire nation. And these peculiarities which I have just mentioned are excused by the custom of a single region, a single corner of the world. Think how much greater the claims

for pardon must be when something is spread throughout the entire human race! (4) All of us are inconsiderate and thoughtless, all of us unreliable, querulous, ambitious. But why use gentler language to conceal a universal sore? All of us are *bad*. Whatever he blames in another, each will find in his own heart. Why point out the pallor of one man and the gauntness of another? We are faced with an epidemic! So we should be more indulgent towards one another. We are bad men living among bad men; and only one thing can calm us – we must agree to go easy on one another. (5) 'He has already harmed me, and I have not harmed him yet!' But perhaps there is someone whom you have already harmed or whom you will. Don't take just this hour or this day into consideration. Consider the whole cast of your mind. You may not be guilty of wrongdoing. But you are quite capable of it.

27 (1) How much more satisfactory it is to heal a wrong than to exact retribution for it![53] Retribution takes much time, exposing itself to a multitude of injuries in its distress over one. Our anger invariably lasts longer than the damage done to us. How much better to go the other way and not confront fault with fault! No one, surely, would look very stable if he kicked back at a mule or bit back at a dog. (2) 'But animals don't know that they are doing wrong', you may say. Well firstly, how unfair it is that the fact of being human should spoil the chances of winning pardon! And secondly, if other animals are to escape your anger because they have no understanding, you should place any person without understanding in the same position. Why should his other differences from dumb animals matter at all, if he resembles them in the one excuse for any wrong-doing they do – darkness of mind? (3) 'He has done wrong!' Is this the first time? Is this the last time? You have no reason to believe him, even if he says 'I won't do it again.' He will – and others will do him wrong. His whole life will be tossed from one error to another. Gentleness is the only treatment for the ungentle.

So will you ever stop being angry?
(4) A standard and highly effective argument against mourning can also be used against anger: are you ever going to stop – or never?

---

[53] Cf. II 10. 7: the wise man sees the wicked as patients.

If you are, how much better to take leave yourself of anger, and not the other way round! Or is this commotion going to be permanent? Can you not see what a restless life you are threatening to give yourself? What will it be like if you are constantly on the boil? (5) Besides, however well and truly you inflame yourself, however much you rehearse your reasons for being provoked, your anger will disappear of its own accord. Time will undermine its strength. How much better that the defeat of anger should not be its own doing but yours![54]

28 (1) You will be angry with one person after another, with slaves and then freedmen, with your parents and then your children, with acquaintances and then with people unknown to you; everywhere you will find occasion for anger – unless the mind steps in to intercede. Your rage will sweep you this way and that, that way and this. New provocations will constantly be cropping up and your fury will never stop. Poor man, will you ever find yourself *liking* people? What a waste of precious time on a bad business! (2) How much better right now to make friends, to mollify enemies, go into public service or turn your efforts to private business, than to look round for possible harm to do someone, for damage to inflict on his reputation, his estate or his person. You just cannot manage it without conflict and danger, even if you are fighting a lesser man. (3) You can take delivery of him tied up and ready for anything you see fit to have done to him – even so, it can often happen that too strong a blow dislocates a joint or leaves a muscle caught in the teeth which it just broken. Bad temper has left many crippled or enfeebled, even when the victim was passive. Besides, nothing is naturally so weak that it perishes without endangering its killer. Weaklings turn out equal to the very strongest through the force of pain or circumstances.

Make allowances. Be magnanimous. Take your time
(4) What of the fact that most of what angers us causes more annoyance than harm? Moreover, there is a great difference between opposing my will and just failing to support me, between grabbing and just failing to give. And yet it is all one to us whether someone

---

[54] A good example of this argument, used in a consolation, is Chapter 20 (112b–c) of the *Consolation to Apollonius*, traditionally ascribed to Plutarch.

takes away or refuses to grant, whether he cuts short or just puts off our hopes, whether he is acting against us or for himself, for love of another or through hatred of us. (5) There are people who not only have just cause to stand against us, but for whom it is positively honourable to do so. One may be protecting a father, another a brother, a third his country, a fourth his friend. Yet we refuse to forgive them for doing what we would blame them for not doing. On the contrary (and this is quite incredible), we often think well of the deed and ill of the doer. (6) But, good heavens, a man of true greatness and justice looks up to those of the enemy that are bravest and most stubborn in the fight for the freedom and salvation of their country, praying to have such men as fellow-citizens and soldiers.

29 (1) To hate a person whom you should praise is shameful. How much more shameful must it be to hate someone for reasons which make him worthy of pity. He may be a prisoner of war, suddenly reduced to slavery but holding on to the remains of his freedom, with little energy for demeaning, toilsome tasks. He may be out of training and unable to keep up on foot with his master's horse and carriage, or exhausted from regular night-duty and overcome by sleep. He may hold out against labour in the country or approach it half-heartedly, after being transferred from the holiday of service in the town to really hard work. (2) We should draw a distinction between being unable and being unwilling. Many will be acquitted if once we start to sit in judgment before losing our tempers. As it is, we follow our first impulse. Then, however empty the provocation, we keep up our anger, lest we look as though we had no reason for starting it. Most unfairly of all, its unfairness makes us all the more stubborn. We hold on to our anger and increase it, as though its violence were proof of its justice.[55]

False accounting

30 (1) We would do better to look at its beginnings. How trivial and harmless they are! What you see happening to dumb animals you will also find in man. We are upset by empty trifles. Bulls are provoked by the colour red, snakes rise up at shadows, bears and lions are roused by a towel: any creature fierce and furious by

---

[55] See the story of Gnaeus Piso (I 18. 3–6).

nature is unsettled by things of no substance. (2) The same occurs with restless and brutish characters: they are wounded by mere suspicions of how things are – so much so that they can even, on occasion, speak of anything less than a great favour as a 'wrong'. In such favours lies the commonest, certainly the bitterest, material for anger. We are angry with those whom we love most because they have granted us less than we had imagined that they would or less than others have got from them. In both cases, a remedy lies at hand. (3) If more has been bestowed on somebody else, we should enjoy what is ours without making comparisons – no one will be happy if tormented by the thought of someone else who is happier. Again, I may have less than I hoped for. But perhaps I was hoping for more than I should have. This factor is what we have most to fear. It generates the most dangerous forms of anger, threats to all that is most sacred. (4) The killers of our deified Julius included more of his friends than his enemies. He had failed to satisfy their insatiable hopes. He had wished to do so, of course – no one made more generous use of victory than he did, laying claim to nothing save the power to hand things out to others – but how could he have satisfied such unconscionable appetites? Every one wanted what only one could have. (5) So he saw his comrades-in-arms with their swords drawn around his chair, Tillius Cimber,[56] the keenest of his partisans a little while before, and others who had become Pompeians only after Pompey's death. That is what has turned a king's weapons against him, driving on his trustiest followers to plot the death of the man for whom and before whom it had been their prayer to die.

31 (1) No one who has his eye on others and what they have is content with what he himself has. Hence even the gods incur our anger because some one is ahead of us. We forget how many are behind us or what a huge weight of envy follows at the back of one who himself has few to envy. But such is human impertinence that, having received much, people think themselves wronged if they could have received more. (2) 'He gave me the praetorship,

---

[56] Lucius Tillius Cimber, praetor in 46 BC, designated governor with proconsular power of Bithynia and Pontus for 44 BC, owed his rise to Julius Caesar. On the Ides of March 44 BC, he approached Caesar, ostensibly to plead for his brother's pardon, and grabbed his toga, as a signal to his fellow conspirators for the assassination. He died with Brutus and Cassius at the battle of Philippi in 42 BC.

but I had hoped for the consulate.'[57] 'He gave me the twelve fasces,[58] but did not make me a regular consul.' 'He was willing for the year to be dated with my name,[59] but did nothing to get me the priesthood.' 'I got elected into a college of priests, but why into only one?' 'He raised me to the highest status, but contributed nothing to my private fortune.' 'He just gave me what he had to give to someone, nothing from his own pocket.'[60] (3) Come now, be thankful for what you have received! Stand by for the rest and be glad that you are not yet full. One of life's pleasures is to have something left to hope for. Suppose that you have beaten everyone – rejoice that you come first in a friend's affections. Suppose that many are beating you – think how many more are behind than in front of you. What is your greatest failing, you ask? False accounting. You put too high a value on what you have given, too low a value on what you have received.

Take your time

32 (1) Various motives should deter us from anger: fear in some cases, respect in others, or disgust – it would be a grand achievement, I suppose, to send some poor slave to prison! Why the hurry to inflict a whipping immediately or have his legs broken at once? (2) Our power to do these things will still be there, if we put it off. Wait for the time when we ourselves give the orders, instead of speaking, as we do now, at the command of anger. When it is gone, we shall see how to assess the damages. Here is where we make our biggest mistake, resorting to sword and capital punishment, using chains, prison and starvation to punish a matter which needs only a light beating to correct it.

[57] Magistracies at Rome were held in ascending order – quaestorship, praetorship, consulate, censorship. By Seneca's time, they were in the gift of the emperor, as were priesthoods.

[58] As a mark of office, consuls at Rome had an escort of twelve lictors carrying fasces or bundles of rods with axes in the middle. See I 19. 3, n. 46.

[59] In other words, 'he made me a regular consul'. The consulate came in two forms. The two *consules ordinarii* who entered office on 1 January and after whom the year was named were distinguished from an indefinite number of 'suffect' or supplementary consuls.

[60] The theme reappears at *On Favours* II 27. 4, in a discussion about ingratitude, and also in Plutarch's essay *On Good Spirits* (470b). Eyeing people better off than yourself is an obvious way to make yourself ungrateful for what you have, discontented and bad tempered. The warning against it goes back to Democritus (Fragment 191 Diels–Kranz), and was a stand-by in the literature of popular ethics.

You attach great value to little things

(3) 'How', you may ask, 'are we to keep in mind the pettiness, the wretchedness, the childishness of what we take to be harm done to us?' I would, assuredly, advise nothing more than to acquire a lofty mind and insight into the things for which we go to law, run about and lose our breath. How mean and sordid they are! How unfit for the attention of anyone who has ever had a single high and noble thought!

33 (1) Most of the row is about money. That is what wears out the courts, sets father against son, mixes the poison in, puts the sword in the hands of assassin and legion alike – money smeared by our blood! That is what makes the nights noisy with quarrels of wife and husband, what packs the crowds into the magistrates' courts, what leads to savagery and pillage by kings, when they overthrow states erected by the long toil of centuries, to probe for gold and silver in the cinders of cities. (2) People love to look at their money-bags lying in the corner. These are why they shout till their eyes burst out, why the courts resound with the din of legal proceedings, why jurors summoned from distant parts are in session to judge who has the better claim for his greed. (3) What if it is not even a bag of money, but a fistful of pennies or a few pounds[61] charged to his account by a slave, that drives an old man on the point of dying without an heir to split his sides with fury? What if interest of one per cent per annum drives an ailing money-lender, with twisted legs and hands no good any more for doing the counting, to shout aloud in the very throes of his illness demanding guarantees for his pennies? (4) If you offered me all the money from all the mines that are now most exploited, if you threw before me whatever lies concealed in the treasure-chambers (returned to the depths below the ground by the very greed which first took it out to no good purpose), this whole hoard would not, I think, be worth the frown on a good man's forehead. Laughter, and a lot of it, is the right response to the things which drive us to tears![62]

34 (1) Come now, run through the other factors – food and drink and the pretentious refinements devised on their account,

---

[61] Latin *denarium*. A denarius in the time of Seneca would be worth roughly £4 in 1994. See *On Favours* III 2 nn. 2 and 3, and IV 39. 2.
[62] See II 10. 6 on Democritus and Heraclitus. Cf. 37. 3 below.

abusive language, disrespectful gestures, restive beasts of burden, lazy slaves, suspicions and the malign misconstructions of what someone else has said. (They make the gift of speech one of the wrongs done by nature to man.) Believe me, they are trivial things which make us flare up in a far from trivial way, the sort of things which rouse children to quarrels and brawls. (2) None of those things, which we handle with such ill humour, is serious or important. And there, I tell you, lies the start of your insane anger. You attach great value to little things. 'He wanted to take my inheritance.' 'He denounced me to the man whom I had long been courting for his last will and testament.' 'He fancied my mistress.' What should be the bond of love has become a source of discord and hatred – I mean the desire for the same thing. (3) A narrow path provokes altercations between those who go along it, while a broad, open highway can take whole crowds without their colliding. The objects of your desire, likewise, because they are petty and cannot be transferred to one person without being snatched from another, stir up fights and brawls among those who are striving for the same things.

35 (1) A slave has answered back and you are indignant – or was it a freedman? or your wife? or a dependant? And then you complain that freedom has been abolished in the commonwealth, when you have abolished it in your home! Again, if he stays silent under questioning, you call it recalcitrance. (2) Well, let him talk, let him be silent, let him laugh! 'What! In front of his master?' No, in front of the family head. Why shout and make a noise? Why fetch the whip in the middle of dinner, just because the slaves are talking, and the commotion of a public assembly cannot be combined with the silence of the desert? (3) You were not given ears simply to hear things tuneful and soft, sweet and sedate. You must also listen to laughter and weeping, blandishments and quarrels, good news and bad, human speech and the growling or barking of animals. What makes you jump, poor wretch, if a servant shouts, or the brass reverberates, or the door slams? However spoiled you are, you you cannot help hearing the thunder. (4) Take what I have said about hearing and apply it to sight. The disgust will be just as bad, if the eyes have been badly trained. They will be offended by a spot, by dirt, by silver with a poor shine to it, by a pool which is not clear down to the bottom. (5) But, of course,

those whose eyes at home can only bear to look upon freshly polished marble of varied colour and tables with a rich grain in the wood, who refuse to walk except upon flooring costlier than gold, observe with the greatest equanimity, once they are outside, the rough, muddy surface of the path, the filth on most of the people whom they run into, the holes, the chinks, the unevenness on the walls of the tenements. So what is it that in public fails to annoy them but at home provokes them? Simply their own opinion, reasonable and tolerant out there, moody and cross at home.[63]

Examine your conscience every day

36 (1) All our senses, in fact, must be trained to endure. They are naturally capable of endurance, once the mind stops corrupting them. It should be summoned each day to give account of itself. Sextius[64] used to do this. At the day's end, when he had retired for the night, he would interrogate his mind: 'What ailment of yours have you cured today? What failing have you resisted? Where can you show improvement?'[65] (2) Your anger will cease or moderate itself, if it knows that each day it must come before a judge. Could anything be finer than this habit of sifting through the whole day? Think of the sleep that follows the self-examination! How calm, deep and unimpeded it must be, when the mind has been praised or admonished and – its own sentinel and censor – has taken stock secretly of its own habits.

(3) I make use of this opportunity, daily pleading my case at my own court. When the light has been taken away and my wife has fallen silent, aware as she is of my habit, I examine my entire day, going through what I have done and said. I conceal nothing from myself, I pass nothing by. I have nothing to fear from my errors when I can say:[66]

---

[63] Much of the material in Chapters 34 and 35 recalls the chapters on credulity and self-indulgence in Book II (22–5), but the register has changed. Serious warning has given place to satire.

[64] See above on II 36. 1.

[65] By Seneca's time, the nocturnal self-examination and critical recollection of the day's doings was a standard spiritual discipline (cf. *Letter* 28. 10; Horace, *Satire* I 4. 133–8; Epictetus, IV 4. 46, etc.). It appears to have originated in the Pythagorean school where it was as much a mnemonic as a moral exercise (see Cicero, *On Old Age* 39).

[66] What follows is of a piece with Seneca's earlier moralizing to Novatus. Some of its material has already occurred; and it is hard to judge quite where his homily to himself comes to an end. After 37. 5? Or, as we take it here, after 38. 2?

(4) 'See that you do not do this any more. For the
I excuse you. In that dispute, you spoke too pugn
Don't have anything in future to do with ignorant ¡
those who have never learned don't want to learn!
'You were franker than you should have been in adm(
that person.[67] You did not help him – you just annoyed him.
In future, don't just consider the truth of what you are saying,
but whether the person to whom you are saying it can endure
the truth. While good men are glad to be admonished, the
worse a man is, the more keenly he resents any guidance.

37 (1) 'At the party, certain people made jokes and remarks
at your expense which struck home. Remember to keep away
from low company. They let themselves go too much when
they have been drinking – even when sober, they have no
modesty.

(2) 'You saw a friend who had lost his temper with the
door-keeper of some lawyer or plutocrat for barring his
entrance. You yourself, on his behalf, lost your temper with
that utterly insignificant slave. Are you going to lose your
temper with the dog on the chain? Even he, after barking a
lot, will calm down if you throw him something to eat. (3)
Stand back and laugh! As it is, the man there thinks he is
somebody for guarding a threshold besieged by a crowd of
litigants, while the man inside is on top of the world and thinks
it a mark of power and prosperity to be inaccessible, not
realizing that the hardest door to pass through is that of a
prison.

'Get it into your mind beforehand that you will have much
to endure. No one, surely, is surprised at feeling cold in winter,
sick at sea, or jostled about on the road. The mind can meet
anything bravely, if it comes to it prepared.

(4) 'Denied a place of honour, you began to grow angry
with your host, with the master of ceremonies, with the guest
who had been placed above you. You lunatic, what difference
does it make what part of the couch you put your weight on?
Can a cushion add to your honour or your shame?

(5) 'You cast an unfriendly eye on some one who had spoken
ill of your talent. Is this to be a rule? If so, Ennius[68] whose

---

[67] A new point. Seneca is presenting himself as the moral teacher, for whom frank, if
friendly, admonition and reproach is a duty. Needless to say, the limits of acceptable
frankness were a problem. The Epicurean Philodemus wrote a whole treatise on
the subject.

[68] Quintus Ennius (239–169 BC), a major poet regarded as hopelessly archaic by Seneca's contemporaries.

work you dislike would hate you, Hortensius[69] would declare his hostility and Cicero would be your enemy for mocking his poetry. If you stand for office, you really must put up with the way people vote.'

38 (1) 'So someone insulted you. It cannot surely have been worse than what happened to Diogenes the Stoic philosopher.[70] At the very moment that he was lecturing on anger, a cheeky adolescent spat on him. He bore it gently and wisely. "No," said he, "I am not angry. But I am not sure that I should not be." (2) Our Cato did even better. He was pleading a case when Lentulus,[71] that figure of uncontrollable factiousness as our fathers recall him, worked up a thick mass of spittle and landed it right on his forehead. He wiped it off his face with the words: "I will swear to anyone, Lentulus, that people are wrong to say that you cannot use your mouth!" '

(III) How to cure anger in others

39 (1) We have done it, Novatus! We have calmed the mind. It will now be impervious to bad temper, or will rise above it. Let us now see how to appease that of others, since our wish is not just to be healed, but to heal.

(2) At the start, we should not venture to soothe a person's anger with words, since it is deaf and mindless. We should give it time. Remedies do their work in periods of abatement. We do not tamper with eyes when they are swollen, if we want our massage to stimulate the force in them that is fixed in a stare, nor with other faults in their time of inflammation. The cure for disease in its first stage is rest. (3) 'What a lot of use your remedy is,' you may say, 'if it merely quiets the anger as it subsides of its own accord!' Well, firstly, it has the effect of making it subside sooner while, secondly, it guards against a recurrence. Moreover, it tricks the very impulse which it dares not appease, by taking away all means of retribution, by feigning anger so as to play the part of assistant and fellow-sufferer and thus have more influence in its

---

[69] Quintus Hortensius Hortalus (114–50 BC), the leading forensic orator at Rome before Cicero, practised a florid 'Asianic' style of rhetoric.

[70] Diogenes of Babylon (c. 240–152 BC), Fragment 50 (*SVF* III).

[71] Perhaps Publius Cornelius Lentulus Sura, executed in 63 BC for complicity in Catiline's conspiracy. The exact point of Cato's witticism is uncertain.

decisions, by contriving delays and using the quest for greater punishment as a way to postpone any for the time being. (4) Every device should be used to give the man's rage a rest. If it is on the violent side, some irresistible shame or fear should be knocked into him. If it is less intense, one can bring in conversation of a pleasant or novel kind and distract his curiosity. There is a story of a doctor treating a princess and unable to do so without surgery. Gently bathing her suppurating breast, he inserted the knife concealed in a sponge. The girl would have resisted the treatment if it had been openly applied, but because she did not expect it, she put up with the pain. Some things are only cured by deception.

40 (1) To one person you might say, 'Perhaps your enemies are enjoying your bad temper', to another: 'Take care that the greatness and strength of mind with which you are credited is not weakened. I myself am outraged, heaven knows. My distress knows no limit. But we must bide our time – he will be punished all right. Bear that in mind. When you can, you shall make him pay for the delay as well.'

(2) To reproach a person in a temper, however, and to lose your temper in turn is to provoke him. You should approach him with a variety of blandishments, unless you happen to be a person of such importance that you can shatter his anger, as our deified Augustus did when dining with Vedius Pollio.[72] One of the servants had broken a crystal cup. Vedius ordered him to be seized and executed in an unusual way – he was to be thrown to the giant lampreys which were kept in a pool (not for their owner's self-indulgence, as you might think, but to sate his savagery). (3) The boy struggled free and fled to Caesar's feet, asking only for some other form of death, just not to be eaten. Shocked by the unprecedented cruelty, Caesar had him released, ordering all the crystal to be broken in front of him and the pool to be filled in. (4) For Caesar it was right to reprove a friend in this way. He made good use of his power. 'Are you giving orders at a banquet for a man to be seized and shredded in a newfangled kind of punishment? Your cup has been broken – must a man therefore be disembowelled? Are you so pleased with yourself as to command an

---

[72] A friend of Augustus, belonging to the equestrian order, loyal and useful if unspeakable. Also mentioned at *On Mercy* 1 18. 2.

execution in the very presence of Caesar?' (5) If someone has the power to approach a person's anger from a position of superiority, he should certainly deal harshly with it in this way – but only if it is that sort of anger that I just mentioned, fierce, monstrous and bloodthirsty, incurable without some greater object of fear.

Conclusion

Life is too short to waste it being angry

41 (1) Let us give the mind that peace that we shall only give it by constantly practising wholesome precepts, by good conduct, by concentrating our attention and desire on virtue alone. Let us meet the demands of conscience, and not toil for reputation. Let even ill-repute come after us, so long as we have deserved well. (2) 'But the crowd admires spirited actions; the audacious are held in honour and the peaceful are taken for sluggards.' At first sight, perhaps. But as soon as the peaceful tenor of their lives proves that theirs is not sloth but peace of mind, the populace will revere and admire them. (3) So this gruesome, aggressive affection contains nothing of value. On the contrary, it contains every evil, the sword and the flames. Trampling shame underfoot, staining its hands with slaughter, scattering the limbs of its children, it leaves nothing free of crime. Without any thought for glory or fear of infamy, it stands beyond all correction once it has hardened from anger to hatred.

42 (1) Let us rid ourselves of this evil, clearing the mind of it, root and branch – however tiny the pieces, wherever they attach themselves, they will grow again. Instead of moderating our anger, we should eliminate it altogether – for how can there be moderation of a thing that is bad? Moreover, we can do this, if only we make the effort.

(2) Nothing will help more than a meditation on our mortality. Each of us should say to himself and to others: 'What joy is there in acting as though we were born to live for ever, declaring our anger and squandering our momentary span of life? What joy is there in turning the days which could be spent in honest pleasure to the pain and torture of others? These things cannot survive the waste, we have not the time to lose. (3) Why rush to fight, why

bring conflicts upon ourselves? Why forget our frailty and take on huge hatreds? Why rise up, easily broken as we are, to break others? At any time now, these hostilities which our mind conducts so implacably may be cancelled by a fever or some other ailment of the body; at any time now death may come between the fiercest pair of opponents and part them. (4) Why such commotion, why such turbulent confusion of life? Fate looms above our heads, chalking up the days as they go to waste, approaching nearer and nearer. The time which you have allotted for someone else's death may well be close to your own.

43 (1) Why not, rather, gather your brief life together, calming it for yourself and for others? Why not make yourself a person to be loved by all while you live and missed when you have made your departure? Why this longing to drag down a man who holds his head too high in his dealings with you? And what of the man who barks at you, a low and despicable person, of course, but a sharp-tongued nuisance to his betters? Why the all-out effort to crush him? Why the anger with your slave? Your master? Your king? Your dependant? Wait a little. Death is on its way, to make you all equal. (2) We regularly see, in the morning show at the amphitheatre, the match between bull and bear tied together; when the one has worn down the other, the slaughterer awaits them both. Our act is the same; we assail an opponent who is tied to us, while the end, and that right early, looms alike over victor and vanquished. In peace and quiet, rather, let us pass what is left of our lives. Let no one look upon our lifeless body with hatred. (3) It often happens that a brawl is broken up by a shout of 'Fire!' in the neighbourhood, that the arrival of a wild animal sends brigand and traveller in different directions. There is no time to struggle with lesser evils when a greater terror has come into view. Why the bother with struggles and snares? Surely you cannot wish the object of your anger to suffer anything more than death. Even if you stay quiet, he is going to die. You waste your effort if you want to cause what will happen anyway. (4) 'I don't necessarily want to kill him,' you may say, 'but just to inflict exile, disgrace and ruin on him.' I am readier to pardon the wish to wound an enemy than the wish to give him a blister. For that shows not merely a bad but a small mind. But whether you have the extreme or the lesser penalties in mind, how very short is the time for his

punishment and torture or for your evil delight at it! At any moment now, we shall spit forth this life of ours. (5) In the meantime, while we still draw breath, while we still remain among human beings, let us cultivate our humanity. Let us not bring fear or danger upon any one. Let us look down on damages and wrongs, insults and carping criticisms. Let us bear with greatness of mind our short-lived troubles. As they say, we have only to look back, only to turn round – quick now, here comes death!

---

[72] A friend of Augustus, belonging to the equestrian order, loyal and useful if unspeakable. Also mentioned at *On Mercy* 1 18. 2.

To Nero
On Mercy

Ad Neronem
De Clementia

Introduction

Addressee and date

On Mercy was composed for Seneca's pupil the young emperor Nero, to celebrate the start of his principate, to admonish him on how to conduct it, and to stress the need for mercifulness in all his dealings. The work describes him as 'eighteen years old' (I 9. I). Since Nero was born on 15 December, AD 37, it will thus have been written between December 55 and December 56. Unfortunately, it also credits him with the 'magnanimous boast' that in the whole world he has 'not shed one drop of human blood' (I 11. 3). This has inspired attempts by some scholars to date the work earlier. For Nero, who was proclaimed emperor in October 54, had already, in early 55 AD, arranged for his step brother by adoption, Britannicus, to be poisoned;[1] Seneca can hardly himself have been ignorant of the crime, and the claim which he puts into Nero's mouth makes the young emperor look scandalously hypocritical. But we do not know how widely reports of Nero's guilt may have circulated at the time among the reading public, for whom Seneca was writing. For *On Mercy* was not only a work of advice for the young emperor; it was also intended to reassure that wider public about the character of the new regime[2] and

---

[1] See Suetonius, *Nero* 33. 2–3 and Tacitus *Annals* XIII 15–17.
[2] See Griffin, p. 138. Much of what follows is heavily indebted to the chapter 'Ideology for a New Regime' (pp. 129–71).

to show that Nero's adviser was by no means as harsh in his
attitudes as Stoics were commonly thought to be (II 5. 2).[3]

Subject and organization

Seneca refuses to give a single definition of his subject, speaking
of mercy as among other things, 'leniency', or 'a tendency to
be lenient', 'towards an inferior in determining punishments'
and 'moderation in stopping short of penalties which could
deservedly be imposed' (II 3. 1). His refusal is understandable.
If acts of mercy – pardoning the criminal, sparing the vanquished enemy, and so forth – are easily recognized, Seneca's
concern is with the virtue, the specific quality of mind,
expressed in such actions, that is with 'mercifulness'. For this
there was no exact Greek equivalent or available school definition. The standard translation in Greek for *clementia* was to
be ἐπιείκεια, a term generally understood as 'reasonableness'
in interpreting or applying the law [4] and in not pressing your
lawful claims to the utmost. But the Latin concept also had
much to do with πρᾳότης, 'mildness' in the control of anger,
and with φιλανθρωπία 'love of mankind'.[5] *Clementia*, however,
had one obvious feature which made it an eminently suitable
topic for an address to a prince. It was a virtue exercised
towards inferiors. You can only show mercy to someone who
is 'at your mercy'; and *clementia* had been recognized since the
time of Caesar as supremely the virtue of a conqueror or
autocrat who, at least in theory, has everyone else in his power.
Seneca (I 3. 1) proposed to write *On Mercy* in three parts:
one on leniency[6] and its value to the prince, one on defining

---

[3] 'Mercy,' *clementia*, was in fact a slogan of the new reign. Nero began his principate
with a show of leniency in recalling a certain Plautius Lateranus from exile,
'pledging himself to clemency in numerous speeches which Seneca had placed in
his mouth to show what honest advice he was giving' (Tacitus, *Annals* XIII 11. 2),
[4] Aristotle devotes a short chapter of the book on justice in the *Nicomachean Ethics*
(V 10. 1137a31–8a3) and two pages in the *Rhetoric* (1376a18–b23) to ἐπιείκεια
so understood.
[5] See Plutarch, *Life of Caesar* 57. 3: 'it was thought right to decree the temple of
Clemency ['Επιείκεια], as a thank-offering for his mildness' [πρᾳότης]. A striking
early example of [ἐπιείκεια] meaning virtually the same as *clementia* is in Thucydides' account of the debate on whether or not to spare the people of Mitylene
(III 40. 2 f., 48), where the term is closely linked with 'pity'.
[6] The text here, unfortunately, is hardly intelligible and requires emendation. See n. 30.

mercy and distinguishing it from vices that somehow resemble it, and one on how to establish this virtue in the mind. Each part would probably have had a book to itself, though that is merely conjecture. *On Mercy* was thus planned on broadly the same lines as *On Anger*, a work in which theoretical questions on anger were followed by advice on how to cure it and preceded by an extended passage on its horrors. But the text, as we have it, ends after only seven chapters in Book II.[7] Moreover, the opening discussion of leniency, of its glory and value to the prince, has a book to itself. It may seem illogical – it would certainly be contrary to the conventional procedure of philosophers – for Seneca to sing the praises of 'mercy' at such length before defining what quality he has in mind. But this first book is virtually a separate treatise on kingship, a most appropriate subject on which to be seen instructing the new emperor. And there would be no need to define *clementia*, a concept long familiar to Roman readers, so long as his purpose is simply to claim that it is the most important of all virtues for a king to possess.[8]

Seneca on kingship

Book I of *On Mercy* falls itself into three main parts.[9] After the introductory address of Nero (1 1 f.), possibly our earliest example of a 'mirror of princes' telling a prince how to behave by praising him for already behaving as prescribed, Seneca argues, firstly (3. 2–8), that mercy, while incumbent on everyone, is above all a virtue of monarchs, a claim which he illustrates with an extended story about Augustus (9–11. 3) and rounds off by contrasting the life of a king with that of a tyrant (11. 4 –13). Next (14–19), he discusses the duties of a monarch, comparing him with other figures of power – father,

---

[7] Four brief and inconsequential quotations from a work of Seneca on mercy, which are not to be found in the extant essay, are preserved in a letter, apparently from 1102, of Hildebert, archbishop of Tours (J. P. Migne, *Patrologia Latina*, 217 vols. (Paris 1844–55), CLXXI p. 145).

[8] Only in the next book, as Seneca sets about distingishing the virtue from 'the vices that resemble it' (1 3.1) are clear definitions essential. As he says at 1 3.3, 'these matters are better discussed in their proper place'.

[9] With what follows, compare Griffin, p. 143.

schoolmaster, army officer, slave owner, queen (or, rather, king) bee – and showing that in all cases leniency is the best policy. Thirdly and finally (20–4), he deals in a fairly systematic way with the principles of punishment, before concluding with a peroration on the horrors of cruelty (25 f.).

Throughout the book, the moral is the same: 'mercy enhances not only a ruler's honour, but his safety' (11. 4). These are traditional ways of recommending a course of action – Seneca is arguing *per honestum et utile*; and they would have their effect on a prince as vain and timid as Nero. But Seneca also argues, in more metaphysical terms, that a king is the 'mind' of the commonwealth, which he must spare as he would his own body (I 3. 5–1 5 and 1 7). Time and again, Seneca returns to the theme of the prince's special position. All men, born as they are for the common good, should be merciful and even-tempered – in this context, a certain amount of material familiar from *On Anger* reappears.[10] But a prince should have these virtues to a greater extent, since his scope is so very much greater. If his virtues can do more good, his misdeeds can do more harm and earn him more hatred (18. 3). Private individuals can be excused for quarrelling; but a king cannot (7. 3) – and, anyway, he has no need to throw his weight about (21. 3). He has to be more careful than an ordinary citizen to demonstrate his disinterestedness (15. 3), since the eyes of all are constantly and constrainingly upon him – so much so that being king amounts to a 'noble servitude' (8. 1–5).

Soul and body require one another. So do prince and commonwealth – it would disintegrate without him. Seneca writes as a monarchist, accepting the historical inevitability of the principate. Elsewhere,[11] he levels two criticisms at those who assassinated Julius Caesar for fear that he was intending to make himself king. They had not realized, firstly, that the best form of government is that under a just monarch. A Stoic, of course, could equally well be a republican – several of the school (foremost among them, Caesar's opponent, Cato the

---

[10] Notably in 5–7: the appeal to magnanimity in 5 (echoing *On Anger* I 20 f., II 32. 4), the reflection in 6 that 'we have (all done wrong' (cf. *On Anger* II 6–10, 28. I) and the (7. I f.) theme of imitating the gods cf. *On Anger* II 16. 2, 27. I).
[11] *On Favours* II 20.

Younger) had been. Orthodox Stoic political theory could serve
to support either monarchy or government by the Senate.[12]
But secondly and more seriously, Caesar's assassins had been
unrealistic, imagining that 'civic freedom', 'equality of rights
and a due supremacy of law could still be maintained' in a
degenerate age. They had not seen, in other words, that kingship was now the only workable form of government. What is
striking about Seneca's account of monarchy is its frankness
and absolutism.[13] For centuries, the Romans had hated the
very word 'king'. Julius Caesar had been assassinated because
it was thought that he was intending to make himself king.
Augustus had prudently contented himself with the more
modest title of *princeps* or 'first citizen', carefully avoiding any
behaviour that smacked of royal 'pride'. Seneca praises and
recommends this tactful style of behaviour (13. 4, 15. 3); but
he makes no bones about speaking of 'princes and kings and
whatever other title there may be for guardians of public
order' (4. 3). Moreover, what he understands by 'kingship' is
a monarchy on a Hellenistic, indeed oriental model.[14] Nero
has been chosen to act as the representative of the gods on
earth (1. 2), and he is not answerable to any earthly authority.
He may do well, of course, to stay on the right side of his
guards and the populace: the power and security of a Roman
emperor depended on his being accepted by them. But nowhere

[12] For the Stoics, the ideal, best form of government is a mixture of democracy,
kingship and aristocracy (Diogenes Laertius VII 131). The monarchical element
is found in the single, sovereign authority of human and divine reason in establishing the law and governing human affairs; while those who possess reason in
perfected form are a limited group of 'best people' (aristocrats) entitled to political
recognition as such. The element of democracy comes in through the idea that
the whole body of true citizens under the ideal government would be persons of
such perfected understanding. When differences of emphasis are allowed for, this
position could obviously be applied concretely so as to defend either the senatorial
or the kingly rule in Rome.
[13] For numerous parallels between *On Mercy* and earlier Greek writing on kingship,
see Griffin pp. 144 f.
[14] In the Greek world there had been two styles of kingship. A king like the Spartan
Agesilaus, as his ancient biographers describe him, or the Cypriote Nicocles in
the speech written for him by Isocrates (*Oration* III), could justify his position on
the grounds of his moral excellence. But a monarch could equally present himself
as the regent on earth of the gods or even as himself a deity. This was the style
which Alexander the Great had copied from the kings of Persia.

in our text is he told to defer to 'the Senate and people of Rome'. He may well watch over himself 'as though the laws ... will call him to account' (1. 4); but the operative phrase here is 'as though'. Nero is fully entitled to break the law if he can save lives by doing so (5. 4). Saving lives matters more than obeying the laws or observing some political system of checks and balances. The nature of Senecan kingship comes out at its clearest in his comparison of the king with the tyrant (11. 4–13). The classic difference between them had been that the king rules, as the tyrant does not, 'according to law over willing subjects'[15] whose rights he has to respect. For Seneca, the difference is purely moral: a king is merciful, a tyrant is not. Because of his cruelty, Sulla can be branded as tyrant, despite the fact that he stepped down from office and restored senatorial government (12. 1–3). Everything comes down to the character of the ruler, 'whatever the manner of his accession to power and whatever its legal basis' (19. 1). It may have been only realistic of Seneca to disregard the constitutional niceties in this way. But the trust which in consequence he had to place in the good nature and malleability of his pupil was to be cruelly disappointed. Soon enough, Nero kicked over the traces; and Seneca was to be remembered for his pains, by at least one writer, as τυραννοδιδάσκαλος, the tyrant's teacher.[16]

The quality of mercy

After another flattering preamble about the emperor's kind-heartedness, Book II goes on to define *clementia*. Seneca (II 3. 1) offers no less than five definitions: mercy means 'self-control by the mind when it has the power to take vengeance' or (2) leniency towards an inferior when punishing him, or (3) a tendency to be lenient in such cases, or (4) a 'moderation that remits something of a deserved and due punishment' or at least – and the qualification is important – (5) 'stops short of *what could deservedly be imposed*'. Mercy is thus a mental con-

---

[15] Xenophon, *Memorabilia* IV 6. 12, Aristotle, *Politics* 1285a25–9.
[16] Dio Cassius, LXI 10. 2.

dition; its field is vengeance or, rather, punishment; and it manifests itself as leniency and restraint in imposing less by way of punishment than could justifiably be imposed. Its contrary, Seneca continues (4. 1), is not 'sternness', an inclination presumably to impose the maximum due punishment,[17] but rather 'cruelty' or a savage spirit in punishing that goes beyond the limit of what is humane and justifiable (4. 1–3). Neither should mercy be confused with pity. For pity, in Stoic eyes, is no more than a sentimental compassion for the unfortunate, which comes from overestimating the significance of their misfortunes. It is thus an emotional malady, no less than is anger or cruelty, whereas mercy is a function of uncorrupted reason (4. 4–5. 1). Seneca offers a number of arguments to show that the wise man will not feel pity (5. 2–6) before arguing further (7) that neither will he forgive. Then the text breaks off.

'The wise man neither pities nor pardons' – the Stoics were notorious, as Seneca acknowledges (5. 2) for the alleged harshness of their doctrine. To pardon a person's crime or misdeed, they maintained, is to allow that it was not that person's fault, whereas in fact it was, since all misdeeds result from the agent's own badness. Nor will the good man be 'reasonable' (ἐπιεικής) in remitting a deserved punishment, since that would mean his assuming that the legally prescribed punishment is more than what is deserved.[18] We have seen that ἐπιείκεια was the Greek equivalent for *clementia*; and Seneca's positive evaluation of mercy might seem like a serious departure from orthodox Stoicism. But probably Seneca did not regard it so. 'Reasonableness', as Greek Stoics – and Aristotle, too – understood it, meant 'going against' or 'cor-

---

[17] This is guesswork. *Severitas* or 'sternness' is not discussed in the text as it survives. But see Tacitus, *Annals* XIV 49.

[18] This summary of Stoic attitudes to pardoning and to ἐπιείκεια is a paraphrase of that in Stobaeus (II pp. 95. 24–96. 9 (= *SVF* III 640). There is, however, a certain unclarity here, since 'law' in Stoic thought, could mean either the statutes of a community or it could mean the internal voice of prescriptive reason, the 'moral law' (See General Introduction, p. xxv). Stobaeus promptly goes on to define law in the latter sense, as 'right reason commanding what should be done and forbidding what should not be done' (II 96. 10–2). On this definition, the Stoic rejection of ἐπιείκεια is a condemnation of departures from strict morality, or rather from laws correctly enacted on that basis; it is not a doctrine of blind obedience to any old statute enacted by any old law-giver.

recting' the written law where it was judged not to do justice to the circumstances of some particular case.[19] But references to the written law are notably sparse in *On Mercy*.[20] Seneca's concern is primarily with cases in which there is no single punishment fixed by law. The context of the discussion in Book II appears to be the *cognitio*, the judicial investigation before the Senate or the emperor's council of crimes for which there was no statutory penalty. It was possible there to impose, with equal justice, punishments of varying harshness. The verdict could be 'strict' in exacting the maximum penalty, or 'merciful' in settling for something less. Here Seneca's claim that mercy is superior to forgiveness and pardon, because it is more complete, acquires some plausibility. Forgiveness means failing to punish what you have judged should be punished. Pardon is the remission of a penalty that you have judged to be due. But the function of mercy is to judge in the first place that the penalty is not due; and it can do so on a variety of grounds – not only the possibility that the malefactor was acting under compulsion or did not know what he was doing, but also considerations of his age, his social standing, his chances of being reformed, or the glory that might result from acquitting him or treating him mildly. The wise man can take all these factors into account and so do far more good to his fellow men than ever he could by just feeling pity for them.

Mercy is characterized by freedom of decision. 'It judges not by legal formula, but by what is equitable and good' (7. 3). Here, as in Book I, the written laws can be disregarded.[21] What matters is the prince's sense of what is equitable and good. But that, in Nero's case, was an unreliable factor. Before long, he discovered that it was quite possible to engineer trials for treason, where the Senate would obligingly propose some

---

[19] In the *Rhetoric*, Aristotle describes reasonableness as 'the justice that is contrary to the written law' (1374a26–8), in the *Nicomachean Ethics* as a 'correction of legal justice' (1137b12 f.).

[20] And when they do occur it is only the emperor, not an ordinary magistrate, who is allowed to break them. See I 5. 4.

[21] That is, by the prince. Seneca's concentration on the quality of mercy in a prince leaves it unclear what scope he would allow for mercy in an ordinary citizen or magistrate – although, as we have seen, he says explicitly that mercifulness is a virtue for everybody (I 3. 2, 5. 2–3).

truly horrible punishment, and he could then show his clemency in remitting it.[22]

Epilogue

Book II of *On Mercy* breaks off in mid-sentence. We can only guess what may have followed – or whether the work was completed at all. Seneca would perhaps have had further distinctions to make, and he could well have gone into the casuistry of mercy. At I 12. 3, he promised, in connection with Sulla, to deal with the question of what wrath to visit on vanquished enemies, especially if they are fellow-citizens on the opposite side in a civil war.

We can guess, too, how Seneca would have set about establishing the virtue of mercy in the mind. The second, therapeutic half of *On Anger* consists largely of thoughts from the earlier theoretical chapters, reformulated and amplified in such a way as to leave the strongest possible impression. Some of this material, as we saw, reappears in Book I of *On Mercy*. We can be pretty sure that it would have surfaced yet again in the last part of the treatise, reworked and enriched with numerous examples, in the attempt to turn the kindly impulses which Seneca piously detects in his pupil into a firmly and rationally grounded habit.[23]

[22] See Griffin, pp. 162 f., 171.
[23] See II 2.2.

Book I

Preface

A mirror for the prince

1 (1) I have undertaken to write on mercy, Nero Caesar, in order to act as a kind of mirror, showing you to yourself on the point as you are of attaining the greatest of pleasures. The true satisfaction from good deeds is, of course, to have done them, and there is no reward worthy of virtue apart from virtue itself. Yet it is enjoyable to inspect and to go through the good state of one's conscience, and then to cast one's eyes on the huge crowd here – quarrelsome, factious, uncontrolled, as likely to run riot for its own as for another's downfall, if it breaks the yoke now on it – and to say to oneself:

> (2) 'Have I, of all mortals, found favour with the gods and been chosen to act on earth in their stead? I am the judge with power of life and death over nations, I have the fate and condition of everyone in my hands. All dispensations of fortune to mortals are made through pronouncements on my lips. My verdict is what gives peoples and cities cause to rejoice. No region anywhere flourishes but by my will and favour. These swords in their countless thousands, sheathed through the peace that I bring, will be drawn at my nod. The extermination or banishment of nations, the granting or loss of their liberty, the enslavement of kings or their coronation, the destruction or rise of cities – all this comes under my jurisdiction. (3) Such is the extent of my power. Yet I have not been driven to unjust punishment by anger or youthful impulse, nor by the rashness

and obstinacy of men, which wrenches the patience from even the calmest breasts, nor even by the glory, fearsome but common among those of high command, of parading one's power through terror. My sword has been sheathed, indeed hung away altogether. I have spared to the utmost even the meanest blood. There is no one, whatever else he may lack, who has not the name of man to commend him to my favour. (4) My sternness I conceal, my mercy I hold at the ready. I watch over myself as though the laws, which I have summoned from decay and darkness into the light, will call me to account.[1] I have been touched by the first flush of one person's youthfulness, by another's extreme old age. I have granted pardon to one man because of his high position, to another because of his low estate. Whenever I could find no other ground for pity, I have shown mercy to *myself*. This very day, should the gods demand it, I can render account for the whole human race.'

(5) This you can say boldly out loud, Caesar, that everything entrusted to your guardianship is kept safe, that nothing has been taken from the commonwealth by violence or secret fraud on your part.[2] You have aspired to the rarest of praise, praise as yet never granted to a prince – that of guiltlessness.[3] Nor has that singular goodness of yours been wasted. It has found men neither ungrateful nor unfavourable in their appraisal. You have your recompense. No one human being was ever so dear to another human being as you are to the Roman people, its great and lasting blessing. (6) But the burden which you have taken upon yourself is huge. No one now speaks of our deified Augustus or the early years of Tiberius Caesar; no one seeks an example for you to imitate – apart from yourself. Your reign is being judged by the taste which we have had of it.[4] This would be hard were that goodness of

---

[1] Seneca is having Nero proclaim 'a return to legality after the harsh arbitrariness of Claudius' reign' (*ibid* p. 138). But note the 'as though'. The emperor is not in fact bound by any written laws. The Stoics described kingship as ἀρχὴ ἀνυπεύθυνος, an office whose holder cannot be called to account (Diogenes Laertius, VII 122 = *SVF* III 617).

[2] Reading (with Gertz) *omnia quae in fidem tutelam*<que venerint tuam tuta ha>*beri* and (with Hosius) *nihil per te neque vi neque clam* <adimi> *reipublicae*.

[3] A year earlier, in fact, Nero had already poisoned his brother by adoption, Britannicus, though public opinion may not yet have credited him with the murder.

[4] Reading *principatus tuus ad gustum exigitur*.

yours not innate but put on for the moment. No one can wear a mask for long; pretences soon fall back into their true nature. But anything with truth underlying it – with firm ground to sprout from, so to speak – grows with the sheer passing of time into something greater and better. (7) Great was the risk run by the Roman people; it was uncertain what direction these noble talents of yours were taking. But now the prayers of the populace rest in safety. There is no danger of your suddenly forgetting yourself. People, of course, are made greedy by too much good fortune. No appetites are ever so moderate as to cease at the point of attainment. They progress from great to greater, and the most insatiable hopes are embraced by those who have succeeded beyond their hopes. And yet all your citizens are now compelled to acknowledge that they are fortunate and that nothing henceforth can be added to these blessings, provided that they last.[5] (8) Much constrains them to this acknowledgment, the last that men are prepared to make: security deep and abundant, law raised above all violations of law. The happiest form of commonwealth meets[6] their eyes, with supreme liberty in want of nothing save the licence to ruin itself. (9) But what, above all, has touched the greatest and the humblest alike is admiration for your mercy. Other blessings are experienced or expected by each, according to his circumstances, in different degrees. Mercy inspires the same hope in all. There is no one so satisfied at his own guiltlessness as not to rejoice that mercy should stand before his eyes, ready for human error.

2 (1) There are some, I know, who think of mercy as a support for the worst sort of men; superfluous except when a crime has been committed, this is the one virtue that is inoperative among the guiltless. First of all, however, just as medicine is of use to the sick but is prized also by the healthy, so mercy, while invoked by those who deserve punishment, is also revered by the guiltless. Moreover, there is scope for it even in their case, since there are times when luck has the same effect as guilt. Nor is it just innocence that is aided by mercy; often virtue is, seeing that the times give rise to actions which, while praised, can be punished. You can add that the majority of mankind are capable of returning to innocence,

---

[5] Reading MS *ut*, rather than *nisi ut*.
[6] Reading *obversatur*.

if pardoned.[7] (2) It is not proper, however, to pardon as a general rule. When you take away the distinction between the good and the bad, the result is chaos and an outburst of vice. You need to avoid extremes and know how to distinguish curable from hopeless characters. Mercy should not be indiscriminate and general; but neither should it be excluded. To pardon everyone is as much a cruelty as to pardon no one. We should keep to a mean. The balance, however, is hard to maintain, and any departure from parity should tip the scale to the side of human kindness.

Division of the subject

3 (1) But these matters are better discussed in their proper place. For the moment, I shall divide the entire material here into three parts. The first is on relaxing your animosity, on lenience.[8] The second is to demonstrate the nature and disposition of mercy. For since there are vices which imitate the virtues, they can only be separated if branded with marks to distinguish them. In the third place, we shall enquire how the mind may be led to this virtue, how it may establish it firmly and by practice make it its own.

The excellence of mercy

Mercy the royal virtue

(2) Of all the virtues, in truth, none befits a human being more, since none is more humane. That is a necessary point of agreement not only among ourselves with our view that man should be seen as a social animal born for the common good, but also among those who give man over to pleasure and whose every word and

---

[7] Something has fallen out after *si*. Something like <*ignoscas*> (Préchac) needs to be understood.

[8] Reading, with Kronenberg, *animi remissionis*, a term meaning literally 'relaxation of mind' – in particular, of the mind as the seat of anger. Cicero contrasts *animi remissio* with *severitas* as an attitude which an orator can inspire (*On the Orator* II 72, cf. *Letters to his Friends* V 2. 9). Lenience and its importance to the prince are the theme of *On Mercy* I, while II discusses the nature of mercy and distinguishes it from failings which resemble it, before breaking off. The missing parts of the work presumably dealt with the questions of moral training .

action looks to their own advantage.[9] For if a man seeks calm and leisure, he acquires here a virtue which, with its love of peace and restraint on action, suits his nature. (3) Of all men, however, mercy becomes no one more than a king or a prince. What gives great might its grace and glory is its power for good; strength to harm is simply pernicious force. He alone has a firm, well-founded greatness whom all know to be not only above them but also for them, whose vigilant care for the safety of each and every one they experience every day, whose approach is not like the leap of an evil, dangerous beast from its lair, before which they scatter in flight, but rather that of a bright and kindly star. Racing each other they fly towards him, in total readiness to throw themselves on to the blades of those who lie in wait for him, to cast their own bodies to the ground if human slaughter is needed to provide the foundation of his road to safety. They watch over his sleep at night. They protect his person, making themselves a barrier to encircle it. As danger approaches, they interpose. (4) There is reason behind this unanimity of peoples and cities in their protection and love of kings, in their sacrifice of themselves and their own, whenever the safety of their commander requires it. It is not through lack of self-esteem or of sanity that thousands face the sword for one person and rescue, by a multitude of deaths, one life – sometimes that of a feeble old man. (5) Compare the way in which the body is entirely at the service of the mind. It may be ever so much larger and more impressive. The mind may remain hidden and tiny, its very location uncertain. Yet hands, feet and eyes do its business. The skin that we see protects it. At its command, we lie still. Or else we run restlessly about, when it has given the order. If its avarice masters us, we scan the sea for material gain. Its lust for glory has long since led us to thrust our right hand into the flame[10] or plunge of our own free will into the

---

[9] The reference here is to the Stoics ('ourselves') and to the followers of Epicurus. Here, as in *On the Private Life* 2. 2–3, 7. 1, Seneca stresses the agreement of the two moral theories on a particular issue, despite the radical opposition of their basic principles. Elsewhere (see especially *On Favours* IV 2–8, 16–25) this opposition is what he emphasizes. Passages like the present one do not imply any compromise with Epicureanism or weakened commitment to fundamental Stoic doctrine.

[10] Seneca is recalling the story of Mucius Scaevola (Livy, II 12.13). See on *On Favours* IV 27. 2, n. 50.

earth.[11] In the same way, this vast multitude of men surrounds one man as though he were its mind,[12] ruled by his spirit, guided by his reason; it would crush and shatter itself by its own strength, without the support of his discernment.

4 (1) Their own safety is thus what men have at heart when for one man they lead ten legions into battle, rushing at the front line and baring their breasts to the wounds, lest their emperor's standards be overthrown. For he is the bond which holds the commonwealth together; he is the breath of life drawn by these several thousands. They themselves would be nothing but a burden, a prey, were that mind of the empire to be withdrawn.

> While he survives, in concord and content
> The commons live, by no divisions rent,
> But the great monarch's death dissolves the government.[13]

(2) Such a disaster would be the end of the Roman peace, driving the fortunes of our great people to ruin. That people will only escape the danger for so long as it can endure the reins. Should it break them, should it find them shaken off and not allow them to be put on again, the unified structure of this far-flung empire will shatter into a multitude of parts, and this city's dominance will have ended with its willingness to obey. (3) No wonder, then, that princes and kings and whatever other title there may be for guardians of public order, should meet with a love surpassing even the bonds of private affinity. For if men of sense put public interests before private, it follows that their affection will also be greater for one on whom the whole commonwealth turns. Long ago, in fact, Caesar so worked himself into the commonwealth, that neither could be separated without the ruin of the other. He needs the strength, and the commonwealth needs a head.

5 (1) My discourse may seem to have digressed some way from its subject. In truth, it bears closely on the real question. For if,

---

[11] Reading with Préchac *voluntari<i in terr>am subsiluimus*. The reference is probably to the heroism of Marcus Curtius who, to save his country, leaped on horseback into a chasm which had appeared in the Forum (Livy, VII 6. 5).

[12] Reading with Leo (*Hermes* 40. 1905, 610) *uni ut animo circumdata*.

[13] Vergil, *Georgics* IV 212 f. (Dryden's translation), a passage comparing the kingdom of the bees with the monarchies of Egypt, Lycia, Parthia and Media.

as has just been shown, your commonwealth is your body and you are its mind, you can see, I think, how necessary mercy is. You are sparing yourself, when you appear to spare another. So even culpable citizens should be spared in the same way as unsound limbs. If ever there is need for blood to be let, you should stay the knife,[14] lest it cut beyond what is needed. (2) Mercy, as I said, is natural to all human beings. Yet it most becomes emperors, finding when among them more to save and greater scope for revealing itself. How tiny is the harm done by the cruelty of private individuals! But the raging of princes means war. (3) There is, to be sure, a concord among the virtues. Each of them is as good and honourable as the other. Yet one may be more suitable to some people. Greatness of mind befits any mortal, even the poorest – is anything greater or braver than to beat back the force of ill fortune?[15] But this greatness of mind has freer scope in good fortune, and is shown to better effect up on the magistrate's bench than down on the floor. (4) Mercy, whatever house it enters, will make it happy and calm. In a palace, its rarity renders it the more amazing. For what is more remarkable than that one whose anger has nothing to resist it, whose severest sentence commands the assent of the very people who perish by it, whom no one is going to sue or even entreat, if he has been too fiercely incensed – that this very man should take hold of himself, putting his power to better, more peaceful use with this very thought: 'Anyone can break the law in order to take a life. No one except for me can do so to save a life!'? (5) A great mind is an adornment to great fortune, but it must rise to it and stand above it – or else bring down fortune, too, to the ground. Now the characteristic of a great mind is to be peaceful and calm, looking down from above at injuries and affronts. It is for women to rave in anger, for wild beasts – and not even the noble ones at that – to bite and worry the fallen. Elephants and lions walk past what they have struck down;[16] relentlessness is the mark of an ignoble animal. (6) Savage, inexorable

---

[14] Reading *acies* with Préchac.

[15] Compare *On Anger* I 20 f. Note how Seneca adapts his Stoic theme. If greatness of mind is a virtue which anyone, even a slave, can exercise, nonetheless the prince has more scope than anyone for doing so. In the same way, everyone can and should imitate the gods; but the prince can do so to much greater effect.

[16] Compare *On Anger* II 32. 3.

anger is not becoming to a king. He cannot tower much above
any person on whose level he has placed himself by growing angry.
But if he grants life and dignity to men who have risked and
deserve to lose them, he does what none save a man of power can
do. One can take the life of even a superior; one cannot grant it
to anyone except an inferior. (7) To save life is the prerogative of
high good fortune, never more admirable than when it attains the
same power as the gods, by whose favour we are brought into the
light of day, good men and bad alike. So a prince should adopt
as his own the attitude of the gods. Some citizens, because they
are useful and good, he should look upon with pleasure, others
he should leave to make up the number, rejoicing in the existence
of some, enduring that of the others.

6 (1) Consider this city where the crowd flows without pause
through its broadest streets, crushed if anything stands in the way
to hold back the swift current of its movement, where the capacities
of three whole theatres are required at one and the same time,[17]
where produce grown all over the world is consumed – think what
an empty waste there would be if nothing were left of it save those
whom a stern judge would acquit![18] (2) How few investigators there
are who would not be found guilty under the very law by which
they make their investigation! How few accusers are blameless! Is
anyone more reluctant, I wonder, to grant pardon than he who
has all too often had reason to seek it? (3) We have all done
wrong, some seriously, some more trivially, some on purpose, some
perhaps under impulse or led astray by the wickedness of others.
Some of us were not firm enough in our good intentions, losing
our innocence unwillingly, clutching at it as we lost it. Nor have
we merely transgressed – to the end of our lives we shall continue
to transgress. (4) Suppose, indeed, that someone has so purged
his mind as to be beyond further reach of confusion or deception.
His innocence has been reached, none the less, through doing
wrong.

7 (1) Having mentioned the gods,[19] I can do no better than to
make them a model for the prince: he should wish to be to the

---

[17] Translating (roughly) Hosius' *tribus eodem tempore theatris caveae postulantur.* The
three theatres were those of Balbus, Marcellus and Pompey.
[18] Compare *On Anger* II 10. 2–6, 28, etc.
[19] At 5. 7.

citizens as he would wish the gods to be to him. Can it be good that the powers of heaven should be inexorably set against sin and error, hostile to the very point of our final destruction? Could any king in that case be safely assured that his limbs would not have to be gathered together by the sooth-sayers?[20] (2) But if the gods, neither implacable nor unreasonable, are not given to pursuing the crimes of potentates immediately with their thunderbolts, how much more reasonable is it for a man set in authority over men to exercise his command in a gentle spirit and to reflect: When is the world's state more pleasing to the eye and lovelier? On a day serene and bright? Or when all is shaken by frequent thunderbolts and the lightning flashes hither and thither? And yet the look of a calm, well-ordered empire is like that of the sky serene and shining. (3) A reign that it cruel is troubled and overcast. All there tremble and start up at any sudden noise. Nor is the cause of the universal disturbance himself unshaken.

Private individuals are more easily pardoned if they avenge themselves relentlessly. They can be hurt; they are open to pain from wrongs done to them. Besides, they are afraid of contempt, and not to pay back in kind those who harm them looks like weakness, not mercy. But those to whom vengeance is easy can do without it and gain sure praise for their gentleness. (4) Men of humble position are free to use violence, go to law, rush into brawls and indulge their anger – blows between equals are slight. For a king, it hardly accords with his majesty so much as to raise his voice or use intemperate language.

8 (1) You may think it hard that kings should be deprived of that freedom in speaking which even the humblest enjoy. 'This is *slavery*,' you may say, 'not supreme command.' What! Are you not aware that this supreme command means *noble* slavery for you?[21] The situation is different for those who lurk in the crowd without leaving it, whose virtues have to fight long to come into the open and whose vices have the cover of darkness. But what you say and do is seized on by rumour; and that is why none should care more

---

[20] I.e. after having been struck by lightning.
[21] Reading, with Wilamowitz, *istud nobilem esse tibi servitutem*. The phrase 'noble servitude' was that of the Macedonian king Antigonus II (cf. Aelian, *Varia Historia* II 20), who may have been echoing the views on kingship of the Stoic philosopher, Perseus.

about their reputation than those whose reputation, whatever their deserts may be, is going to be great. (2) How much there is that you are forbidden but we, thanks to you, are allowed! I can walk without fear wherever I will in the city, with no escort to follow me, with no sword either at home or at my side. You, in the peace that you guarantee, must live under arms. You cannot escape your lot. It besets you; wherever you descend, it follows you with its mass of trappings. (3) The slavery of being supremely great lies in the impossibility of ever becoming anything less. But this constraint is one which you share with the gods. They too are held bound to the heavens. No more is it granted to them than it would be safe for you to come down. You are fixed to your pinnacle. (4) When we move, few notice. We can go, come back, change costume unnoticed by the public. You have no more chance than the sun of not being seen. A flood of light meets you face to face, and the eyes of all are turned towards it.[22] You think you are setting out – in fact, you are rising. (5) You cannot speak without your voice being heard by the nations everywhere; you cannot show anger without everything trembling at it, since you cannot strike anyone without throwing whatever is around him into turmoil. When thunderbolts fall, few are endangered, but all are terrified. In the same way, punishments by mighty potentates cause more terror than harm – and not without reason: it is not what he has done, but what he may do, that people consider in the case of one who can do anything.

(6) Consider this, too. Private individuals are likelier to have wrongs done to them by putting up with wrongs which already have been done. For kings, however, the surer way to security is through gentleness, since frequent punishment, while it crushes hatred in a few, arouses it in everyone. (7) The wish to rage should cease, sooner than the occasion. Otherwise, in the same way that trees which have been chopped down sprout again with a multitude of branches and many plants are pruned to make them grow thicker, the cruelty of a king increases the number of his enemies by removing them. Parents and children of those slain, kinsmen and friends, take the place of each single victim.

---

[22] Reading, with MSS, *multa* contra *te lux est*. The image, familiar in Egyptian pharaonic iconography, is that of the monarch turned towards the sun, illuminated

The example of Augustus

9 (1) To remind you how true this is, I would like to take an example from your own family. Our deified Augustus was a mild prince – if you begin your judgment with his principate. Admittedly, while the commonwealth was still ruled in common with others,[23] he did wield the sword. At the very age which you are now, eighteen years old, he had already plunged his dagger into the bosom of friends, already plotted to assassinate the consul Mark Antony, already been a partner in the proscriptions.[24] (2) But when he was over forty, in Gaul, information was brought to him that Lucius Cinna, a dim-witted man, was organizing a plot against him.[25] He was told where, when and how the attack was to be made – one of the accomplices was the informant. (3) He resolved to be avenged and ordered a council of his friends to be summoned. He spent a restless night reflecting that a young man of noble birth and otherwise blameless, a grandson of Gnaeus Pompeius,[26] was to be condemned. By now he could not bring himself to kill even one man, though it was he to whom Mark Antony had dictated an edict of proscription at dinner! (4) He groaned from time to time, and came out with a variety of conflicting utterances: 'Well? Am I to let my assassin walk about in safety while I am seized with anxiety? Is he then to escape punishment? Here am I, attacked in vain in so many civil wars, survivor of so many battles by land and sea – and there he is, now that peace on land and sea has been established, making up his mind to kill me, or rather to dispatch me as a sacrifice at the altar!' (The plan had been to attack him as he offered sacrifice.) (5) Silence would intervene and then again he would come out with much louder anger against

---

by it and reflecting its light. See P. Grimal, *Révue des Etudes Latines* (1971), pp. 207–11.

[23] Reading, with Lipsius, *in communi quidem republica.*

[24] Seneca's chronology here is vague. The proscriptions occurred after Augustus had been voted triumvir in November 43 BC, when he was twenty years old, not eighteen. A year earlier, he had been charged with plotting against Antony, and he was suspected of having had the consuls Hirtius and Pansa killed in April 43 BC.

[25] The conspiracy of Gnaeus Cornelius Cinna Magnus (Lucius was the name of his father), not mentioned by Tacitus or Suetonius, may have taken place during Augustus' absence in Gaul (possibly 17–13 BC). The story is repeated by Dio Cassius (LV 14–22).

[26] Pompey the Great (106–48 BC).

himself than against Cinna: 'What do you go on living for, if so many people stand to gain by your death? What end will there be to punishment and bloodshed? Yes, of course I am the target for young nobles, of course they are going to whet their swords against my person. Life is not worth it, if my survival means that so many must perish.' (6) Finally Livia, his wife,[27] interrupted him. 'Will you take a woman's advice?' said she. 'Do as doctors do. When the usual remedies do no good, they try the opposite. Sternness so far has got you nowhere. Salvidienus was followed by Lepidus, Lepidus by Murena, Murena by Caepio, Caepio by Egnatius,[28] not to mention others whose very audacity I blush to recall.[29] Now see how mercy works for you. Pardon Lucius Cinna. He has been caught. He cannot now do you any harm. But he can do your reputation some good.' (7) Glad to have found a supporter, he thanked his wife. He promptly sent a message to his friends cancelling the council and had Cinna brought to him alone. Sending everyone else from the room, he ordered a second chair to be fetched for Cinna. 'First', he said, 'I request that you don't interrupt me when I am speaking and don't raise an outcry in the middle of what I have to say. You will be given time to speak. (8) I found you, Cinna, in the enemy camp. You had not been made my enemy – you were that by birth.[30] Yet I saved you. I let you have all your father's estate. Today you are so prosperous and wealthy as to make the victors envy you your defeat. You sought the priesthood. I passed over several whose fathers had fought on my side. But despite such services to you on my part, you have made up your mind to kill me.' (9) At these words, Cinna cried out that

---

[27] Livia Drusilla (58 BC–AD 29), Augustus' second wife, mother (by an earlier marriage) of the emperor Tiberius.

[28] Quintus Rufus Salvidienus, an early associate and general of Augustus, had been executed for treasonable approaches to Antony in 40 BC. For conspiring to assassinate Augustus on his return from his Egyptian campaign, Marcus Aemilius Lepidus, son of the triumvir, had been executed in 30 BC. Aulus Terentius Varro Murena had been implicated in a conspiracy headed by Fannius Caepio. Both were executed in c. 22 BC. Marcus Egnatius Rufus, popular politician, aedile and praetor, was imprisoned and put to death in 19 BC. The same catalogue of conspirators appears in Suetonius, *Life of Augustus* 19.

[29] Perhaps Plautius Rufus, Lucius Paulus, Lucius Audasius, Asinius Epicadus and the slave Telephus, who are next to be mentioned by Suetonius (*ibid.*).

[30] Gnaeus Cinna's mother was Pompey's daughter; his father, Lucius Cornelius Cinna, publicly approved of the murder of Julius Caesar.

he was far from such lunacy. 'You are not keeping your promise, Cinna. We agreed that you were not to interrupt. I tell you, you are planning to kill me', said Augustus, also naming the place, the accomplices, the date, the plan of action and the man with the dagger. (10) He saw that the other was rooted to the spot, no longer constrained by their agreement but by his conscience into holding his tongue. 'What was your purpose in doing this?' he asked. 'To be prince yourself? My goodness, the Roman people must be in a bad way if I am your only obstacle to power. You cannot even protect your own household. Only the other day, the influence of a mere freedman was enough to defeat you in a private law-suit.[31] All the more reason why nothing should be easier for you than to summon up help against Caesar! Come now, suppose that I am the only one to block your hopes, will Paulus or Fabius Maximus put up with you, will a Cossus, a Servilius or that great host of nobles with more than an empty name to put on show, I mean those who add lustre to their ancestry?'[32]

(11) So as not fill up a great part of this book by going over his entire speech (we know that he spoke for longer than two hours, drawing out this punishment which was going to be enough for him on its own) – 'Your life', he said, 'I grant to you once more, Cinna, formerly my enemy, now a plotter and parricide.[33] From this day on, let friendship begin between us. Let us see which of us keeps better faith, I in granting you your life, or you in owing it to me.' (12) Afterwards, he gave him the consulate on his own initiative, complaining that Cinna had not dared to seek it.[34] In Cinna he had his warmest and loyalest friend. He became his sole heir. No further plots were hatched against him by anyone.

---

[31] We have no other information about this law-suit.

[32] The references are probably to Lucius Aemilius Paulus (consul AD 1, husband of Augustus' granddaughter Julia, executed for conspiracy AD 8), Fabius Maximus Paulus (consul 11 BC, friend and toady of Augustus, propagator of the imperial cult), Cossus Cornelius Lentulus (consul 1 BC) and Marcus Servilius (consul AD 3). All these, like Cinna, were members of old noble families who briefly did well and were able to pursue their ambitions under the monarchy of the despised commoner Augustus; all of them duly achieved the most coveted political prize, the consulate. See Syme, pp. 419–23.

[33] Legally, in pardoning Cinna, Augustus would be acting *ultra vires*, not that that would have mattered. Cf. 5. 4: 'Anyone can break the law in order to take a life. No one except for me can do so to save a life!'

[34] Cinna was consul in AD 5.

Book I

10 (1) Your great-great-grandfather[35] spared the vanquished. If he had not, whom would he have had to rule? Sallustius,[36] a Cocceius,[37] a Dellius,[38] indeed his whole inner circle of friends[39] were recruited from the enemy camp. As it was, he had his mercy to thank for a Domitius,[40] a Messala,[41] an Asinius,[42] a Cicero[43] – in fact for the flower of the state. Lepidus himself was allowed a very long time to die! For years on end, Augustus suffered him to keep the insignia of a leading citizen. Only on his death did he allow the Chief Priesthood to be transferred to himself.[44] He wanted it to be an honour, not a trophy. (2) This habit of mercy brought him safety and security, popularity and favour, although he had placed his hand on a Roman people that had never yet bowed its neck. To this day it guarantees him a glory that even living princes

[35] I.e. Augustus: Nero was the son of Agrippina the Younger, daughter of Germanicus and the elder Agrippina, daughter of Julia, only child of Augustus.
[36] Gaius Sallustius Crispus, grandnephew and adopted son of the historian Sallust, succeeded Maecenas as chief minister, confidant and henchman of Augustus and then of Tiberius.
[37] Lucius Cocceius Nerva, Marcus Cocceius Nerva (consul 36 BC) and Gaius Cocceius Balbus (consul 39 BC) had all been partisans of Antony (see Syme, p. 267). The former served Octavian (i.e. Augustus) in his negotiations with Antony.
[38] Quintus Dellius, addressee of a well-known ode by Horace (II 3), was famed for his political agility, having deserted Dolabella, Cassius and Antony in turn.
[39] The Latin phrase here (cohortem primae admissionis) refers to a practice which, according to Seneca (On Favours VI 34. 2), had been introduced by Gaius Gracchus in the late second century BC. A great man's clients and well-wishers were expected to pay him a formal morning courtesy call (the salutatio). If he was sufficiently important, the number of callers would be such that only a select few, the cohors primae admissionis, could actually be admitted into the house. The rest had to stay in the courtyard or the street.
[40] Gnaius Domitius Ahenobarbus (consul 32 BC) had been a republican and then a supporter of Antony, before going over to Augustus, shortly before the battle of Actium. Another member of the family was Lucius Domitius Ahenobarbus (consul 16 BC), Nero's grandfather.
[41] Marcus Valerius Messalla Corvinus (64 BC–AD 8), soldier, statesman and patron of letters, had been on the republican side and then supported Antony. In 36 BC he had transferred his allegiance to Augustus, with whom as consul in 31 BC he took part in the battle of Actium.
[42] Gaius Asinius Pollio (76 BC–AD 4, consul 40 BC), on whom see further On Anger III 23.5, had supported Antony and engaged in polemic with the young Augustus (Syme, p. 211).
[43] Marcus Tullius Cicero (consul 30 BC), dissolute son of the great orator, had served under Brutus and Sextus Pompeius.
[44] Marcus Aemilius Lepidus, appointed triumvir in 43 BC with Antony and Augustus, had been forced into private life in 36 BC but retained the offfice of Pontifex Maximus till his death in 12 BC.

141

can hardly command. (3) We believe him to be a god – and without being ordered to do so; we acknowledge that Augustus was a good prince, richly deserving the name of 'parent',[45] for the simple reason that the insults offered to him, which princes usually find more bitter than injuries, were never avenged with cruelty, that he smiled at the abuse directed at him,[46] that he appeared to be suffering punishment when inflicting it, that, so far from killing those whom he had condemned for adultery with his daughter,[47] he sent them away for their safety, giving them passports. (4) That really is forgiveness: when you know that there will be many who would feel anger on your behalf and humour you by killing some who has nothing to do with them, you not merely grant the person his safety but guarantee it!

11 (1) These things Augustus did in his old age or just on the verge of it. In his youth, he was hot-headed; he burned with anger; he did many things which he did not like to look back on. No one would dare to compare the kindness of our deified Augustus with yours, even if the contest were between years of youth and an overripe old age. He may have shown moderation and mercy. Of course he did – after staining the sea at Actium with Roman blood, after shattering the fleets (his own and the other side's) in Sicily, after the sacrifices at Perusia and the proscriptions![48] (2) But mercy is not the name that I would give to exhausted cruelty. True mercy, Caesar, is what you have shown. It is not something that starts with remorse at savagery – it means spotlessness, it means never having shed a citizen's blood, it means supreme power exercised with the truest self-control, an embracing love for the human race as though for oneself,[49] it means not being corrupted by greed or natural impetuosity or examples set by earlier princes into testing how far one can go against one's fellow-citizens; it

---

[45] Augustus had been acclaimed *pater patriae*, 'Father of the Fatherland', in 2 BC.
[46] See the anecdote at *On Anger* III 23. 4–8.
[47] Reading, with Erasmus and most editors after him, *filiae*. When Augustus' daughter Julia was banished in 2 BC for immorality, one of her paramours, Iullus Antonius (son of Mark Antony), in fact was put to death. See Syme, pp. 426 f.
[48] Seneca is referring, in reverse chronological order, to the naval battle of Actium in 31 BC (which eliminated Antony as a rival of Augustus), the costly defeat of Sextus Pompeius, son of Pompey the Great, in Sicily in 37/36 BC, the capture and sack of Perusia in 40 BC and the proscriptions of November 43 BC.
[49] Keeping the Hosius text, but putting a semi-colon after *amor*.

means blunting the edge of one's imperial power. (3) You have given us, Caesar, a state unstained by blood. Your magnanimous boast that in the whole world you have not shed one drop of human blood is the greater and more amazing in that no one ever had the sword entrusted to him at an earlier age.

King versus tyrant

(4) Mercy, then, enhances not only a ruler's honour, but his safety. The glory of empire, it is at the same time its surest protection. For what has allowed kings to grow old and bequeath their kingdoms to their children and grandchildren? Why is the power of tyrants accursed and short-lived? What is the difference between a king and a tyrant? – after all, their show of fortune and their power are the same. It is simply that tyrants act savagely for their pleasure, whereas kings do so only for a reason and out of necessity.

12 (1) 'What do you mean? Are not kings also in the habit of killing?' Yes, but only when the public good dictates it. A tyrant's savagery comes from the heart. What distinguishes a tyrant from a king are his actions, not the name. Dionysius the elder[50] was rightly and deservedly preferable to many kings. And why should not Lucius Sulla[51] be called a tyrant?[52] His killing only came to an end when he ran out of enemies. (2) He may have climbed down from the office of dictator and returned to civilian life. But what tyrant ever drank so greedily of human blood as he did? He ordered seven thousand Roman citizens to be slaughtered. Sitting nearby in the temple of Bellona, he heard the cry of thousands groaning beneath the sword. To the terrified Senate he said: 'To work, gentlemen! It is only a few mutineers being killed on my orders.' (3) He was not lying – to Sulla they did seem few. But more about Sulla anon, when we come to the question of the anger appropriate for enemies, especially if fellow-citizens from the same class as ourselves have broken away and come under that

---

[50] Dionysius I (c. 430–367 BC), ruler of Syracuse, was remembered, thanks largely to his connection with Plato (see Plato, *Seventh Letter*), as a tyrant in the grand manner.

[51] See Biographical Notes and *On Anger* I 20. 4.

[52] I.e. despite the fact that he confined himself to the forms of republican government and tried to restore the primacy of the Senate.

label. Meanwhile, as I said, it is mercy which makes there be a great distinction between king and tyrant.[53] Each may be fenced around with arms as much as the other. But the one has them as a bulwark for peace, the other in order to repress great hatred with great fear. Nor can he look upon the very hands into which he has entrusted himself without anxiety. (4) Contradictory motives drive him to self-contradiction. He is hated because he is feared, and being hated makes him want to be feared. He invokes that accursed verse which has sent many to their ruin: 'let them hate, provided that they fear,'[54] in ignorance of the fury which arises when hatred grows beyond measure. In moderation, you see, fear does inhibit the mind. But if it is continuous and intense and threatens death, it arouses even the sluggish to boldness, inducing them to try anything. (5) That is how wild beasts are trapped and held in by a line strung with feathers.[55] But these same creatures, should a horseman with javelins attack them from behind, will try to flee through the very things which they have been fleeing from. They will trample down what scares them. Courage is at its keenest when forged by the threat of death. Fear should leave an element of security undisturbed, holding out much more in the way of hope than of danger. Otherwise, when the peaceful have as much to dread as anyone else, they find it a pleasure to incur danger and to squander lives that are not theirs anyway.

13 (1) A calm, indulgent king has trustworthy guards, as you would expect, since he employs them for the common safety. Eager for glory, his soldiers see that their service is for the public security and willingly undergo any hardship in guarding, as it were, a parent. But the tyrant, fierce and bloodthirsty, can only arouse the resentment of his lackeys. (2) No one can hold the good will and

---

[53] Traditionally, what distinguished a king from a tyrant was not his clemency, but the constitutional limits on his power: the king 'rules by law over willing subjects' (Aristotle, *Politics* 1285a27). Only where, as with the Roman emperor, the laws offer his subjects no guarantee of their rights and their wishes are of no decisive importance, does a moral quality such as clemency on the part of the monarch become the decisive criterion.

[54] Accius, Fragment 148 (*Remains of Old Latin*, Loeb edn. (1936), II, p. 382), also quoted by Seneca at II 2. 2 and at *On Anger* I 20. 4 (again in connection with Sulla).

[55] See *On Anger* II 11. 5.

loyalty of servants whom he employs to work the instruments of torture, such as the 'pony',[56] and the weapons of death, throwing men to them as though to the beasts. Gloomier and more troubled than any defendant in court (as well he might be, having gods and men to fear as witnesses and avengers of his crimes), he has reached the point where he cannot change his ways. For quite the worst thing about cruelty is that you have to press on with it. There is no way back to something better. The only protection for crime is more crime. And what could be more wretched than to be, as he now is, *obliged* to be bad? (3) A pitiable creature he is, at least from his own point of view – it would be wrong for anyone else to pity him! Wielding power by slaughter and pillage, he arouses suspicion in all his dealings abroad and at home alike. Resorting to arms though afraid of arms, with no trust in the loyalty of friends or the piety of his children, wherever he looks around at what he has done or what he is going to do, he uncovers a conscience full of crimes and torment. Often fearing yet more often longing for death, he is more hateful to himself than to those who are his slaves.

(4) Contrast him with one whose care is for all without exception. While guarding some things more than others, he nurtures every part of the commonwealth as though it were part of himself. Inclined to the milder course, even when it may be of use to punish, he reveals his reluctance to apply harsh remedies. Free in mind from all trace of enmity or wildness, he exercises his power in an indulgent and beneficial manner, eager only to win the approval of the citizens for his commands, abundantly happy in his own eyes if he can share his good fortune with the public. Affable in conversation, accessible and easily approached,[57] amiable in expression (which is what most wins over the people), favourably disposed to requests that are reasonable without being harsh even to ones that are not, he is loved by the whole state, protected and courted. (5) What people say about him is the same in secret as in the open. They are eager to rear children; the childlessness once imposed by public misfortune is reversed, since no one doubts that his children will have cause to thank him for letting them see

---

[56] Apparently a sort of rack; see *On Anger* III 3. 6, 19. 1.
[57] These are all aspects of princely 'civility'. See below, n. 61.

so happy an age. Such a prince, protected by his own good deeds, has no need of guards. He wears his armour purely for decoration.

'Father of the Fatherland'[58]

14 (1) What, then, are his duties? Those of good parents, whose habit it is to reproach their children sometimes gently, sometimes with threats, on occasion even punishing them with lashes. No one in his right mind, surely, would disinherit a son for a first offence. Only when his patience has been overcome by serious and repeated wrong-doing, when he has more to fear than to condemn, will he pen the decisive legal document. He first makes many an attempt to reclaim a character still not set though already inclined to the worse. Only when all hope is lost does he resort to extreme measures. No one comes to the point of inflicting punishment until he has run out of remedies. (2) That is how a parent, and also a prince, ought to act. If we call him 'Father of the Fatherland', it is not empty flattery that has led us to do so. Other titles may simply be honorific. We speak of men as 'the Great', 'the Fortunate', 'the August', loading their ambition and greatness with every possible title. We do this as a tribute to them. But we have given the 'Father of the Fatherland' that name to remind him that he has been granted the power of a father, the most moderate of powers, in caring for children and subordinating his own interests to theirs.[59] (3) A father would be slow to sever one of his limbs; having done so, he would long to restore it; while doing so, he would groan and hesitate often and long. Condemning in haste, you see, comes close to condemning with pleasure, punishing too hard to punishing unfairly.

15 (1) I can remember Tricho, a Roman knight who had flogged his son to death. The populace stabbed him with their styluses in the forum. The authority of Augustus Caesar was hardly enough to rescue him from the violent hostility of fathers and sons

[58] This title, which had been held by Augustus (see 10. 3 above), had been offered to Nero on his accession (Suetonius, *Life of Nero* 8). He adopted it in late 55 or AD 56, i.e. at roughly the time that *On Mercy* was being written.
[59] This was a characteristic regularly ascribed to the good king. See Cicero *Republic* II 47. The theme can be traced back to Xenophon (*Education of Cyrus* VIII 1. 1).

alike. (2) But Tarius, who had caught his son in a plot to kill him and found him guilty after an enquiry into the case, won everyone's respect by contenting himself with a sentence of exile, and a comfortable exile at that. He confined the parricide to Massilia on the same allowance that he had regularly received while still innocent.[60] The effect of this generosity was that, in a city where there is always someone to speak up for scoundrels, no one doubted that the accused had deserved his condemnation, condemned as he had been by a father incapable of hating him.

(3) This very case, moreover, will give you a model with which to compare the good father – the good prince. Before starting the enquiry into his son, Tarius called Caesar Augustus to the council. Augustus duly entered a private dwelling, took his seat and assisted at someone else's council. He did not say 'No, come to my house! ' If he had, the enquiry would have been Caesar's, not the father's.[61]

(4) When the case had been heard and everything sifted through, both what the young man had to say for himself and what was brought against him, Caesar asked that each should put down his judgment in writing, in case all should come out with the same judgment as he.[62] Next, before the tablets were opened, he swore that he would not accept any bequest from Tarius, a man of some wealth. (5) Some might say, 'It was small-minded of him to worry about the impression he might give of opening up his own prospects by the son's condemnation.' I think the opposite. Any one of us faced with hostile opinion ought indeed to have relied simply on his own conscience. But princes should give much weight even to rumour. So Caesar swore that he would not accept a bequest, (6) depriving Tarius indeed, on the very same day, of a further heir, but redeeming his own freedom of judgment. And after proving his sternness to be disinterested (something which a prince should

---

[60] Lucius Tarius Rufus, a man of humble provincial origins, had a long and distinguished career, rising to the rank of consul (16 BC) and acquiring considerable wealth. Massilia (modern Marseille) was a Greek city on the southern coast of France.

[61] Augustus' behaviour here is a model not only of clemency but of another virtue important for a Roman *princeps* – *civilitas* or the rejection of kingly pretensions and 'pride' for the modest style of an ordinary citizen, a *civis*. In practice, this meant making oneself 'affable in conversation, accessible and easily approached' and 'aimiable', as Seneca puts it at 13. 4.

[62] Nero in fact adopted this practice, making members of his council submit their judgments in writing (Suetonius, *Life of Nero* 15. 1).

always take care to do), he decreed banishment to wherever the father saw fit. (7) He did not decide on the sack and the snake[63] or on prison. His mind was less on the subject of his verdict than on the man whose council he was attending. So he said that the mildest sort of punishment should suffice a father in the case of a youthful son driven to a crime carried out in a timid – that is, almost innocent – way: namely, banishment from the city and from his father's sight.

Patterns of command

16 (1) How worthy was Caesar to be invited to parental councils, and share the inheritance of the children who were not guilty! Such mercy befits a prince. Wherever he goes, he should make everything milder. No one in the eyes of a king should be so worthless as to perish unnoticed. Whatever the man may be, he comes under his command.

(2) For the great forms of command we should seek a pattern in the lesser forms. There is no one way of exercising it. A prince has command over his citizens, a father over his children, a teacher over his students, a tribune or centurion over his soldiers. (3) The worst sort of father, surely, would seem to be one who curbs his children with unremitting blows for even the smallest offence. And which is the worthier teacher of liberal studies: one who flays the students if memory fails them or if the eye lacks agility in reading and gets stuck[64] – or one who prefers to correct and teach by admonition and appeal to their sense of shame? Show me a savage tribune or centurion: he just breeds deserters – and ones whose crime is pardonable. (4) Can it be fair to lay harsher and heavier commands on a man than are laid on dumb animals? Yet the horse is not regularly lashed into a state of terror, if its trainer has any experience. It will become nervous and obstinate unless you soothe it by gentle handling. (5) A huntsman worth the name does the same, whether training puppies to follow the trail or using hounds

---

[63] The traditional punishment for a parricide, to which Seneca also alludes at 23. I and *On Anger* I 16. 5, was to be sewn alive in a sack – along with a dog, an ape, a cock and a serpent – and thrown into the river.

[64] A problem perhaps commoner in the ancient world than now. Punctuation was primitive and texts were written without separating the words.

already practised to start and chase down the prey. Without making constant threats (for that breaks the spirit and shatters with a degenerate fear whatever native character they may have), he does not allow them, either, to wander and stray about freely in all directions. You can also think of those who drive the more sluggish beasts of burden. Born to abuse and wretchedness, such creatures can be goaded by excessive cruelty to throw off the yoke. 17 (1) But no animal is moodier than man. None requires more skilful handling or greater forbearance. Nothing could be stupider than to blush at venting anger on beasts of burden and dogs, but to be reduced to the very worst state by a human like yourself.

We cure diseases – we do not lose our temper with them. Yet here, too, we have a disease, of the mind. It requires gentle medicine and a doctor with no hostility of his own towards the patient.[65] (2) To despair of making a cure is the mark of a bad doctor. Likewise, in cases where the mind is affected, the right course for the one entrusted with everyone's health is not to abandon hope too quickly and pronounce the symptoms fatal. It is, rather, to wrestle with the failings and stand up to them, to make some ashamed of their illness while deceiving others with gentle treatment. The cure will be swifter and better if the remedies are disguised. The aim of the prince should not just be to restore health, but to avoid an embarrassing scar. (3) No glory can come to a king from punishing savagely – who doubts that he can do that? On the contrary, his greatest glory is to hold back his power, rescuing many from the anger of others, while exposing no one to his own.

18 (1) Restraint in ordering slaves about is praiseworthy. Even if someone is your chattel, the question is not how far you can get away with making him suffer, but what is essentially reasonable and good and how much that allows you. This principle tells you to spare even the captive and the slave whom you have bought; and it tells you, with still more justice, not to abuse the free, the free-born, the well-born as though they were chattels, but to treat them as people simply of lower degree who have been entrusted to you not as slaves but as wards. (2) Slaves have the right to seek refuge at a god's statue; and though you have the right to do

---

[65] Compare *On Anger* I 6. 2, II 10. 7.

anything to a slave, yet there are things which the law common to all living creatures forbids you to do to a human being.[66] Who did not hate Vedius Pollio[67] more than his slaves did, for fattening his lampreys with human blood and ordering those who offended him to be cast into his fish-pond – or should I say, his snake-pit? Ah, there was a man who deserved a thousand deaths, whether he meant to eat the lampreys to whom he threw his servants as food, or whether he was just keeping them in order to feed them in this manner! (3) Cruel masters have the whole city pointing at them with hatred and loathing. So, too, with kings. The wrongs which they do have a wider scope. The infamy and odium is passed on over the centuries. How much better never to have been born than to be classed as one whose birth was a public misfortune!

19 (1) No one could conceive of anything more becoming to a ruler than mercy, whatever the manner of his accession to power and whatever its legal basis. We may, of course, acknowledge it to be the more beautiful and magnificent, the greater the power behind it – a power which ought not to be malign, if disposed in accordance with the law of nature. (2) For kingship has been devised by nature herself, as you can see from bees,[68] among other animals. Their king has the most spacious cell in the central and safest place, doing no work himself but supervising that of others. If he goes, the swarm breaks up, and they refuse to have more than one king, seeking out the best by combat. He stands out in appearance, distinct from the others in size and splendour. (3) The greatest difference, however, is that bees are highly irascible and, for their size, highly pugnacious, leaving their stings behind in the wound, whereas their king himself has no sting.[69] Not wishing him to be savage or to exact a costly revenge, Nature took away his weapon and left his anger unarmed. A mighty example for great kings!

[66] On the theme of the equal humanity of slaves, see further *Letter* 47 and *On Favours* III 18–28.

[67] On whom see also *On Anger* III 40. 2.

[68] Mistaking their sex, the ancients spoke of 'king' bees. The political analogy goes back to Plato (*Republic* 520b). It was developed by Vergil in a passage (*Georgics* IV 210–18) already recalled at 4. 1. Its point, for Seneca, is not that kingship is the 'natural' ideal form of government, but rather that in the bees we have a natural model of what government by a king should be like.

[69] Aristotle (*History of Animals* 553b5–7) had judged differently: 'king' bees do have a sting, but do not use it.

Nature has a way of revealing herself[70] in small things, and piling up tiny demonstrations of mighty principles.[71] (4) It would be shameful not to draw morals from tiny creatures, seeing that the mind of man needs a greater moderation to match its greater violence and power to harm. If only there could be the same law for man, that his anger should be shattered along with its instrument, that it should be impossible to do harm more than once, or to use others to wreak his hatred! His fury would readily abate, if he could find satsfaction only through his own resources and discharge his violence only at the risk of his own life. (5) But even as it is, he has no safe course. He is bound to feel as much fear as he would like to inspire, to keep an eye on everyone's hand and, even when no one has laid hold of him, to think himself under attack and never for one moment to feel free from fear. Would anyone bear to live such a life, when he might be harmless to others and hence secure, exercising to the gladness of all a beneficent right to power? It is a mistake to think that the king is safe, if nothing is safe from the king. Security comes at the price of reciprocity. (6) There is no need for him to raise aloft high citadels or to fortify hills steep to climb, nor to cut off the mountainside and fence himself in with a multitude of walls and towers – mercy will assure the king's safety even in the open. He has one impregnable bulwark – the love of the citizens. (7) What could be lovelier than to live while all pray for him to live, voicing their prayers under no surveillance, while the slightest uncertainty about his health arouses in men not their hope but their fear, while nothing is so precious to any one that he would not exchange it for the safety of his guardian, (8) considering all that happens to him as something befalling himself?[72] In his life he has shown by numerous demonstrations of kindness not that the commonweath belongs to him, but he to the commonwealth. Who would dare to contrive any danger for such a man? Who would not wish, could he do so, to drive ill-fortune away from one beneath whose sway justice, peace, purity, calm and worth all flourish, and the state in its wealth overflows with an abundance of all things good? It looks

---

[70] Reading, with Erasmus, *exerere se.*
[71] Reading *documenta minima aggerere.*
[72] Translating, for want of anything better, Erasmus' *omne illi quod contingit, sibi quoque evenire deputet.*

on its governor with the very same mind that we, were they to grant us the power to see them, would look upon the immortal gods – with veneration and worship. (9) He must surely be second only to the gods if his conduct accords with their nature, if he is beneficent, generous, powerful for good? This should be your aspiration, this your ideal – to count as greatest only by counting, at the same time, as best.

Principles of punishment

20 (1) A prince has normally one of two reasons for inflicting punishment: to avenge himself or somebody else. I shall discuss first the case where he is personally involved. For moderation comes harder when retribution is required by one's own distress, rather than by the need to set an example. (2) There would be no point here in reminding him not to give easy credence, to sift out the truth, to side with innocence and be seen to do so, to realize that the interests of the accused are no less important than those of the judge.[73] All this is a matter of justice, not mercy. What I now urge on him is that he respond to damage openly inflicted on himself by keeping his mind under control, by remitting the punishment if he can safely do so or, if he cannot, by moderating it, and that he should be far easier to placate when wronged himself than when others are wronged. (3) A man of great mind is not one who is generous with what belongs to others, but who gives at the cost of depriving himself. In the same way, I would not apply the word 'merciful' to one who is easy about suffering inflicted on another, but to one with goads of his own to drive him on but who still does not leap into action, who understands that the mark of a great mind is to endure wrongs done to him even where his power is supreme, and that nothing is more glorious than a wronged prince unrequited.

21 (1) Retribution normally provides one of two things: consolation for the injured party or security for the future. But the prince's station is too grand to need solace and his power too manifest for him to seek a reputation for strength through ill done to another. I speak here of cases where he has been attacked and

---

[73] Reading, with Lipsius, *et appareat, ut non minorem agi rem ... sciat.*

dishonoured by inferiors. For if he now sees his former equals at his feet, he has had vengeance enough. A king can be killed by a slave, by a serpent, by a mere arrow; whereas no one has ever saved anyone without being superior to the person saved. (2) So he should use in a noble spirit the great gift which the gods have given him – his power to grant life and to take it away. Above all, with those whom he knows to have been on the same royal pinnacle as he. When he has gained control over them, his retribution is already complete. He has done all that is needed for true punishment. To owe one's life is to have lost it. Anyone who has fallen from the heights to his enemy's feet and has had to wait for another to pass sentence on his life and kingdom, survives to the glory of his saviour, contributing more to that renown by his safety than if snatched from sight. He offers a lasting spectacle of the other's excellence. In a triumphal procession, he would soon have passed out of sight. (3) And of course, if his kingdom can safely be left in his charge, if he can be restored to the state from which he fell, the praise will be hugely increased for one who was content to take from a conquered king nothing beyond his glory. To do this is to triumph over one's own victory, to testify that one has found nothing among the vanquished worthy of a victor. (4) Towards his own citizens, if they are unknown or of low degree, the prince should act all the more moderately because their destruction matters less. Some you may be happy to spare, some you may disdain to punish. You must stay your hand, as you do with animals that are small but messy if crushed. And there are those whose pardon or punishment will be on the lips of the whole city. The occasion for conspicuous mercy should be grasped.

22 (1) Let us pass on to wrongs done to others. In punishing them there are three principles which the law follows and which a prince, too, should follow: either to correct the person punished, or to improve others by his punishment, or else to remove the wicked so that the rest may live in greater security. The wicked themselves you will find easier to correct by a lighter punishment – one takes more care how one lives, if there is something left to lose. No one has any thought for his dignity when it is gone. To afford no scope for further punishment is a kind of immunity. (2) Again, public morals are better put right by a sparing use of punitive measures. For wrongdoing becomes the general practice

if there are numerous wrongdoers; the stigma is less serious if lost in a crowd of condemnations; and sternness forfeits, through constant application, what most makes it a remedy – its force of example. (3) A prince will establish good morals in a state and cleanse it of its vices by patience – which does not mean that he approves of them, but rather that he is unwilling, indeed highly distressed, to reach the point of chastisement. Men are inhibited from doing wrong by the very mercifulness of the ruler. Punishment seems far more serious, if decreed by a mild man.

23 (1) You will observe, too, that crimes are often committed if often punished. In a five-year period, your father[74] had more people sewn into the sack than there had been, or so we are told, in all the centuries before him. Offspring were far less bold in committing the ultimate sacrilege, so long as the crime had no law to cover it. With supreme sagacity men of the deepest wisdom and insight into nature preferred to pass it by as a crime beyond belief and beyond human boldness, rather than to demonstrate, by punishing it, that it could be committed. Parricides came into being with the law against them. The penalty showed them the way to the misdeed. Filial piety in fact reached its lowest point after the sack had become a commoner sight than the cross.[75] (2) In a city where men are seldom punished, innocence becomes the agreed way to behave, something allowed free play as a public good. Give the city an idea of itself as innocent, and it will be. It will be the angrier with departures from the common sobriety, if it sees that they are few. It is dangerous, believe me, to show the city how great a majority the wicked are.

24 (1) A proposal was once made in the Senate to distinguish slaves from free men by their costume.[76] Then it became clear what a danger would threaten us, if the slaves started to count our number. You can be sure of having the same thing to fear, if no one is pardoned. It will soon be clear how much the worse elements

---

[74] The emperor Claudius, by whom Nero had been adopted as a boy, was an enthusiast for punishing parricides in this way (Suetonius, *Life of Claudius* 34. 1). See also 15. 7, n. 63.

[75] Crucifixion was the standard mode of execution for slaves (see 1 26. 1), for non-citizens and, later, for citizens too, if they were members of the lower orders.

[76] We have no information about when or under what circumstances this proposal may have been made. The story reflects the (not unfounded) anxieties of wealthy slave-owners. See Griffin, p. 267.

of the city preponderate. For a prince a multitude of punishments is as shameful as a multitude of funerals is for a doctor. Authority more relaxed is better obeyed. (2) The human mind is naturally obstinate. It struggles against opposition and difficulty, readier to follow of its own accord than to be drawn. Just as horses of good breed and pedigree are better controlled on an easy rein, so a willing innocence follows spontaneously upon mercy, which the state finds worth maintaining in its own interest. More good, accordingly, is done this way.

The horrors of cruelty

25 (1) Cruelty is utterly inhuman, an evil unworthy of a mind so mild as man's. It is bestial madness to rejoice in wounds and blood, to cast off the man and turn into an animal of the forest. What difference is there, I ask you, Alexander, between throwing Lysimachus to the lion or rending him yourself with your own teeth?[77] Its mouth is yours, its ferocity yours. How keenly you would long to be endowed with its claws yourself, with its jaws yawning wide enough to devour men alive! My demand to you is not that your hand, certain death as it was to your intimate friends, should actually save someone; it is not that your ferocious mind, that insatiable curse of whole nations, should be satisfied with anything short of blood and slaughter – what I now call mercy is simply that for killing a friend you should choose a *human* executioner. (2) What makes savagery especially loathsome is that it goes beyond the bounds first of custom and then of humanity. Seeking out new forms of punishment, summoning its ingenuity to think up devices for varying and extending the pain, it delights in human affliction. This is when that[78] dire disease of the mind has reached the ultimate insanity. Cruelty has become a pleasure, killing men a positive delight.[79] (3) Hard in pursuit of such a man come abhorrence, hatred, poison, the sword. He is menaced by dangers as numerous as the people whom he himself has endangered. He finds himself beset at times by private plotting, at other times by public uprising.

[77] See *On Anger* III 17. 2.
[78] Reading, with Erasmus, *ille.*
[79] See *On Anger* II 5. 3.

Minor disasters affecting private individuals leave the city as a whole unmoved. When the fury spreads and attacks everyone, it is struck down on all sides. (4) Tiny snakes go unnoticed. There is no public hunt for them. But when a serpent has exceeded the normal size and grown into a monster, poisoning the wells with its spittle, scorching whatever it breathes on and crushing everything in its way, the engines of war are brought out to attack it. Evil things, if tiny, can talk their way out and get off. If they are huge, everyone goes straight at them. (5) In the same way, a single sick person does not disturb even his own household. But where deaths come thick and fast and there is obviously a plague, you get an outcry and flight from the city, you see hands raised in supplication to the gods. If there are signs of fire in a single house, family and neighbours pour water on it. But a vast blaze, which has already destroyed many homes, takes a good part of the city to smother it.

26 (1) The cruelty even of private individuals has met with retribution at the hands of slaves in danger of certain crucifixion. The cruelty of tyrants has set nations and peoples, both those afflicted and those threatened by it, to work at their destruction. There have been times when their own guards have risen up against them, practising on them the perfidy, faithlessness, ferocity and whatever else they had learned from them. What can you expect, after all, from one whom you have taught to be bad? Wickedness is never at your service for long, nor will it confine its wrongdoing to what you command. (2) But imagine cruelty exercised in safety – what would its kingdom be like? It would look like cities fallen to the enemy; it would have the terrifying face of public fear. Everywhere you would see sorrow, trepidation, confusion. Entertainments themselves would arouse fear. No one could go without anxiety to parties where, even in his cups, his tongue must be carefully guarded, or to public shows where material is sought for accusing people and putting them in jeopardy. They can certainly be put on at huge expense, with royal resources and performers of the choicest reputation – but who would enjoy the games in prison? (3) Good God! What an evil it is to kill, to rage, to delight in the noise of chains and to cut off the heads of citizens, to pour out a mass of blood wherever you go, to terrify people and send them running by your very appearance! Would life be any different, if lions and bears had the kingdom, if serpents and the most noxious kind of animal were given power over us? (4) Such creatures, devoid of reason and damned by us for their monstrousness, do leave their own kind alone. Even among wild beasts, there is safety in physical resemblance.[80] But the tyrant's frenzy refuses to hold back even from his closest friends. Men inside and outside his circle it treats the same. The more it is exercised, the more excited it grows. From the slaughter of individuals it creeps on to the massacre of nations. To set fire to houses, to drive the plough over ancient cities it sees as real power. Orders for the killing of just one or two individuals are not enough, it believes, for a commanding officer. Unless at the same time a whole drove of wretches awaits the blow, it thinks its cruelty reduced to the ranks.

(5) Happiness that deserves the name lies in giving salvation to many, recalling them to life from the throes of death and earning by mercy the civic crown.[81] No ornament – no weapon torn from the vanquished enemy, no chariot gory with barbarian blood, no spoils acquired in war – is lovelier or worthier of the prince's high estate than that crown for the saving of citizens. Such is the power of a god – to save men in droves, to save whole peoples. To slaughter multitudes indiscriminately is the power of a conflagration or a collapsing edifice!

---

[80] Compare *On Anger* II 8. 3.
[81] The 'civic crown', made of oak leaves, was an award for saving the life of a citizen in battle.

Book II

Preface

1 (1) What most drove me to write on mercy, Nero Caesar, was one remark of yours which, I remember, I heard with admiration when it was uttered and reported admiringly to others. A noble, great-minded utterance of great kindness, not premeditated or intended for others to hear, it burst out suddenly, bringing into the open the conflict between your leniency and your lot in life. (2) Burrus, your prefect,[1] a remarkable man, born to serve a prince such as you, was about to execute two robbers. He was pressing you to write their names and your reason for wanting them executed. This had often been put off, but he insisted that it should be done. His reluctance met yours, as he held out the document and handed it over to you. You exclaimed, 'Oh that I had not learned to write!' (3) An utterance fit for all nations to hear – those who inhabit the Roman empire, those in precarious independence on its borders, those who rise against it with military force and martial spirit! An utterance to be addressed to an assembly of all mankind, to command the sworn allegiance of princes and kings! An utterance befitting a general innocence of the human race, an utterance to bring back that age long past! (4) Now indeed would be the proper

---

[1] Sextus Afranius Burrus had been appointed praetorian prefect (commander of the emperor's bodyguard) by Claudius in AD 51, and continued in that office under Nero. Nero's tutor and adviser for many years, he was responsible, with Seneca, for governing the empire in the first years of the reign. See Introduction, p. XIV.

time for men to act in unison for the right and the good, to drive out that greed for the property of others from which arise all the evils of the human mind; for piety and integrity, for good faith and modesty to rise again; for vice, after the long misuse of its reign, to give way at last to a pure and happy age.

2 (1) That this will in large measure come to be, Caesar, I am pleased to hope and trust. The gentleness of your mind will be transmitted to others; little by little, it will be diffused over the whole body of the empire. All will be formed in your likeness. Health springs from the head, the source of lively alertness or of drooping langour in all things, according to the vitality or faintness of the soul in them. There will be citizens, there will be allies worthy of this goodness. The whole world will see the return of right morals. Your hands everywhere will be spared the need to punish.

(2) Allow me to linger awhile on this point, and not just to charm your ears – that is not my habit. I would rather offend you with the truth than please you with flattery. What, then, is my motive? I wish you to be as familiar as possible with your good deeds and words so that what is now a matter of natural impulse in you may become a matter of settled judgment. Apart from that, I have in mind a great many powerful but hateful remarks which have come into human life and are in frequent circulation, like 'Let them hate, provided that they fear'[2] with its likeness to the Greek verse about 'confounding earth with fire when I am dead'[3] and others of that sort. (3) Somehow, men of monstrous and hateful character have always found more promising material for expressing[4] forceful and passionate sentiments. I have yet to hear from a good and gentle person an utterance that was at all spirited.

What then is the moral? That sometimes, however seldom, unwillingly and hesitatingly, you do have to write the very thing which brought you to hate all writing – but only, as in fact you would, hesitatingly and with repeated procrastination.

---

[2] Accius, Fragment 148 (p. 382), also quoted at I 12. 4 and *On Anger* I 20. 4.

[3] Nauck–Snell, *Adespota* 513. Nero himself was later to rephrase the line as he set light to Rome: 'Be earth with fire confounded while I *live*' (Suetonius, *Life of Nero* 38. 1).

[4] Reading, with Lipsius, *ingenia immania et invisa, materia secundiore expresserunt* . . .

The nature of mercy

Definitions and contraries

3 (1) But lest we be taken in by the attractive name of mercy and led into something opposed to it, we should look at what mercy is, what it is like and what its limits are.

Mercy means 'self-control by the mind when it has the power to take vengeance' or 'leniency on the part of a superior towards an inferior in imposing punishments'. It is safer to put forward several definitions; one on its own might fail to cover the subject and, so to speak, lose its case.[5] So it can also be called a 'tendency of the mind to leniency in exacting a punishment'. (2) The following definition will meet with objections, although it comes very close to the truth. We might speak of mercy as 'moderation that remits something of a deserved and due punishment'. The cry will go up that no virtue ever gives any one less than his due. But everyone realizes that mercy is something which 'stops short of what could deservedly be imposed'.

4 (1) Its opposite, or so the ill-informed think, is sternness. But no virtue is the opposite of a virtue. What, then, is the opposite of mercy? Cruelty, which is nothing other than grimness of mind in exacting punishment. 'But there are people who do not exact punishment and yet are cruel, like those who kill strangers whom they encounter, not for gain but for the sake of killing, and are not content just to slay – they are positively savage, like the notorious Busiris or Procrustes[6] or the pirates who beat their captives with whips and throw them alive to the flames.' Yes, that certainly is cruelty. But it does not involve a pursuit of retribution (they suffered no damage), nor anger at someone's misdeed, since there was no preceding crime. So it falls outside our definition,

---

[5] The Latin legal expression *formula excidere* means literally 'to lose one's case by failure to use the correct form of pleading' (*Oxford Latin Dictionary*), the *formula* being the official document drawn up by the plaintiff (in conjunction with the defendant and the magistrate) summarizing the legal issue in a suit and instructing the judge to pass judgment.

[6] Two mythical brutes. Busiris, a king of Egypt with the unpleasant habit of slaughtering on the altar of Zeus all foreigners who entered the country, was finally slain by Hercules. Procrustes, a robber in Attica who would kidnap travellers and force them to lie on one of his two beds, hammering them out, if they were too short to fit it, or lopping them, if they were too long, met the same fate at the hands of Theseus.

which covered simply the lack of self-control by the mind in exacting punishment. We might say that it is not 'cruelty' but a 'bestiality' that takes pleasure in being savage. We might call it 'madness', since there are various kinds of madness and none more obvious than that which reaches the point of slaughtering men and tearing them to pieces. (3) Those, then, whom I call cruel are people who have reason to punish but no moderation in doing so, as in the case of Phalaris.[7] His savagery was never actually turned on the innocent, we are told. It just went beyond the limit of anything humane or justifiable. We can avoid the quibble by defining cruelty to be a 'tendency of the mind to the harsher course'. Such a tendency would be repudiated by mercy and told to keep its distance. But mercy is quite compatible with sternness.

Mercy, pity, forgiveness

(4) Here it is relevant to ask what commiseration or pity[8] is. There are many who praise it as a virtue, and call the man of pity a good man. But this, too, is a mental failing. Not only in the area of sternness, but also in that of mercy, there are things which we should avoid. Under the guise of sternness we fall into cruelty, under that of mercy into pity. In the latter case, the error may be less dangerous. But error is error just the same, in any departure from the truth.

5 (1) In the same way, then, that religion serves to worship the gods while superstition dishonours them, mercy and gentleness are qualities displayed by all good men, while pity is something that they will avoid. The fault of a petty mind succumbing to the sight of evils that affect others, it is a feature very familiar in the worst kind of person. There are women, senile or silly, so affected by the tears of the nastiest criminals that, if they could, they would break open the prison. Pity looks at the plight, not at the cause of it. Mercy joins in with reason.

---

[7] See *On Anger* II 5. 1.
[8] The Latin noun here and in what follows is *misericordia*, the verb *misereri*. The obvious English translation for both is 'pity'. Unfortunately, Seneca associates them with *miseria*, 'misery'; and the only way in English to bring out this association is to use 'commiseration' and 'commiserate' as alternative translations, treating these as synonymous with 'pity'.

(2) I know that the Stoic school has a bad reputation among the ill-informed for being too hard and most unlikely to give good advice to princes and kings. The objection is that it will not allow the wise man to pity or pardon. Take these ideas out of context and they are hateful. They apparently leave no hope for human error; they would bring all lapses to punishment: (3) But if that is so, what on earth is this science which tells us to unlearn our humanity and closes our surest refuge against fortune, which we find in mutual assistance? In fact no school of philosophers is kinder or more lenient, more philanthropic or attentive to the common good – so much so that a Stoic's avowed objective is to be of use and help, taking thought not for himself alone but for each and all. (4) Commiseration is 'sorrow of the mind caused by an impression of miseries affecting other people' or 'sadness induced by bad things which happen to others without, so it thinks, their deserving them'. But no sorrow befalls the wise man. His mind is serene and nothing can occur to cloud it over. Again, nothing more befits a man than a great mind. But a mind cannot both be great and also grieving, (5) since grief blunts the wits, debases and shrivels them. And that is something which will not happen to a wise man even in his own misfortunes. On the contrary, he will beat back fortune's anger and break it at his feet. He will always have the same calm, unshaken expression,[9] which he could not do if he were open to sadness.

6 (1) Consider this, too. The wise man sees ahead and has his course of action at the ready. But nothing ever comes clear and unclouded from a disturbed source. Sadness is ill adapted for seeing how things are, for thinking out what might be useful, for avoiding what might be dangerous and working out what would be fair. So he will not feel pity or have commiseration, since that would entail a miserable state of mind. (2) Everything else, however, which I would wish to see done by people who feel pity he will do with a glad and lofty mind. He will help others in who are in tears without joining his tears to theirs. He will extend his hand to the shipwrecked traveller, his hospitality to the exile, his alms to the needy – not throwing them down in the insulting way that most of those who would like to seem full of pity do, disdaining

---

[9] The paradigm here was Socrates. See *On Anger* II 7. 1.

those whom they help and fearing to come into contact with them, but as one man giving to another man from the common store. He will grant to the weeping mother her son, order the captive to be unchained, release the gladiator from his school, give burial even to the criminal – but he will do such things with his mind calm and his countenance unchanged. (3) A wise man then, will not feel pity. But he will be of help and service, born as he is to assist the community and promote the common good. Of this help he will give each a part. Even unfortunates who deserve reproach and correction will be allowed a due measure of his kindness. But those in their affliction who struggle more valiantly[10] will receive much readier assistance from him. Whenever he can, he will intervene against fortune. What better use could there be for his resources or wealth than to restore what chance has overthrown? To be sure, his face will not fall, nor his heart sink, at the sight of a withered limb or of emaciation in rags or of old age leaning on its stick. None the less he will help all who deserve help, looking favourably, like a god, on the ill-fated.

(4) <Furthermore,> commiserating comes close to feeling miserable, having an element of it and owing something to it. As you must know, weak eyes are the ones which water at the sight of someone else's inflammation, just as it is an out-and-out sickness and not a matter of jollity always to laugh when others do, or for one's own mouth to gape open when anyone yawns. Pity is a fault of minds unduly frightened by misery. To demand this from the wise man is very close to demanding that he lament and groan at the funerals of strangers.

7 (1) 'But why will he not forgive?' Come now, let us make up our minds as to what pardon is, and we shall realize that a wise man ought not to grant it. Pardon is the remission of deserved punishment. The reason why the wise man ought not to grant this is given at greater length by those whose theme it is.[11] I for my part, as though to summarize a case that is not my own, would say: a person can only be forgiven if he deserves to be punished.

---

[10] Reading *fortius laborantibus.*

[11] Seneca could be referring simply to doxographical accounts of Stoic ethics, like that in Diogenes Laertius (VII 84–131), one whole section of which goes to questions about the wise man (117–25) and does indeed assert that the wise will 'not be pitiful nor pardon anyone' (123).

But the wise man does nothing that he ought not to do and omits nothing that he ought to do. So he will not excuse a punishment which he ought to exact. (2) But what you want to achieve through pardon can be granted to you in a more honourable way. The wise man will spare men, take thought for them and reform them. He will do the same as he would if he forgave them – but without forgiving, since to forgive is to confess that one has left undone something which ought to have been done. In one case, he may simply administer a verbal admonition without any punishment, seeing the man to be at an age still capable of correction. In another, where the man is patently labouring under an invidious accusation, he will order him to go scot-free, since he may have been misled or under the influence of alcohol. Enemies he will release unharmed, sometimes even commended, if they had an honourable reason – loyalty, a treaty, their freedom – to drive them to war. (3) All these are works of mercy, not pardon. Mercy has a freedom of decision. It judges not by legal formula, but by what is equitable and good. It can acquit or set the damages as high as it wishes. All these things it does with the idea not of doing something less than what is just but that what it decides should be the justest possible. Forgiveness, on the other hand, is failing to punish what in your judgment should be punished, while pardon is the remission of a penalty that is due. Mercy is superior above all in declaring that those released ought not to have suffered anything different. It is completer than pardon and more honourable. (4) In my opinion, the dispute is about words. On the facts, there is agreement. The wise man will remit many punishments, he will save many whose character is unsound but capable of being made sound. He will follow the example of good farmers. It is not only the straight and tall trees that they tend, but also those which for some reason are crooked – they apply poles to straighten them. Others they prune so as not to impair the height with side-branches. Where trees are weak because of the soil, they fertilize them; where they are struggling in the shade, they clear an opening for the daylight. (5) The wise man will see which character requires which method of treatment, which way to render the crooked straight . . .'

To <Serenus>
On The Private Life

Ad <Serenum>
De Otio

Introduction

Title, transmission, and addressee

On the Private Life is a fragment. It begins halfway through a word, and ends abruptly eight chapters later. Preserved in our principal manuscript[1] for Seneca's *Essays*, it is simply tacked on to chapter 27 of *On the Happy Life*[2] – the scribe must have skipped a couple of pages or more. But the table of contents in the manuscript indicates that the essay *Ad Gallionem de beata vita* (*To Gallio On the Happy Life*) was followed there by one *Ad* [erasure of seven letters] *de otio*; and *otium*, or 'the private life', is the subject of our fragment. The name of its addressee is usually restored as 'Serenus'. In that case, the work will have been addressed to Annaeus Serenus, a younger friend, possibly a relative, of Seneca's, and the addressee of two other essays, *On the Wise Man's Constancy* and *On Peace of Mind*. It will have been written before the end of 63 AD, the year of Serenus' untimely death.[3]

---

[1] The *Ambrosiana*, produced around 1060–85 at the abbey of Monte Cassino near Naples and presented c. 1605 to the newly founded Ambrosian Library in Milan by cardinal Frederico Borromeo.

[2] Which is why, in the oldest printed editions, it begins at Chapter 28!

[3] In *Letter* 63 Seneca pays tribute to Serenus, who had risen to become Nero's captain of the guards and died suddenly, probably in the year 63 or the year before, after eating a poisonous tree-fungus (something like a mushroom) at a banquet (Pliny, *Natural History* XXII 96).

Subject

The Latin word *otium*, conventionally translated as 'leisure', had the specific meaning of leisure from public activity, freedom from public responsibilities. It is in this sense – above all, as freedom to devote oneself in private to cultural and philosophical interests – that Seneca advocates it here. (That is why we have opted to translate the title with *On the Private Life*, instead of the conventional *On Leisure*.) He broaches the subject in two other essays, in *On Peace of Mind* and *On the Shortness of Life*, an exhortation to his father-in-law Paulinus to retire from public activity, as well as in a number of *Letters* (19, 21, 55, 68). But his most thorough theoretical treatment of it is in the *De Otio*, which advocates the private life in terms of what the Stoic wise man, the fully perfected human being, rather than ordinary mortals like Paulinus or Serenus or Seneca himself, should be doing.

Seneca's thesis was controversial, as the incredulous opposition of his addressee shows (1. 4, 6. 1, 6. 5, 7. 2). From the beginning the Stoics, unlike Aristotle, had insisted that philosophical or scientific enquiry was of value only for its benefit to human life. They rejected any category of 'higher' – theoretical or contemplative – studies to be pursued for their own sake. Human reason, they believed, is essentially practical; its natural function is to acquire and then to apply the knowledge necessary for leading a good, active human life. At the same time, this knowledge embraces not only ethics, but logic and physics, which itself includes natural science and theology. To live good human lives, we must understand ourselves accurately as functional parts of a divinely directed world-order, while the processes and structures of reasoning studied in logic are the very processes by which that world-order is constituted. Seneca is therefore on solid ground in arguing that Stoicism does at least support a deep devotion to philosophical studies, since a 'practical' life, if it is to be led well, must be grounded in such studies. And he can claim with some plausibility (6. 4) that Zeno and Chrysippus, in fact, 'did' more for their fellow men by inactive lives spent in thinking and writing than they could ever have done by public 'activity'.

Argument

Our fragment starts somewhere near the beginning of the work. Its opening exhortation to the private life (1. 1–3) meets with the objection that this sounds more like advice from Epicurus – famous for the slogan 'Live unnoticed!' – than from a Stoic (1. 4 f.). Whereupon Seneca, following the standard rhetorical procedure, moves on to *propositio* and *divisio*, to stating his claim and 'dividing' what he has to say into parts (2). He will argue, firstly, that Stoic principles permit one to give oneself over 'entirely, even from earliest youth' to philosophical study – in other words, to abstain from public life altogether – and, secondly, that 'one has every right to do this on completion of service', that is, after formal retirement. (The fragment breaks off before this second topic is reached.)

Stoics and Epicureans alike say that the wise man will abstain from public life – Seneca here would stress the agreement between the two schools.[4] The difference between them is simply that Epicurus recommends such abstention on principle, the Stoics only when there are special reasons for it. There are, broadly, two such reasons. Either the public realm is beyond redemption, or the wise man himself may not be up to the job of redeeming it. He may not have enough influence, or his health may be be bad (3. 1–3). So he is entitled to remain in private life, where he can still be of use to others (3. 4 f.). For in fact there are *two* public domains, *two* commonwealths, as Seneca goes on to argue in an eloquent exposition of a Stoic theme (4). We all belong, not only to some particular political community such as Athens or Carthage, but also to the grander, divinely ordered cosmic community of gods and men, which we can serve by studying and instructing others about the natural world and how to live a fully human life there. Nature has intended us to make such enquiries (5), to contemplate as well as to act. The two entail one another (5. 8), since action presupposes the insights acquired through contemplation, while contemplation issues in action. Seneca goes on to argue (7) that the three things traditionally regarded

---

[4] Rather as he does at *On Mercy* 1 3. 2.

as worth doing in life – contemplation, public activity or just enjoying oneself – all involve one another and that all schools of philosophy really approve of the contemplative life.

Chapters 4 and 5 are quite the most impressive in the essay as we have it. Between them, they certainly suggest that the contemplative life, if it means sharing with God the governance of the whole cosmos, is something vastly superior to participation in the politics of some particular community. The founders of the Stoa had in fact been prevented from taking part in Athenian public life (6. 4 f.). That was one of the two special reasons mentioned at the beginning (3. 3) which the Stoic wise man might have for resigning himself to a private existence. In the final surviving chapter (8), Seneca moves onto the other main reason, and makes a much stronger claim. On the principle laid down by Chrysippus, he says, the Stoic wise man is not merely allowed, he can freely choose – even if he is in a position to play an effective part in public life – to abstain from doing so, since no commonwealth in the world as we know it is good enough for him. But that is virtually to claim that he will abstain, like the Epicurean wise man, on principle: under all actual circumstances, he will prefer to neglect practical politics and to devote himself to private study and writing. This goes against what Seneca says elsewhere.[5] And it conflicts with other Stoic teaching.[6] Seneca's language in fact suggests that he is out of sympathy with this argument.[7] It looks as though he is on the point of asserting the intellectual independence proclaimed at 3. 1 and taking Chrysippus to task, as he does elsewhere[8] – or else of denying that these really are implications of Chrysippus' principle. But the text breaks off, and we cannot say what came next.

[5] Notably at *On Peace of Mind* 5. 3, where he cites the courage of Socrates at the time of the thirty tyrants as proof that 'even when the state is in ruins there will be occasion for the wise man to show his worth'. On the apparent discrepancies between this work and the final chapter of *On the Private Life*, see Griffin pp. 331–4.

[6] According to Stobaeus (II p. 94. 8–11), the Stoic wise man will indeed take part in public life, particularly in those states which hold out some chance of being perfected. Similarly (p. 111, 3–5), a man of sense would be willing to rule as a king, or to live as an adviser to one with a promising moral disposition.

[7] See n. 20 to 8. 1.

[8] See *On Favours* I. 4.

We can only speculate about the subsequent arguments for retirement after a career of public service and how these would have tied in with those in the surviving text for abstention from public life altogether. Nor can we do more than make guesses about the relation between *On the Private Life* and Seneca's own career. Was he himself contemplating retirement when he wrote it? Or had his experience with Nero led him to doubt whether philosophy could ever have its due influence on the conduct of public affairs? The fragmentary character of our text does not permit an answer.

On The Private Life

Preface

1 (1) ***** with great accord they urge vices upon us.[1] Even if we do nothing else for our well-being, our retreat will itself do us good; we shall be better on our own. And what if we retreat into the best company[2] and select a model there for our lives? That only happens in retirement. It is then that decisions once made can be realized, when no one intervenes with the help of the populace to deflect a judgment which is still weak.[3] It is then that life, fragmented by an enormous variety of aims, can follow an even, unitary course. (2) For the worst of our evils is that we vary our vices themselves. Thus we cannot even manage to persist in evil already familiar. One thing after another appeals to us, and we have the further vexation that our judgments are not only perverse but fickle. We fluctuate, and grasp one thing after another. We abandon what we sought and seek again what we abandoned. We alternate between desire and regret. (3) We depend entirely on the judgments of others; what seems best to us is what the many pursue and praise, not that which deserves pursuit and praise; nor do we judge a path to be good or bad by itself, but by the number of footprints on it – and none of them coming back![4]

[1] The beginning of the essay has clearly been lost. See Introduction, p. 167
[2] By 'the best company' Seneca means the company of great writers, particularly that of the leading Stoic philosophers.
[3] The Stoics saw the influence of other people as one of the two main factors in the 'perversion' of human reason in childhood, the other being the sheer persuasiveness of external things (*SVF* III 228).
[4] I.e. these are ways of no return, they lead to moral annihilation. Seneca is alluding (as Horace does to rather similar effect at *Epistles* I 1. 70–5) to the fable of the fox and the lion.

Can a Stoic choose the private life?

Stoic and Epicurean attitudes

(4) You will say to me: 'What do you mean, Seneca? Are you deserting your party? Surely your Stoics say: "Till the final extremity of life we shall remain in action. We shall not cease to devote ourselves to the good of the community, to aid the individual, to raise an aged hand to assist even our enemies. We are the ones who grant no respite for age – as that excellent author puts it,

we press the helmet to our grizzled hair.[5]

We are they for whom there is not a moment's inactivity till death – so much so that death itself, if we had our say, would not be inactive." Why are you, in Zeno's own headquarters, uttering precepts of Epicurus?[6] If you are displeased with your party, why not defect outright, instead of betraying it?'

(5) For the moment, I shall just answer: 'Surely you can only want me to be like my leaders? Well then, I shall not go where they send me but where they lead.'

Division of the subject

2 (1) Next, I shall prove to you that I am not abandoning the precepts of the Stoa. It is not even that the Stoics themselves have abandoned them, though I would have every excuse for following not their precepts but their example. I will divide what I have to say into two parts. Firstly, that one can give oneself over entirely, even from earliest youth, to the contemplation of truth, seeking the principle of living and practising it in secret. (2) Secondly, that one has every right to do this on completion of service, when the best of life is over, and to turn the mind to other activities,[7] like the Vestal virgins[8] whose years are allotted to different duties; they

---

[5] Vergil, *Aeneid* IX 612.
[6] On Zeno, the founder of the Stoa, and Epicurus, see Biographical Notes.
[7] Reading, with Lipsius, *ad alios actus animum referre*. Only the first topic in Seneca's programme, that an initial decision to abstain from politics can be justified on Stoic principles, is handled – and that incompletely – in the text as we have it. Some of Seneca's views on the subject of retiring after active service can be extracted from other works, notably *On the Shortness of Life* and *On Peace of Mind*.
[8] Concerning whom see also *On Favours* I 3. 1.

learn to perform the sacred rites and, having learned them, teach them.

3 (1) I shall show that the Stoics too have this doctrine. It is not that I make it a rule not to do anything contrary to what Zeno or Chrysippus[9] say. Rather, the facts themselves allow me to go along with their opinion. To follow one person all the time is to belong not to a court, but a clique. If only things were all fully grasped! If only truth were open and acknowledged, and we never changed our principles! As it is, we must search for the truth along with the very people who would teach it.

(2) Two schools, on this point as on others, are particularly at variance, the Epicureans and the Stoics. But each of them directs you, by a different route, to the private life. Epicurus says: 'The wise man will not go into public life, unless something interferes.' Zeno says: 'He will go into public life, unless something impedes.' (3) The former aims for a private life on principle, the latter on special grounds. But these grounds are wide in extent. If the public realm is too corrupt to be helped, if it has been taken over by the wicked, the wise man will not struggle pointlessly nor squander himself to no avail. If he has too little authority or strength, if the public realm will not accept him or his health impedes him, in the same way that he will not launch a battered ship onto the sea or register for military service if disabled, he will not embark on a course which he knows he cannot manage.

The two commonwealths

(4) So it is possible even for one whose resources are still intact, before experiencing any storms, to settle in safety, apply himself thenceforth to liberal arts and demand uninterrupted retirement, a devotee of the virtues which even the quietest can exercise. (5) What is required, you see, of any man is that he should be of use to other men – if possible, to many; failing that, to a few; failing that, to those nearest him; failing that, to himself. For when he makes himself useful to others, he busies himself for the community. In the same way that he who makes himself worse harms not himself alone but everyone whom he could have benefitted had he

---

[9] The third head of the Stoa. See Biographical Notes.

become better, so anyone who serves himself well is of use to others by the very fact of preparing what will be of use to them.

4 (1) We must grasp that there are two public realms, two commonwealths.[10] One is great and truly common to all, where gods as well as men are included, where we look not to this corner or that, but measure its bounds with the sun. The other is that in which we are enrolled by an accident of birth – I mean Athens or Carthage or some other city that belongs not to all men but only a limited number. Some devote themselves at the same time to both commonwealths, the greater and the lesser, some only to the one or the other. (2) We can serve this greater commonwealth even in retirement – indeed better, I suspect, in retirement – by enquiring what virtue is, whether it is one or many, whether nature or art makes men good; whether this receptacle of earth and sea and of things attached to earth and sea is one, or whether God has strewn abroad a multitude of such bodies; whether the matter from which all things come to be is altogether continuous and a plenum, or dispersed, with an intermixture of void and solid bodies; where God resides, whether he views his handiwork in idleness or acts upon it, and whether he surrounds it from without or pervades its entirety; whether the world is immortal, or to be numbered among things that collapse and are temporal.[11] What service to God is there in this contemplation? That the greatness of his work be not without witness.

Nature, contemplation and action

5 (1) We[12] regularly say that the highest good is to live according to nature; and Nature has begotten us for both – to contemplate reality and to act. Let me now prove what I just said. And yet,

---

[10] With what follows compare the very similar assertions of the Stoic speaker Balbus in Cicero's *On the Nature of the Gods* (II 154 f.).

[11] Seneca here lists the principal questions of moral and natural philosophy disputed among the various philosophical schools in the Hellenistic period. He formulates the questions of natural philosophy in the context especially of the dispute between Stoics (who believed in a creative and provident god pervading a single continuous world-order) and Epicureans (atomists who believed in many world-orders coming into being and passing away by purely natural causes without any influence from the gods).

[12] I.e. we Stoics.

why should I? It will be proved, if each consults himself on the extent of his appetite for knowledge of the unknown and his excitement at any report of it. (2) There are people who sail the seas and endure the toils of the longest journey for the sole reward of coming to know something hidden and far away. That is what packs the crowds into public spectacles, what compels people to pry into things barred to them, to search out things ever more hidden, to unravel antiquities and hear about the ways of barbarous nations. (3) Nature has given us a mind full of curiosity.[13] Aware of her own skill and beauty, she brought us into being to view the mighty spectacle. She would lose all satisfaction in herself, were she to display works so great and glorious, so delicately drawn, so bright and, in more ways than one, so beautiful, to a lonely solitude. (4) You can realize that her wish was to be viewed, and not just seen, if you look at the place that we were given. We were established in her midst and given a commanding view of all things. Not only was man stood upright. To fit him for contemplation, enabling him to follow the stars from their rising as they glide to their fall and to turn his face with the turning world, she raised his head aloft and placed it upon a neck which he can move. Moreover, she caused six signs of the zodiac to rise by day and six by night, revealing every region of herself, so that through those things which she had made visible to his eye she might arouse an appetite for the rest. (5) We cannot cast our eyes upon all things or their true extent. But our perspicacity has uncovered a way of investigation and put down a basis for truth, allowing enquiry to proceed from the obvious to the obscure and discover things older than the world itself. What was the source of these stars? What was the condition of the universe before the different elements separated to form its parts? What is the principle which unfolded them while they were immersed and indistinct? Who put things in their place? Was it by their nature that heavy things fell and light things rose – or, quite apart from physical thrust and weight, did

---

[13] For a Greek or Roman reader, this would be a paradox. *Curiositas* was generally seen as a matter of prying into things that are none of one's business, and these were commonly thought to include the secrets of nature. To claim, with Seneca or Aristotle at the start of the *Metaphysics*, that men were intended by nature to enquire into her secrets, was to express a view that was by no means universally accepted.

some higher power lay down the law for them? What is the truth of that argument for the divine spirit in men, that a part of it – sparks, as it were, from the stars – leaped down to earth and was caught in an alien environment?

(6) Our speculation has burst through the ramparts of heaven, not content to know merely what is shown to it. 'I investigate', it says, 'what lies beyond the world. Is it a vast abyss or has it limits of its own to enclose it? And what is the condition of things outside? Are they shapeless and indistinct, taking up the same room in all directions? Or are they also arranged in some order? Are they contiguous with this world or withdrawn far from it, leaving it to turn in a vacuum? Is it out of indivisible bodies that anything which has been or will be born is constructed? Or is their matter a continuum, subject throughout to transformation? Are the elements contrary to one another – or is it that, rather than clashing, they work variously together?'

(7) Man was born to ask such questions. Think how little time he has, even if he claims every moment for himself! Suppose that he allows nothing to escape him through self-indulgence, nothing to slip away through carelessness, that he hoards his hours with the utmost parsimony, that he reaches the ultimate limit of human life and that nothing in him decreed by nature is deranged by fortune – none the less, for knowledge of things immortal, man is all *too* mortal. (8) So I live according to Nature if I devote myself wholly to her, if I marvel at her and worship her. Nature wished me to do both – to act and to be free for contemplation. I am doing both. Even contemplation involves action.

6 (1) 'But it matters', you may say, 'whether you go to it just for pleasure. You could be seeking nothing besides uninterrupted contemplation without any outcome – contemplation is agreeable and has its attractions.' To this my reply will be: it matters just as much what your attitude is in your political life. Are you always on the go, allowing yourself no time to turn from things human to things divine? (2) To seek wealth, without any love of virtue and without mental cultivation, and merely to make exertions are not at all commendable (these all need to be combined with one another and intertwined). In the same way, virtue is an incomplete and feeble good when wasted on a retirement without activity, never displaying what it has learned. (3) No one would deny that

virtue should test its progress by action; that, instead of just pon-
dering what should be done, it should at some stage put a hand
to it and turn its ideas into reality. But suppose that the wise man
himself is not the cause of delay, that there is nothing lacking in
the agent, just a lack of things to do – you will surely allow him
his own company then?

(4) What is the wise man's attitude as he retreats into retirement?
One of knowing that, even then, he will be doing things for the
benefit of posterity. We are certainly ones to claim that Zeno and
Chrysippus accomplished more than if they had commanded armies,
held public office and passed laws – and they did pass laws, though
not for just one state but for the entire human race! So why should
such retirement be wrong for the good man, if it enables him to
govern the centuries to come and address not just a few men but
all men of all nations, present and future? (5) In short, I put the
question to you, did Cleanthes[14] and Chrysippus and Zeno live by
their teachings? You will certainly reply that they did live as they
said one should live. Yet none of them administered the affairs of
a commonwealth. 'But they did not have the fortune or the standing
that normally gets people into public administration.'[15] None the
less, they did not lead idle lives. They found a way to make their
very repose more profitable to men than the bustle and sweat of
others. Hence they can be seen to have done much, though they
did nothing in the public realm.

7 (1) Moreover, there are three kinds of life,[16] and it is regularly
asked which is the best. One is given to pleasure, the other to
contemplation, the third to action. If we first put aside all conten-
tiousness and that implacable hatred which we declare on those
who follow a different rule from ours, we can see that all three
come to the same conclusion under one label or another. The man
who favours pleasure has not dispensed with contemplation, nor
the contemplative with pleasure; nor has he whose life is dedicated

---

[14] Cleanthes of Assos (331?–232 BC), the second head of the Stoa.
[15] Zeno from Citium in Cyprus, Cleanthes from Assos in north-west Asia Minor
and Chrysippus from Soli in Cilcia were none of them free-born Athenian ctizens.
As mere resident aliens they were not entitled to take part in Athenian public life.
[16] This classic distinction goes back to Aristotle (*Nicomachean Ethics* 1095b15–19)
and earlier.

to action dispensed with contemplation. (2) 'But it makes a very great difference', you may say, 'whether a thing is an objective or an accessory to some other objective.' The difference, I grant you, is great. Yet you cannot have one without the other. The contemplative cannot contemplate without action, the man of action cannot act without contemplation; nor does that third character, of whom we have agreed to think ill, favour an idle pleasure but one which he has made stable by his reason.[17] So this very school of voluptuaries is also committed to activity. (3) Why should it not be? Epicurus himself says that he will sometimes withdraw from pleasure and even go for pain, if the pleasure is threatened by remorse, or a lesser pain is to take the place of one more serious.[18] (4) My point is that all schools approve of contemplation. Others make for it directly. We treat it as an anchorage, not a harbour.

Is any commonwealth fit for the wise?

8 (1) Note also that the law[19] laid down by Chrysippus allows you to live in retirement – I do not mean just putting up with retirement, but choosing it. Our school says that the wise man will not attach himself to just any commonwealth. But what difference does it make how the wise man comes to retirement, whether it is that the right commonwealth is unavailable to him or that he himself is unavailable to the commonwealth, if no such commonwealth is going to be available to any wise man? But there will never be one available to the choosy.[20] (2) I ask you, what commonwealth is any wise man going to attach himself to? The Athenian? That was where Socrates was condemned, where Aristotle had to

---

[17] Seneca is recalling Epicurus' theory that the good is not to be found in 'kinetic', sensual pleasures of eating, drinking and sex, but rather in 'static' pleasure: enjoying the stable condition that comes about when one is experiencing no distress or physical need. And that requires the use of reason, not bodily titillation. See e.g. Cicero, *On Ends* II 9–10; Epicurus, *Letter to Menoeceus* 131–2.

[18] See Epicurus, *Letter to Menoeceus* 129–30.

[19] I.e. the principle that Seneca cites above (3. 2) as Zeno's, that the wise man 'will go into public life, unless something impedes'.

[20] The Latin word here, *fastidiose*, is not a term of praise. If it is only if they are 'choosy' that wise men will always opt for a private life, perhaps it does not follow after all, for Seneca, that 'retirement becomes a necessity for all wise men' (as he infers below, 8. 3). See Griffin, pp. 332 f.

flee to avoid condemnation,[21] where envy oppresses the excellent.[22] You cannot be telling me that the wise man will attach himself to *that* commmonwealth! The Carthaginian, then? That seat of unremitting sedition, where the best men were menaced by liberty, where fairness and goodness were held in utter contempt, where inhuman cruelty towards enemies extended to enmity even towards its own citizens! He will flee that one as well. (3) Were I to go through each commonwealth, I would not find one that could endure the wise man or be endured by him. But if no commonwealth is to be found of the kind that we imagine, retirement becomes a necessity for all wise men, because the one thing which could be preferred to retirement nowhere exists. (4) If someone says that sailing is best and then says that you should not sail on a sea where shipwrecks regularly occur and there are often sudden storms to sweep the helmsman off course, he would be telling me, I think, not to weigh anchor, though speaking in praise of sailing. *****

---

[21] In the outburst of anti-Macedonian feeling at Athens which followed the death of Alexander in 323 BC, Aristotle (whose close association with both Philip and Alexander was widely known) found himself accused of impiety and 'rather than let the Athenians sin twice against philosophy', retired to Chalcis where he died the following year.

[22] A complaint regularly levelled against democracies.

To Aebutius Liberalis
On Favours

Ad Aebutium Liberalem
De Beneficiis

Introduction

Addressee and date

On Favours is dedicated to a certain Aebutius Liberalis, a native of Lyons[1] whose generosity Seneca praises at V 1. 3. We know next to nothing about him apart from what we learn from Seneca himself. Quite conceivably, he was chosen as the addressee of a work on acts of kindness simply because of his highly appropriate name, Liberalis.[2]

The work was written after the death in AD 56 of the infamous Caninius Rebilus (Tacitus, *Annals* XIII 30), whom Seneca mentions at II 21. 6 in terms quite impossible if he were still alive, and probably after that of Nero's mother, Agrippina, in AD 59. Had she still been alive and powerful, he would not have written so favourably of Crispus Passienus (I 15. 5), her second husband who had been murdered at her instigation. The bulk of the work must have been completed before the composition, in summer AD 64, of *Letters* 81 which refers to 'our books on favours'.[3] In fact it probably antedates the earthquake of 62 which destroyed a great part of Pompeii (Tacitus, *Annals* XV 22).[4] This sensational disaster inspired Seneca to an eloquent meditation on human mortality

---

[1] His distress at its destruction by fire in AD 64 is the starting-point of Seneca's *Letter* 91.
[2] See Griffin, p. 455 and p. 319 n. 5.
[3] 81. 3. The letter is itself on the same subject.
[4] Not to be confused with the earthquake of AD 78 which finished off the town altogether.

(*Investigations into Nature* VI Pref.). Had it occurred by the time he was writing *On Favours*, he might have been more hesitant than he is at IV 6. 2 in describing the world as a large habitation 'without risk of fire or subsidence'.

Title and subject

The standard rendering of *De beneficiis* by translators of Seneca into English, from Thomas Lodge in 1613 onwards, has been 'On Benefits',[5] in much the same way that Cicero's *De officiis* was known for generations as 'Tully's Offices'. Unfortunately, the Latin *beneficium* means, strictly, 'benefaction' or 'kindly deed', whereas the ordinary sense of 'benefit', in modern usage, is 'advantage, profit, good'. A 'benefit' is something which results – something which you receive – from a benefaction.[6] But Seneca's concern is very much with the activity and its motives, and the easiest English translation for *beneficia*, almost all the time, is 'favours',[7] though there are places where 'kindnesess' or even 'acts of kindness' read better.[8]

What counted as a *beneficium*? Covering 'both an action that does good and an object bestowed by that action – for instance, a sum of money, a house, a robe of office' (II 34. 5), the word could describe any action or gift, official or private, for which the recipient might have reason to be grateful.[9] Seneca himself offers some orientation. At I 11, he distinguishes three kinds

---

[5] *The Workes of Lucius Annaeus Seneca both Morall and Naturall* (London 1614). An earlier translaton, by Arthur Golding (1578), had paraphrased the title, verbosely but not inaccurately, as '*The woorke of the exellent Philosopher Lucius Annaeus Seneca concerning Benefyting, that is to say the dooing, receyving and requyting of good Turnes*'.

[6] In the same way, 'to benefit' someone implies more than *bene facere*, doing him a kindness. It suggests that he really *does* derive some advantage or profit. In Lodge's day, the range of the term was wider. 'Benefit' could indeed then mean a 'good deed,' a 'kindly deed,' as in the Authorized Version Epistle to Philemon 14: 'that thy benefit should not be as it were of necessity, but willingly'.

[7] This requires a slight change of idiom from the Latin. Seneca speaks of 'giving' as well as 'receiving' and 'returning' a *beneficium* (*dare, accipere, reddere*). In ordinary English, a 'favour' or 'kindness' is 'done' rather than 'given', though it can be 'granted', and it can certainly be 'accepted' or 'returned'. We adopt those idioms in our translation.

[8] E.g. I 4. 6, 15. 1.

[9] Cf. Veyne, p. 348 f.

of *beneficia*: indispensable, useful and agreeable. The paradigm of the first is rescuing someone from mortal danger – from proscription (II 11. 1), from pirates (I 5. 4) or shipwreck (IV 37) – or defending his reputation in court and preserving his liberty (II 35. 3) or saving his son's life or pardoning his father (II 25. 1); the 'useful' kind covers all sorts of political, social or material assistance – awards of public office (I 5.1, II 27. 4), grants of citizenship, gifts of land, property and money, not to mention taking on a person's debts (II 7. 2); while 'agreeable' *beneficia* include presents of books and wine. Elsewhere Seneca provides further information, and begins to impose his own philosophical principles. To count as a *beneficium*, a good turn must be substantial – a triviality like throwing a coin to a beggar is not enough; and it must be done for the sake of the beneficiary (IV. 29). It must also be *voluntary*. A favour is a spontaneous action (I 6. 1), an expression of unconstrained good will towards the recipient. (As such, it can be distinguished from an *officium* or 'duty'.) It is not an acknowledgment of some right or some undeniable claim on the recipient's part.[10] Nor does a favour create any legal obligation. It has no 'market value'. For there is no agreement as to what constitutes any particular favour nor about its extent (III 7. 6); the imponderables – the attitudes of the parties involved, their circumstances and so forth – are just too many. Thus favours cannot be exchanged with the precision possible for transactions in goods and services which do have a market value,[11] – and this means that ingratitude, while detestable, can never be, as fraud is, a proper subject for litigation (III 6–17). Of course, favours should be repaid. But their repayment, though it may certainly be found adequate or inadequate, cannot be accurately measured against them. It will often be unequal and incommensurable, since 'a favour can be done in one way and returned in another' (III 9. 3). A rich man, for instance, might provide oil for the public baths and, in return, be awarded a statue in his honour.[12]

---

[10] Hence *beneficium* can be contrasted with *iudicium*, a judgment of merit based on compelling grounds. See below on I 15. 5.

[11] When Seneca uses commercial language and describes a favour as 'a loan that cannot be repaid' (IV 12. 1 f.), he is admits that he is resorting to metaphor.

[12] The example used by Veyne and Murray (in his introduction to Veyne, p. xiv).

Indeed, to revert to Seneca's examples, the proper return for the money, the house or the robe of office might sometimes be just good will and gratitude. The Stoics were merely exaggerating an elementary fact when they claimed paradoxically that, in general, 'to accept a favour gladly is already to have repaid it' (II 31).

Background and sources

On Favours is a work about acts of kindness by individuals to other individuals.[13] Seneca is not concerned with the spectacular benefactions – the erection of lavish public buildings, the financing of festivals and so forth – by monarchs, magistrates and local notables – to entire communities,[14] important though these were in the ancient world. But he can still speak of favours as 'the thing which, more than anything else, holds society together'.[15] He was appealing to a long-recognized fact of life. Ancient society was very much a nexus of allegiances created and sustained by favours of one sort or another. (So, to a lesser extent, is modern society.) Their significance for social cohesion had been noted by Democritus (Fragment 255), and Aristotle touches on the subject in ways that anticipate Seneca. He too looks at the question of how to gauge the extent of a favour (*Nicomachean Ethics* VIII 13, 1163a9–23). He draws the same sort of analogy as Seneca does (II 33. 2) between the attitude of a benefactor and that of artists towards their creations (IX 7. 1167b33–68a3). And in the *Rhetoric*, he

---

[13] Hence the need to discriminate, to ask yourself 'What to do for whom, how and when?' (see I 15. 1–3, II 15. 3, IV 9. 2–11, etc.). The only passage where Seneca touches on benefactions to the community at large is when he takes the kindness of the gods to mankind as a whole and discusses the problem which this poses to individual human beings who seek to imitate the gods: IV 28).

[14] On which, see Veyne, *passim*. The purpose of such benefactions, rather like that of the precious gifts that Homeric heroes presented to their visitors (on which see O. Murray, *Early Greece* (London 1980), pp. 50–2), was to make friends for the benefactor and influence people, to acquire honour and create good will. On the ancient 'gift economy', of which these practices are just one aspect, see *ibid.*, p. xiv and, more generally, M. Mauss, *The Gift*, English edn., (London 1954) p. 2.

[15] (I 4. 2). Cicero had likewise seen favours and gratitude as the very 'bonds of concord' (*On Ends* II 117).

Introduction

defines χάρις (Latin *gratia*)[16] in terms of 'a service to someone who needs it, not in return for anything nor for the advantage of the person doing the service but for the other person'.[17]

Seneca's principal inspiration, however, came from earlier Stoic works *On Favours*.[18] Cleanthes, the second head of the school, had written one,[19] so had Chrysippus.[20] But Seneca's main source would seem to be Hecaton, a pupil of Panaetius and like him the author of a work *On Duties*, which very probably included a discussion of favours.[21] Apart from a few fragments, these writings are all lost. But we are fortunate that Seneca's excellent and comprehensive essay has preserved so much Stoic thought about favours. He writes as a convinced Stoic, proud of the doctrine that man is a 'social animal born for the common good' (*On Mercy* I 3. 2), 'begotten for mutual assistance' (*On Anger* I 5. 2).[22] His school found evidence for this in the 'mutual attraction' that human beings naturally feel for one another and that is evident already in the behaviour of infants.[23] Not that we should or can live our adult lives simply on the basis of such natural feelings. But they do indicate that concern for others and mutual assistance are among the 'natural norms'[24] which serve to define the proper sort of life for a human being. Accordingly, as adults no longer acting by instinct but by our own understanding of what the proper life is, we should recognize that mutual assistance and

[16] On the meanings of the Greek term see n. 5 on I 3. 2. They include the 'benevolence' which leads you to do a kindness and the 'gratitude' that you may feel on receiving one, as well as the act of kindness itself.
[17] II 7, 1385a17–19. The question of how to judge a favour was to find its way into the rhetorical curriculum. See Cicero, *De Inventione* II 112.
[18] Seneca's sources for *On Favours* are discussed at length by F.-R. Chaumartin, *Le De Beneficiis de Sénèque, sa signification philosophique, politique et morale* (Paris 1985), pp. 31–154.
[19] περὶ χάριτος, Diogenes Laertius, VII 175. Seneca's three references in *On Favours* (V 14. 1, VI 10. 2 and 12. 2) to Cleanthes may derive from that work.
[20] Seneca discusses Chrysippus' views at I 3. 8 ff., II 17. 3 and 25. 3, and III 22. 1.
[21] Seneca cites Hecaton at I 3. 9, II 21. 4 ff., III 18, VI 37. 1.
[22] See also *On Mercy* II 5. 3, 6. 3; *On the Private Life* I. 4, 3. 5. In *On Favours* IV 18. 2–4 the theme recurs in the guise of that 'fellowship' (*societas*) which he says god or nature endowed human beings with, along with reason, for their mutual protection against the predations of physically much better endowed animals.
[23] See Cicero, *On Ends* III 62–3.
[24] See General Introduction p. XXIII.

187

concern for the good of others are important elements in it. If some sorts of assistance, such as giving a stranger directions to the next town, are mere duties of common humanity, the more substantial and more personal forms that count as 'favours' (IV 29) are the most important expression that this recognition can take. As always with the Stoics, it is the spirit in which favours are done and received – when they are done solely for their own sake or that of the recipient and are gratefully received on that basis – that gives them their human value. In this way, Seneca's complex and detailed discussion of doing, accepting and repaying favours grows into a grander discussion of human morality in general and of the ties which bind individual human beings together to form a society.

Argument

Our translation of *On Favours* covers only the first four of its seven books. Seneca himself says that everything essential to the subject has been defined and discussed in them; what remain for the other three books are ancillary questions, attractive but unnecessary, that 'do not really repay the effort, but are not entirely a waste of it' (V 1. 2).

The subject itself, Seneca tells us (V 1. 1), is bounded by the questions how to do a favour and how to accept one. He gives these a thorough and systematic treatment in Books I and II, texts – by his standards – of quite unusual perspicuity and single-mindedness. Book I begins with a vivid Introduction (1–4) which culminates in a memorable image of the three Graces. Holding hands as they dance, they symbolize that 'sequence of kindness, passing from one hand to another', coming back to the initial giver and passing on again from that person, which is at its 'loveliest' if the 'succession is maintained' (3. 4). Seneca then defines what a favour is: an act of spontaneous good will (6. 1). Sharply distinguishing the performance of this act from its vehicle, the 'material' aid or gift which, confusingly, can also be described by the word 'favour' (*beneficium*), he illustrates the distinction with a story about Socrates and his pupils (8–9. 1). After a digression of uncertain length (there is a gap in the text) on the special odiousness of ingratitude (9. 2–10), the rest of the book (11–15) goes to discussing what favours one should grant. Next comes the manner in which one should grant them – promptly, sometimes openly sometimes in secret, never arrogantly, and always with regard for the beneficiary's true interests. This is discussed in the first half of Book II (1–17). There follows a second major analogy, between the exchange of kindnesses and a game of ball (17. 2–8). After this, the second half of the book (18–35) deals with questions about accepting favours – whom to accept a favour from (18. 3–21) and the right way to accept it: one should do so cheerfully and with grateful acknowledgment of the benefactor's good will (22–5). Then comes another digression on ingratitude, this time on its motives (26–31, a passage with some notable reminiscences of *On Anger*), after which the book returns to its proper subject with a vigorous defence of the Stoic paradox that 'to accept a favour gladly is to have repaid it' (31–6).

Already in Book II Seneca has shown signs of abandoning the strict plan of 'how to do a favour' and 'how to accept one' for the looser and more comfortable format of 'questions' to do with favours. Books III and IV are entirely in that format. Illuminating the main subject from a variety of angles, they make their most important points obliquely in the course of answering various specific questions about favours. Book III opens with yet further reflections on ingratitude – or rather on forgetfulness, the worst form of it (1–5). It then asks whether ingratitude should be made subject to legal prosecution. Seneca's answer, not surprisingly, is that it should not. But the discussion is revealing, in several ways. That he should think the question worth such attention reveals how seriously he regards ingratitude. As a violation of social good order, it is comparable to many offences which are indeed subject to legal penalties. What renders favours unsuitable for this particular form of public sanction is simply their personal, subjective character. And that is the crucial point. You cannot treat a favour as a business transaction without ruining it (14. 4). You cannot hedge it with guarantees. You can only rely on the good faith of the other party. The discussion culminates with a satirical picture of the legal devices used to secure a business transaction (15. 1 f.) 'What a shameful acknowledgment of human fraudulence!', cries Seneca (15. 3). The fact that Roman law in the previous century had made some progress in bringing bad faith to book[25] is of no concern to him. He is writing not as a social or legal reformer, but as a moralist urging the reader to transcend the squalid commercial attitudes of ordinary life – to copy the gods, not the money-lenders (15. 4) – and become a better person. (His attitude here matches that in *On Mercy*, which found the decisive factor in the well-being of the state not in some constitutional reform, but simply in the moral excellence of the prince.)

The same tacit exhortation to rise above the roles and limitations of normal social life can be found in the rest of Book III (18–38), where Seneca enquires whether a slave can do his master a favour (18–28) and whether a child can outdo the favour done by its parent in bringing it into the world (29–36). 'Favours', involving as they do no prior obligation, can be distinguished from the menial 'services' which a slave has to do and from the 'duties' incumbent upon a member of a family (18. 1). It might seem as though, strictly speaking, a slave can never do his master a favour and what might otherwise look like favours by a son, whose legal position in Roman law was not altogether unlike that of a slave,[26] are merely a discharge of filial duty. In arguing the contrary, Seneca is not only defending, as impressively as any ancient writer, the essential dignity – we might almost say, the essential rights – of all human beings.[27] He is also inviting us to rise above conventional roles and attitudes to a more generous morality of which all rational animals – master or slave, parent or child – are capable.

[25] Notably in the celebrated *formulae de dolo* by Cicero's contemporary Gaius Aquillius Gallus (praetor 66 BC). See Cicero, *On Duties* III 60; *On the Nature of the Gods* III 74.
[26] See Crook, pp. 107–13.
[27] At III 18.2, Seneca does in fact speak of a slave's *ius humanum*, 'human rights'. Recalling as it does a legal concept like *ius Latii* 'Latin rights' (a qualified form of Roman citizenship), Seneca's *ius humanum* might well suggest citizenship in the world-wide human community, in the cosmic city of gods and men (see General Introduction, p. xxv). But, just in case we might be tempted to translate the suggestion into some political doctrine of universal human rights, Seneca promptly and typically adds: 'what matters is *the state of mind*, not the status'.

Book IV takes a more philosophical turn. Seneca defends at length (1–25) the Stoic doctrine that doing favours and being grateful are things 'to be chosen for their own sake' against the Epicurean view that they originated, and are practised to this day, solely because they increase our common safety and mutual pleasure. The defence begins and ends with theology (4–9, 25). With much eloquence, Seneca argues that our favours, like those of the gods towards us, should be done without thought of future recompense. We should model our actions on theirs, since our natures as rational beings can only be perfected if we follow the lead of those rational beings whose actions are already perfect; and the gods, in favouring us with the world order and all that it provides for the enhancement of our lives, have no thought for anything but the intrinsic value of what they are doing. This does not mean, however, that our favours should be indiscriminate, but rather that we should discriminate on some principle other than that of our own mercenary advantage (9. 2–11). In fact we are willing to do favours even at the cost of danger and loss, since we love our good deeds (12. 2–15). With that we come to the heart of Stoic ethics. Kindness and gratitude, like other things that are honourable and morally good, have a beauty which leads us to choose them for their own sake (16–18, 20–2) – Epicurus' own piety is an example of this disinterested attitude (19). In the same way, we marvel at the splendour of the cosmos, quite forgetting the benefits that it showers upon us (23–4. 1).

With IV 1–25, an exercise in Stoicism at its most elevated, the whole work comes to a climax. The remainder of Book IV is less exalted, as Seneca addresses three questions: 'If I am to imitate the gods, will I knowingly do the ungrateful a favour?' (26–32); 'What do I do if I am not sure about the other person?' (33–9); and 'Should favours always be returned?' (40). In answering them he once more draws extensively on Stoic theories. He distinguishes two kinds of ingratitude, the vice familiar to us and the inability of all but the wise man to be grateful in a perfect way (26–7). Seneca explains that, while a favour must be done for the sake of the recipient, it is quite in order to follow the example of the gods and do someone a favour who does not deserve it, for the sake of someone connected with him who does (28–30), combining this explanation with a spirited defence of providence (31 f.). He invokes the Stoic doctrine of holding back or 'reservation', of not counting your chickens before they are hatched (34. 3–5), and explains how one is perfectly justified in changing one's mind when circumstances change. But the discussion grows perfunctory towards the end, as though these questions were already among the ancillary matters to be discussed in the next three books.

Book I

Preface

Errors in doing and accepting favours

1 (1) Among the many different errors of those who live reckless and thoughtless lives, I could hardly mention anything more shameful,[1] most excellent Liberalis, than our incompetence in doing or accepting favours. For its consequence is that, ill allotted, they are ill acknowledged. They are not returned, and we complain too late. They were lost when they were granted. (2) No wonder that among our numerous major vices none is more common than ingratitude.

I see several causes for this. The first is that we do not select the right people on whom to bestow our favours. We would not lend money on account to anyone without looking carefully into his estate and way of life; we would not scatter seed on exhausted and infertile soil. But our favours, with an utter lack of discrimination, are thrown away rather than granted. (3) Nor could I say at all easily whether it is more shameful to repudiate a favour, or to demand its return, since this is the kind of debt that can only be recovered if the repayment is voluntary. To plead insolvency here is especially infamous, for the very reason that what is required for discharging the obligation is not money but an attitude of mind: to acknowledge a favour is to repay it. (4) But while those who will not even utter thanks are blameworthy, so too are we. We encounter much ingratitude but create still more by our oppressive

---

[1] Reading *nihil propemodum indignius ... dixerim.*

reproaches and demands, by fickle changes of mind when a gift has been given, by complaining and picking on trifles. We spoil the effect entirely, not just afterwards, but while we are doing the favour. (5) Has ever a gentle request been enough for any of us? Or just one request? No, at the first suspicion of being approached for something, we have frowned and looked away, pretended to be busy, made use of lengthy conversations, endlessly drawn out on purpose, to deny the petitioner his opportunity, and used a variety of tricks to escape his pressing needs. (6) When cornered, we have either put off the favour – which is a cowardly way of saying 'No' – or promised it, but reluctantly, with furrowed brows, with the grudging words forced out of us. (7) But no one likes to acknowledge something that was not so much accepted as extorted. No one can feel gratitude for a favour haughtily tossed down or angrily thrust on him or granted out of weariness to avoid further trouble. It is a mistake to expect a positive response from someone exhausted by delay and tortured by suspense. (8) A favour is acknowledged in the same spirit in which it is granted. So it should not be granted unthinkingly; a man thanks only himself for what someone has given him unawares. Nor should it be late; in any service, much value is placed on the agent's willingness, and lateness amounts to prolonged refusal. Above all, it should not be humiliating; nature has arranged that insults should go deeper than any services, and that these should fade swiftly away while insults are tenaciously remembered. So what can you expect, if you cause offence while placing someone under an obligation? It will be thanks enough if the favour is forgiven.

(9) But the sheer number of the ungrateful is no reason for reluctance to do good turns. In the first place, as I have said, we increase their number. Nor, secondly, is the kindness, lavish and unceasing, of the immortal gods themselves deterred by sacrilege or indifference to them. They act by their nature, doing good to all things, even to people who ill appreciate their gifts. We should follow their lead, so far as our human weakness allows. The favours that we do should be gifts, not investments. You deserve to be cheated, if you thought of the return as you gave. (10) Suppose that it has gone badly. Children and wives have also been known to disappoint, yet we still raise children and get married. So resistant are we to experience that we go to war after being defeated and

to sea after being shipwrecked. How much more seemly to stay firm in doing favours! Refusing to do them because they have not been returned means that you did them for the sake of the return. It provides a good excuse for ingratitude, a disgrace only if freely permitted.[2] (11) How many people are unworthy to see the light of day! Yet it dawns. How many people complain that they were ever born! Yet nature begets new progeny and allows the very people who would rather not have existed to go on existing. (12) The mark of a great and good mind is not to seek a reward for doing favours, but just to do them and, even after finding bad men, to search for a good man. What is the glory of helping many, if no one has disappointed you? As it is, however, virtue consists in doing favours which will not with certainty be returned, though any one of distinction profits at once from doing them. (13) We should not be put off by these considerations or made sluggish in doing what is in fact something very fine. Indeed, were I to lose hope of ever finding gratitude, I would rather that my favours were not returned than not granted. For refusing to grant is to anticipate the fault of ingratitude. I will explain what I mean. Not to return a favour is the greater wickedness, but not to do one is the earlier.

2 (1) If on the crowd you would your favours cast,
     That one be well placed many must be lost.[3]

In the first line there are two points to object to: favours should not be showered on the crowd, and it is not right to cast anything about – least of all, your favours. Take away the element of judgment and they cease to be favours; they fall under some quite different heading. (2) But the sentiment which follows is admirable: one favour well placed makes up for the loss of several that have gone astray. But wait, I beg you. It might be truer and better suited to the moral stature of the benefactor, if we urged him simply to give, even if none of his favours is going to be well placed. For it is false to say 'many must be lost'. None are lost,

---

[2] Seneca's thought seems to be that to do a favour in order to receive something in return, is tantamount to requiring the return as a strict obligation, a *quid pro quo*; in which case there would be no moral disgrace in refusing to make the return, since moral disgrace (or credit) implies that one had a free choice of what to do and was not obliged to act in one particular way. See III 7. 2–3, where Seneca makes the corresponding point about the praiseworthiness of returning a favour.

[3] The author of these lines is unknown.

because loss presupposes calculation. (3) But with favours the accounting is simple. It is purely a matter of paying out. Any return is sheer gain; if there is none, no loss is incurred. I gave for the sake of giving. Favours are not something which one enters into an account book and calls in, like a rapacious debt-collector, at a set date and hour. A good man never thinks of them, unless reminded by their return. Otherwise they come to look like debts. To note down a favour as an outlay is vile usury. (4) However your earlier favours turned out, you should go on conferring them on others. Better that they lie fallow among the ungrateful who may one day, through shame or circumstance or example, learn to become grateful. Don't stop. Finish the job. Keep up the role of the good man. Assist people, be it with money, credit, influence, advice or sound instruction. (5) Even wild beasts are susceptible to acts of kindness. No animal is so savage as not to be softened and made affectionate by your attention. The lion's mouth is stroked with impunity by his trainer; the elephant's fierceness is coaxed into the docility of a slave if you give him food.[4] So true is it that even creatures that cannot understand or see the value of a favour are won over, none the less, by persistent, unremitting kindness. Perhaps one favour has met with ingratitude – a second may not. Suppose that they have both been forgotten – a third may recall the others as well, which have slipped from the memory. 3 (1) Favours will be wasted if you jump to the conclusion that they have been wasted. If you press on and pile one on top of another, you will wring gratitude from even the hard, unmindful breast. In face of so many, the man will not have the nerve to lift his eyes. Wherever he turns in his effort to forget them, you must make him see you. Besiege him with your favours.

The three Graces[5]

(2) What is the essence, the special character of such favours? I shall tell you, if first you allow me a rapid digression on some

---

[4] Compare *On Anger* II 31. 6.

[5] The Latin noun *gratia* ('grace') translates the Greek χάρις, a word covering outward 'grace', 'graciousness' towards someone and 'gratefulness' for something, as well as concrete a 'favour'. Goddesses personifying beauty, charm, and the joy aroused by nature's fertility, the Graces or 'Charites' were at first indefinite in number, and they had a variety of names. From Hesiod onwards, their usual

questions that are not strictly relevant. Why are the Graces three
in number and why are they sisters? Why are they holding hands?
Why are they smiling and youthful and virgin? Why is their costume
loose and transparent?

(3) Some would have it thought that there is one to do the
favour, a second to receive it and a third to return it. According
to others, there are three sorts of people who do favours – those
who earn a claim to favours by doing them first, those who return
favours, and those who receive them in such a way as to return
them at the same time.[6] (4) You can take your pick of these two
theories. What use is this knowledge to us? And what is the point
of their holding hands in a dance that goes back on itself? That
there is a sequence of kindness, passing from one hand to another,
which comes back none the less to the giver, and that the beauty
of the whole is lost if the sequence is anywhere interrupted, while
it is loveliest if it hangs together and the succession is maintained.
In the dance, however, a greater dignity falls on the elder sister,
as it does to those who earn a claim to favours by doing them

number was three. Associated with the Muses (*Theogony* 64) and still more with
Aphrodite, goddess of love (Homer, *Cypria* Fragment 5), they were regularly
represented by ancient artists (and later by those of the Renaissance) in the
manner described by Seneca. Their variety of names made them a fertile subject
for allegorical interpretation by philosophers like Chrysippus. Seneca himself may
be somewhat offhand about the myth and its meaning. Yet it provides him with
one of his two main images for the role of favours in human society, the other
(also taken from Chrysippus) being that of the ball game at II 17. 3–7 and 32.
On the later history of this highly influential theme, see the chapter on 'Seneca's
Graces' in Edgar Wind's *Pagan Mysteries of the Renaissance* (London 1958).

[6] We cannot definitely identify the authors of these two interpretations, but the
context suggests that they were Stoic philosophers, and Seneca goes on just below
(3. 8 ff.) to criticize other views of Chrysippus and Hecaton on the Graces. On
the first interpretation, the three Graces represent three stages of a benign process:
giving, accepting, returning a favour. On the second, they symbolize three kinds
of benign activity: taking the initiative, returning the favour and accepting it with
a graciousness that is tantamount to returning it – the graciousness which Seneca
has in mind when he writes that 'to accept a favour gladly is to have returned it'
(II 30. 2). Neither allegorization of the three Graces as they are usually depicted
(e.g. that in the fresco from Pompeii in the museum at Naples) is satisfactory.
The process of giving, accepting and returning a favour only needs two participants,
while the central figure in most representations, the one who graciously gets and
gives, is not returning the gift so much as passing it *on*. Seneca himself does a
better job of interpretation when he goes on here to talk (though vaguely) about
a 'sequence of kindness.' Aristotle (*Nicomachean Ethics* v 5, 1133a3–5) speaks of
a triple process, in which a favour is granted, and returned, and then later the
recipient does the donor a new favour.

first. (5) Their faces are cheerful, as faces usually are when favours are granted or accepted. They are young, because the memory of favours ought not to grow old. They are virgin, because favours are unspoiled and unblemished and seen by all as holy. There should be no tie or restriction to them. So their garments are loose – and indeed transparent, since favours long to be visible.

(6) Some may be so enthralled by the Greeks as to pronounce such considerations necessary. But there can be no one who sees any relevance to our subject in the names which Hesiod attached to the Graces. He called the eldest Aglaie, the second Euphrosyne, the third Thalia.[7] The meaning of these names is twisted by everyone to suit himself, in an effort to bring it into line with some theory or other. In fact Hesiod just gave his girls the names he fancied. (7) In the same way, Homer changed the name of one, calling her Pasithea and promising her in marriage.[8] (You can see that these virgins are not Vestals!)[9] I can think of another poet[10] who has them in girdles and brings them on in robes of thick, in fact of Phryxian, wool. And Mercury stands with them,[11] not because kindnesses need argument or speech to commend them, but because the painter felt like it.

(8) Chrysippus, too, with his well-known sharpness and shrewdness in getting to the innermost truth, with his way of speaking to the point and not using more words than are needed to make himself understood, devotes his entire book[12] to such frivolities – to the extent of saying very little about the duty itself of doing, accepting or returning a favour. Nor does he graft these stories onto his argument, but the other way round. (9) For besides what

---

[7] *Theogony* 906–10. The names stand for concepts which were regularly associated. Aglaie means 'splendour', Euphrosyne 'merriment' and Thalia 'feasting'.

[8] At *Iliad* XIV 267–9, Hera promises Hypnos that, if he will put Zeus to sleep, she will give him as his bride 'one of the younger Charites ... Pasithea for whom you yearn all your days'.

[9] At Rome, the sacred fire of Vesta the hearth goddess was guarded and fed by six virgins known as 'Vestals'. Forbidden to marry for thirty years, a Vestal could be entombed alive for unchastity.

[10] It is not known what poet Seneca has in mind.

[11] As he does in Botticelli's *Primavera*. Mercury, as the messenger of the gods, was specially associated with oratory and skill at pleading a case.

[12] Presumably the work entitled *On Favours* to which Philodemus once refers (*SVF* II 1081). Seneca cites Chrysippus again in II 17. 3, II 25. 3, and III 22. 1, perhaps from the same work.

Hecaton copies from him,[13] Chrysippus says that the three Graces are daughters of Jupiter and Eurynome, younger than the Hours[14] but a bit better looking, which is why they were given to Venus as companions. Their mother's name, too, he thought relevant. She was called Eurynome or 'the Wide-spreading' because it takes an extensive fortune to hand out favours. As though a mother normally gets her name after the daughters, or the poets are accurate with names! (10) In the same way that a butler[15] announcing someone makes good his loss of memory with effrontery and invents a name, when he cannot recall the right one, so too the poets see no point in telling the truth. Either out of necessity or corrupted by the beauty of it all, they have anyone called whatever name goes neatly into the verse. Nor is it dishonesty on their part to put a new name on the list – the next poet that comes along will have them called a name of his choosing. You can see that in the case of Thalia, with whom we are particularly concerned. She appears in Hesiod as a Grace, in Homer as a Muse.[16]

4 (1) But so as not to do what I am blaming in others, I shall leave all this aside. It is off the point, indeed it has nothing remotely to do with it. But do come to my defence, if any one accuses me of taking Chrysippus down a peg. He was a great man, of course, but still a Greek. His sharp mind is too subtle; it loses its edge and often turns on itself. Even when it seems to be getting somewhere, it

[13] Hecaton of Rhodes, Stoic philosopher of the first half of the First century BC, author of works on ethics now lost; like his famous associate Posidonius, also of Rhodes, he was a pupil at Athens of Panaetius. Hecaton is reported to have written a work *On Duty* (or *On Duties* – Cicero refers to it twice, once each way, in his own *On Duties*, III 63, 89), to which this and Seneca's other mentions of his views in *On Favours* (see II 21. 4 ff., III 18) may refer.

[14] Personifications of the seasons, especially those of life and growth, the *Horai* or 'Hours' were associated with Aphrodite and the Graces (as at Hesiod, *Works and Days* 73–5). Chrysippus here would be making a commentary on Hesiod, *Theogony* 901–27, a catalogue of Zeus' various wives, which relates (901–3) that the 'Hours' were daughters by his second marriage to Eunomiê ('Law and Order'), while the 'fair-cheeked Graces' were children of his third wife Eurynome, the 'wide-spreading' one (907–9).

[15] Lat. *nomenclator*: a servant who stands beside an official or nobleman and tells him the names of people as they come into view, e.g. at a reception.

[16] Seneca is mistaken: the nine Muses are mentioned by Homer at *Odyssey* 24. 60, but he never in fact names them. Hesiod, however, does list them by name (*Theogony* 77–9), calling one of them 'Thaleia' (Θάλεια). At 907, one of the Graces receives the related but slightly different name of 'Thalia' (Θαλία). Both Greek words would have been spelled the same in Latin.

only pricks – it does not get through. (2) But what is the use of sharpness here? Our task it to talk about favours, to sort out a matter which, more than anything else, holds human society together. A law must be laid down for our lives lest, under the guise of generosity a thoughtless indulgence should come into favour, and lest liberality, which ought never to be lacking nor yet excessive, should find itself hamstrung, in the course of being restrained, by this very vigilance. (3) Men must be taught to give gladly, to take gladly, to give gladly back. They must be taught to set themselves the mighty challenge of not merely matching but surpassing in deed and spirit those to whom they are under obligation, since anyone with a favour to return can only make it up by going beyond it. The one must be taught to ignore what is owed him, the other to acknowledge a still greater debt. (4) To this most honourable of competitions, between one favour and another, Chrysippus urges us on as follows. Perhaps, he says, if the Graces are Jupiter's daughters, ungratefulness may be a sacrilege and cause offence to such attractive young ladies! (5) No! Teach me how to do more good myself and to be more grateful to those who have done me good, how to provoke in the minds of those who have obliged and those who have been obliged that contest which makes the giver forgetful and prolongs the memory of the debtor. And let the frivolities of which I speak be left to poets, whose purpose is just to delight the ear and weave a sweet story. (6) But if you would cure people's characters, if you would hold on to trust as a factor in human affairs and engrave[17] on men's minds a memory of services received, you must speak in earnest and act with force – unless perhaps you suppose that frivolous talk and fables and old wives' tales can prevent that most disastrous of things, an annulment of kindnesses altogether.[18]

---

[17] Reading, with Madvig and Gertz, *incidere*.

[18] Stoic philosophers were unusually frank and independent-minded in their use (and criticism) of their predecessors' work; Seneca is no exception (see also *On the Private Life* 1. 5–3. 1 and 8. 1–4, and *On Favours* II 21. 4, III 18). But his criticisms of Chrysippus here are also tinged with a certain impatience at what Romans saw as a typically Greek excess of ingenuity and persistence in exploring the logical, conceptual and linguistic minutiae. We know from other sources that the sort of allegorizing to which Seneca objects so scathingly here was not uncommon in Chrysippus' writings. And it had a solid basis in Stoicism, which

What is a favour?

5 (1) But passing quickly over the needless questions, the first point that I do need to explain is this: we must learn what it is that we owe on receiving a favour. One person might say that he owes the money which he received, another the consulate, a third the priesthood, a fourth the province. (2) But these are mere signs of services rendered, not the services themselves. A favour cannot possibly be touched by the hand; the transaction takes place in the mind. There is a great difference between its material and the favour itself. So it is not the gold or the silver, or any of those things which are accepted as so important, that constitutes the favour, but rather the good will of whoever bestows it. The ignorant, however, take note only of what meets the eye, what can be handed over and held in possession, while attaching little value to what is dear and precious in itself. (3) What we can hold or look upon, what our covetousness fixes on, can be taken away from us by misfortune or malice. The favour, even when its vehicle is lost, remains. It is a right action[19] and no force can undo it.

(4) Suppose that I have ransomed a friend from pirates, and that some other enemy has caught him and put him in prison; it is not the favour, but the use and enjoyment of my favour, that has been taken away from him. Suppose that I have snatched a person's children from shipwreck or a fire and restored them to him, only for some illness or some other iniquitous mischance to carry them off; even in their absence, the favour done in my action towards them remains. (5) All those things that wrongly assume the name of favours are no more than services that allow a friendly good will to display itself. Elsewhere, too, it can happen that the

saw both the physical and the 'moral' universe as totally rational. God's thought pervades and indeed constitutes all things; the function of philosophy is to recover the 'original', divine way of conceiving and describing them. Adapting the standard Greek view, the Stoics regarded the ancient traditional poets Homer and Hesiod as inspired men whose names, genealogies and other tales of the gods, if only we can learn to interpret them correctly, convey this original account of things. The results of independent philosophical argument and poetic exegesis must in the end confirm one another, and the latter becomes an essential part of a full investigation of many philosophical questions.

[19] Latin *recte factum*, which translates Greek κατόρθωμα, referring in Stoic theory to an action that fulfils all the requirements of virtue: it is a right action done for the right reasons and from a fully and permanently virtuous state of mind.

appearance of a thing is different from the thing itself. (6) A general may award the military collar, the wall-crown or the civic crown.[20] Is there anything precious about the crown itself – or the robe of office, the fasces, the dais and the triumphal car? None of these is an honour; they are simply badges of honour. In the same way, what strikes the eye is not the favour itself, but the trace and mark of a favour.

6 (1) What then is a favour? An act of benevolence bestowing joy and deriving joy from bestowing it, with an inclination and spontaneous readiness to do so. Thus what matters is not the deed or the gift but the mentality behind them: the kindness lies not in the deed or gift but in the mind itself of the person responsible for the deed or gift. (2) There is a great difference between these, as you can see from the fact that a kindness is good without qualification, whereas the deed or gift is neither good nor bad.[21] The mind is what raises small things high, casts lustre on dingy things, discredits things that are great and valued; the objects of desire are themselves neutral by nature, neither good nor bad; what matters is the end towards which they are directed by that governor[22] who gives things their form. (3) It is not the kindness itself that is counted out or handed over. In the same way it is not by the sacrificial victims, however fat and glittering with gold, that the gods are honoured, but by uprightness and holiness of will in the worshippers. Good men with no more to offer than groats and meal-paste are devout, while the wicked cannot avoid impiety, however much they stain the altars with blood.

7 (1) If favours were a matter of objects, rather than of the wish to do a favour, they would be the greater the greater the objects are that are given to us. But that is false. We are sometimes

---

[20] The military collar of twisted metal (or 'torque'), worn in battle by ancient Gallic, German and British soldiers, was adopted by the Romans as a military ornament and decoration. The wall-crown, with turrets, was awarded to the first soldier to scale a besieged city's wall. The civic crown, a garland of oak leaves, was awarded for saving the life of a fellow citizen and soldier (see also *On Mercy* I 26. 5).

[21] The Stoics held that virtuous states of mind and actions that express them are the only things that are good by their natures and in themselves. Other normally valuable things, such as health or money or honours or physical gratification, etc., are neither good nor bad but 'indifferent', and are only 'preferred'. See General Introduction, p. xxii, and Long–Sedley, Chapter 58.

[22] I.e. the mind; reading, with Gronovius, *ille rector*.

under the greater obligation to someone who made small gifts magnificently, whose 'mind was equal to the wealth of kings',[23] who bestowed little but gladly, who forgot his own poverty while having regard for mine, who had not just the wish but a burning desire to help, who thought that he was receiving a kindness while he was doing one, who gave without any intention of ever getting it back and took it back without any thought of having given it in the first place, who went out to look for the chance to help and seized it. (2) Against that, as I have said, favours deserve no thanks, however substantial or spectacular they may seem, if they have to be screwed out or just fall out through inattention. A gift is much more welcome from a ready than from a full hand. (3) It was a slight service that one man did me – but he could not do more. The other man's gift was great – but he hesitated, he put it off, he groaned as he gave it, he gave it haughtily, he flaunted it about; it was not the beneficiary whom he wished to please; he did it for his ambition, not for me.

8 (1) Once when everyone was offering Socrates what he could, his pupil Aeschines[24] who was poor said, 'I can find nothing to give you that is worthy of you. In this alone I feel myself to be poor. So I present you with the one thing that I have – myself. Take this gift in good part, I beg you, whatever its value. Bear in mind that others, while giving you much, have left more for themselves.' (2) To which Socrates answered, 'How could your gift to me be anything other than great – or do you hold yourself of little account? I shall make it my care to return you to yourself a better man than I received you.'[25] With this gift, Aeschines surpassed Alcibiades, whose spirit matched his wealth.[26] He surpassed the entire bounty of the opulent young.

---

[23] Adapted from Vergil's account (*Georgics* IV 13) of an old man who lived on his few acres as contentedly as a king.

[24] Aeschines of Sphettus, a writer of Socratic dialogues, much esteemed for their style, substantial fragments of which survive. Diogenes Laertius includes him in his *Lives of Eminent Philosophers*, II 60–4.

[25] A less elaborate version of this story is found also in Diogenes Laertius II 34.

[26] I.e. he was as great-spirited and generous as he was wealthy. See Aelian's story (*Varia Historia* IX 29), about Alcibiades' attempts to lavish gifts on Socrates. The classic picture of the relations between the two men is in Plato's *Symposium*. For the career of the notorious Alcibiades (c. 450–404 BC), see Thucydides, V–VIII, and Plutarch's *Life of Alcibiades*.

9 (1) You see how the mind can find the means to be generous even in the straits of poverty! I seem to hear Aeschines saying, 'You have achieved nothing, Fortune, by wishing poverty on me. I shall provide none the less a worthy gift for this man. If I cannot give him anything from your resources, I shall do so from mine.' And you have no reason to think that he was cheap in his own eyes – the price he put on himself was – himself! Clever young man: he found a way of giving Socrates to himself as a gift! It is not the extent of the favours but the character of their authors which should concern us . . .[27]

Ingratitude, the worst form of human depravity

(2) . . . he craftily keeps himself accessible to men with immoderate appetites and, without intending to give them any real help, fosters their unconscionable expectations with words. On the other hand, his reputation will suffer if his tongue is sharp and his face severe as he flaunts invidiously his own good fortune. People court, and loathe, the prosperous. They would do the same, if they could – but they hate him for doing it. (3) Having their fun with other people's wives, and not even in secret but openly, they put their own wives at the disposal of others. A man is boorish, rude, ill-mannered, and counts as a horrible match among the married women, if he forbids his wife to set herself up for hire in a litter, allowing everyone to have a look at her as she travels around on view from all sides. (4) Anyone who makes himself conspicuous by not having a mistress, anyone without an allowance paid to someone else's wife, gets a name among married women as a low sort of person with sordid tastes and an eye for the maidservants. So the surest way[28] to get engaged is to commit adultery; to be

---

[27] The sudden change of subject here points to a lacuna in the text (possibly quite substantial. This might partly explain the notable brevity of Book I compared with the others). Conceivably, it contained some objection that not everyone is as worthy as Socrates of our wholehearted generosity or likely even to be grateful, thus launching Seneca into the digression that follows on ingratitude and the evils of human nature, past and present (with which compare *On Anger* II 9). He would then be meeting this objection at 10. 5, where he lists a few favours which even the undeserving may expect from us.
[28] Reading with N *inde certissimum*.

an ex-spouse or still unmarried is the general rule;[29] and no one takes a wife without having taken her away from someone. (5) Men now vie with one another to squander what they have seized, to recoup with a fierce, belated[30] avarice what they have squandered, to cast aside their scruples, to look down on the poverty of others, while fearing their own more than any other evil, to disturb the peace with acts of violence and oppress the weak with force and threats. No wonder that provinces are looted and venal judgments, when the bidding has been heard on both sides, are knocked down to one or the other – to sell what you have bought is a universal law!

10 (1) But my enthusiasm has carried me too far – the subject set me going – and I must conclude by not resting the blame on our own generation. Our ancestors complained about it, so do we, so will our descendants – the overthrow of morals, the reign of wickedness, the decline of human behaviour and collapse of any feeling for what is right.[31] Yet all this remains and will remain where it was – with a slight movement in one direction or the other, like the waves which the tide, as it rises, lifts further inland and constrains, as it ebbs, to the inner line of the shore. (2) At one moment, adultery will be more prevalent than other misbehaviour, as chastity kicks over the traces. At another, there will be a rage for dinner-parties and that most repulsive source of ruin to an estate, the kitchen. Or else you will find excess in adorning the body and a concern for personal appearance that exhibits a deformity of mind. At yet another time, an ill-regulated freedom will break out into impudent boldness. Or there will be a movement towards cruelty in individuals and peoples and the profanation, in the madness of civil war, of all that is holy and sacred. Or again, drunkenness may at times be held in honour, with a larger capacity than anyone else's for wine counting as a virtue. (3) Vices never stay in one place waiting for you. They are constantly on the move, in turbulent disagreement with each other. One thing, however, will aways be the same, the verdict that we have to pass on ourselves: we are bad, we have been bad; and, I hate to add, we

---

[29] Reading with Gertz *viduitas caelibatusque*.
[30] Reading *sera et acri avaritia*.
[31] Reading with N *fas labi*.

will go on being bad. (4) There will always be murderers, tyrants, robbers, adulterers, plunderers, temple-thieves, traitors.

And lower than all these is ingratitude. Of course, it may be that they all spring from ingratitude, without which no major crime comes to its full size. Beware of it as the greatest of crimes you can commit. But forgive it as the most trivial, if someone else commits it. For the wrong done to you adds up simply to this, that you have wasted a favour, while the best part of it remains safely yours – to have done it.

(5) Now, just as we must take care to concentrate our favours on those who will be grateful, so there are some favours which, even if our expectations of people are poor, we will do and grant – and not only if we reckon that they are going to be ungrateful; we will do so even if we know that they have been. For example, if I can bring back someone's children to him, rescuing them from great danger with none to myself, I shall not hesitate to do so. If he deserves it, I shall protect him and take his side even at the cost of my own blood. If he does not, and I can save him from robbers by merely shouting, that cry which means safety to a human being will not be slow in coming.

(I) What favours to grant

11 (1) The next point to discuss is: what favours to grant, and how? First of all, we should give things that are indispensable; secondly, things that are useful; thirdly, things that are agreeable. In every case, they should be things that will last.

Let us begin, then, with things that are indispensable. Anything vitally important has a different impact, as they say,[32] from that of anything which merely makes life more elegant or convenient. A person can look down on what he can easily do without, on something of which he can say: 'Take it back. I don't want it. I am happy with what I have.' And there are times when you don't just feel like returning what you have received – you feel like throwing it on the floor. (2) Indispensable favours comprise, in the first place, those without which we could not live; secondly, those

---

[32] Reading with Préchac *quod aiunt*.

without which we ought not to live; thirdly, those without which we would prefer not to live.

(3) The first are of this kind: rescue from the hands of the enemy, from the tyrant's wrath, from proscription and the other various, unpredictable dangers which beset the life of men. Whichever of these we have shaken off, the greater and more dreadful it is, the greater will be our gratitude. The thought will ever recur of how great an evil we have been spared, and it greatly enhances the service to have fear preceding it. But of course, we should not be slower than we have to be in saving anyone, simply to give our service an added weight through fear. (4) Next come the things which we could live without, though death would then be a better fate – such as liberty, undefiled modesty and a sound mind. After these, we should put things dear to us through kinship and blood, through old habit and long familiarity, such as children, wives, home and anything else that the mind becomes so attached to as to make it harder to be torn from it than from life itself.

(5) Then follow the useful favours, of which there is an abundant and varied supply. Here you will find the provision of money – not to excess, but in healthy moderation – as well as honours and advancement for those who wish to rise in life. Nothing is more useful than to be of use in that field.[33]

From this point onwards, the remaining favours are extras, which stimulate self-indulgence. Here the rule to follow is that their appropriateness should make them welcome. They should be out of the ordinary, things possessed by few – or by few in the relevant age-group or by few in this particular way; and, even if they have no intrinsic value, they should acquire one from their timing or place. (6) We should see what present will give the greatest pleasure, what will frequently attract the attention of its possessor and bring us to mind whenever he comes into contact with it. At all events, we should take care not to send presents that are pointless, such as gear for the hunt to a woman or an old man, books to a country bumpkin or hunting-nets to a scholar and man of letters. Conversely, we should be on the alert lest, in our wish to send someone something to his taste, we cast a slur on his weaknesses – for instance, by sending wine to a drunkard or medicine to a

---

[33] Reading with W. H. Alexander, *Classical Quarterly* 31 (1937), p. 55, *ibi.*

hypochondriac. A gift turns into a taunt when it draws attention
to the faults of the recipient.

12 (1) If we have any control over what to give, we should go
for things that will last, so that our gift should be as imperishable
as possible. Few are so grateful as to think of what they have
received, even when they cannot see it. But even the ungrateful
will be assailed by memory when they have the gift before their
eyes and are not allowed to forget it; its author is thrust upon
them and drummed in. We should seek out the favours that will
endure, for the very reason that we ought never to issue reminders.
The object itself should arouse the flagging memory. (2) I shall
be happier to give a silver artefact than silver coin, a statue rather
than a garment or something that may wear out after brief use.
There are few whose gratitude outlasts the thing given to them; it
is commoner for gifts to stay in mind only for so long as they stay
in use. For my part, if I can avoid it, I do not wish my gift to be
used up: it should stay in existence, cling to my friend, live with
him.

(3) No one is so stupid as to need telling not to send a present
of gladiators or animals for the arena when the show has already
been put on, of summer clothes in winter or winter clothes at
midsummer. Favour should be done with common sense. The time
and the place should be studied, as should the people involved,
since small considerations are what make some things welcome or
unwelcome. How much more acceptable it is if we give a person
what he does not have rather than what he has in abundance, what
he has long sought without finding rather than what he is going
to see everywhere. (4) Presents should not be costly so much as
unusual and choice, such that even a rich man can find a place
for them, just as ordinary apples, of which we will be tired in a
few days' time, give pleasure if they come out of season. And there
will be some distinction, too, about things which no one else has
given them or which we have given to no one else.

13 (1) Alexander of Macedon had conquered the East and was
rising in thought above his human station, when the Corinthians
sent an embassy to congratulate him and grant him the citizenship
of their state. He laughed at this kind of civility till one of the
ambassadors said, 'No one has ever been given our citizenship
except you and Hercules.' (2) Alexander was glad to accept such

an undiluted honour. He honoured the ambassadors with invitations to his table and with other courtesies. His thoughts were not on who was granting him their citizenship but on who had been granted it. Devoted to glory (with no idea of its true nature or limits), he followed in the footsteps of Hercules and Bacchus without even halting where they had stopped.[34] He turned his eyes from the authors of his honour to his partner in it, as though he already occupied heaven, to which he aspired in his utter vanity, because he was being placed on a level with Hercules. (3) But what similarity was there to that hero in this crazy young man whose claim to virtue was no more than rashness blessed with good fortune? Hercules conquered nothing for himself. He crossed the world, led not by lust but by considered judgment in his choice of what to conquer, enemy of the wicked, avenger of the good, bringer of peace on land and sea. Alexander, from boyhood onwards, was a robber and looter of nations, ruin to foes and friends alike. One whose highest good was to terrify the whole of mankind, he forgot that it is not merely the fiercest but the most cowardly of animals that are feared for their venom.

14 (1) But to return to the subject. A kindness accorded to just anyone wins gratitude from no one. No one at an inn or tavern sees himself as a personal guest. Nor will he think himself the guest of the host at a public banquet, where it can be said: 'What, after all, has he done for me? Just the same as for that man over there whom he hardly knows, or for that one, a positive enemy of his, a disgusting fellow. He cannot have thought there was anything in me to deserve it. He was just indulging his own particular weakness.'[35] If you want it to be received with gratitude, make it

---

[34] The hero Hercules and the god Bacchus were claimed by Greek writers (e.g. Diodorus Siculus, II 38 f.) to have brought civilization to India. The claim rested on information about the Indian deities Shiva and Krishna picked up by Greeks in India and interpreted as information about figures in Greek prehistory. Alexander's wish to rival these mythological figures was a commonplace, not entirely without foundation, in Hellenistic and Roman literature. He was prevented from pushing his conquests further east, past the Punjab, only by his soldiers' refusal to follow him.

[35] The Latin *morbo suo* means literally 'his illness'. For the Stoics vices are afflictions, diseases of the mind, which disturb its normal and natural functioning in much the same way that a bodily disease disturbs some bodily function. Seneca elsewhere defines 'disease' in this sense as 'a persistent perversion of the judgment' (*Letters* 75. 11). In the present case the vice is presumably frivolity and self-importance.

scarce. If you do, anyone will allow the debt to be charged to him. (2) But no one should take this to mean that I would hold back liberality and keep it on a tighter rein. No, it can go as far as it likes; but it should really *go*, and not meander. You can cast your gifts around, but in such a way that no one, even if there are many other recipients, should think himself one of a crowd. (3) Everyone should be given some particular token of friendship to suggest some special degree of familiarity, allowing him to say: 'I got the same as this other person, but without any prompting', 'I got the same as that one did, but quickly – he took a long time to earn it', 'Others have had the same, but without the same words or the same friendliness with which it was conferred on me', '*He* got it, after asking – I had not even asked', 'He got it, but he could easily give it back; his old age and lack of any encumbering heir promised much. So I was given more, though given the same, because there was no hope of getting it back from me.' (4) A courtesan shares herself in such a way as to leave each of her several admirers with some token of special affection. Anyone, likewise, who wants to be loved for his kindnesses, will think up ways of obliging many while giving each of them something to make him feel a cut above the others.

15 (1) No, I would certainly not put any restraint on acts of kindness. The more they are and the greater, the more honour they will do you. But you must use your judgment – you will not win any hearts by casual or careless presents. (2) So if anyone thinks that these precepts of ours are meant to narrow the boundaries of generosity and restrict the course open to it, he has misheard our advice. Is there any virtue which we Stoics respect more or do more to stimulate? Is anyone better fitted to encourage it than we are with our stress on the sanctity of human fellowship? (3) So what am I saying? Since there is nothing morally good in any mental drive, even one which begins with good intentions, unless it becomes a virtue through moderation, I am insisting that liberality should not be prodigal. A kindness will be received with pleasure, indeed with open palms, when reason guides it to the deserving, but not when it is dispatched to all and sundry by chance and thoughtless impulse. It must be something which a person is glad to display and assign to himself. (4) Can you call them kindnessess, if you are ashamed to mention their author? How much more

gratefully received they are, how much more permanently ensconced in the mind, if you find more pleasure in thinking of the benefactor than the benefaction!

(5) Crispus Passienus[36] used to say that from some people he would prefer a favourable judgment to a favour, and from others the other way round. He gave an example: 'From our deified Augustus I would rather have the judgment, from Claudius the favour.'[37] (6) I for my part think that no favour should be sought from anyone if he has a low judgment of you. 'You mean, he should not have accepted what Claudius was giving?' Yes, he should – but in the way that you accept something from fortune, knowing that she can turn nasty in a flash. 'So why distinguish what in fact are a thorough mixture?' Because you cannot have a favour if the best part of it is missing – the judgment that went into doing it. Besides, a huge sum of money given without reflection or the right intention is not a favour but a windfall. Indeed, there are many things which you should take – but without feeling any indebtedness.

[36] A rich friend of Seneca's father, Crispus Passienus was married to Domitia, Nero's aunt, and then to Agrippina, Nero's mother, who had him murdered, sometime between AD 44 and 48, so as to inherit his property. The fact that Seneca mentions him here with approval suggests that at the time of writing Agrippina (herself murdered in AD 59) was no longer alive and dangerous.

[37] The two terms, *beneficium* ('favour') and *iudicium* ('judgment'), were commonly contrasted with one another: *beneficium* being an expression of arbitrary good will, as against a 'judgment' of merit, a decision based on esteem for the recipient. To describe the award of an honour as a *beneficium* could thus imply that, in the eyes of the donor, it was not entirely deserved, though how far the implication caused offence would depend on what the recipient thought of his own merits as well as of the donor and his powers of judgment. Seneca wishes here to play down the distinction between two terms: no gift can be a favour, properly speaking, without expressing the donor's esteem, if not for the recipient's distinctive merit, then at least for his humanity. See also I 2. 1 above.

Book II

(II) How to do a favour

(1) Be prompt

1 (1) Let us now consider, most excellent Liberalis, what still remains from the first part of our subject: how to do a favour.[1] In this matter, I think I can show you the easiest route to take: we should give as we would wish to have things given to us – (2) above all, gladly, without delay, and without any hesitation.

No gratitude is felt for a favour which has long stuck to the hands of whoever granted it, which he seemed unhappy to let go, giving as though he were robbing himself. Even if some delay should intervene, we should do everything to avoid the appearance of having had to think whether to do it. Hesitation is the next thing to refusal. It never inspires gratitude. For quite the pleasantest thing about a favour is the willingness shown in bestowing it, while procrastination itself is an admission of unwillingness. It means that nothing has really been given; that the gift was just a matter of poor resistance to the other person's inducement. In fact, there are many whose liberality is due simply to the lack of a firm frown. (3) The greatest gratitude goes to favours that are prompt, easily come by and unsolicited, where the only delay comes from regard for the delicacy of the recipient. The best thing is to anticipate a person's wishes, the next best to follow them. It is better to get

---

[1] At I 11. 1 above, Seneca divided what was to follow into two topics: what favours to do, and how to do them. The first of these was handled in I 11–15. He now comes on to the second topic, how we should grant our favours (II 1–17).

in first before the request is made; a good man's lips freeze together as he makes it, and he blushes all over; to spare him the torture is to make the service several times more valuable. (4) To be given something after asking for it is not to get it for nothing. In the view of our ancestors, the weightiest of authorities, nothing costs more than something bought by entreaty. Men would be more sparing with their vows to the gods, if they had to speak them openly. Even to the gods, whom it is no dishonour to supplicate, we prefer to pray in silence, in the secrecy of our hearts.

2 (1) 'I am asking you' – what a distressing and burdensome thing to say! It can only be uttered with downcast eyes! A friend and anyone whose friendship you intend to earn by doing a service should be excused it. However much you hurry, the favour will be done too late, if it is done upon request. You must guess what he wants and, having grasped what it is, you must free him from the crushing need to make the request. The favour to delight him and live on in his heart is the one which comes out to meet him. (2) If we cannot anticipate it, we should cut short any prolonged request. To give the impression not of having been asked but merely informed, we should make an immediate undertaking and prove by our very haste that we were on the point of acting, even before we were approached. In sickness, food at the right moment makes for health, and water given at the proper time is as good as a remedy. A favour, likewise, may be trivial and commonplace; but, if it is promptly done without your wasting so much as an hour, it gains greatly in force and is more welcome than any costly present which is slow in coming and long considered. Anyone who acts so promptly is, quite undoubtedly, glad to act. He acts with joy, and he wears his state of mind on his face.

3 (1) Enormous favours have been spoiled by silence, by a slowness to speak that gives an impression of grim severity. They were promised with a look of reluctance. How much better to add kind words to kind deeds, to grace your offer with expressions of courteous benevolence! (2) To make the petitioner reproach himself for his slowness in asking, you might add a friendly rebuke: 'I am quite annoyed with you for wanting something without wishing me to know about it long ago' or 'for making so much ado about asking' or 'for bringing in a third party' 'but I am flattered that it did suit you to test my feelings. In future, if you want anything,

demand it as of right. Just this once, your gaucheness is excused!' (3) This will have the effect of his putting more value on your mental attitude than on whatever it was that he came to beg. Generosity and kindness are seen at their best when the man says to himself as he leaves: 'I have made a great gain today. I would rather have found him to be a man like that than have got several times the sum that I mentioned by some other way. I can never be grateful enough for the attitude which he took.'

4 (1) But there are many who make their kindnesses hateful by rough words and superciliousness. Their language and arrogance are such as to leave you regretting that your request was ever granted. And then, after the promise is made, come further delays. But nothing is more painful than having to ask for the very thing which you have already been granted. (2) Favours ought to be put into immediate effect – but from some people it is harder actually to get the favour than to get the promise of one. You have to request one man to remind them and another to bring the business to a conclusion. All the while, a single good turn passes through several hands and gets worn away. This leaves very little good will for the person who undertook to do it, since everyone who subsequently has to be asked takes some of the credit from him. (3) So if you want your offering to be appreciated, you will take care that the favours reach those who were promised them whole and undiluted, without anything, as they say, 'knocked off'. No one should take them over or slow them up. When it comes to a gift on your part, no one can create gratitude for himself without reducing the gratitude due to you.

5 (1) Nothing is so bitter as long suspense. Some people indeed are less upset at seeing their hopes dashed than deferred. Yet a great many have the fault of putting off, through perverse ostentation, what they have promised to do, so as to keep up the number of their petitioners. Servants of the crown are an example. They enjoy prolonging their show of arrogance, thinking their power diminished unless they treat one individual after another to a prolonged and frequent show of it. They do nothing forthwith, nothing once and for all. Swift to insult, they are slow to do favours. (2) There is nothing truer, you can be sure, than the words of the comic poet:

What! Have you not realized yet,
The more you stall, the less the gratitude you get?'[2]

Hence those utterances of honest vexation: 'If you are going to do something, do it!' and 'Nothing is worth that much. I would rather you said "No" at once.' When the mind has grown weary and started to hate the favour while waiting for it, can it really feel gratitude? (3) The harshest cruelty is to draw out the punishment; and swift execution can be a form of mercy, since the final agony brings with it its own end, while the time that leads up to it is the worst part of the punishment that is going to follow. In the same way, the gratitude for a gift will be the greater, the less time there has been for suspense. For good things, too, the waiting can be anxious, and most favours are simply alleviations. To prolong a person's torture, when he could instantly be freed of it, or to postpone his moment of joy is to do violence to the favour. (4) Generosity always moves quickly. The mark of willing action is swift action. Slow assistance, dragged out from day to day, has not come from the heart. Thus the two most valuable things about a favour have been lost: the timing and the proof that you wish to be friendly. Delayed resolutions mean reluctance.

Avoid ungraciousness

6 (1) In any business, Liberalis, by no means the least important factor is the manner in which things are said or done. Swiftness adds a lot, delay takes away a lot. The iron in javelins may be of the same strength, but it makes a vast difference whether the arm shoots out to hurl them or whether they drop limply from the hand. The same sword may simply scratch or it may pierce right through – the pressure of the fingers that grasp it is what matters. Similarly, the gift may be the same; what makes the difference is how it is given. (2) How gracious and precious it will be, if its giver will not even allow himself to be thanked, forgetting as he gives it that he has given it! Again, to reprimand someone at the very moment of bestowing something on him is a crazy addition of insult to service. Acts of kindness must not be made irritating.

---

[2] Author unknown.

No element of unpleasantness should be mixed into them. Even if there is something on which you would like to remonstrate, choose another time to do so.

7 (1) Fabius Verrucosus[3] used to describe a favour rudely granted by a hard man as 'bread with stones in it', not to be forgone, if you are hungry, but not good to eat. (2) Tiberius Caesar was asked by an ex-praetor, Marius Nepos, for help with his debts. He told him to issue him a list of his creditors. That was not giving him anything – it was just calling a meeting of the creditors. When the list had been issued, he wrote to Nepos saying that he had ordered the money to be paid and adding some insulting advice. This left Nepos without his debts, and without any favour to repay; Tiberius had freed him of his creditors, but had not put him under any obligation to himself. (3) Tiberius, though, must have had some object in view. He did not, I think, want more people coming to him with the same request. This may well have been an effective way to shame men into checking their unconscionable appetites.[4] But to do a favour you must follow an entirely different path. Your gift must be prepared in every way that will make it the more acceptable. What Tiberius did certainly does not amount to doing a person a favour, but to catching him out. 8 (1) (Besides, to give you my opinion in passing on a further point, it is not really proper, even for a prince, to grant in order to degrade.) Yet not even in this way, it may be said, could Tiberius escape what he was trying to avoid. A good many people were afterwards found making the same request. He ordered them to give an explanation of their debts to the Senate, granting them certain agreed sums of money on that condition. (2) But that is not generosity so much as the work of a censor.[5] It may be

---

[3] I.e. Fabius Maximus Verrucosus Cunctator, the Roman general who defeated Hannibal by the delaying tactics described at *On Anger* I 11. 5.

[4] Similar instances of liberality and ungraciousness on the part of Tiberius are reported by Tacitus (*Annals* I 75. 3–7) and given the same interpretation: their effect was to make 'the others prefer to suffer poverty in silence rather than win favours from him by acknowledging it' (I 75. 7).

[5] The censors in Rome were magistrates originally charged with making up and maintaining the *census* or official roll of citizens. Amongst other things, they had the power to revise the senatorial rolls and strike off senators guilty of misconduct or unable to meet the property qualification.

assistance. It may be a princely contribution. It cannot be a favour, if I cannot recall it without blushing. I was summoned to judgment, and had to plead my case in order to gain my request.

Do some favours openly, some in secret

9 (1) That is why all who teach wisdom advise that some favours be done openly and some in secret. Openly, when they are glorious to obtain, like military awards, civic honours and anything else that gains in appearance by publicity. Against that, favours which contribute nothing to preferment or prestige, but simply help against infirmity, poverty or degradation, should be done on the quiet, to the knowledge only of those whom they benefit.

10 (1) Sometimes even the person who is being helped must be deceived if he is to have the help without knowing from whom he got it. They say that Arcesilaus[6] had a friend who was poor but concealed his poverty. He fell sick and would not even admit that he had not the means to spend on essentials. Arcesilaus decided that he would have to be helped in secret. He slipped a purse under his pillow without his knowing about it, so that the man who was too bashful for his own good might come upon what he needed, rather than have it given to him. (2) 'You mean, he is not to know who he got it from?' Yes, if that itself is an essential part of the favour. Besides, there will be many other things which I may do or bestow on him to make him realize who was responsible for that favour as well. Moreover, while he may not know that he was given anything, I shall know that I gave it. 'That is not enough', you may say. No, it is not – if an investment is what you have in mind. But if it is just a gift, you should give it in the way that will be the most use to the person who gets it. You should be satisfied to have yourself as a witness. Otherwise the pleasure is not that of doing good but of being seen to have done good. (3) 'But I want him to know, all the same.' You are looking for a debtor. 'I want him to know, all the same.' What? If he would be better off or find it more to his honour or be happier not to know,

---

[6] Famous philosopher, founder of the sceptical Academy. The same story about Arcesilaus (316/5–242/1 BC) is told by Plutarch (*How to tell a Flatterer from a Friend* 22, 63d), by Diogenes Laertius (IV 37), and the fourth century emperor Julian (*Orations* II 1. 103d).

would you not change your position? 'I want him to know.' (4) So you would not save a man's life in the dark? I do not deny that, where circumstances permit, we should think of our joy at a willing recipient. But if he needs to be helped and is ashamed of it, if he takes offence at what we have to give unless we conceal it, I shall not put the favour on the public record![7] Of course not! I am not going to show him that the gift was mine, since one of the first and most important rules is never to reproach a person for a favour done to him or even remind him of it. The rule for a favour between two people is this: the one should promptly forget that he did it; the other should never forget that he received it.

Avoid reminders, add on new favours

11 (1) The mind is frayed and crushed by continual reminders of service rendered. One feels like bursting out in the way that the man saved by some friend of Caesar's from proscription by the triumvirs exclaimed when unable to bear his rescuer's arrogance,: 'Hand me back to Caesar!'[8] Just how long will you keep on saying 'I saved you, I snatched you from death?' Your service, if I recall it at my pleasure, is life to me. If I do so at yours, it is death. I owe you nothing, if you saved me so as to have someone to put on view. Just how long will you parade me about? Just how long will you force me to remember my good fortune? In an official triumph, I would only have been led along once. (2) We should not mention what we have bestowed. To remind the beneficiary is to ask for repayment. You should not dwell on it or refresh his memory, unless by giving a further gift you remind him of its predecessor. Nor should we tell other people. If you have done a favour, you should keep quiet; you should talk only if you have

---

[7] Latin *in acta non mitto*. Official bodies at Rome – law-courts, Senate and the imperial council – kept and published records (*acta*) of their proceedings. Such *acta* were the nearest thing at Rome to a modern newspaper, containing as they did the court news, reports of family events in high society and city news. See also III 16. 2.

[8] I.e. to Augustus who, in November 43 BC, along with Antony and Lepidus, became one of a triumvirate or 'board of three' dictators. Invested with sweeping powers, they tried to get rid of several hundred opponents (the best known of them being Cicero; see *On Anger* II 2. 3) by 'proscribing' them (publicly declaring them to be outlaws and confiscating their property).

received one. Else you will be told what a certain person who was always boasting of a favour he had done was told: 'You must admit that you have been repaid.' 'When was that?' he retorted. 'Many times and many places – every time and everywhere that you talked about it.' (3) What need have you to make speeches and do someone else's work for him? There is someone who can do the job more creditably than you. When he talks about your kindness, you will also be praised for not talking about it yourself. You must think me ungrateful indeed, if your silence is going to mean that no one knows of it! We should avoid any such boasting – so much so that, if somebody does talk about a favour of ours in front of us, our reply should be: 'Of course, he has the highest claim to favours even greater than that. But the case, I know, is rather that I would like to do everything for him, not that I have already done so.' And this should be said without servility and without that show of rejection which some people use towards what they wish to attract.

(4) After that, you should add on every sort of kindness. A farmer will lose the seed he has scattered, if his work ends with the sowing. Much care is needed to bring the seedling to harvest. Nothing comes to fruit without regular cultivation from start to finish. (5) The same holds good for favours. Nothing could be greater than what is bestowed by parents on their children. But the gift remains unfulfilled unless sustained through infancy and nurtured by long devotion. The same goes for other favours. You must aid them – or lose them. It is not enough to have done them – you must tend them. If you wish those under obligation to you to be grateful, you must not simply do them favours – you must love your favours.

(6) Above all, as I said, we must go easy on people's ears. Reminders make for revulsion, reproaches for loathing.

Avoid arrogance

In doing any favour, nothing should be avoided so much as arrogance. There is no need for an insolent expression or language swollen with pride. The act itself puts you on a pedestal. We should rid ourselves of empty boasting. Our acts will speak for us, if we can stay silent. Loathing, not merely lack of gratitude, is the reaction to a favour arrogantly done.

12 (1) Gaius Caesar[9] granted Pompeius Pennus[10] his life, if by 'granting' you mean 'not taking away'. Then, as Pompey thanked him on his acquittal, he stretched out his left foot to be kissed. Some may excuse this and deny that it was meant to be insolent, by saying that he wanted to show off his slipper, which was gilded – or rather golden – and studded with pearls. Yes, indeed! What was the insult here, if the gold and pearls were what this ex-consul was kissing? Quite apart from that, he could not have chosen any other part of Caesar's person as less defiling to kiss. (2) A man fated at birth to transform the manners of a free citizenry into Persian servitude, judged it not enough that a senator, an elderly man and one who had held the highest public office, should in full view of the leading citizens lie before him in supplication, prostrate like a vanquished enemy at the knees of his conqueror. He found the wherewithal, even below the knee, to put freedom down. This was surely to trample on the commonwealth – and, though you may think this irrelevant, with the left foot at that! For it would not have been insolence foul or furious enough for him to be in his slippers[11] while trying a man of consular rank on a capital charge – he had to stuff the senatorial face with the fastenings of his imperial footwear!

13 (1) Arrogance, stupidest evil of high fortune! What a pleasure it is to to receive no favours from you! What a way you have of turning them into ill-treatment! What a discredit they all are to you! The higher you raise yourself, the lower you sink, proving that you have no claim to those blessings that so puff you up. Whatever you give you spoil. (2) I feel like asking her why she thrusts her chest out so, why she distorts her expression and cast of feature so as to wear a mask in preference to a face. Gifts that please are ones bestowed with a look of human kindness, or at any rate of gentleness and indulgence, by one who, as he gave them, was above me but did not exult over me, who was as generous as he could be, coming down to my level and ridding

---

[9] I.e. Caligula.

[10] Possibly the Sextus Pompeius who was consul in AD 14 (Tacitus, *Annals* 1 7. 2). A kinsman of the royal family (Dio Cassius, LVI 29. 5), he could be the fabulously rich Pompeius who Seneca says (*On Peace of Mind* 11. 10) was later starved to death by 'his old kinsman', Caligula.

[11] Caligula's choice of footwear clearly aroused much attention. For another instance of his cruelty in slippers, see *On Anger* III 18. 3–4.

his gift of show, who waited for that suitable moment which makes help timely rather than vitally urgent. (3) One way to persuade these people not to ruin their kindnesses by insolence is to show them that neither will their gifts seem the larger for being given more noisily, nor they themselves the greater to anyone for that reason, that the grandeur of arrogance is an illusion, casting odium even on what is lovable.

Take the beneficiary's true interests into account

14 (1) Some things will harm those who obtain them. The true favour is not to give but to refuse to give these. We shall accordingly consider the interests rather than the wishes of the petitioner. We often desire what is harmful, and we cannot make out how ruinous it is, since our judgment is obstructed by emotion. When the desire has subsided, with the fall of that fiery mental impulse that put our reasoning to flight, we curse those responsible so ruinously for evil gifts. (2) We withhold cold water from the sick, weapons from those who grieve and are angry with themselves; we withhold from those in love[12] whatever the passion demands for their self-destruction. So, in general, things that will do harm may be requested earnestly and humbly, sometimes even piteously – we shall keep on refusing them. The proper thing is to look at both the initial effects of the favours that we do and at the outcome, giving what it will be a pleasure not only to receive but to have received.

(3) There are many who may say: 'I know that it will not do him any good. But what am I to do? He is asking, and I cannot resist his entreaties. That is his look-out. He will have himself to blame, not me.' Wrong. He will have you to blame, and rightly. When he is back in his right mind, when the paroxysm that inflamed him has abated, why should he not resent the assistance which has led to harm and danger? (4) Compliance that ruins the petitioner is a cruel sort of kindness. The finest of actions is to save people even against their will, even if they refuse. Similarly, to lavish what is deadly on people who ask for it is an ingratiating, affable hatred. We should do the sort of favour that will give ever more pleasure

---

[12] Reading, with all the MSS, *amantibus*.

as it is put to use, one that will never turn into an evil. I shall not give money if I know it is going to be paid out to an adulteress. I will not be found an accomplice in any shameful action or plan. If I can, I will restrain a person from crime; if I cannot, I will not assist him. (5) Whether it is anger driving him where it should not or the heat of ambition turning him from ways of safety, any strength for evil must derive only from himself.[13] I will not allow him to say at some future time, 'He ruined me with his love.' Often there is no difference between the services of our friends and the prayers of our enemies. What our enemies would like to happen to us is what we are driven to and equipped for by the inopportune bounty of our friends. Could anything be more shameful than this most frequent of occurrences, that there should be no difference between hatred and a favour?

Avoid doing anything that will cause you shame

15 (1) We should never bestow anything that will come back to shame us. The whole point of friendship is to put your friend on the same level as yourself. Both parties must come jointly into consideration. I shall give to the needy, but without bringing need on myself. I shall help a man on the point of perishing, but without myself perishing – unless that is to be the price for saving a great man or a great cause. (2) Never will I do a favour that it would be a disgrace to ask for. Nor shall I exaggerate what is a small thing – but neither shall I allow what is great to be received as a trifle. Claiming credit for what one has given destroys the gratitude, but to show the extent of the gift is to bring it favourably to the recipient's attention, not to cast any reproaches.

Consider both your own and your recipient's position

(3) Each of us must consider his means and his resources, in case we offer more than we can afford – or less; and we must consider our recipient's role in life, since some favours are too small to come properly from a great man, while some are too great for the recipient. You should compare the two roles[14] and consider, in

---

[13] Translating Gertz' *in nullum malum vires adsumet nisi a semet ipso patiar*.
[14] In speaking of 'roles' (*personae*) in life, Seneca is touching on a prominent theme in Middle Stoicism, discussed at some length by Cicero in *On Duties* (I 107–

that context, what you are going to give. It could be burdensome
for the giver, or too little. Again, it might be beneath the recipient's
dignity, or more than he should accept.

16 (1) Someone was once presented with a city by Alexander,
that lunatic with no conception of anything that was not grandiose.
He took stock of himself and shrank back from such a huge,
invidious present, saying that it was unsuitable for his station in
life. 'What concerns me,' came the answer, 'is not what you can
fittingly get, but what I can fittingly give.'[15] A spirited, royal saying,
it might seem – but very stupid! Nothing, in itself, is ever fitting.
What matters is who does the giving, to whom, when, why, where,
and the other essential elements in any account of an action. (2)
You are indeed the most swollen-headed of creatures! If he cannot
fittingly take it, neither can you fittingly give it. You must pay
regard to his role and standing. Virtue is always a mean, and to
go beyond it is as wrong as to fall short of it.[16] To do so may
well be open to you. Fortune may well have raised you to the
point where whole cities are gifts for you to distribute (but how
much more magnanimous it would have been not to capture them
at all than to throw them around!). All the same, some people are
just not large enough to pocket a whole city.

17 (1) A Cynic asked Antigonus[17] for a talent, only to get the
reply that this was more than a Cynic should ask for. Rebuffed,
he asked for a penny, and the reply came that this was less than

---

25): each of us has, broadly, four *personae* or roles to play, imposd on us by (1)
universal human nature, (2) our individual character, (3) our station in life and
(4) choice of career. Later on, we shall find Seneca playing down the importance
of social roles: you can do favours even 'in the role of a slave' (III 21. 2; cf. III
23. 4), since being a slave does not rob you of the obligations and rights which
you have because you are human.

[15] With some variation, this apothegm is ascribed to Alexander by Plutarch (*Sayings
of Kings and Generals*, 179 f.) and several other writers. See *Gnomologium Vaticanum*
p. 81.

[16] Here, as at I 15. 3, Seneca appears to be recollecting Aristotle's doctrine of
virtue as a mean. His immediate source, however, is likely to have been not a
Peripatetic, but a Stoic writer like Hecaton, whose work he consulted in writing
On Favours (see I 3. 9 above), or Hecaton's teacher Panaetius, whom Cicero in
his *On Duties* may be following when he speaks, rather like Seneca, of 'that
intermediate course between too much and too little which the Peripatetics approve
and rightly approve' (I 89; cf. I 140).

[17] Antigonus the One-eyed, general and successor of Alexander. For other anecdotes
about him, see III 37 (where the story told of him was in fact about his son)
and *On Anger* III 22. 2–5.

a king could decently give.[18] 'That sort of quibbling', <you may retort,> 'is quite disgraceful. Antigonus simply found a way to give neither. When it came to the penny, he kept the role of a monarch in view; when it came to the talent, that of a Cynic. Yet he could also have treated the penny as something to give a Cynic and the talent as a gift from a king. There may be things too great for a Cynic to receive; but there is nothing too trivial to be honourably bestowed by a king with kindness.' (2) If you want my opinion, I approve of the king's reply. To demand and yet despise money <as the Cynic did> is quite intolerable. You have declared your hatred of money. That is your claim, that is the role which you have chosen. Now you must play it. It is utterly iniquitous to acquire money while boasting of poverty. In short, one should consider one's own role in life no less than that of the person whom one is thinking of helping.

The game of ball

(3) I would like to take up an analogy which our own Chrysippus[19] drew with a game of ball. It falls to the ground through the fault either of the person throwing it or of the person receiving it, while it only remains in play by passing, properly thrown and caught, from one pair of hands to the other. A good player needs to send it off differently to a tall partner than to a short one. The same principle applies to a favour. Only if properly accommodated to both the persons involved, bestower and recipient, will it leave the one and reach the other as it should. (4) Again, if the game is with a trained and practised player, we shall be bolder in throwing the ball. No matter how it comes, his hand will be ready and quick to drive it back. Against an untrained novice, we shall not throw

---

[18] Plutarch (*Sayings of Kings and Generals* 182e) tells the same story, but in reverse order, making the Cynic (whose name he gives as Thrasyllus) ask first for a penny (lit., a drachma) then for a talent. It reappears at *Gnomologium Vaticanum* 104 with Alexander and Diogenes the Cynic as the protagonists.

[19] Apart from what Seneca himself says in this passage, we have no knowledge of the context in which Chrysippus produced this important analogy, or the use to which he himself put it; perhaps it was in the work, cited at 1 3. 8 above, on the Graces. Seneca reintroduces it at II 32. 1. He was not the only writer of the period to employ the analogy. Plutarch does so twice, at *On Socrates' Daemon* 582e–f and the *Commentary on Hesiod's 'Works and Days'* Fragment 52 Sandbach.

it so hard or so vigorously but be more relaxed, aiming the ball right into his hands and simply meeting it when it comes back.[20] We should use the same procedure when doing favours. There are some people whom we have to teach, and we should be satisfied if they simply make the effort, pluck up the courage or are just willing. (5) As it is, we very often make people ungrateful and welcome the idea that they should be so, as though our favours could only be great if we cannot be thanked for them, in the same way that a mean sportsman deliberately tries to make his fellow-player look incompetent, even if it means spoiling the game which cannot go on except by mutual consent. (6) Many are so perverse that they would prefer to lose what they have provided rather than be seen to have had any return. They make an arrogant point of what they have done. How much better and more considerate it would be to see to it that recipients too have a part to play, to welcome the idea that you could be thanked, to put a kind interpretation on everything, to listen to professions of gratitude as though they were actual repayments, to be compliant to the point of actually wishing to see the person under obligation to you released from it! (7) A usurer commonly gets a bad reputation for making harsh demands. He gets an equally bad one if, when it comes to repaying him, he drags his feet and makes trouble and seeks to procrastinate.[21] You must accept, just as you must refrain from demanding, the return of a favour. It is best to be a person who gives readily, who never demands repayment, but is delighted to get it, who has genuinely forgotten what he provided and accepts its return as though accepting a favour.

III How to behave in accepting favours

18 (1) There are some who are arrogant not only in doing favours but even in accepting them, an offence that should never be committed. We must now proceed to deal with the second part of the subject: how people should behave in accepting favours.[22]

---

[20] Reading, with Alexander, *Classical Quarterly* 31 (1937), p. 56, *remissae*.

[21] So as to increase the interest due to him.

[22] At I 11. 1 above Seneca divided what was to follow (I 11–II 17) into the two subjects, what favours to do, and how. Now, in retrospect, he counts all that as the 'first part' of his subject; it concerned the doing of favours, whereas the

Any duty involving two people makes equal demands on them both. Having examined what a father should be like, you will know that just as much work remains in order to make out what a son should be like. If a husband has a role to play, the wife has no less of one. (2) The reciprocity in making demands and fulfilling them requires a rule which applies to both alike – and that, as Hecaton[23] says, is a difficult matter. Moral goodness, indeed anything approaching moral goodness, is always uphill.[24] It requires not merely action, but rational action. Reason must be our guide throughout our life; all things, from the smallest to the greatest, must be performed on its instructions; gifts must be given in whatever manner reason suggests.

Be discriminating about whom you allow to do you a favour, and about what counts as one

Now reason's first verdict is that we must not accept things from everybody. (3) From whom, then, are we to accept things? To answer you briefly, from people to whom we would have given them. It may well be that still greater discrimination is needed in seeking a person to be indebted to than a person on whom to bestow things. Quite apart from the awkward consequences (and there are several), it can be agonizing to find yourself in debt to someone to whom you would rather not be. On the other hand, it is highly agreeable to have received a favour from someone whom you would love even after he had done you wrong; a friendship which would anyway be agreeable has found its justification. Quite the most wretched thing for any self-respecting, upright person is having to have a friend whom he does not like.

(4) In all this, I must warn you that I am not speaking of the wise. Whatever they ought to do they also like to do; their minds are under their control; they set down the law for themselves as they see fit and they keep it as they have laid it down. I am

'second part' that he introduces here is a discussion of how to accept them. This takes up the remainder of the present book.

[23] See I 3. 9, n. 13. We do not know in what work or in what context Hecaton discussed this rule.

[24] Contrast *On Anger* II 13. 1–2.

speaking of imperfect human beings who wish to follow the path of virtue but whose emotions often resist before submitting.

(5) So I have to choose from whom to accept a favour. Indeed, I must think more carefully when it comes to a favour, than when it comes to money, about who is putting me in his debt. In the one case, I just have to return what I received; having returned it, I am released, I am a free man. In the other, I have extra payments to make; even when I have returned the favour, the bond between us remains. I am obliged, when I have returned it, to start again, and the friendship stays where it was. And just as I would not grant anyone my friendship if he was unworthy of it, neither shall I grant him that most hallowed of privileges, the rights of a benefactor, which are the source of friendship. (6) 'But', you may argue, 'I am not always in a position to say "No". Sometimes you have to accept a favour, even against your will. Suppose it comes from a cruel, short-tempered tyrant who is going to take it as a personal affront if you disdain his services – am I to refuse it? Or think of being in the same situation with a robber, a pirate, or a king with a robber's or even a pirate's soul – what am I to do? Is he really not good enough to put me in his debt?' (7) When I said you have to choose who is to put you into his debt, I was excluding fear and *force majeure*.[25] If they come into play, all choice vanishes. If you are free, if it is your decision whether you want to or not, you should ponder the matter yourself. If you are under constraint and the decision is out of your hands, you will know that you are not accepting anything – you are just obeying. No one is under any obligation for accepting what he could not refuse. If you want to know whether I wish to say 'Yes', give me a chance to say 'No.' (8) 'But he granted you your life!' It does not matter what the gift is, if it does not proceed from a willing giver to a willing recipient. You may have saved me; but that does not make you my saviour. Poison sometimes acts like a medicine; it still does not count as wholesome. Some things do good without putting you under any obligation. An abscess on a tyrant was lanced by the sword of a man who had come to kill him; but that did not make

---

[25] As Griffin points out, p. 442, Tacitus puts virtually the same sentiment into Seneca's plea to Nero for permission to retire and hand back the indecently large wealth that had been bestowed on him: 'my one defence is that it would have been wrong to struggle against your munificence' (*Annals* XIV 53. 6).

the tyrant grateful to him for treating a complaint, which the doctors had shrunk from taking into their own hands, with remedial harm.[26]

19 (1) You can see that the action itself is of no great importance. A man who has done you good from a bad motive is not deemed to have done a favour. The favour was a matter of luck, the wrong a contribution of the man himself. I have seen a lion in the amphitheatre who recognized one of the gladiators (he had once been its keeper) and protected him from attack by the wild beasts.[27] A savage animal's help cannot surely count as a favour. Not in the least! It neither wanted to do one nor did it act with that purpose.[28] (2) Replace the animal in my example with the tyrant. Both of them have given someone his life; neither has done a favour. A favour is not something that you can be forced to accept. Hence it cannot put you under an obligation against your will. First you must grant me power to decide; then do the favour.

20 (1) It is commonly debated[29] whether Marcus Brutus should have allowed our deified Julius to grant him his life, having decided that it was his duty to kill him. (2) His reason for killing him we shall discuss in another context.[30] (My view is that, great man though he was in other matters, he was badly wrong here and that his action was not true to Stoic teaching. Either he feared the very word 'king',[31] although it is under a just king that a state reaches

---

[26] The tyrant in question is Jason, tyrant (c. 385–370 BC) of Pherae, a city of Thessaly. Cicero (*On the Nature of the Gods* III 70) and Pliny the Elder (*Natural History* VII 51) also mention this incident, but with different details. (See also Plutarch, *How to Profit from One's Enemies* 89c, and Valerius Maximus, I 8, Ext. 6.)

[27] Seneca could be telling the truth. Compare the famous story of Androcles and the lion told by Aulus Gellius (*Attic Nights* V 14). As his source for it, Gellius names Apion Pleistonices, an Alexandrian writer who had lived in Rome at the time of Caligula and Claudius and who claimed to have witnessed the lion's performance there .

[28] Here Seneca is applying the Stoic doctrine that animals are irrational and hence incapable of moral action. (See *On Anger* I 3. 3–8, on the parallel point about animals' emotions: rage in a wild beast has no rational thought-content, and so is a different sort of thing from rage in a human being, which does.)

[29] In the oratorical schools, for training and display. After defeating Pompey in the battle of Pharsalus (48 BC) Caesar pardoned Brutus (among many others) for having fought on Pompey's side; three and a half years later Brutus was among Caesar's murderers.

[30] No such discussion can be found in Seneca's surviving works.

[31] As all loyal republicans had done since the expulsion of Tarquinius Superbus, the last king of Rome, by Lucius Junius Brutus, ancestor of Marcus Brutus. A belief that Julius Caesar was in fact aspiring to be king hastened his assassination.

its best condition.[32] Or he expected civic freedom to survive when the advantages of autocracy and subjection were so great. Or else he thought that the state could be recalled to its former constitution when its ancient ways had been abandoned; that an equality of civic rights and a due supremacy of law could be maintained, at a time when he had seen thousands of men at war over the issue not of whether, but to which of two men,[33] they should be slaves. He had entirely forgotten the facts of human nature and the character of his own city, if he thought that by killing one man he could prevent the appearance of another with the same ambitions, despite the fact that a Tarquin had emerged after the destruction of so many kings by sword and thunderbolt.[34]) (3) But he was right to let Caesar grant him his life without, on that account, having to regard him as a father. Only by doing wrong had Caesar attained the right to do this favour.[35] Failure to kill is not the same as saving a life. What he was granting was not a favour but a reprieve.

21 (1) A more genuinely debatable question is this. What should a prisoner do if a male prostitute infamous for his oral activities offers the money for his ransom? Shall I allow myself to be rescued by the dirty brute? If I have been, how shall I show him my gratitude? Am I to spend my life with a pervert? Or refuse to live with my rescuer? (2) I will give you my opinion. Even from a person like that I would take the money to spend on saving my life. But I would take it as a loan, not a favour. I would pay him back the money. If the chance came to save him from danger, I would do so. But I would not sink to friendship with him, for that means a union of like-minded people. I would class him not as a rescuer but as a money-lender who, I know, must be given back what I got from him.

---

[32] This commonplace of Hellenistic literature on kingship goes back at least to Plato (*Statesman* 294a) and is not particularly Stoic.

[33] I.e. to Caesar or Pompey. The reference is to the civil war between them. Compare Seneca *Letters* 14. 13.

[34] Two early kings of Rome, Tarquinius Priscus and Servius Tullius, had been assassinated; another, Tullius Hostilius, had been struck by a thunderbolt. But that did not stop the still more tyrannical Tarquinius Superbus from ascending the throne.

[35] Caesar's clemency had only been made possible by his victory in an unjust civil war.

(3) Suppose that someone is worthy of my accepting a favour from him, but that it would harm him to do it. I shall refuse to accept, because the help which he is ready to offer me comes at the cost of inconvenience and even danger to himself. He may, for instance, be about to defend me at a trial where his defence will earn him the enmity of the king. I would be his enemy myself, if he were willing to risk danger on my behalf whereas I refused to take the easier course and face the danger without him.

(4) Hecaton cites a pointless and silly example. Arcesilaus, he said, refused to accept money from a youth still under paternal jurisdiction, for fear that the youth might annoy his skinflint father.[36] Is there anything praiseworthy in not receiving stolen goods, or preferring non-acceptance to repayment? Where is the self-restraint in refusing to accept other people's property?

(5) If you do need an example of highmindedness, we can take the case of Julius Graecinus,[37] a man of unusual distinction, killed by Gaius Caesar[38] simply for being a better person than a tyrant finds it useful for anyone to be. He was taking contributions from friends to meet the expense of public games[39] when a large sum of money was sent to him by Fabius Persicus.[40] He refused to take it. Reproached for turning it down by people who were thinking less about the sender than about what had been sent, he answered: 'Am I to accept a favour from him, when I would not even accept a toast?' (6) And when the ex-consul Rebilus,[41] of equal infamy,

---

[36] On Hecaton, see I 3. 9 n. 13. On Arcesilaus, see II 10. 1, n. 6.

[37] Roman senator, father of Gnaeus Julius Agricola the famous governor of Britain, Julius Graecinus is described by Tacitus, Agricola's son-in-law, as a man of renown in rhetoric and philosophy, whose very virtues aroused Caligula's wrath; ordered to prosecute Marcus Silanus, he refused and was executed (*Agricola* 4. 1). Seneca quotes another of his bon mots in *Letter* 29. 6.

[38] I.e. Caligula.

[39] 'One of the rules of friendship in the senatorial class for a friend when he became aedile' and had to put on public games (Veyne, p. 213).

[40] One of the old nobility and a friend of Claudius', Paullus Fabius Persicus (consul AD 34) is described by Seneca later in *On Favours* (IV 30. 2) as the very type of the degenerate aristocrat.

[41] According to Tacitus (*Annals* XIII 30. 3) Caninius Rebilus, 'outstanding in legal learning and wealth', committed suicide in AD 56, to the surprise of all since 'no one had thought he had the courage for this, because of his notorious effeminacy'. Since Seneca would hardly have spoken of Rebilus as he does had he still been alive, this part of *On Favours* must have been written after that date.

had sent a still greater sum, insisting that he should order its acceptance, he said: 'I beg your indulgence. I refused to take money even from Persicus.' Was it a question here of accepting money – or of selecting a Senate?[42]

Accept cheerfully

22 (1) When we have decided to accept, we should do so cheerfully. We should express our delight and make it obvious to our benefactor so that he gets an immediate reward. To see a friend joyful is due cause for joy, still more to have made him joyful. We must show how grateful we are by pouring out our feelings and bearing witness to them not only in his presence but everywhere. To accept a favour gratefully is to pay back the first instalment of it.

23 (1) There are some who will only accept a favour in secret. They avoid any witness or accessory to the act. You can be sure that their intentions are bad. While anyone making a present should draw no more attention to it than will give pleasure to its recipient, the person receiving it should invite a whole assembly to see him do so. What you are ashamed to acknowledge, you should not accept. (2) Some express their thanks furtively, in a corner, in your ear. But that is not diffidence – it is just a way of disclaiming the favour. You are being ungrateful, if you only express your thanks in the absence of anyone who might pass judgment. Some refuse to be put down as borrowers on the account or to introduce people as sureties, to call in witnesses to the document or have a document at all.[43] The same thing is done by people who try to make any favour conferred on them as inconspicuous as possible. (3) They shrink from taking it openly, in case they should be said to owe their success less to their own merits than to assistance by others; and they are still more remiss in their obligations towards those to whom they owe life and social position. Afraid to be thought dependents, they incur the graver reputation of being ungrateful.

24 (1) Others speak worst of those who have done best by them. It can be safer to offend some people than to do them a

---

[42] I.e. the high-minded Julius Graecinus was acting not like an intended beneficiary but rather a censor, a magistrate empowered to revise the senatorial rolls and decide who should be struck off them. See II 8. 2, n. 5.

[43] Legal devices for safeguarding a transaction. See below, on III 15. 1 f..

good turn. They try to prove by hating you that they owe you nothing. And yet we must see to it, more than anything else, that our memory for services done to us stays fast. It needs refreshing from time to time. For one can make no repayment without remembering, and remembering is itself a repayment. (2) The manner of acceptance should not be disdainful, though neither should it be humbly submissive. If a man shows indifference in accepting a favour when it has all the charm of novelty, what will he do when the first pleasure of it has cooled? (3) One person may be disdainful in his acceptance, as if to say 'I really have no need of it. But since you want it so much, I will permit you to put me under an obligation.' Another may be apathetic, leaving its author in doubt as to whether he so much as noticed it. A third barely opens his mouth and shows even less gratitude than if he had stayed silent. (4) You, therefore, must express yourself the more extravagantly to match the importance of the matter, adding words like, 'You have put more people than you think in your debt!' (everyone is delighted to find the scope of his favours wider than he had thought); or, 'You do not know what you have done for me, but I must tell you how much more it is than you think!' (one immediately shows gratitude if one heaps up the burden on oneself); or, 'I can never repay you but at least I shall never stop telling everyone that I cannot.' **25** (1) Nothing that Furnius did served more to win the favour of Caesar Augustus and make him ready to grant other requests than his remark on winning pardon for his father, who had taken the side of Antony: 'I hold this one thing against you, Caesar. You have ensured that I should live and die without discharging my gratitude.'[44] There is no mark of gratitude like an utter dissatisfaction with oneself and a positive despair of ever being able to match the favour.

(2) With these and similar utterances, we should see to it that our intentions are not concealed, that we bring them into the open and make them shine forth. Words may fail us, but if we feel the

---

[44] Gaius Furnius, a distinguished orator, had been a republican closely allied with Cicero till 44 BC and then a partisan of Antony's under whom he governed Asia 36/5 BC. Pardoned by Augustus after Actium on the plea of his son, also called Gaius Furnius, he was later enrolled in the Senate. The son went on to become governor of Spain in 25 BC and consul in 17 BC.

indebtedness that we should, our awareness of it will show on our faces.

(3) Anyone who is going to be grateful should immediately, on accepting a favour, think on how to repay it. Chrysippus[45] indeed describes him as a man all set for a race, held at the barrier and obliged to wait for the moment when the signal is given, as it were, and he can spring forward. He will certainly need great effort and great speed to catch up with the person who has the start of him!

Ingratitude: its principal causes are self-regard, greed and envy

26 (1) We must now examine the principal causes of ingratitude. These are: undue self-regard (the failing, innate in mortals, of admiring oneself and whatever belongs to oneself), greed and envy.

(2) Let us start with the first of these. Everyone judges himself generously. Hence he thinks that everything he has got is his due: he takes it as payment – and still does not think that he has been appreciated at his true value. 'He did give it to me. But how long he took! How much trouble it cost me! I could have got so much more by cultivating So-and-so or So-and-so instead – or myself!' 'I had not expected this! He treats me as one of the crowd. Was I worth so little to him? It would have shown more respect to have passed me by.'

27 (1) Gnaeus Lentulus, the augur,[46] a prime example of wealth before his freedmen reduced him to poverty, a man with four hundred million sesterces to look at (I was speaking precisely – he never did more than look at them), had a barren mind and a spirit no less feeble. He was the greatest of misers, but freer with coins than talk, so dire was his poverty of speech. (2) He owed

---

[45] *SVF* III 726. Seneca may be referring to a passage of Chrysippus' *On Favours*, the work mentioned at 1 3. 8f..

[46] Consul in 14 BC, Gnaeus Cornelius Lentulus Augur (so called in order to distinguish him from his contemporary of the same name who was consul in 18 BC) served Augustus as proconsul in Asia in 2/1 BC and governor of Illyricum where he won an honorary triumph in warfare against the Getae (Tacitus, *Annals* IV 44. 1). He died in AD 25 – having been driven, it was believed, to suicide (Suetonius, *Life of Tiberius* 49) and leaving his considerable wealth to Tiberius. Tacitus speaks much more favourably of him than Seneca does.

all his advancement to Augustus. Having brought to his association with Augustus nothing more than poverty labouring under the burden of a noble name, he had become a leading citizen in wealth and influence. But he regularly complained about Augustus, saying that he had taken him away from his studies, that nothing of what had been heaped upon him could make up for what he had lost through giving up oratory. But this too was one of the favours bestowed by our deified Augustus. It had freed him from wasting his effort and making himself ridiculous.

(3) Greed allows no one to be grateful. Its immoral hopes are never satisfied with what comes to it. The more we get, the more we covet; and our avarice is far more excited when assigned the task of accumulating enormous wealth, in the same way that the force of a flame is vastly the greater, the greater the conflagration from which it flares out. (4) Nor is ambition any better about allowing one to rest content with that measure of public honours which was once its shameless prayer. No one gives thanks for a tribunate, but complains at not being advanced all the way to the praetorship. Nor is that welcome, if there is no consulate to follow it. Nor is even a consulate enough, if it is the only one.[47] Our covetousness keeps stretching further, and has no idea of how well off it is. It never looks back at its beginnings, only forward to its objectives.

28 (1) A fiercer and more insistent evil than any of these is envy. It disturbs us with comparisons – 'He gave me this, but gave more to him, and sooner to that person over there.' In the second place, it never takes anyone else's situation into account but always favours itself. How much more straightforward and sensible it would be to magnify the favour received, realizing that no one can be as esteemed by others as he is by himself! (2) 'I should have got more, but it would have been hard for him to give more. He had to spread his generosity widely.' 'And this is just the beginning. We should take it in good part and encourage him by receiving it gratefully. He did not do enough, but he will do it more often.' 'Yes, he preferred that person to me. But he also preferred me to many others.' 'That person may not have my good qualities and merits, but he had his charm.' 'Grumbling will not make me worthy

---

[47] Cf. *On Anger* III 31. 2.

of more; it will just make me unworthy of what I have been given. More may have been given to those utter scoundrels. So what? Fortune rarely shows any judgment.' (3) Every day we complain that the wicked prosper. All too often, the hail passes over the fields of all the worst people and flattens the corn of the best. Everyone has his destiny, in friendship as in everything else. (4) No favour is too ample for ill nature to pick holes in it, none too paltry for a good interpretation to enlarge it. You will never be short of grounds for complaint, if you look at favours from their least favourable angle.

29 (1) See how unfair men are in appraising the gifts of the gods,[48] even men who profess to be wise. They grumble because we are not the equals of the elephant in bodily size, of the stag in speed, of the bird in its weightlessness, of the bull in the force of its charge; because a wild beast's skin is hard, a deer's prettier, a bear's thicker, a beaver's softer; because the dog surpasses us in keenness of smell, the eagle in sharpness of eye, the crow in length of years and many animals in their power to swim. (2) Nature simply will not allow some properties to coexist in the same body – physical agility and brute strength, for instance. Yet they call it an injury that man is not a compound of incompatible advantages, and they accuse the gods of neglecting us because we have not been endowed with a health that is proof against even our vices or with knowledge of the future. They can scarcely restrain themselves from the impudence of loathing Nature for the fact that we stand beneath the gods, that we are not on their level. (3) How much better it would be to contemplate once again the number and quantity of their favours towards us and to give thanks that in this loveliest of habitations they were willing for us to be their lieutenants, putting us in charge of things on earth. How can anyone compare us with animals when the power over them is in our hands? We were only denied what could never have been granted. (4) Accordingly, whoever you are in your unfair judgment of our human condition, consider what our Father has bestowed upon us, how much stronger those animals are and yet we have

---

[48] The following digression, like the similarly theological passage at *On Anger* II 27. 1 f., is a good example of Stoic natural philosophy at the service of ethics (see Introduction to *On the Private Life*). Reflection on the divine order of the cosmos provides a basis for the virtues of gratitude and good temper.

yoked them, how much swifter they are and yet we catch them, how there is nothing mortal that lies beyond our reach. (5) We have been given so many excellences, so many skills, and a mind, moreover, which can penetrate anything with the force of its application, swifter than the stars whose courses, many centuries hence, it anticipates. And what a wealth of harvests we have, of riches, of treasures one piled up on top of the other. You may go round all creation and, finding nothing which in its entirety you would rather be, pick out from everything individual gifts which you would like to have – if you make a true judgment of Nature's kindness, you must confess that you are her favourite. (6) The fact is that we have been, and are, dearest to the immortal gods. They have bestowed the greatest honour possible on us by placing us next to them. Much we had given to us. We had no room for more.

30 (1) All this, dear Liberalis, I thought to be necessary. I had to say something about the greatest favours, if we were to speak of trivial ones; and it is here that the impudence of this loathsome vice which seeps into everything else has its source. Will a person answer anyone with thanks, will he think of any present as great and something to be returned, if he despises the greatest favours of all? Will he feel indebted to anyone for his safety or for the breath that he draws, if he denies that he has been granted his life by the gods from whom he seeks it every day? (2) To teach gratitude is to come to the defence of men and gods alike. The gods want for nothing, placed as they are beyond all need. None the less, we can repay them. There is no reason for anyone to seek an excuse for his ingratitude in weakness or poverty, saying, 'What am I to do? And how? When am I to repay those superior beings? They are lords of everything.' Repayment is easy. You may be stingy, but it will not cost a penny. You may be idle, but no effort is needed. At the very moment that you find yourself under an obligation, you can even things out with anyone, if you so wish. To accept a favour gladly is to have repaid it.

To accept a favour gladly is to have repaid it

31 (1) Among the paradoxes of the Stoic school this, in my view, is the least astonishing and the least hard to believe:[49] to accept a

---

[49] The 'paradoxes' of Stoical ethical theory were a commonplace of philosophical discussion in Hellenistic times; see Cicero, *The Paradoxes of the Stoics*. The most

favour gladly is to have repaid it. Since we refer everything to the mind, a person acts only to the extent that he willed his action; and since piety, good faith, justice – in short, every virtue – is complete in itself, even if it is prevented from raising a finger, human gratitude, too, can be an act of will alone. (2) Whenever a person achieves what he intended, he reaps the reward of what he has done. Now what is the intention of someone doing a favour? To help and to please the recipient. If he accomplishes what he wanted, if his state of mind gets through to me and inspires me with a joy that we both share, he has gained what he was after. He did not want anything in exchange – or it would not have been a favour that he was doing, but a deal. (3) A voyage is successful if it ends at the port of its destination. A dart thrown by a sure hand does its job, if it hits the mark. A person doing a favour wants it to be accepted with thanks. If it is well received, he has what he wanted. 'But he must have expected to get something!' Then he cannot have been doing a favour – its special feature is not to think of the return. (4) What I accepted I accepted in the same state of mind as that in which it was given. So I have repaid it. Otherwise the best of things would be tied to the worst of conditions. To be grateful, I would be thrown back on chance. But if chance goes against me and I cannot respond in kind, my state of mind is response enough to his. 'What do you mean? Am I not to do whatever I can to make repayment? Shall I not seek out every occasion, every time and circumstance? Shall I not long to line the pocket of one who has given to me?' Yes, but favours would be in a poor way were gratitude never allowed to be empty-handed.

32 (1) 'The recipient of a favour', you may object, 'may accept it in quite the friendliest state of mind – he still has not done all that he should. There remains the part about paying it back, just as in the ball game it is indeed something to catch skilfully and carefully, but a man is only described as a good player if he makes a swift and accurate *return* of what he has caught.' (2) The analogy is false. Why? Because the point of the game lies in bodily motion

prominently mentioned are these: that only what is 'honourable' (possessed of moral worth: *honestum*, καλόν) is good, that virtue is sufficient for happiness, that wrong actions are all equally bad and right actions all equally good, that only the wise man is free and every 'fool' a slave, that only the wise man is wealthy. See further IV 26. 2–27. 1.

and agility, not in a state of mind; everything which the eye has to judge must be spread out to view. And even so I would not call him a bad player if he caught the ball as he should but was prevented through no fault of his own from returning it. (3) 'The player's skill may leave nothing to be desired,' you may say, 'but the very fact that he has done part of what he should and is able to do the other part, which he failed to do, means that the game itself, which comes to fulfilment by alternate serves and returns, is incomplete.' (4) I shall not spend any more time refuting this. Let us grant that this is the case – it is the game, not the player, that leaves something to be desired. Likewise, in the subject under discussion, there may be something missing when it comes to the gift, if some other part[50] is still due, but not when it comes to the mind at work in the gift, if it has met with a mind to match itself and, to that extent, achieved what it wanted.

33 (1) Suppose someone has done me a favour, and I have accepted it in the way that he wished it to be accepted. He has got what he is after, indeed the one thing that he is after. And this means that I have shown gratitude. He may expect me to be of use to him afterwards, he may expect some benefit from a grateful human being. But that is not the missing part of a duty that has not yet been fully performed. It is just an addition to one that has. (2) Suppose that Phidias[51] makes a statue. His art brings him one reward, the work of art quite another. The reward from his art is to have made what he wanted. The reward from the work of art is to have made a profit from making it. Phidias' work is complete, even if it remains unsold. His work brings him three kinds of reward: one consists in his consciousness of it, which comes to him when the work is finished; one in his reputation; while the third is the benefit to be derived from the good will created, from the sale of it, or from some other sort of advantage. (3) In the same way, the first reward for doing a favour is in one's consciousness of it (one gets this when the good turn goes where

---

[50] Reading with the MSS *pars*.
[51] The greatest sculptor of the fifth century BC, Phidias designed, amongst other things, the sculptures on the Parthenon at Athens. The analogy between benefactor and artist goes back to Aristotle (*Nicomachean Ethics*. IX 7, 1167b31 ff.): in the same way that artists love the product of their artistry, Aristotle says, benefactors love those they have benefitted, since they are their 'handiwork'.

one wanted it to go), while both one's reputation and the things which might be bestowed in return are a secondary reward. So when a favour has been accepted in a friendly way, its author has already received a repayment in good will, though not, as yet, a material recompense. I still owe him something extra. But the favour itself, by accepting it properly, I have repaid in full.

34 (1) 'What do you mean – "paying it back," when one has not done a thing?' Well, firstly, one has. To have a good state of mind is to offer him something good – while remaining, as a friend should, on terms of equality. Then, secondly, loans and favours are paid off in different ways. But don't expect me to wave the repayment before your eyes – the transaction takes place between two minds. (2) What I am saying will not seem difficult (though it may at first go against your own opinion), if you pay attention and reflect that there are more things than there are words for. A huge number of things have no name. The terms which we use to indicate them are not proper to them; they belong to other things and have been borrowed. We speak of our own foot, a foot on a bed, a foot of a sail,[52] a foot in a verse; of a dog for hunting, of a dogfish, of the Dog Star. We have not the resources to give every object its own name and, when need arises, we borrow. (3) Courage, strictly, is the art[53] of despising the danger which it is right to despise or the science of danger – of warding it off, meeting it, courting it. Yet we can speak of a gladiator as a courageous man, as we can of a worthless slave driven by rashness to a scorn of death. (4) Frugality is the science of avoiding unnecessary expenditure or the art of due measure in managing property. Yet 'very frugal' is our expression for a petty-minded and stingy person, though there is a vast difference between due measure and meanness. These are essentially different things, but the poverty of our language has the effect that we call either type of person 'frugal', while the word 'courageous' is applied both to one who despises the blows of fortune, having reason to do so, and to one who runs into danger for no reason at all. (5) In the same way, a favour, as I have said, covers both an action that does good and an object

---

[52] At least, you could in Latin. The 'foot' of a sail was the rope by which its lower two corners were affixed to the vessel.

[53] Reading, with W. Alexander, Classical Quarterly 28 (1934) p. 54, *fortitudo est <ars> pericula iusta contemnens.*

bestowed by that action – for instance, a sum of money, a house, a robe of office. The name is the same for either; their meaning and effect are very different.

35 (1) So pay attention, and you will realize that I am not saying anything from which your own opinion should recoil. The favour which came to fulfilment in the action has been repaid, if it was accepted with good will. The other favour consisting in the object has not yet been returned, though we shall wish to return it. We have requited the act of will with our own act of will; for the object, we remain in debt. Thus while we can say that the favour has been repaid if gladly accepted, we would still urge a repayment in something similar to what was received.

(2) Some of what we Stoics say goes against ordinary usage but then comes back to it by a different route. We deny that the wise man can be wronged, and yet the person who punches him will be sentenced for wrongful injury. We deny that a fool can possess anything, yet anyone who steals from a fool we condemn for theft. We say that everyone is mad, but we do not dose everyone with hellebore.[54] The very people whom we describe as mad we entrust with the vote and authority to administer justice.[55] (3) In the same way, we describe one who has received a favour with a good mental attitude as having already repaid it, while leaving him none the less in debt, with repayment still to make, even when he has made it. This is not to repudiate the favour. It is to encourage ourselves not to be afraid of favours, not to lose courage beneath an unbearable load. 'I have had good things bestowed on me, my reputation has been defended, the slurs removed from it, my life has been saved along with that liberty which means more than life. How can I repay him? When will the day come for me to show him how I feel?' (4) The very day that *he* showed you how he feels! Accept the favour, take it to your bosom, rejoice not at what you may have received but at what you can repay and are going to owe! You will not be running any risks so great that chance could

---

[54] A drink made from hellebore (varieties of which are popular plants in British and North American gardens) was used as a purgative to cure the madness caused by an excess of black bile in the body. In Greek, 'Drink hellebore!' was a way of saying 'You are mad!'

[55] In a different aspect, the same Stoic paradox about wise men and fools is expounded at greater length at IV 26. 2–27. 1.

make you fail to show your gratitude. I shall put no difficulties in your way, in case you despair, in case at the prospect of toil and long servitude you lose your strength. I am not telling you to put off repaying – you can do it immediately. (5) You will never be thankful, if you are not so at once. So what are you to do? There is no need to take up arms – though sometime, perhaps, there may be. There is no need to cross the seas – though sometime, perhaps, even as the storm threatens, you may find yourself putting to sea. You wish to return a favour? Accept it with good will and you have already repaid it. Not that you should think yourself discharged – you can just be more confident about your debt.

Book III

Ingratitude

Ingratitude: its worst form is forgetfulness

1 (1) Not to return a favour is shameful and is held by all to be so, Aebutius Liberalis. That is why people complain about ingratitude, even when guilty of it themselves. At the same time, we are all of us attached to the behaviour we all dislike, and such is the contradiction that we regard some as our worst enemies not just after – but *because* – they have done us favours. (2) I will not deny that with some people this is due to natural viciousness. But with most people the passage of time is what has robbed them of the memory. What was fresh and vigorous in their minds has faded during the interval.

You and I once had a discussion about such people, I know. You called them 'forgetful' rather than 'ungrateful', as though the cause of a person's ingratitude were an excuse for it, as though the fact that this happens meant that he is not ungrateful, whereas it can only happen because he *is* ungrateful. (3) There are many kinds of ingratitude, just as there are of murder or theft. The fault is one and the same, but with a great variety of subdivisions. It is ungrateful to deny receiving a favour that one has received, ungrateful to pretend that one has not received it, it is ungrateful not to return it, and most ungrateful of all to forget it. (4) In other cases, the debt may not be repaid, but it is still consciously owed. There remains, enclosed in a guilty conscience, at least a trace of the services done. Some day the ungrateful may be brought round for some reason to make repayment – by the promptings of shame, by a sudden desire (of the sort which occurs from time to time even in wicked hearts) to do something honourable or by the inducement of some easy opportunity. But gratitude is impossible if the favour has entirely slipped the memory. Which is worse: failure of gratitude for a favour, or failure even to remember it? (5) Your eyes are faulty if they recoil from the light; they are blind if they cannot see it. Not to love your parents is impiety; not to recognize them is lunacy.

2 (1) Is anyone so ungrateful as one who sets aside what should be in the front of the mind and always occurring to him, who so dismisses it as to have no knowledge of it? It is quite clear that you have not thought often of making repayment, if forgetfulness has crept over you. (2) In point of fact, to repay a favour, you need ability, you need the occasion and the means, you need fortune to favour you. But just remembering it – and with[1] no outlay at all – means that you are grateful. It requires no effort, no resources, no luck; and failure to provide it has no excuse behind which to shelter. You cannot have wanted to be grateful if you have put the favour so far away from you as to lose sight of it. (3) Things that are kept in use, handled and touched every day, are never in danger of decay, while those that are not brought into view and remain unfamiliar, as though unnecessary, accumulate dirt with the passing of time. In the same way, anything practised and renewed by repeated effort of thought never slips the memory, which loses nothing except what it rarely looks back on.

3 (1) Apart from this, there are other reasons, too, why services done to us, often of the greatest value, should be torn from the memory. First and most powerful of all is the fact that we are preoccupied with ever-new desires. Our eyes are fixed, not on what we have, but on what we seek to have. Intent as we are on the object of our appetites, we discount what is in our pockets. (2) But the result is that, where desire for new favours has devalued what you have already received, their author, too, falls in value. We may have loved someone, looked up to him, described him as the very foundation of our position in life, for so long as we were happy with what we had managed to get. Then the idea of how

---

[1] Reading, with Gertz, <*et*> *sine.*

wonderful something else might be bursts in on our minds. We make a rush for it with our human habit of having much and still wanting more. Straightway, whatever it was that we called a favour escapes us; and we no longer have eyes for our own advantages over others, but only for those we see in the good fortune of people ahead of us.[2] (3) But no one can be envious and thankful at the same time. Envy goes with complaints and gloom, thankfulness with joy.

(4) In the second place, none of us is aware of any moment in time except that which is actually passing. So people rarely turn their minds back to the past. That is why our teachers and their kindnesses fall from the memory – we have left our childhood entirely behind us. That is why kindnesses done to us in our youth are lost to us – our youth itself is never relived. No one regards what has been as past, but as perished. So faint is our memory in our concentration on the future. 4 (1) Here I must give Epicurus due acknowledgment. He is constantly complaining that we are ungrateful towards the past, that we never remember any blessing received or count it among our pleasures, although there is no surer pleasure than one which cannot be taken away.[3] (2) Present blessings are not yet entirely on firm ground, since blows of fortune can still interfere with them. Future blessings hang before us uncertainly. Only what is past lies stored in safety. How can anyone be thankful for favours, if he has passed his life dedicated entirely to things present and future? Memory is what makes for gratitude; and memory receives the least attention where hope is given the most.

5 (1) Some things, my dear Liberalis, need only be grasped once to stay in the mind. There are others which, if you are really to know them, it is not enough just to have been taught. The knowledge fails you if it is not kept up. I am speaking of geometry, knowledge of celestial bodies and any other subject that is elusive

---

[2] Compare II 27. 4 and *On Anger* III 31. 2.

[3] Usener prints this section as Epicurus, Fragment 435. See also Epicurus, *Principal Doctrines* 18; *Vatican Sayings* 17, 19, and 55; and Cicero, *On Ends* I 57, 60 and 62; along with his quotation (II 96) from Epicurus' description of his last hours, racked by disease yet happy because of his pleasant memories. This Epicurean theme of gratitude for the past also appears in Plutarch's *On Good Spirits* (478b–e). Like the warning against eyeing those better off than oneself (see 3. 3 above), it appears to have been an established topic in that literature.

because of its detailed precision. In the same way, some favours are not allowed by their sheer importance to escape the mind. Others, less important but very numerous and from separate times, do slip away because, as I have said, they are not regularly handled and we do not like going over our obligations. (2) Listen to what people say as they make their petitions. Everyone claims that the memory will live for ever in his mind; everyone pledges his 'attachment', his 'devotion' and any expression still more abject that he can find for binding himself. A short time goes by. The very same people shun their earlier utterances as base and servile. They reach the state, as I see it, of the worst and most ungrateful – they forget. So much, indeed, is ingratitude bound up with forgetfulness, that a person counts as grateful[4] if the favour simply comes into his mind.

Should ingratitude be made subject to legal prosecution?[5]

6 (1) The question arises: should a fault so hateful as this go unpunished? Should the law that is enacted in the schools of oratory[6] be laid down also for the state, granting the right to bring

---

[4] Reading, with Alexander, *ut [in]gratus sit.*
[5] This general question had become a political issue, in the specific case of freedmen charged with ingratitude by their ex-masters. A slave at his 'manumission' or release from slavery promised obedience and service (*obsequium*) to his master, who remained his patron with certain rights over him. These he might need to enforce: in 50 BC, Cicero had written to Atticus about repudiating the manumission of two freedmen for gross negligence of their duties (*Letters to Atticus* VII 2. 8). But was breach of *obsequium* a legal offence? During the principate, from Augustus to Marcus Aurelius, progressively harsher penalties were prescribed against 'ungrateful freedmen', *liberti ingrati* (see C. E. Manning, *ANRW* II 36. 3, p. 1536). In AD 56, a proposal had been made by the Senate and discussed in Nero's council, where Seneca would have been present, to allow patrons to revoke the manumission of ungrateful freedmen, its purpose being to increase a patron's hold over his freedmen (and their assets) as well as to reduce the threat that they might inform on him. The proposal was rejected, or rather a compromise was reached. Nero ruled that patrons were to have no such sweeping powers, but that in individual cases patrons could make charges and the Senate order re-enslavement (Tacitus, *Annals* XIII 26 f.). In this very limited context, a prosecution for ingratitude was to be possible. In our present text, however, Seneca is writing simply as a moralist, and he condemns the idea altogether. Later on (IV 17.1), he accepts without more ado the fact that ingratitude is not covered by law.
[6] One exercise in the schools of rhetoric was the *controversia*, a mock law-suit on an imaginary case under an imaginary law. A well-worn example of such a case was that of 'the wicked, ungrateful husband' (Juvenal, *Satires* VII 169) who has

a suit for ingratitude? It strikes everyone as fair. 'Why not? Even cities reproach other cities with what they have bestowed on them. Favours conferred on one generation are exacted from its descendants.'[7] (2) Our ancestors, however, who were certainly very great men, pressed their enemies only for restitution of property. When it came to favours, they showed their greatness of mind, in granting them and in allowing them to be unreturned. Except in the Macedonian nation,[8] the right has never been granted to sue for ingratitude.[9] And this is a weighty argument that it should not be granted. We are all in agreement about criminal offences. Homicide, poisoning, parricide and sacrilege may be punished differently in one place than in another, but everywhere they receive some punishment. Yet this most common of charges meets nowhere with punishment, though everywhere with disapproval. It is not that we are excusing it. But it is hard to assess so vague a matter. So we visit it solely with our hatred, leaving it among those misdeeds which we refer to the gods for judgment.

7 (1) In fact, I can think of several reasons why this charge should not be covered by a law. First of all, the best thing about a favour is lost if the right to sue is granted, as it is for a fixed sum of money or for property rented or leased. Its most attractive aspect is that we granted the favour even at the risk of not getting it back, that we left it all to the discretion of the recipient. If I lay a charge and summon him before the judge, it stops being a favour and turns into a loan. (2) Secondly, while showing gratitude is the most honourable course of action, it ceases to be honourable

---

been saved from a tyrant by his wife and then divorces her for barrenness (Seneca the Elder, *Controversiae* II 5) or who has been ransomed by her father but executes her for adultery (IX 1; see also III Praef. 17).

[7] In particular, the emperors expected the wills of persons who owed them favours to reflect their gratitude. Caligula started the practice of invalidating wills that failed to do so (Suetonius, *Life of Gaius* 38. 20).

[8] See the story at IV 37.

[9] Seneca's elder contemporary Valerius Maximus does say that legal action against ingratitude was allowed at Athens (V 3 Ext. 3), that an ungrateful freedman could be stripped of his freedom there by his patron (II 6. 6) and that there was a similar law at Marseilles (*ibid.*). Valerius, however, may be confusing as a 'suit for ingratitude' (in Greek δίκη ἀχαριστίας) the 'suit for desertion' (δίκη ἀποστασίου): an ex-slave at Athens had the status of a resident alien under the patronage of his ex-master and was liable, if he attached himself to a different patron, to be sued for 'desertion' and re-enslaved.

if made obligatory. A person will no more be praised for being grateful than for returning a deposit or for paying off a debt before coming up before a judge. (3) So the two loveliest things in human life are spoiled – the person's gratitude and the favour. There is nothing magnificent about a favour that is not freely granted, but merely loaned, or in a return made not because the person wishes to make it but because he has to. There can be no glory in gratitude if you cannot be ungrateful with impunity.

(4) Consider this, too. All the law-courts in the world would hardly be enough to enforce this one law. Would anyone fail to sue? Would anyone fail to be sued? All exalt their services to other people and exaggerate their contributions, even the slightest. (5) Moreover, issues only come under judicial enquiry if they can be covered by a set form of words[10] that imposes a limit on the judge's freedom. That is why a good case is stronger when sent to a judge than to an arbitrator, since the judge is restricted by the form of words and is given certain limits which he cannot overstep, whereas the arbitrator has only his scruples, free and bound by no constraints; he can add and take away, guiding his verdict not by the promptings of law and justice but by impulses of kindness and compassion. (6) The judge in a suit for ingratitude, far from being tied down, will be in a position of the most sovereign freedom. There is no agreement about what constitutes a favour, nor about its extent; what matters is simply how kind an interpretation the judge puts on it. There is no law to show what constitutes ingratitude; it often happens that even a person who has given back what he has received is guilty of ingratitude, and one who has not is innocent. (7) In some cases, even an inexperienced judge can record a verdict – where, for instance, he has just to state whether something was done or not, where written undertakings are produced to settle the dispute, where some legal principle decides between the disputants. But where a state of mind has to be inferred, where the quarrel is about something which wisdom alone can decide, a judge for the issue can hardly be taken from those

---

[10] The *formula* or 'form of words' was the official document, drawn up by the plaintiff the defendant and the praetor in charge, summarizing the legal issue in a suit and instructing the judge to pass judgment. See *On Mercy* II 3. 1, n. 5.

put on the praetor's list as having the means and the ancestry of a knight.[11]

8 (1) So it is not that the matter is unfit to be brought to judgment. It is rather that anyone fit to judge it has yet to be found. You will not be surprised at this, if you go through the difficulties that will face anyone on whom it should fall to deal with this sort of charge. (2) Suppose someone has given a large sum of money, but was rich and was not going to feel the cost. Suppose someone else gave it, but at the risk of losing his entire estate. The sum was the same, but not the favour. Again, one person may have paid out money to a man bound over for debt, but drawing it from his own resources. Another may have given the same amount, but have had to borrow or beg it, putting himself under a huge obligation. Is their position the same, do you think, if the one had no difficulty in lavishing the favour while the other had to accept a gift in order to make one?

(3) The timing, not the amount, is what makes some favours important. A grant of land fertile enough to reduce the price of grain is a favour; so is a single loaf in a famine. A grant of territories with large, navigable rivers running through them is a favour; it is also a favour to people parched with thirst, scarcely drawing breath down their desiccated throats, if you point out a fountain. Who is to compare these or weigh them against each other? Judgment is difficult when the investigation is not about the thing itself but about its force. The gifts may well be the same; but they were given differently and their weight is not the same. (4) So-and-so did me a favour – yes, but unwillingly, or complaining that he had done so, or giving me a more arrogant look than usual, or so slowly that he would have done more for me if he had promptly said 'No.'[12] How is a judge to start weighing these up, when a person's language or hesitation or the look on his face can ruin the good will which a good turn should communicate?

---

[11] In Roman civil procedure, the judges were private individuals, with no need for any special juridical training, taken from the two higher classes, senators and knights. To be enrolled on the praetor's list as a knight, a person needed to be of citizen birth and to possess 400,000 sesterces (very roughly £400,000 or US $600,000. A sesterce was very approximately equivalent to a Victorian sixpence (see Veyne, p. 9), i.e. to £1 in 1994.)

[12] Cf. II 1–5.

9 (1) And what of the fact that some things are called favours because they are very greatly coveted, while others that are not commonly so labelled are in fact greater ones even if less obvious? (2) You would certainly call it a favour to have granted someone the citizenship of a powerful nation or put him on the equestrian benches[13] or defended him on a capital charge.[14] But what of having given him good advice or stopped him from rushing into crime? What of knocking away the sword as he tried to kill himself, of finding effective consolation for his sorrow, of restoring his will to live when he only wished to follow those whom he had lost? What of attending his sick bed, when his health and safety were in the balance, of seizing on the right moment to feed him, of restoring his flagging circulation with wine, of bringing a doctor to his death bed? (3) Who is to weigh such things up? Who is to direct one favour to be balanced by another when they are quite different? 'I gave you your house.' But I warned you that yours was going to fall on top of you. 'I gave you an estate.' But I gave you a plank when we were ship-wrecked. 'I fought for you and got wounded.' But I saved your life by my silence. A favour can given in one way and returned in another. An equation between the two is hard to establish.

10 (1) Besides, there is no specified date for repaying a favour as there is for repaying a loan. Anyone who has not made repayment may still do so. Tell me in fact, what should the deadline be for ingratitude? (2) The most important favours have no procedure for proving them. They frequently remain unannounced, a secret known only to the two parties – or shall we have it that favours should never be done without a witness?

(3) Again, what penalty are we to lay down for the ungrateful? One and the same for all, though the favours are unequal? Or a penalty varying in proportion to the favour done in any given case? Shall the assessment be in money? What of the fact that some favours are worth as much as life itself – or still more? What penalty is to be decreed here? A penalty less than the favour done

---

[13] Lit. 'on the fourteen' (rows in the theatre). Under the *lex Roscia* of 67 BC these were reserved for members of the equestrian order, the knights.

[14] Lawyers were not allowed to charge for their services which, strictly, were always 'favours'. A successful advocate, however, could expect handsome recompense from a grateful client.

will not be just. To match it, you need a death sentence. But what could be more inhuman than a favour which ends in bloodshed?

11 (1) 'Parents have certain legal prerogatives',[15] you may say. 'They receive a consideration which is out of the ordinary. So, too, should other benefactors.'[16] We have sanctified the state of parenthood because it was desirable for children to be raised. People had to be stirred to the task with its uncertain outcome. There was no possibility of telling them as we tell those who do favours: 'Choose whom to give to. Blame yourself for any disappointment. Help those who deserve it.' In raising children, nothing is left to the decision of those who raise them – it is all a matter of hoping and praying. So, to calm them as they ran the risk, they had to be given certain powers. And because it is useful for the young to be controlled, we imposed on them household magistrates, as it were, to guard them and hold them in check.[17] (2) Again, parents are in a different situation. When they have done favours, they do them again to the same people regardless, and they will go on doing them. Nor is there any danger of their claiming to have done favours they have not. In other cases, it is quite proper to ask not just whether a favour has been returned but whether it was done at all. The services of parents, however, are generally admitted. (3) Again, the favour done by all parents is one and the same; and we have been able to evaluate it once and for all. Other favours are different, unlike each other, an infinite distance apart; and there was no rule which they could all be brought under. It would be fairer to abandon the lot of them than to treat them all as equal.

12 (1) Some things cost the giver much. Some mean much to the recipient but cost nothing to the person bestowing them. Some are made to friends, some to strangers. The same amount may be given, but it means more if given to one whom you only begin to

---

[15] At Athens, under a law attributed to Solon (early sixth century BC), a son could be prosecuted for neglect or maltreatment of his parents and barred from public office, if found guilty. See Xenophon, *Memorabilia* II 2. 13; Aeschines, I 28; Demosthenes, XXIV 103–7. The Roman institution of *patria potestas* gave the head of a family absolute power over its other members; it is to this that Seneca's 'household magistrates' just below refers.

[16] Reading, with Koch, *beneficorum*.

[17] Transposing, with Gertz *et quia utile ... contineretur* (end of 11. 2) to after *potestas fuit*.

know when doing the favour. One man bestows help, another honours, a third consolation. (2) You may find someone who thinks nothing more agreeable or important than to have a place where his misfortune can find comfort; you may find someone else, on the other hand, who would rather one were solicitous for his status than for his safety; and there is the person who feels himself more in your debt for an increase in his security than in his honour. The value of all these things will vary according to the mental inclination of the judge. (3) Furthermore, I can myself choose if someone is to lend me something. But I often find myself being done a favour by someone from whom I do not want it, and I am sometimes put under an obligation without realizing it. What are you to do <in this case>? Are you going to call a person ungrateful if a favour is imposed upon him without his knowledge, which he would have refused, had he known? Will you not call him ungrateful if, however he got it, he fails to repay it? (4) Someone may have done me a favour, and afterwards wronged me. Am I bound by one present from him to put up with all the wrongs he does me? Or will it be as though I have already repaid him, since the favour has been annulled by the wrong which followed it? And then how are you to work out which is greater – the favour received or the harm inflicted? I would need more than a day if I tried to deal with all the difficulties.

13 (1) 'We shall only make people slower to do favours,' you may say, 'by not protecting the favours that are done and not punishing those who would repudiate them.' Yes, but on the other hand, it should also occur to you that people will be much slower to accept favours if they are faced with the risk of legal action, and with finding themselves, though innocent, in a situation of heightened anxiety. (2) Besides, if this is done, we ourselves will be slower to do favours. No one is pleased to give to unwilling recipients. Anyone drawn to act kindly by his own good nature and the sheer attractiveness of the action will be still more pleased to give to people who will only be indebted to the extent that they wish. An act of kindness loses much of its glory, if careful and circumspect.

14 (1) 'Then, in that case, favours may be fewer, but they will be more genuine. What harm is there in restricting people's rashness in doing them?' Yes, this was the very aim of those who refused

to pass a law on this matter – that we should be more careful in making gifts, more cautious in our choice of those on whom to confer our services. (2) To whom are you giving? That is what you must consider again and again. There will be no recourse to legal action, no right of restitution. You are wrong if you think that a judge will come to your aid. No law will put you back where you were. The one thing to keep your eyes on is the good faith of your recipient. That is how favours retain their power and their glory. You will degrade them by making them a subject for litigation. (3) 'Pay back what you owe!' is an utterly reasonable maxim, affirming a universal law.[18] But it is utterly shameful when applied to a favour! 'Pay back!' Yes, but what? The life which one owes? One's status? One's security? One's health? (4) The most important things cannot be repaid. 'Well, in their place, put something of the same value.' But that is just what I was saying! All that is excellent in such a precious activity will come to an end, if we turn a favour into a business deal. There is no need to goad the mind to avarice, to complaints, to dissension. It comes to these of its own accord. Indeed, so far as we can, we should make a stand and cut off any occasion for them which it may be seeking.

15 (1) If creditors could only be persuaded to accept payment solely from those who are willing to pay! If only there were no strict formal contract[19] binding purchaser to vendor![20] If only our agreements and compacts could be guarded without the impress of seals, just preserved through good faith and the cultivation of equity in the soul! (2) But men have put compulsion before ideals. They would rather enforce good faith than await it. Witnesses are brought on by both parties. One person, in a series of ledgers,[21]

---

[18] Latin *ius gentium*, the 'law of nations'. Here the term refers to 'universal' law, the common principles recognized in the law of all peoples.

[19] Latin *stipulatio*. The earliest form of Roman contract, concluded orally in the form of question and answer: 'Do you promise to do (or give) x?' 'I do', this was a matter of 'strict law', *stricti iuris*. That is, it had to be honoured in strict adherence to its wording.

[20] Sale was usually a 'consensual' contract, worked out by oral agreement (*consensu*) and allowing for a more liberal compliance *bona fide* – that is, on principles of 'good faith' and equity – than a *stipulatio* would (see n. 19). Buyer and vendor could also choose, though they were not obliged, to be bound by *stipulatio*.

[21] The moment a purchase or debt was written down, it would become unalterably a matter of 'strict law', usually to the disadvantage of the purchaser or debtor. See Cicero's story of a fraudulently sold house at *On Duties* III 58–60.

puts several borrowers onto his account by inserting the names of those who stand surety.[22] Another is not content with a verbal contract[23] – he has to have the debtor pinned down with his own autograph.[24] (3) What a shameful acknowledgment of human fraudulence and public wickedness! Our signet-rings are trusted more than our souls! What are these distinguished gentlemen brought in for? What is the point of their signatures? Of course, to prevent the debtor denying that he received what he did receive. Are *they* the incorruptible champions of truth, do you think? I tell you, these very people will immediately be subjected to the same procedure when money is entrusted to them. Would it not be less shameful for trust to be disappointed in some cases than for treachery to be feared in all? (4) Our avarice lacks one thing alone to be complete – that we should refuse to do favours without some guarantor. The mark of a noble, magnificent mind is to aid, to do people good. In granting favours, you copy the gods. When you sue to get them back, you copy the money-lenders. Why, in our defence of those who do favours, should we put them in that sordid company?

16 (1) 'More people will be ungrateful, if there is no right to sue for ingratitude.' No, fewer will. Favours will be done with greater discrimination. Besides, it is not a good idea for all to know how many ungrateful people there are. The shame of the thing will be lost in the sheer number of wrongdoers, and there is no scope for ignominy in a reproach that is general. (2) No woman today, surely, blushes at divorce, now that some illustrious, aristocratic ladies keep track of the years not by the consuls[25] but by their husbands, leaving home to get married and marrying to get divorced. Women fought shy of such conduct while it was still unusual. But now that the gazette[26] never appears without a divorce case in it, they have learned to do what they have so often heard

---

[22] A 'surety' (Latin *pararius*) undertook by a separate promise the same liability as the debtor did by his *stipulatio*, and could thus himself count as a debtor.

[23] Latin *interrogatio*, i.e. a mere verbal *stipulatio* in question and answer form.

[24] And perhaps to no avail. See Juvenal, XIII 135–9.

[25] It was customary at Rome to date events by reference to the two holders of the consulate (the highest civil and military magistracy) in that year. Under the empire, when consuls held office for less than a year, reference was made to the two who took office on 1 January.

[26] See II 10. 4, n. 7.

about. (3) Is there anything shameful today about adultery, now
that we have reached the point where no woman will take a
husband except to arouse a lover? Chastity is proof of ugliness.
Where are you going to find a woman so wretched and dowdy
as to be content with just a pair of lovers? Unless she has one
every hour (and even so the day is not enough for them all),
unless she goes for a drive with one and spends the night with
another, she counts as unenlightened and out of date, unaware
that 'being married' is simply a name for having a single lover.
(4) The shame of such misdeeds has vanished now that the practice
has come to be more widespread. In the same way, you will make
the ungrateful more numerous and influential once they start to
count their number.

The punishment for ingratitude

17 (1) 'What do you mean? Is ingratitude to go unpunished?'
What do *you* mean? Is impiety unpunished? What about malice, or
avarice? What about violence or cruelty? Do you really believe that
anything goes unpunished, if it is hated? Can you think of any
worse punishment than public loathing? (2) The punishment for
ingratitude lies in not daring to accept a favour from anyone or to
do anyone a favour, in being pointed out by everyone or thinking
that one is being pointed out, in having lost all sense of the best
and sweetest thing on earth. You would call it a misfortune to be
without sight or to have your ears blocked up by disease. Would
you not describe one who has lost all sense of favours as wretched?
(3) He has the gods to fear, witnesses as they are of all ingratitude.
He burns in anguish at his awareness of having cut short the
favour. And finally, it is punishment enough to derive no enjoyment
from a thing which, as I said, is the pleasantest on earth. But he
who is glad to be a recipient enjoys a continual, unfailing pleasure,
rejoicing less in the object itself than in the intention with which
it was given to him. To the grateful a favour is a joy for ever, to
the ungrateful a joy but once. (4) You can place the two lives
beside each other. The one man is gloomy and anxious, as those
who cheat and repudiate usually are, denying the honour that is
their due to parents, tutor and teachers. The other is joyous,
cheerful, eager for the chance to return the favour and deriving a

great joy from this very emotion, with his eye not on how to default but on how to make a fuller and richer response, not only to family and friends but to those of lower estate as well. Even if such a man is done a favour by his slave, his thought is not on who did it, but on what it was.

Slaves and masters

Can a slave do his master a favour?

18 (1) Some, though, like Hecaton,[27] raise the question of whether a slave can do his master a favour. For there are those who make a distinction between favours, duties and menial services.[28] A favour is done by an outsider (that is, some one who could hold back without being blamed); a duty is the work of a son, of a wife, of anyone with ties of kinship to rouse them and compel them to help; while a menial service is performed by a slave whose lot is to be in a situation where nothing that he provides will give him any claim on his superior.

(3) <But>[29] if a favour cannot be done to his master by a slave, neither can it be done by anyone to his king, nor by a soldier to his commander. If you are under absolute rule, does it matter what sort it is? If a slave is prevented, by the constraints and extreme intimidation to which he is subject, from claiming to have deserved well, the same obstacles stand in the way of anyone under a king or a commander. Their titles are different; their power over you

---

[27] See I 3. 9, n. 13.

[28] Latin *beneficia, officia, ministeria*. The author of this interesting distinction is unknown. The context here strongly suggests that Hecaton at least employed it, and he may have been its originator: a distinction between favours, duties and menial services would be quite in place in the work *On Duty* which Hecaton wrote and in which Seneca may have found him raising the question whether a slave can do his master a favour.

[29] Something must have dropped out of the text at the end of 18. 1, perhaps the conclusion that favours cannot be done to the head of a family by his slaves since that would be a 'menial service', nor even by subordinate members of the family, since that would be a 'duty'. Seneca deals with the first claim at 19–28 and with the second, or something coming under it, at 29–38.

With Sonntag, we transpose 18. 2 and 18. 3, in order to provide a suitable connection for the 'Besides' at the beginning of 18. 2, and to preserve the striking continuity of thought between 18. 2 and 4.

is the same. And yet kings and generals have favours done to them. So too, then, can masters. (2) Besides, to deny that a slave may sometimes do his master a favour is to ignore his rights as a man. What matters is the state of mind, and not the status, of whoever bestows it. No one is barred from being good. Virtue is open to everyone, admits everyone, invites everyone – freeborn, freedman and slave, king and exile. It does not have to choose the great house or the great fortune; it is content with the naked man. What safety could there be against sudden changes, what grandeur could the mind promise itself, if its sure virtue were transformed by a change of fortune? (4) A slave can be just, he can be brave, he can have greatness of mind. So he can also do a favour. For that, too, belongs to virtue. Slaves can indeed do their masters a favour – so much so that often the very existence of their masters has depended on their favour.

19 (1) There is no doubt that a slave can do a favour to anyone you like. So why not also to his master? 'Because he cannot put his master in his debt if he gives him money.[30] Otherwise he would place him under obligation every day. He accompanies him on travels abroad, looks after him in sickness, wears himself out working on his farm. Bestowed by anyone else, all these kindnesses would be called favours; bestowed by a slave, they are just a menial service. A favour is something done by someone in a position not to do it. But a slave has no power to refuse. He bestows nothing; he just obeys orders. Nor can he boast of doing anything that he could not help doing.' (2) Even on these terms I can win the argument. I can draw the slave to conclude that he is free in many things.[31] Meanwhile, tell me this. Suppose I show you someone fighting for his master's safety without regard for his own, riddled with wounds yet pouring out from his very entrails what blood is left there and seeking, so as to give his master time to escape, a respite for him at the cost of his own life – would you deny that he has done a favour, just because he is a slave? (3) Suppose I show you someone uncorrupted by any of a tyrant's promises

---

[30] Not being capable of legal ownership, a slave could not strictly be owed money by his master, since any property that he might manage as more or less his own already belonged by law to his master.

[31] First of all in the free use of his own mind (see Chapter 20), and then in any action that goes beyond the services normally required of a slave (Chapters 21–2).

into betraying his master's secrets, unintimidated by any threats, unmastered by any tortures,[32] who has deflected, so far as he could, the suspicions of his inquisitor and paid for his fidelity with his life – would you deny that he has done his master a favour, just because he was a slave? (4) May it not be that a display of virtue in a slave is the greater for its rarity and the more welcome for the fact that, while subjection to orders is generally hateful and all constraint burdensome, the common hatred of his condition has been overcome in an individual slave by love for his master? A favour is not prevented from being one because it comes from a slave. It is all the greater because even his slavery has not sufficed to deter him from it.

20 (1) It is a mistake to think that slavery penetrates the entire man. The better part of him is exempt. Bodies can be assigned to masters and be at their mercy. But the mind, at any rate, is its own master, so free in its movements that not even this prison which shuts it in can hold it back from following its own impulse, from setting mighty projects in motion, from faring forth into the infinite to consort with the stars. (2) The body, therefore, is what fortune hands over to a master, what he buys and sells. That inner part can never come into anyone's possession. Whatever proceeds from it is free. For neither can we command everything from our slaves nor are they compelled to obey us in everything. They are not obliged to carry out orders against the commonwealth nor, if any crime is involved, to lend a hand.

21 (1) Some things are neither prescribed nor forbidden by law. Here the slave has the material for favours. So long as what he provides is what is ordinarily demanded of a slave, it counts as a menial service. When it is more than what a slave has to do, it is a favour. When it comes into the province of friendly feeling, it can no longer be called a menial service. (2) There are things which a master ought to provide for his slave – food and clothing, for instance. No one would describe these as a favour. But suppose that he has been lenient with him, given him something of a liberal education, taught him the arts in which free men are schooled – that really is a favour. The same holds good, conversely, when the

---

[32] In Roman criminal procedure, slaves were regularly subjected to interrogation with torture.

role is that of a slave. Whatever goes beyond the provisions of the slave's duty, whatever he provides not because he has been told but because he wishes to do so, is a favour – with the sole proviso that it should be significant enough to count as one were it provided by anyone else.

22 (1) A slave, according to Chrysippus, is a 'hireling for life'.[33] In the same way that a hireling does a favour, if he provides more than what he has hired himself for, so too a slave – when good will towards his master carries him beyond the bounds of his station, when he dares to raise his sights and act in a way that would be a credit even to men born under a luckier star, when he exceeds his master's hopes, a favour has been encountered within the household. (2) Is it fair, do you think, for us to be angry if they do less than they should, but not to feel gratitude if they do more than they are meant or accustomed to do? Do you want to know when it is not a favour? When you can say 'Well, he had better *not* refuse me!' When he has provided in fact what he could have refused to do, his willingness deserves to be praised.

(3) Favours and wrongs are contraries of each other: one can do one's master a favour if one can be wronged by him.[34] But wrongs are done by masters to slaves; they come under the jurisdiction of an official,[35] charged with curbing their cruelty, lust and meanness in supplying everyday necessities. 'And so? Does that mean that a favour can be done to a master by his slave?' No. To one human being by another. (4) After all, he did what was in his power. So he did his master a favour. Not to accept it from a slave would be quite within your power. But who is so important that fortune cannot compel him to stand in need of even the humblest?

---

[33] Printed as *SVF* III 351. This definition of Chrysippus' implies what was also held by Roman jurists, that, contrary to what Aristotle had maintained, there are no 'slaves by nature'. Cicero (*On Duties* I 41) cites with approval, without indicating the author, the injunction that slaves should be treated as 'hirelings'.

[34] Seneca is employing the logical principle that if something falls within the range of one contrary then it is the sort of thing that *can* fall under the other. His claim is that doing a favour to someone and being wronged by him are contraries to which this principle applies.

[35] I.e. the *praefectus urbi*, a magistrate charged primarily with controlling the slave population and other unruly elements in the city (Tacitus, *Annals* VI 11).

Examples of favours done by slaves to their masters

23 (1) I shall now recall several examples of such favours, all of them different, some quite contrary to one another. One slave granted his master life, another granted him death; one saved him from perishing and, if that were not enough, saved him by perishing himself; one helped his master to die, another tricked him out of dying.

(2) Claudius Quadrigarius[36] relates in Book XVIII of his *Annals* that, when Grumentum[37] was under siege and had been reduced to the final extremity of hopelessness, two slaves deserted to the enemy camp and proved their worth there. Then with the city captured and the conquerors running everywhere this way and that, they ran ahead through paths familiar to them to the house where they had been in service and drove out their mistress before them. Asked who she was, they asserted that she was their mistress, and a most cruel one at that, whom they were taking off to punishment. Having led her then outside the city walls, they concealed her with the greatest care, till the wrath of the enemy had subsided. Then, once the soldiery had had its fill of plunder and quickly returned to Roman ways, they too returned to theirs and re-entered, of their own free will, their mistress's service. (3) She granted them both their freedom on the spot, thinking it no shame to owe her life to men over whom she had once had power of life and death. Indeed, she could take this as grounds rather for congratulation. Rescued in any other way, she would have had the benefit of a familiar and ordinary mercy. Rescued in the way that she was, she was a story of note, a pattern for two cities. (4) In such confusion at the capture of the town, as each took thought only for himself, all deserted her save the deserters; yet they, to show the intention behind their earlier change of side, deserted from the victor to the woman captive, in the guise of murderers from within the

---

[36] An annalist of the first century BC, Claudius Quadrigarius wrote a history of Rome in at least twenty-three books (all now lost, except for isolated quotations in later ancient writers), from its sacking by Celtish marauders in 387 to about 80 BC.

[37] An inland town in Lucania some distance south of Naples, Grumentum was besieged in the Social War, 90–88 BC, a revolt by Rome's Italian allies which ended with their being granted full Roman citizenship.

household; and the best part of the favour that they did was that they thought it worthwhile, lest their mistress be killed, to give the impression of having killed her. It is hardly, believe me, a mark of a low – let alone of a servile – mind[38] to do an outstanding deed at the cost of a criminal reputation.

(5) Vettius, chief of the Marsi,[39] was being led to the Roman general. His slave drew the sword of the very soldier who was dragging him along. He first killed his master and then, with the words, 'It is time to think of myself. I have already freed my master', ran himself through with a single blow. Show me any one who rescued his master in a more magnificent way!

24 (1) Caesar was besieging Corfinium.[40] Domitius was trapped. He ordered the doctor, who was also his slave, to give him poison. Seeing him hesitate, he said: 'What are you waiting for? You are acting as though this entire matter were in your control! I demand to die, and I have weapons.' The other agreed, and gave him a harmless drug to drink. When Domitius had gone to sleep, he went to the son and said, 'Put me under guard till you learn from the outcome whether I gave your father poison.' Domitius lived on. His life was spared by Caesar. But first it had been spared by a slave.

25 (1) A master under proscription during the civil war was concealed by his slave, who put on his rings and costume, went up to the men who were looking for him and, saying that he would make no plea to prevent their carrying out their orders, held out his neck for execution. What a man! To wish to die for his master at a time when it was unusual loyalty not to wish the master to die! To be found merciful amid universal cruelty, loyal amid universal treachery! With huge rewards on display for betrayal, to long for death as the reward of loyalty!

26 (1) I shall include some examples from our own age. Under Tiberius Caesar, there was a widespread, almost universal craze for bringing in accusations.[41] It wrought destruction, heavier than

---

[38] Reading, with Préchac, *non est, mihi crede, non dico servilis, sed* vilis *animi*.

[39] The Italian tribe whose revolt initiated the Social War.

[40] In 49 BC, during the civil war between Pompey and Julius Caesar, Corfinium, a town about midway between Rome and Pescara, was garrisoned by forces under Lucius Domitius Ahenobarbus, before being besieged and taken by Caesar.

[41] Under Tiberius, especially after AD 23, charges of *maiestas* – *lèse majesté*, ill-intentioned action against the state and the head of state – became increasingly

any civil war did, on the citizenry in a time of peace. Drunken conversation and candid jokes were seized on. Nothing was safe. Any occasion for savagery was good enough. Nor did people await the outcome for the defendant; there was only one. Paulus, an ex-praetor, was at a banquet wearing a ring with the portrait of Tiberius prominently embossed on the stone. (2) It would be very foolish of me to search now for words with which to say that he picked up a – chamber-pot. The action was promptly noted by Maro,[42] a well-known spy of that time, and by the slave of the man against whom he was plotting. He seized the ring from his drunken master; and as Maro[43] called the banqueters to witness that the portrait had been applied to something unmentionable, and was already composing his denunciation, he displayed the ring, slave as he was, on his own hand. If you call that man a slave, you will call the other a banqueter!

27 (1) Under our deified Augustus, words were not yet a source of danger to people, though already they could cause trouble. Rufus, a man of senatorial rank, had expressed at dinner a wish that Caesar should not return safely from the travels that he planned, adding that every bull and calf would have the same wish.[44] There were people whose business it was to listen carefully. As dawn broke, a slave who had stood at his feet as he dined told him what he had said at dinner in his cups, urging him to get to Caesar first and report himself. (2) He took the advice, ran up to Caesar as he made his way down from the palace and, swearing that he had been quite mad the day before, wished that his words would rebound upon himself and his children, asking him to forgive him and restore him to favour. (3) Caesar consented. 'But no one will believe that you have restored me to favour, unless you give me some present', he said, and asked for a sum of money that, even from someone well disposed towards him, was not to be scorned. He got it. 'In my own interest', said Caesar, 'I shall take

---

frequent, often on grounds as trivial as that in the present story. See Suetonius, *Life of Tiberius* 58.

[42] Outside this passage, Paulus and Maro are not mentioned by Seneca or any other ancient writer.

[43] Reading and punctuating, with Alexander, *insidiae. Ei ebrio anulum extraxit, et cum Maro . . .*

[44] Bulls and calves would be sacrificed in large numbers to give thanks to the gods for Caesar's safe return.

care never to be angry with you!'[45] (4) Caesar acted honourably in forgiving him and crowning his clemency with generosity. Anyone who hears of this case is bound to praise Caesar – but only after praising the slave first. You need not wait for me to tell you that, having done this, the slave got his freedom. Not that it came gratis. The money for his freedom had already been paid out by Caesar.

Conclusion: the one nobility is virtue

28 (1) After so many examples, is there any doubt that a master can be done a favour by a slave? Why should the slave's action be diminished by his station and not, rather, his station be dignified by the action itself? All of us have the same beginnings, the same origin. No one is nobler than the next man, save he whose nature is more upright and more inclined to virtuous action. (2) Those who display their family busts in the reception-room and set out in the ante-chamber the names of their family, in a long list tied in with numerous twists of genealogy, are surely more notorious than noble. We all have one common parent – the cosmos. The stages between may be splendid or sordid, yet everyone's origin can be traced back there. Do not be deceived by those who in reviewing the rolls of their ancestors foist in a god wherever an illustrious name is wanting. (3) And do not look down on anyone, even if the names of those with whom he belongs are sunk in oblivion, ill assisted by any indulgence of fortune. Whether your precursors rank as freedmen, slaves or foreigners, raise your minds boldly aloft. Leap over any obscurity in between. At the top of your family tree a grand nobility awaits you.[46] (4) Why are we raised in our arrogance to such a pitch of vanity that we think it beneath us to accept a favour from slaves, that we eye their condition and forget their merits? Are you to call anyone a slave, slave as you are yourself to lust and gluttony, to a mistress – no, the common possession of numerous mistresses? (5) Are *you* to

---

[45] I.e. 'because restoring you to favour has become so expensive'. Instead of exacting reparation for the offence and thereby profiting from it, Caesar has himself had to pay out.

[46] Seneca is recalling the Stoic doctrine that all rational beings are related to and derive their reason from the divine cosmic reason. Cf. *Letters* 44. 1: 'all human beings, if traced back to their first origins, come from the gods'.

call anyone a slave? Where, tell me, are those porters who carry your litter around hurrying you off to? Those men in cloaks, decked out in uncommonly fine military dress – where, I ask, are they carrying you? To some doorkeeper's door, to gardens in the charge of some slave who does not even have any regular duties. And then you say that you cannot be done a favour by a slave, when you count it a favour to kiss the hand of someone else's slave![47] (6) What a gross contradiction! At one and the same time, you look down on slaves and court them, imperious and violent at home, but grovelling outside, an object as much as an agent of contempt. None are more apt to degrade themselves than those who are unconscionably self-exalted. None are readier to trample on others than those who have learned to insult through accepting insult.

Parents and children

Can children outdo the favour done by their parents in begetting them?

29 (1) I had to say all this. I needed to crush the insolence of men who depend for everything on fortune, and to claim for slaves the right to do favours – so that the claim might be made for sons as well. There is, in fact, a question whether at any time children can do their parents greater favours than they have received.

(2) It will be admitted that there have been many sons who were greater and more powerful than their parents, and likewise better. If that is agreed, it is quite possible that they did better service, having greater luck and a better will. (3) 'But whatever a son gives his father', you may object, 'is inevitably less; his very power to give is owed to his father who can never be outdone by any favour, since the very fact that he is outdone is a favour on his part.' Well, first of all, there are some things which take their beginning from other things and yet are greater than their beginnings. Nor is a thing prevented from being greater than what it took its start from by the fact that it could not have progressed as far as it has without having made a start. (4) There is no thing that does not

---

[47] Kissing someone on the hand was a gesture of supplication. Compare Seneca, *Letters* 118. 3; Epictetus, IV 1. 148, 7. 23, etc.

greatly surpass its origins. Seeds are the cause of all things and
yet are a tiny part of what they generate. Consider the Rhine, the
Euphrates or indeed any famous river – what would they be if you
judged them simply at their source? Whatever they have to make
them feared or to win them renown has been acquired in their
progress. (5) Consider the tree-trunks, the tallest (if height is what
you are judging) or the broadest (if you are judging their thickness
and the spread of their branches). Compared with these, how tiny
is the volume embraced by the slender root-fibres. But do away
with the root and no more will woods arise nor mighty mountains
be clothed.[48] The temples and battlements[49] of the city rest upon
their foundations. Yet the base thrown down for the whole edifice
lies hidden. (6) The same occurs everywhere else: origins are
overwhelmed by the greatness that follows. I could not have
achieved anything without prior favours on the part of my parents.
But that does not mean that whatever I have achieved is less than
what I needed in order to achieve it. (7) Had a nurse not nourished
me in my infancy, I could not have done any of the things which
I now perform by brain and hand, I could not have risen to the
renown and distinction which my efforts in war and peace have
merited. Surely you would not treat such supreme activities as less
important than the functions of a mere nurse. But where do the
cases differ? Without a father to favour me I could not have gone
on to my later activities, but equally so, not without a nurse. (8)
And if I owe to my beginnings whatever I can now do, you should
reflect that my beginning was not in my father, not even my
grandfather. There will always be something further back, from
which the source of my immediate source derives. But no one is
going to say that I owe more to ancestors unknown to me and
beyond reach of memory than I do to my father. Yet I do owe
more, if the very fact of his having begotten me is something which
my own father owes to his ancestors.

30 (1) 'Whatever I have done for my father, even if it is a lot,
falls short in value of his service to me; it could not have come
about had he not begotten me.' On that reasoning, if someone had

---

[48] Transposing, with Haase, the sentence *tolle radicem . . . montes vestientur* from the
end of section 4 to after *complectitur*.
[49] Reading something like *templa et illa <fastigia> urbis.* See Alexander.

cured my father of a fatal illness, I could do nothing for that person to match the favour; my father would not have begotten me, had he not been cured. But perhaps a truer evaluation would be that what I have been able to do and what I have done are mine, the product of my powers and my will. (2) Consider the bare fact of my birth and what it amounts to. What do you see? Something insignificant, indeterminate, with potential for good or evil; a first step, certainly, to everything else, but not more important than everything else just because it comes first. (3) Suppose that I have saved my father's life, that I have raised him to the highest position and made him a leading citizen of his state; suppose that not only have I made him famous by my own achievements but that I have given him enormous and ready scope for achievements of his own, without risk but full of prestige; suppose that I have heaped on him honours, riches, whatever attracts the mind of man, and that, though placed above all others, I have yet placed him above myself. (4) Just you say, 'The very fact that you could do this was thanks to your father', and I shall reply: 'Yes of course, if merely to be born is all that is needed for doing all this. But if merely being alive is the least important factor in living well and you have bestowed on me the very thing which I share with wild beasts and with some of the smallest creatures, even some of the vilest, do not give yourself the credit for something which did not arise from – even if it could not have arisen without – any favour of yours.

31 (1) Suppose that I have given you your life in return for the life that you gave me. In that case too, my gift has surpassed yours. I gave to a conscious recipient, conscious myself of giving. Nor was I giving you life for the sake of my own pleasure or, at any rate, by way of pleasure. And holding on to the breath of life is a greater thing than just being given it, in the same way that dying weighs less on you if you have not yet come to fear death. (2) My gift of life was to one who would use it immediately; yours was to a creature who would not even know that he was alive. I gave you life as you shuddered at death; you gave me life to make death a possibility. The life which I granted you was complete and whole; what you begat was a creature without reason, a burden on others. (3) Do you want proof that the gift of life on those terms

is no great favour? You might have exposed me, doing me a positive wrong by having begotten me.[50] What does that prove? That the copulation of father and mother is a very small favour without the addition of others to follow up this prelude to a gift and confirm it with other services. (4) The good is not merely to live, but to live a good life. And, I grant you, I do live a good life. But I could also have lived badly. Your sole contribution is that I live at all. If you claim credit from me for mere life, naked and irrational, and boast of it as a great good, you should reflect that you are taking credit for a good that is shared by flies and worms. (5) And then – to boast of nothing more than having applied myself to virtuous action and taken a straight course in life – in the very favour that you did me you got back more than you gave. You gave me a self that was rude and inexperienced. I gave you a son whom you could be glad to have begotten.

32 (1) Yes, my father supported me. If I do the same for him, I give back more than he gave me. He can rejoice not just at being supported, but at having a son to support him, deriving a greater pleasure from my state of mind than from the conduct itself. The nourishment that he provided went no further than my body. (2) Now suppose that someone has got so far as to be internationally renowned for eloquence or impartiality or martial prowess, covering his father too in greatness and glory while dispelling the obscurity of his birth with the brightness of fame; has he not done his parents an incalculable favour? (3) Would anyone know of Ariston or Gryllus except through their sons, Plato and Xenophon?[51] It is Socrates who saves Sophroniscus from perishing altogether.[52] It would take long to list the others who have survived simply because the distinction of their children has handed them on to posterity. (4) Was the greater favour done to Marcus Agrippa by his father, a man obscure even afterwards? Or was it done to his father by the Agrippa who won the distinction of the naval

---

[50] It was not unheard of for defective or otherwise unwanted infants (usually girls) to be abandoned at birth in the open countryside.

[51] Xenophon (c. 428–c. 354 BC) was an Athenian general and author of a number of surviving works, ranging from a treatise on hunting (especially hare-hunting) and another on estate-management to important historical works and several books of Socratic dialogues. The Plato mentioned is, of course, the philosopher (c. 429–347 BC).

[52] Sophroniscus was Socrates' father.

crown, gaining a decoration unique among military honours, and who raised in the city buildings of such grandeur as to surpass the magnificence of earlier times and to remain unsurpassed by later ones?[53] (5) Was the greater favour done by Octavius to his son, or to his father by our deified Augustus – even if the father was lost in the shadow of the adopted parent?[54] What pleasure Octavius would have had to see him, with the civil wars fought to an end, presiding over peace and security. Hardly acknowledging the good that was due to him, he would scarcely have believed, whenever he looked at himself, that this man could have been born in his household. Why should I now go on to the others who would have been swallowed by oblivion had not their children's glory saved them from darkness and shed lustre on them to this day?

(6) Moreover, our question is not which son has in fact responded with greater favours than those received from his father, but whether a son could do so. Even if the examples that I have given are not yet enough to cap the favours done by their parents, nature is still capable of what has not yet been realized at any time. If no action on its own can outdo the magnitude of a father's services, a plurality of them taken together may do so.

33   (1) Scipio saved his father in battle.[55] Not yet an adult, he spurred his horse into the midst of the enemy. Perhaps it is not enough that, in order to reach his father, he disregarded all the dangers, which at that time were at their thickest around the supreme commanders, and all the difficulties in his path; that to reach the front line the new recruit galloped over the bodies of

---

[53] Marcus Vipsanius Agrippa (c. 64 BC–AD 12), a lifelong friend and associate of Augustus, was awarded the naval crown after his naval victories at Mylae and Naulochus in 36 BC (see Pliny, *Natural History* XVI 8). Immensely rich, he built at his own expense the Pantheon, the first great public baths in Rome, a new bridge over the river Tiber and two new aqueducts.

[54] Augustus had begun life as Gaius Octavius in 63 BC, the son of Gaius Octavius who died in 59 BC and of Atia, niece of the dictator Julius Caesar who adopted him and made him his chief heir. Recognized as Caesar's adopted son in 43 BC, he took the name of Gaius Julius Caesar Octavianus, receiving in 27 BC the title Augustus.

[55] While still an adolescent, Publius Cornelius Scipio Africanus Major (236/5–c. 183 BC), subsequently victor over Hannibal at Zama, fought under his father Publius Cornelius Scipio at the battle of Ticinus (218), Hannibal's first victory over the Romans in Italy. He is said to have saved his father's life there. The elder Publius Cornelius Scipio died seven years later fighting in Spain.

veterans; that he outstripped his years at one bound. (2) Then suppose also that he defends his father in court, rescuing him from the machinations of powerful enemies;[56] that he heaps on him a second consulate and a third, along with honours that even men who have been consul would covet; that he hands over to him in his poverty the spoils of war and – most impressive of achievements for a military hero – enriches him with plunder actually seized from the enemy. (3) If that is still not enough, suppose also that he prolongs his father's provincial governorships and extraordinary powers; that after the destruction of the greatest cities, he becomes protector and founder of a Roman empire that is to extend unrivalled from East to West, thus giving an illustrious man a still greater lustre – to be called 'Scipio's father'. Is there any doubt that by his extraordinary devotion and valour – I can hardly say whether it brought the city itself more protection or more honour – he has surpassed the ordinary favour that parents do in begetting children?

(4) Again, if that is not enough, imagine that someone has shaken the instruments of torture from off his father, taking them upon himself. You can extend a son's favours as far as you like, whereas his father's gift is straightforward and easy, a source of sensual pleasure as he gives it, one which he must have made to many even without realizing it, a gift in which he has a partner, in which the law, his country, the rewards of parenthood, the continuity of home and family will have been considerations – anything rather than the recipient. (5) I ask you, if someone has attained to wisdom and transmitted it to his father, would we still be arguing about whether he had now given more than he received? What he has given in return is the life of happiness. What he received was merely life.

34 (1) 'But whatever you do and whatever you can do for your father', one might object, 'is thanks to him.' Yes, and it is thanks to my teacher that I have progressed in the liberal disciplines. But we go beyond those who passed on those disciplines to us,[57]

---

[56] Scipio Africanus did in fact defend his *brother*, Lucius Cornelius Scipio Asiaticus, at a trial instigated by Cato the elder in 187 BC, from a charge of accepting bribes from Antiochus, king of Syria.
[57] The 'liberal disciplines', subsequently classified as a canon of seven 'liberal arts' (grammar, rhetoric dialectic, arithmetic, geometry, astronomy and music) were a

especially those who taught us the first rudiments. No one can achieve anything without them. But that does not mean that, in whatever one does achieve, one is their inferior. There is a vast difference between what comes first and what is most important. Nor is what comes first equivalent to what is most important simply because without it the other could not come into being.

Five summary Stoic syllogisms

35 (1) And now it is time to produce something coined, so to speak, in our Stoic mint.[58]

> If someone has done a favour and there is something better than it, he can be surpassed. The father has given his son life. But there is something better than life. So the father can be surpassed, because he has done a favour and there is something better than it.
>
> (2) And again, if a man who has made the gift of life to another is more than once saved from death, he has accepted a greater favour than the one which he did. But a father has made the gift of life. He can, therefore, if he is frequently saved by his son from danger of death, receive a greater favour than the one which he did.
>
> (3) A favour received is the greater the more that it is needed. But life is more needed by one who lives than by one who has not been born, since the latter cannot need anything at all. So the father has received a greater favour in being

---

staple of secondary education. In *Letters* 88, Seneca expounds his view that they are a necessary preliminary to – but not a substitute for – philosophy or the pursuit of wisdom.

[58] What follow are five arguments whose logical validity was exhibited in the Stoic elaboration of what corresponds to contemporary propositional logic. The first three and the last are (or can readily be reduced to) examples of *modus ponens* (Chrysippus' 'first indemonstrable'): they consist of an 'If ... then' statement, together with the assertion of the content of the if-clause, from which the content of the then-clause follows logically. The fourth, though somewhat unclear in its formulation, is an example of *modus tollens* (Chrysippus' 'second indemonstrable'): it consists of an 'if ... then' statement, together with the denial of the content of the then-clause, from which follows logically the denial of the content of the if-clause. The Stoics made it a practice to accumulate such simple, valid arguments in support of their major contentions in the sphere of ethical and political theory. Since they thought that the world itself, being the product of and pervaded by the rational thoughts of god, is structured by such logical connections, it was very important to them to exhibit the realm of moral facts as being so constituted.

given his life by his son than a son has from his father in being born.

(4) 'Favours done by a father cannot be surpassed by a son's favours. Why? Because he was given his life by his father and could not, without having been given it, have done any favours at all.' That is something which a father shares with all who have given a person his life. For he would not have been able to show gratitude, if he had not been given his life.[59] So neither can a doctor be shown more gratitude <than his favour requires> (for a doctor regularly gives people their lives) nor can a sailor if he has rescued you from shipwreck. But favours done by these and by others who in some way have given us our lives can be surpassed. So, therefore, can those done by fathers.

(5) If someone has done me a favour which had to be supplemented by favours from many others, while I did him a favour which needed assistance from no one, I have done a greater favour than I received. A father has granted his son a life that would come to an end without many accessories to preserve it. If the son gives the father life, he gives him a life which needs no help for its continuation. So the father who has been given his life has been done a greater favour by the son than that which he himself did him.

These arguments will make filial devotion the livelier

36 (1) These arguments are not the destruction of reverence for parents. They serve not to make children worse towards them, but actually better. Virtue has a natural thirst for glory and longs to outstrip its precursors. Filial devotion will be the livelier, if it approaches the return of favours in the hope of surpassing them. Fathers themselves will be willing and happy for this to happen, since there are many things in which it pays us to be surpassed. (2) On what other basis could you find so welcome a contest? Or parents so fortunate as to acknowledge themselves no match for their children in favours? Unless we take this view of the matter, we merely provide an excuse for our children and make their gratitude more sluggish, when we ought to spur them on, saying:

---

[59] Reading *non potuisset . . . accepisset.*

'To work, my brave boys! We have set an honourable competition between parents and children, to see who has given or got the more. (3) Nor have the parents won, just because they came in first. Only take heart, as befits you, and do not lose courage. You are going to win – they want you to. Nor is there any lack, in so glorious a contest, of leaders to encourage you to actions like their own, commanding you to follow in their footsteps to a victory over parents that has often been won in the past.

37 (1) 'Victory went to Aeneas over his father. In his infancy he himself had been light and easy to carry; his father was heavy with age. Yet he bore him through the ranks of the enemy, through the city as it fell in ruin around him, while the pious old man, clasping his household gods and objects of worship, made a double burden to weigh down his stride. Through the flames he bore him and – filial devotion can manage anything – bore him through to safety, establishing him up for veneration among the founders of the Roman empire.[60]

(2) 'Victory went to the young men of Sicily. As Aetna, roused with unusual force, poured fire over cities, over fields, over most of the island, they carried their parents with them. The fires parted, so it is believed. The flames retreated on either side to open a pathway, a passage for young men worthier than any others to venture much and yet come to safety.[61]

(3) 'Victory went to Antigonus. Having vanquished the enemy in a mighty battle, he transferred the prize of war to his father and gave him dominion over Cyprus. That is true kingship: not to be king, when you could be.[62]

---

[60] From at least the third century BC the story was prevalent that the Romans were descended from Aeneas and his followers who had come to Italy after the sack of Troy. Seneca is recalling the authoritative version of the story in Vergil's *Aeneid*, in particular the account in Book II of Aeneas' filial piety.

[61] The story of Amphinomus and Anapius, heroes of Catana, a town situated beneath Mount Etna in Sicily, was well known in antiquity. It is told in a surviving Latin poem, *Aetna* (lines 603–45), composed sometime in the first century AD.

[62] Seneca is speaking of Antigonus the 'One-Eyed,' one of Alexander's generals and successors (also mentioned above II 17 and at *On Anger* III 22). Here, however, the exploits are those of Antigonus' son, Demetrius Poliorcetes (336–283 BC), who defeated the forces of Ptolemy (king of Egypt) in 306 and won Cyprus for his father. Here, as at *On Anger* III 23. 1, Seneca has blundered. Perhaps he meant to write 'the son of Antigonus'. Or perhaps he did not care. In his youth, as his father noted (*Suasoriae* VI 16), he had not taken much interest in history.

'(4) Victory – over a tyrannical father, too – went to Manlius. Having earlier been banished for a time by his father for youthful loutishness and stupidity, he went to the tribune of the people, who had served a summons on his father. He asked for an interview, which was granted in the hope that he would betray a father whom he hated. (Indeed, the tribune thought that he had done him a good turn by treating the young man's exile as the most serious charge that he was laying against Manlius.) Having gained a private audience, the youth drew a weapon concealed in his clothing and said, "Unless you swear that you will remit the summons against my father, I will run you through with this sword. It is up to you which way my father escapes accusation." The tribune swore, and he kept his oath. He gave the assembly his reason for abandoning the action. No one else ever got away with putting a tribune in his place.[63]

38 (1) 'One example after another can be found of men who snatched their parents from peril, who raised them from the humblest to the highest position, who took them from the unnoticed mass of the common people and left them on the lips of generations for ever. (2) No force of words, no power of natural intelligence can express how needful, how laudable, how quite unforgettable it is to be able to say, "I obeyed my parents. I yielded to their supremacy, whether it was fair or unfair and harsh. I showed myself compliant and submissive. In this alone I was obstinate – never to be surpassed in doing them favours!" (3) Strive, I beseech you! Even in your weariness, renew the fight! Happy are they who win. Happy are they who lose. Is anything more glorious than a youth who can say to himself (for it would be wrong to say it to anyone else), "I surpassed my father in my favours to him"? Is anything more fortunate than an old man who can declare to all men everywhere that he has been surpassed in favours by his own son? Could there be a happier outcome than to admit defeat?'

---

[63] Cicero, whom Seneca is probably following here, tells the same story in *On Duties* III 112, adding the name of the tribune, and the further information that this Manlius (forenamed Titus) was son of Lucius Manlius, dictator in Rome in the early fourth century BC, and the same person as the famous Manlius who defeated a Gaulish warrior in single combat and wrenched from his neck his torque, thus acquiring the surname Torquatus.

Book IV

Are favours and gratitude desirable in themselves?

The Stoic as against the Epicurean view

1 (1) Nothing in all the questions that we have handled, Aebutius Liberalis, is so vital, it would seem, or 'more in need', as Sallust puts it,[1] 'of careful discussion' than what is now before us: are doing a favour and showing gratitude in return things to be chosen for their own sake?

(2) You find people who cultivate honourable action for gain and have no liking for virtue without reward. But there is no grandeur in it, if there is anything venal. Nothing is more shameful than for anyone to calculate a good man's worth. Virtue invokes neither profit to attract nor loss to deter. So far is it from corrupting anyone by raising hopes or making promises that, on the contrary, it calls for sacrifice and is more often a matter of offerings freely made. You must trample on your own interests to approach it; you must go wherever you are summoned or sent, without regard for your property, at times without even a thought for your own blood; nor must you ever try to evade its commands. (3) 'What am I to gain by acting bravely or showing gratitude?' The gain of having done so. Nothing else is on offer. If some advantage happens to come your way, you can treat it as a bonus. Things that are honourable contain their own reward. If anything honourable is to

---

[1] Gaius Sallustius Crispus, *Historiae* (II Fragment 72 in *Salustii Historian Reliquae* ed. B. Maurenbecher (Leipzig 1891–3)). Seneca cites the same phrase, without naming the author, at *On Providence* 5. 9 and *On Peace of Mind* 14.10.

be chosen for its own sake, and if a favour is something honourable, it can only come on the same terms, being of the same nature. And that anything honourable is to be chosen for its own sake has been often and abundantly proved.[2]

2 (1) On this point, we are in arms against the Epicureans, that self-indulgent and sheltered crowd of dinner-party philosophers, for whom virtue is the handmaid of pleasure, obeying it, serving it, seeing it as of higher rank. 'Yet you cannot have pleasure without virtue', you may say.[3] (2) But why put it in front of virtue? Do not think that this is simply a disagreement about precedence. The whole question of virtue and its authority is at issue. It will not be virtue at all, if it can come second. It has a right to the leading role – to go first, to give orders, to stand in the highest position. And you want it to ask for a signal before acting! (3) 'What difference does it make to you? I, too, deny that without virtue a happy life is possible. Pleasure itself, though I follow it and have made myself its slave, I repudiate and condemn, if virtue be absent. There is only one point of disagreement: is virtue the cause of the highest good or is it the highest good itself?'[4] Suppose this alone

---

[2] Seneca could be thinking of Cicero (see *Laws* 1 48) or, more generally, of the famous Stoic proofs that 'everything morally valuable [καλόν or *honestum* – "honourable"] is good' and, likewise, that 'only what is morally valuable is good' (see e.g. Cicero, *On Ends* III 27–8, and cf. III 36; Plutarch *On Stoic Self-contradictions* 1039c). He goes on himself to argue at 11. 4–6 and 15–17 that doing favours is a good to be chosen for its own sake.

[3] Here Seneca begins a debate with an interlocutor who raises difficulties for the Stoic theory, advocating until about Chapter 20 the Epicurean view on the self-interested good of doing favours. The interlocutor is simply a foil for the exposition of Seneca's own view that doing favours has intrinsic value, an exposition which, with intermissions and variations, goes on till nearly the end of the book.

[4] Stoics and Epicureans alike constructed their ethical systems around the concept of a 'final and ultimate good', an 'end for the sake of which everything else is done but which is not itself done for the sake of anything' (Stobaeus II 77. 16 ff. = 63A Long–Sedley). Where they disagreed was over the identity of the highest good. Epicurus identified it with pleasure (provided that pleasure itself was correctly understood), and emphasized the importance for a pleasant life of the absence of avoidable pain. The Stoics saw it as a 'life in conformity with nature' – one's own nature and that of the cosmos – which they could describe simply as 'virtue', understanding by that a quality of mind together with the decisions and actions to which it gives rise in shaping one's life. These radically different conceptions of the highest good were the starting points for radically different systems of ethics. That is why Seneca begins his discussion by distinguishing between the attitudes of the two schools on this question.

were the question: are you thinking simply of a change of precedence? To put last things first is a real muddle, of course, an obvious lack of vision. (4) But what outrages me is not that virtue should be placed after pleasure, but that it should be placed alongside pleasure at all. It despises and hates pleasure, recoiling as far as it can from it, having more to do with the manly inconveniences of toil and pain than with this effeminate 'good' of yours.

3 (1) I had to insert these remarks, dear Liberalis, because doing a favour, which is what we are now discussing, is a function of virtue, and nothing is more shameful than doing one for any purpose other than that of doing it. For if we gave in the hope of getting back, we would give to the wealthiest, not the worthiest. As it is, I would prefer a pauper to an unsuitable rich man. It is not a favour at all if it considers a person's fortune. (2) Besides, if advantage were all that induced us to help, those who could most easily spread their favours would be under the least obligation to do so – I mean the rich and powerful, I mean monarchs with no need for aid from others. The very gods would not make the gifts that they do in such numbers, pouring them forth unceasingly day and night. In everything their own nature is enough to keep them fully provided, safe and inviolate. No one would receive any favour from them, if the one motive for doing it lay in looking to oneself and to one's own advantage. (3) You are not doing a favour, you are making an investment, if you cast your eyes around to see not where your outlay would do the most good, but where it would be the most profitable and the returns the easiest. Since the gods are far from this sort of consideration, it follows that they will not be liberal. If the one motive for benefaction is the benefactor's own advantage and a god can expect no advantage from us, there can be no motive for a god's beneficence.

God does favours with no thought of a return

4 (1) I know the answer which will be given here: 'Yes, and that is why a god does not do favours. Free of care and of care for us, he turns his back on the world and pays no attention. Or rather, and this is what Epicurus sees as the greatest happiness, he does nothing at all. Nor is he any more responsive to favours

done to him than to wrongs.'[5] (2) Whoever says this has closed his ears to the sound of prayer, of vows made in all places, in private and public, with hands raised to heaven. This would not happen, I tell you, it could not be that nearly all mankind would have joined in the lunacy of addressing deities that cannot hear and gods that cannot act, unless we had some knowledge of their favours towards us, of favours sometimes brought to us of their own accord, sometimes granted in answer to prayer, of favours great and timely that free us from mighty threats by their coming. (3) Is anyone so wretched, so forgotten, born to so hard and punitive a destiny, as not to sense such divine munificence? Cast your eyes on those who bewail their lot and complain of it; you will find that they have not been entirely deprived of favours from heaven, that there is none without some drop trickling onto him from that most generous of springs. Was it too small a gift that was bestowed upon all alike at birth? Even if we pass over what follows and has not been given in equal measure, was it too small a gift that Nature gave us when she gave us herself?

5 (1) 'God does no favours.' Where then is the source of what you have, and give, and refuse to give, of what you save and what you seize? Of those countless things that beguile your eyes, your ears, your mind? Of that copious supply that suffices for luxury too (it is not only for our necessities that provision has been made – we are loved to the point of indulgence)? (2) Of trees in such number with their several ways of bearing fruit? Of so many wholesome herbs? Of food in so many varieties distributed throughout the year that even those who do nothing can chance upon nourishment that the earth provides? Of living creatures in every kind, some born on the dry solid ground, some in moisture, some descending through the air up on high, that every region of the natural world might confer something upon us?[6] (3) Of rivers that gird the plains in most delectable meanderings or offer a road to

---

[5] On Epicurus' theory, a god is a totally serene and happy being, who cannot possibly be involved either in maintaining the world-order or sponsoring the morality of human beings. Concern for such things would inevitably expose him to worry, distress, even anger, thus doing away with his essential serenity and happiness. See Epicurus, *Letter to Herodotus* 76–7, 81–2; *Letter to Menoeceus* 123–4; *Principal Doctrines* 1.

[6] The Stoics believed that everything in the world has been providentially made for the benefit of god and man. See Long–Sedley, 54 N–P.

commerce as they proceed in their vast and navigable course, some of them in summer being marvellously increased in volume, so that regions parched under a burning sky may be watered by the sudden force of a summer torrent? Of channels that gush forth healing springs? Of warm waters bubbling out on the very sea-shore? Of

> thee, mighty Larius, and, Benacus, thee,
> That rise in waves and groaning like the sea?[7]

6 (1) If someone had made you a gift of a few acres, you would say that you had been done a favour – are you denying that the vast expanse of earth wide open before you is a favour? If someone makes you a gift of money and (since this seems important to you) filled your coffer, you will call it a favour. But think of the mines which God has placed underground in such numbers, of the rivers which he has drawn from the earth in such numbers, bearing gold over the beds they flow down along, of the silver, copper and iron in huge quantities which he has buried in every place, while giving you the power to track them down and setting signs on the earth's surface of its hidden riches – are you denying that you have been done a favour? (2) If a house is given to you with some marble gleaming in it and a ceiling bright with its scattering of gilt or paintwork, you call it a considerable present. But God has built a huge residence for you; it holds no risk of fire or subsidence; what you see in it are not flimsy panels of veneer, thinner even than the blade which cut them out, but whole masses of the most precious stone, whole blocks of varied and differentiated material, the tiniest crumbs of which set you marvelling; its ceiling gleams in one way by night, in another by day – are you denying that you have been given any present at all? (3) You value what you possess – are you acting like a man without gratitude? Are you judging yourself indebted to no one? Where did you get that breath which you draw? Or that light which enables you to arrange and order your actions? Or the blood which holds in the warmth of life with its circulation? Or those delicacies which excite your palate with their rare flavours long after you have eaten enough? Or those stimulants of pleasure when it has flagged? Or the repose in which you wither and rot? (4) Surely, if you were grateful you would say:

---

[7] Vergil, *Georgics* II 159–60, on the theme of Lake Como and Lake Garda.

These blessings, friend, a deity bestow'd:
For never can I deem him less than god.
The tender firstlings of my wooly breed
Shall on his holy altar often bleed.
He gave my kine to graze the flow'ry plain;
And to my pipe renew'd the rural strain.[8]

(5) 'A deity it is' that has sent out not just a few oxen, but whole herds of them through the entire world, who provides fodder for flocks everywhere as they roam in all directions, who changes summer for winter pastures. Not merely has he taught men to sing to the pipe and compose a song, rustic and unrefined though with some regard for rules – all these arts, all these modulations of the voice, all these sounds, through our own breath or through breath from outside, which go to make music, are his invention. (6) Nor can you describe what we have discovered as 'ours', any more than the fact of our growth or the occurrence at a fixed time of bodily processes – the loss of our milk-teeth, the onset of puberty with advancing years and the transition to a stage of greater vigour, the appearance of the final wisdom-tooth marking the end of youth's advancement. All the ages of man, all his skills, have their germ within us. It is God, our teacher, who draws forth our genius from the hidden depths.

7 (1) 'No. It is nature that bestows these things upon me.'[9] Do you not realize that, in saying this, you are merely giving a different name to god? For what is nature if not god and divine reason pervading the entire world and its parts? As often as you will, you may find some different way to address the author of all that we have. You may call him 'Jupiter supremely Good and supremely Great'. You may call him 'Thunderer' and 'Stayer', though not for the reason given by the historians that, in answer to a prayer,[10] the battle-line of fleeing Romans stood firm; it is

---

[8] Vergil, *Eclogues* I 6 ff. (Dryden translation), expressing Vergil's own indebtedness to Octavian (Augustus).

[9] This and the next paragraph (down to 'he fills his own creation'), minus the reference to Roman history in 7. 1, are printed (quite conjecturally) by von Arnim as a fragment of Chrysippus (*SVF* II 1024). Certainly, what Seneca says here agrees with what we know about Chrysippus' views on divinity (see Diogeries Laertius VII 147). For Seneca, as for Stoics generally, there is just one god (the cosmic reason), who, however, has many personalities, in accordance (as Seneca puts it just below) with the different 'powers or products of things in the heavens'.

[10] On the part of Romulus in a battle against the Sabines (Livy, I 12. 6).

because all things stay firm thanks to him, that he is said to stay them and make them stable. (2) To speak of him also as 'Fate' would not be a fabrication, since fate is simply a chain of connected causes[11] and he is the first cause of all, on which everything else depends. Whatever names you want, they will fit him exactly, if they connote some power or product of things in the heavens. His titles can be as many as his services to us.

8 (1) Our school thinks of him also as Father Liber,[12] as Hercules, as Mercury: as Father Liber, because he is the parent of all, who first discovered the seminal force that was to arrange, by way of pleasure, for the perpetuation of life;[13] as Hercules, because his strength is unconquered and, when wearied by the works that issue from it, will retreat into fire;[14] as Mercury,[15] because reason belongs to him, together with number and order and knowledge. (2) Wherever you turn, you will find him coming to meet you. Nothing is void of him; he fills his own creation. You waste your time, most ungrateful of mortals, if you say that you owe yourself not to god but to nature. You cannot have nature without god, nor god without nature. Each is the same as the other, differing only in function. (3) If you said that the money which you got from Seneca is owed to Annaeus or Lucius, you would not be changing creditors, just the name. Whether you spoke the first name, the family name or the surname, he would still be the same person. In the same way, you can call on Nature, Fate

---

[11] Seneca here is recalling the Stoic doctrine that everything happens in accordance with a fated, necessary sequence of causes, identical with the reason or thought-process of the divine mind that inheres in and controls the world-order. See Long–Sedley, 55 J–S, especially L (= Cicero, *On Divination* I 125–6).

[12] An Italic god of vegetation, identified in classical times with the Greek god Dionysus, i.e. Bacchus. For what follows, compare Plutarch, *On Isis and Osiris* 367e (*SVF* II 1093).

[13] Reading, with Préchac, *per voluptatem <vitae perpetuitati>*.

[14] In the myth, Hercules ended his days on a pyre on Mount Oeta in Thessaly. The Stoics took this to symbolize their cosmological theory that the world is periodically consumed by turning into a mass of fire, to reconstitute itself again into the same world order – with exactly the same structure, development and history, down to the smallest details – that we now experience. See Long–Sedley, Chapter 46.

[15] Mercury, messenger of the gods, was readily associated by Greek allegorists with *logos*, which means not only 'reason' but 'speech' (see above, I 3. 7). Seneca's particular explication, however, is not to be found in any other surviving Stoic text.

or Fortune. All are names of one and the same god variously exercising his power. Justice, probity, prudence, courage and temperance are good qualities of one and the same mind. Whichever of these has met with your approval, it is in fact the mind that you are approving.

9 (1) But (so as not to go off on another discussion) God confers on us the greatest and most important favours without any thought of return. He has no need for anything to be conferred, nor could we confer anything on him. Doing a favour is, therefore, something to be chosen for its own sake. The one advantage to be considered is that of the recipient, and we should approach it by putting aside any interests of our own.

Discrimination will still be needed

(2) 'But you all say,' someone might object, 'that we should be careful in selecting those to whom we do favours, since neither do farmers commit their seed to the sand.[16] But if that is true, we do pursue our own advantage in doing favours, just as we do in ploughing and sowing. For neither is sowing something to be chosen for its own sake. Besides, you examine the questions where and how to do a favour.[17] You would not have to do so if doing a favour were something to be chosen for its own sake. In whatever circumstances and whatever manner it was done, it would still be a favour.' (3) Yes, what is honourable we pursue for no end other than itself. And yet, even if nothing else is to be pursued, we do ask what to do and when to do it and how. Such factors are what make the act honourable. So in selecting the person to whom I do a favour, I am seeing to it that it really is a favour, since, if it is done to someone vile, it cannot be honourable, nor can it be a favour.

10 (1) To return a deposit is something to be chosen for its own sake. But that does not mean that I shall invariably return one, at any place or time whatsoever. Sometimes there is no

---

[16] Seneca used the same metaphor, to different effect, at II 11. 4; he may be allowing his Epicurean objector to turn the tables here by converting the example to support the Epicurean theory.

[17] Seneca examined them respectively at I 11.5–12 (in the course of discussing 'what favours to do') and II 1–17 above.

practical difference between returning it and outright repudiation.[18] I shall consider the interest of the person to whom I am returning it, and if the deposit is going to harm him, I shall say 'No.'[19] (2) When it comes to a favour, I shall do the same, considering when to do it, to whom, how and on what grounds. Nothing should be done without reason. It is only a favour if it is done with reason, since reason must accompany anything that is honourable. (3) How often we hear people blaming their thoughtless donations with the utterance, 'I would rather have lost it than have given it to him!' Thoughtless donations are the most shameful kind of loss. It is far more serious to have done a favour badly than not to have had it returned. That it was not returned is someone else's fault; our failure to select the recipient properly is our own. (4) In making the choice, however, the last consideration that I shall have in mind is the one you would expect, my chances of getting the favour back. I am selecting someone who will be grateful, not someone to repay me. It often happens that someone who is not going to pay me back is grateful and, that, likewise, someone may be ungrateful even though he has paid it back. (5) I judge people by their cast of mind. I shall pass by the rich but unworthy, giving to the poor and virtuous. In utter destitution, such a one will be grateful. Though all else fail him, his cast of mind will remain.

11 (1) In doing a favour I am not grasping at profit, nor at pleasure, nor at glory. Content to please one person only, I shall give for the sole purpose of doing what ought to be done. But 'ought' means choice; and what sort of choice, you may ask, shall I make? I shall choose a man of integrity and straightforwardness, a man with gratitude and a good memory, someone who can keep his hands off other people's property without clinging stingily to his own, a kind man. When I have chosen such a man, fortune may well deny him any way of showing his gratitude – the business will still have been done to my own satisfaction. (2) If a sordid calculation of my own advantage is what makes me liberal, if I assist no one unless he can assist me in return, I shall not find myself doing a favour to anyone who is setting out for distant

---

[18] Reading, with Lipsius, *palam an* for *an palam* of the mss.
[19] See Plato, *Republic* I 331c: if someone has left a weapon with you for safe-keeping, and asks for it back when out of his mind, it cannot be required by justice that you give it back.

foreign parts, never to return, nor to anyone so ill as to have no hope of recovery. Nor if my own powers are failing, for I shall not have the time to get it back. (3) And yet, to show you that benefaction is something to be chosen for its own sake, foreigners who have only just arrived in our harbours and are due to depart immediately receive help from us. We give the shipwrecked stranger a ship to carry him back, and equip it for him. He leaves us hardly knowing who is responsible for his rescue. Never expecting to come into our sight again, he entrusts the gods with his debt to us and prays them to repay us, while we, in the meantime, have the awareness of our favour, unrewarded though it has been, to gladden us.

(4) Tell me, moreover, when we reach the end of our lives and draw up a will, are we not distributing favours that will be of no profit to us? But think of the time we spend debating with ourselves how much to give to whom! What does it matter whom we give to, if we are not to be repaid by anyone? (5) But we are never more careful in our giving, never are our judgments more agonized, than when all personal advantage is gone and only what is honourable stands before us. We are bad judges of what we ought to do, so long as it is distorted by hope and fear and that slackest of vices, pleasure. But where death has intercepted all these and brought in an uncorrupted judge to pass sentence, we look for the worthiest to receive what belongs to us; nor is there anything that we organize more scrupulously than this matter of no concern to us. (6) Yet, good heavens! a great pleasure comes over a person as he thinks, 'This man I shall make richer. This man's standing, with the increase of wealth, will gain a new splendour from me.' If we only did favours intending to get them back, we would have to die intestate.

In what sense is a favour 'a loan that cannot be repaid'?

12 (1) 'You speak of a favour as "a loan that cannot be repaid".[20] But a loan is not a thing to be chosen for its own sake.' Yes, but when we speak of a 'loan,' we are using an image, a metaphor. In the same way, we speak of law as 'the rule which determines

---

[20] See II 18, 5 above.

what is just and unjust.'[21] A rule, too, is not something to be chosen for its own sake. We resort to such language in order to explain the matter. When I say 'loan', you should understand 'like a loan' – as you can see, when I add 'unrepayable'; in real life there is no such thing as a loan that cannot or should not be repaid.

Favours must be done even at the cost of danger and loss

(2) So far is it from being the case that favours should be done for personal advantage that often, as I said, they have to be done at the cost of danger and loss. That is what brings me to the defence of a man surrounded by robbers, though I could go on in safety. That is how I move to protect a defendant in trouble with influential opponents, thereby turning a clique of powerful persons against me and perhaps laying myself open to the very charge, by the very same accusers, from which I have got him off, though I could pass by on the other side and look on unconcerned at struggles that have nothing to do with me. That is what makes me stand surety for a person who has been condemned. That is what leads me, when a friend's assets have been frozen, to tear down the notice, thereby making myself liable to his creditors.[22] That is what inspires me to save a man under proscription, at the risk of being proscribed myself. (3) No one out to get a place at Tusculum or Tibur[23] as a healthy summer retreat argues about the price–yield ratio.[24] No, having bought it,[25] one just has to look

---

[21] Here Seneca may well be quoting Chrysippus, whose treatise *On Law* in its opening sentence, as cited by the Roman jurist Marcian (third century AD), described or defined law as a 'rule or standard of things just and things unjust' (κανὼν δικαίων καὶ ἀδίκων) (see Long–Sedley, 67R).

[22] Cf. Cicero *For Quinctius* 25 f. On the humiliations of bankruptcy at Rome, see Crook, pp. 173–8.

[23] Tusculum, an ancient hill-town near modern Frascati, where Cicero composed several of his philosophical works, and Tibur (modern Tivoli), where Catullus, possibly Horace, Augustus, and Hadrian all had villas, were fashionable resorts, not too far from the city, for rich Romans.

[24] Latin *quoto anno empturus sit disputat* (or perhaps *annuo fructu* – the ablative, in either case is one of price, not time). I.e. 'nobody argues about how many times the yearly income from the property he will have to pay for it.' (*anno* is equivalent to *annuo fructu* – the ablative, in either case, is one of price, not time. See D. R. Shackleton-Bailey, *Cicero's Letters to Atticus* (Cambridge 1968), p. 376, on IX 9.4.)

[25] Reading, with Erasmus, *cum emerit*.

after it.[26] (4) The same principle applies to favours. If you ask what the return is, I shall answer 'a good conscience'. What is the return on a favour? You tell me: what is the return on justice, on innocence, on greatness of mind, on modesty, on temperance? You are not seeking these things themselves, if you are seeking anything besides them. (5) What leads heaven to complete its orderly changes? What leads the sun to lengthen and shorten the day? All these are favours. They are done to help us. It is the function of heaven to bring round the ordered cycle of things, of the sun to change the position of its rising and setting, and to do this for our well being without recompense. In the same way, it is a man's function, amongst other things, to do favours. Why should he do them? To avoid not doing them and losing the chance to do good.

13 (1) Pleasure for you <Epicureans> is to turn your little bodies over to slothful ease, to pursue a calm that resembles nothing so much as stupefaction, to lurk in thick shade, to beguile the paralysis of a drooping mind with the softest thoughts (you call it 'tranquillity'), to stuff those bodies pale from inaction with food and drink in your garden retreat.[27] (2) Pleasure for *us* is to do favours. And these can be toilsome, so long as they relieve the toils of others. They can be dangerous, so long as they rescue others from danger. They can be a burden to our finances, so long as they relieve the wants and straitened circumstances of others.

(3) What difference does it make to me if I get my favours back? Even after getting them back, I still have favours to do. A favour is for the benefit of its recipient, not for ours. Otherwise, we are just doing it for ourselves. That is why many things that bring the utmost advantage to others lose any claim on their gratitude by having a price. A merchant may be of help to the cities that he visits, a doctor to his patients, a slave-dealer to his merchandise. But they all come to benefit others for their own benefit, and so place no obligation on those whom they help. There is no such thing as a favour with gain as its object. To 'give this and get that' is just a commercial transaction. 14 (1) I would not describe as

---

[26] Cf. II 11. 4 f.
[27] Epicurus' house at Athens had a large garden attached, from which the school obtained its nickname of 'the Garden'.

chaste a woman who repulsed a lover in order to inflame him, or was just afraid of the law or of her husband. As Ovid says,

'She did not since she could not' means 'She did.'[28]

She deserves to be classed with the offenders if she owes her chastity to fear rather than to herself. In the same way, someone who did a favour in order to get it back did not do one. (2) Would you say, then, that we are doing animals a favour when we rear them with a view to working them or eating them, that we are doing orchards a favour when we tend them so that they will not suffer from the dryness or hardness of ground untilled and neglected? (3) No one turns to agriculture as an exercise in justice and kindness, nor to anything else where there is profit. The motive for a favour cannot lie in thoughts of sordid greed, but rather in a humane and generous eagerness to give, even when you have already given, to pile new and fresh gifts on old, with one single concern – the future good of the recipient. Otherwise, it is a low, unpraiseworthy, inglorious thing, to be of help simply because it is expedient. (4) There is nothing magnificent about loving yourself, sparing yourself, grabbing for yourself. True eagerness to do favours is a call away from all this, an inducement to face loss, a farewell to personal advantage in the utter delight of doing good.

The moral beauty of favours is motive enough

15 (1) Can there be any doubt that favours and wrongs are contraries?[29] In the same way, then, that doing an injury is something to be avoided and shunned for its own sake, doing a favour is something to be chosen for its own sake. In the one case, the shamefulness of the crime works against all inducements towards it; in the other, the attraction lies in its moral beauty which is enough by itself to make us act. (2) It would not be false to say that there is no one who does not love the favours which he has done, no one with such a mind as not to enjoy seeing the recipient of his largesse,[30] no one who does not find reason for doing another

---

[28] *Amores* III 4. 4, misquoted so as to change the tenses from present to past.
[29] See III 22. 3 above.
[30] Cf. II 32 above and Aristotle, *Nicomachean Ethics*, IX 7, 1167b311 ff.

favour in the fact that he he has done one already. This would not happen unless we took delight in the favours themselves. How often you hear someone saying: (3) 'I just can't let him down, having saved his life and snatched him from danger. He is asking me to take up his cause against men of great influence. I don't wish to, but what am I to do? I have already been his advocate more than once.' Can you not you see that the thing has a power of its own? It compels us to do favours, firstly because we should, and then because we already have. (4) Where we would have no reason, if this were the start of the matter, to do anything for someone, we do it, because we have done it in the past. So far removed from any personal advantage is our impulse to do favours that we go on looking after and cherishing things that are of no advantage at all to us, solely for love of the favour which we have done. It may have turned out badly, but we show it the same natural indulgence that we show our children when they are naughty.

16 (1) These same people[31] claim that *they* show gratitude not because it is honourable, but because it is advantageous to do so. That is not so; and the proof is all the easier because the very same arguments used to show that doing a favour is something to be chosen for its own sake can be used to show this too.

(2) Our fixed principle, from which we proceed to prove the rest, is that what is honourable is cherished simply because it is honourable. No one will dare to dispute whether gratitude is honourable. Everyone loathes the ungrateful; they are useless even to themselves. Well, suppose somebody tells you: 'His friend did him the greatest favours and he showed no gratitude.' How would you react? As though he had done something shameful, or as though he had missed out on something valuable which would have helped him? You would judge him, I think, to be a bad man, in need of punishment, not of someone to look after him. That would not happen if gratitude were not something honourable and to be chosen for its own sake. (3) Other qualities perhaps show

---

[31] Seneca is still arguing against the Epicureans. Having defended his own view and answered their objections to it (Chapters 9–15), he now examines and attacks their theory that our practice of doing each other favours began originally and is still continued for the sake of our mutual advantage. Against this, he argues (Chapters 16–25) that, when it comes to practice, Epicureans do not and cannot see things in this way.

their worth less obviously. Their moral status may need interpretation. But gratitude is on show for all to see and is too lovely for its splendour to shine forth at all doubtfully or inadequately. Is anything so praiseworthy, is there anything that our minds so universally approve, as gratitude for services rendered?

17 (1) What induced this attitude in us? Surely not gain. You have to despise it if you are not to be ungrateful. Surely not ambition. How can you boast of having paid what you owe? Nor can it be fear. The ungrateful have none, since this is the one thing we have not covered by any law[32] – we thought that nature had guarded sufficiently against it. (2) There is no law commanding love of parents[33] or kindness towards offspring, since we have no need to be forced on where we are going anyway. No one has to have self-love urged upon him – the instinct comes to him at the moment of birth. Nor, likewise, need he be urged to seek for its own sake what is honourable, since its very nature will make it attractive.[34] Virtue has such a charm that even bad men are instinctively inclined to approve of what is better. There is no one who would not wish to seem beneficent and would not aspire, in the midst of his crimes and wrong-doing, to a reputation for kindness, who would not put some appearance of rectitude on even his most intemperate actions, and would not wish it to seem that even those whom he has harmed have been done a favour. (3) So they put up with thanks from their victims,[35] and pretend to be kind and generous, since they cannot be so in reality. This they would not do, if there were not some love of honour as something to be pursued for its own sake[36] compelling them to seek a reputation contrary to their character and to conceal a wickedness desired for its results but hateful and shameful in itself. No one has rebelled against nature's law and shed his humanity to the

---

[32] Though Seneca did discuss at length (III 6–17) whether there should be such a law.

[33] Though, as we saw (III 11. 1), there were laws to punish *neglect* of parents.

[34] The Latin *honestum*, meaning literally 'honoured' or 'honourable', the standard term for 'morally good', translates a Greek word with a somewhat different resonance, καλόν, which means 'beautiful' as well as 'fine' and 'good'. Stoic claims for the 'charm' and 'beauty' (see below, IV 22. 2) of moral goodness owed much of their original persuasiveness to this resonance.

[35] Compare *On Anger* II 33. 2.

[36] Reading, with Castiglioni, *honesti ut per se expetendi*.

extent of being bad purely for the pleasure of being so. (4) Ask anyone who lives off what he has plundered whether he would not prefer what he gets from theft and robbery to come to him honestly. His wish, though his livelihood comes from prowling and striking down passers-by, will be to find it rather than snatch it. You will discover no one who would not rather enjoy the fruits of his wickedness without being wicked. Nature's greatest service to us is that virtue sends its light into every mind, seen even by those who refuse to follow it.

18 (1) That ingratitude is a thing to be shunned for itself is evidence that gratitude is a state of mind to be pursued for itself. Nothing so dissolves and disrupts the concord of mankind as this fault. Our safety depends on the fact that we have mutual acts of kindness to help us. What alone equips us in life and fortifies us against sudden attack is our exchange of favours. (2) Suppose that we were isolated individuals. What would we be? The prey of animals, their victims, the best and easiest blood for them to shed. Other animals have enough strength for self-protection. Those that are born to wander and live apart are armed. Man with his frail skin to cover him, without any powerful claws or teeth to make him a terror to other animals, is protected in his nakedness and weakness by fellowship. God has given that vulnerable creature two things that make him strongest of all, reason and fellowship. That is how, no match for anything if he lived in isolation, he comes to be master of all things. (3) Fellowship has given him dominion over all animals; fellowship dispatched this creature of the land to rule over an element not his own and authorized him to be lord even of the sea. It is what has held back the onslaught of disease, spied out supports for his old age, comforted him in pain. It is what gives us courage, because we can invoke it against fortune. (4) Take away this fellowship and you tear apart the unity of mankind that sustains our life. And you will indeed take it away, if you make ingratitude something to be avoided not for its own sake but for the consequences which the ungrateful have to fear. For there are numerous people who can safely be ungrateful. And anyway, the name I would give to gratitude through fear is ingratitude.

19 (1) No one in his right mind fears the gods. For it is madness to fear what does you good, nor can anyone love those whom he fears. You at any rate, Epicurus, disarm god. You have

taken away all his weapons and all his power, and, so that he should arouse fear in no one, you have cast him beyond the reach of fear.[37] (2) Having confined him with a huge, impassable wall, withdrawn from mortal contact and view, you have no reason to respect him; he has not the means to do good or harm. Abandoned in the space between this world and another, without animal or man or inanimate object for company, he avoids the collapse of worlds as they fall above and around him, deaf to prayers and without any interest in us.[38] (3) Yet this is what you want it to seem that you are venerating with the same gratitude, I suppose, as you would your father. Or, if you do not wish to seem grateful, since you have not had any favours from him, but have been congealed out of atoms and these motes of yours by blind chance, why are you venerating him? (4) 'For his surpassing majesty and unique nature.' Yes, I will grant you, you may well be doing this without any reward or hope to induce you – and that means that there is something that is to be chosen for its own sake, something that attracts you by its very worth, that is, something honourable. But what is more honourable than gratitude? This virtue has a scope as vast as life itself.

Our personal advantage is irrelevant

20 (1) 'But this good has also some element of personal advantage.' What virtue has not? But a thing is only said to be 'chosen

---

[37] See IV 4. I and n. 5. Because, on Epicurean theory, no god can be concerned about human events or behaviour, it is irrational to fear punishment by the gods for any human action or failure to act. Likewise it is irrational to fear natural disasters as if they were the consequence of divine displeasure or caprice. The Stoics agreed that it was irrational to fear God, but for different reasons. Given the moral goodness they thought essential to God, his providential concern for his creation, and his total control over it, it was guaranteed in advance that anything that happened that might affect any of us in any way would be for our good. And it is irrational to fear what is good for you. See the passages collected in Long–Sedley, Chapter 54, and General Introduction, p. xx f.

[38] According to Lucretius (III 18–24, V 146–7) and Cicero (*On the Nature of the Gods* I 18; *On Divination* II 40), both writing in the mid first century BC, Epicurus located the immortal gods somewhere in the otherwise virtually empty space between worlds; in later authors this understanding of Epicurus was widespread and, as far as we know, uncontradicted. But there is no evidence for it in the remains of Epicurus' writings, and it is difficult to see how it can be compatible with his atomic theory of matter, since all atoms constituting any entity must eventually fall apart and destroy it. See Long–Sedley, Chapter 23.

for its own sake' if any extra benefits which it may contain are set aside and removed and it still attracts. Yes, it pays to be grateful. But I will be grateful even if it harms me. (2) What is the aim of gratitude? To win further friends and favours? Well, suppose that someone is going to arouse resentment, suppose he realizes that, far from gaining anything by doing a favour, he may have to lose much that is in reserve or recently acquired; will he not gladly face the loss? (3) Ingratitude means being grateful with an eye to a further gift, it means paying back while cherishing hopes. Ungrateful is what I would call the person who attends a sick-bed because a will is about to be made, who has time to think of an inheritance or legacy. He may well do everything that a good and dutiful friend should do. But if the idea of gain comes into his mind, he is simply fishing, sinking the hook. In the way that carrion birds keep close watch on cattle worn out with disease and on the point of dropping, he is lying in wait for the death and hovering round the dead body.

21 (1) A grateful mind is one that is captivated by the sheer goodness of its intentions. I can show you that this is so and that such a mind need not be corrupted by any personal advantage. There are two kinds of gratitude. A person is called grateful if he has given something back in return for something received. Quite possibly, he can show off; he has something to boast about, to flaunt. But a person can also be called grateful if he receives with a cheerful mind and owes cheerfully.[39] And that is a matter for his own private knowledge. (2) What advantage can come to him from his hidden feelings? And yet, even if he can do nothing further, he is showing gratitude. He feels love, accepts his debt, longs to repay. Whatever else may be missing, he himself has not failed. (3) You are still an artist, even if you have not the equipment for practising your art. Your skill in singing is undiminished though your voice is made inaudible by the noise of a hostile crowd. I wish to repay; but I have still to do something, not about being grateful, but about discharging the debt. It often happens that one who repays is ungrateful, and one who does not repay is grateful. The assessment of this as of any other virtue depends entirely on his mental attitude. If it is as it should be, anything missing will

---

[39] This was the theme of II 31–5.

be the fault of fortune. (4) You can still be articulate even when silent, brave even when your hands are folded, indeed when they are tied. A helmsman is still a helmsman, even on dry land. His knowledge is complete and has nothing missing, even if there is some obstacle to prevent its being put to use. In the same way, a man can be grateful by simply wishing to make a return, even if he has no one but himself to witness the wish. (5) Indeed I will go further, and say that sometimes a person can be grateful while seeming to be ungrateful, having been misinterpreted and traduced by people's opinion. Such a man can only follow his conscience. Eclipsed though it be, it brings him joy, protesting against reputation and public opinion. Relying on itself for everything, when it sees a vast crowd on the other side with a verdict contrary to its own, it refuses to count the ballots but carries the day with its own one vote. (6) If it sees loyalty subjected to the penalties of treason, it remains on its pinnacle, steadfastly surmounting the punishment. 'I have what I wanted,' it says, 'I have what I sought. I have no regrets, nor shall I have any. No outrage of fortune shall bring me to exclaim: "What did I want for myself? What use to me are my good intentions now?"' They have their use even on the rack, even in the flames. Though these be applied to one limb after another, though little by little they make their way round my living body, though my very heart in the fullness of its good conscience drip with blood, it will rejoice in the flames through which its loyalty shines forth.

22 (1) Now is the time to bring on again the following argument, though I have already expounded it.[40] Why is it that we wish to seem grateful when we die? Why do we weigh up services done to us by different people? Why set the memory to pass judgment over an entire lifetime lest we appear to have forgotten a service from anyone? Nothing is left for hope to reach out to. Yet, at this turning-point, we wish to take our leave of human affairs with as much gratitude as possible. (2) You can see what a great reward for the action lies in just doing it, that anything honourable has enormous power to attract the minds of men, that its beauty floods the spirit, enchants it and seizes it with wonder at its light and radiance. (3) 'Yet many advantages do arise from it. The better

---

[40] See IV 11, 4–6 above.

men are, the securer their life is, the more they can count on the
love and approval of the good, while their days are the freer from
care if innocence and gratitude attend on them.' Yes, Nature would
have been most unfair had she made so great a good wretched,
risky and fruitless. Consider this, though. The way to this virtue
is often safe and easy. But if your journey there is through stones
and rocks, with wild animals and snakes infesting it, would you
not still go there? (4) A thing does not cease to be worth pursuing
for its own sake, if it has some additional reward attached to it.
Nearly everything of surpassing beauty comes with many added
attractions. These, however, it brings in its train, leading the way
itself.

23 (1) There can be no doubt that this residence of the human
race is regulated by the sun and the moon in their alternating
courses. The heat of the one brings bodies to life and softens the
ground, checks any excess of water and breaks the grimness of
winter that holds all in its grasp. The gentler heat of the other,
effective and penetrating, controls the ripening of fruit, while its
cycle is matched by that of human fertility. The sun has brought
the year into view by its revolution, while the moon with its shorter
circuits has done the same for the month. (2) But take all this
away – would not the sun be a fitting sight for the eyes, a worthy
object of veneration, simply if it passed over us? The moon would
merit our upward gaze if it merely moved as an idle star on its
way. Heaven itself, when it spreads its fires through the night and
glitters with stars innumerable, has all eyes fixed intently upon it.
Is anyone thinking, as he marvels at those things, that they are of
use to him? (3) Look at those bodies that glide in so great a
concourse above us, at how they take on the guise of an artefact
standing motionless and thus hide their speed from us! What a
multitude of actions occur in that night-time which you observe
simply for counting and dividing the days from each other! What
a throng of events unroll in this silence! What a chain of destinies
is drawn out in that defined zone[41] of heaven! (4) Those stars,
which you see simply as scattered for decoration, are each one of
them at work. There is no reason to think that only seven move
this way and that, while the rest are fixed. A few have motions

---

[41] I.e. that occupied by the signs of the zodiac.

that we can follow; but there are countless deities, further away beyond our vision,[42] that come and go; and those that do suffer our eyes to see them proceed at an imperceptible pace, driven on in secret.[43] 24 (1) Tell me, would not the sight of so great an edifice grip you, even if it did not cover you and protect you, nurture you and beget you, suffusing you with its spirit? These beings are indeed of prime value to us, necessary and vital, yet their sheer grandeur is what takes over the mind entirely.

In the same way, all virtue, especially that of a grateful mind, has much to give you, but it would not have you hold it dear for that reason. It contains something more, and is not fully understood if merely counted as something useful. (2) Suppose that you are grateful because it is in your interest to be so – does that also imply *so far as* it is in your interest? Virtue has no time for a mean admirer. You must approach with an open wallet. The ungrateful may think: 'I did want to repay. But I fear the cost and the risk. I shrink from causing offence. No, I will act instead in my own interest.' But it cannot be the same principle that produces grateful and ungrateful people. Their actions differ, and so must their objectives. The one is ungrateful, though he ought not to be, because it is his interest to be; the other is grateful, though it is not in his interest, because he ought.

25 (1) Our objective is to live according to nature and follow the example of the gods.[44] But the gods, in whatever they do, follow no principle other than that of just doing it. Or perhaps you think that they get some reward for their work in the smoke of entrails and smell of incense! (2) See the extent each day of their labours and largesse, of the fruits with which they fill the earth, the timeliness of the winds towards every coast with which they stir the sea, the sudden showers with which they soften the soil and refresh the dried channels that feed the well-springs,

[42] I.e. so far away that we cannot detect their motion.
[43] It was Stoic doctrine that all the stars, and not just the planets, are in individual motion, the so-called 'fixed' ones advancing in coordination, and that their continual and marvellously regular motion is an indication of the divine mind within them. See Cicero, *On the Nature of the Gods* II 54 f.
[44] Seneca speaks as a Stoic: 'To live in agreement with nature' had been the Stoic formulation, from the time of Zeno onwards, of the 'end' for human beings, the key to a good, well-lived life. For later Platonists, too, 'assimilation to god' was the 'end' of human life.

renewing them with nourishment filtered secretly in. And all this they do without any reward, without any advantage accruing to them. (3) That is the principle which our human reason too, if it keeps faithfully to its model, should observe: not to approach what is honourable in a mercenary spirit. We should be ashamed to put a price on a favour. We have the gods for free.

Should I knowingly do the ungrateful a favour?

26 (1) 'If you are imitating the gods, the ungrateful too will receive your favours. The sun rises on criminals too, and pirates have the seas open to them.' That raises the question of whether a good man will do a favour to an ungrateful man, knowing him to be ungrateful.[45]

Let me put in a remark here so as not to be trapped by the question. The Stoic system gives you two kinds of ingratitude. (2) One is the ingratitude of folly. A fool will also be a bad person; being bad, he will have all the vices; so he will also be ungrateful.[46] Thus all bad people, on our account, are intemperate, greedy, sensual and spiteful, not because all individual bad people are greatly and evidently possessed of these vices, but because they have the potential to be. Indeed, they are, though latently so. The other kind of ingratitude is what is commonly given the name, and is a natural propensity to the vice. (3) A person ungrateful in the first sense, who has this fault because he has every fault, will indeed be done favours by the good man. If he excluded such

---

[45] Having emphasized from the outset (I 1. 2; see also I 10. 5, etc.) that favours should be done with discrimination, with careful attention to the character and mental attitude of potential recipients, Seneca now responds to an objection from the interlocutor (still an opponent but no longer specifically an Epicurean) that this is inconsistent with the principle just enunciated (25. 3), that we ought to do all our actions in imitation of the way in which the gods as perfectly rational beings do theirs.

[46] A 'fool' is the opposite of a 'wise man': someone lacking the deep-seated, permanent understanding of how to behave that the wise man possesses. As a result everything that he does, even if it is not materially a bad action, is badly done, and he has all the vices from which the wise man, thanks to his knowledge, is exempt. Since wisdom is so rare as to be hardly encountered among human beings, virtually all of us count for the Stoics as 'fools'. With what follows compare the similar, if shorter, exposition of the same fundamental Stoic paradox at II 35. 2.

people he would have no one to do favours to. But he will not do them to the other sort, the ungrateful who defraud you of favours and have a natural inclination to do so, any more than he will entrust a defaulted debtor with money or place a deposit with one who has already disavowed several. **27** (1) A person can likewise be called timid because he is a fool; for this too goes with being a bad person, plunged as bad people are in every failing without exception. But we call people timid in the strict sense, if they are naturally given to shuddering at a mere noise. A fool has every failing, but he is not naturally prone to all of them. One may be prone to avarice, another to sensuality, a third to impudence. (2) So it is a mistake to ask the Stoics: 'does this mean that Achilles is timid? that Aristides,[47] a byword for justice, is unjust? that Fabius[48] who saved the day by his hesitation is rash? that Decius[49] fears death? that Mucius[50] is a traitor and Camillus[51] a deserter?'. We are not saying that everybody has every fault in the prominent way that particular faults stand out in some people, but simply that bad and foolish people are not free of any. We would not absolve even the rash from fear or pronounce even the prodigal to be free of avarice. (3) A man has all five senses, but not all men have eyesight like Lynceus.[52] In the same way, anyone who is a fool

---

[47] Athenian statesman and general of the early fifth century BC, subject of a biography by Plutarch. His reputation for honesty goes back to his contemporaries, perhaps partly by way of contrast with his political rival, the great Themistocles, who seems to have engineered his ostracism, in 482 BC.

[48] Fabius Cunctator: see II 7. 1 above and *On Anger* I 12. 5.

[49] Publius Decius Mus, consul in 340 BC. He was popularly believed to have ensured the Romans' victory in a battle against the Latins in Campania by dedicating himself and the enemy to the gods of the underworld and then charging into the enemy ranks to his death (see Livy, VIII 9). Probably this story involves some conflation with a somewhat similar act of his son in a later war.

[50] The legendary Gaius Mucius Cordus Scaevola, a byword for endurance. Captured after a vain attempt to kill Lars Porsenna, the Etruscan king, he showed his patriotism and contempt for physical pain by placing his hand in the fire at the altar. Before making his way into the Etruscan camp, he had notified the Senate of his intentions, so as not to be thought a deserter. See Livy, II 12.

[51] Marcus Furius Camillus, a Roman statesman and general of the early fourth century BC, credited with a 'second founding' of Rome after the Gallic invasion from northern Italy of 387/6. The tradition was that he had been exiled from Rome on charges of embezzlement, but rallied to the city's defence when the Gauls invaded, raised an army and defeated them, recovering the gold with which the Romans had futilely tried to buy them off. There is a life of him by Plutarch.

[52] One of the Argonauts in Greek mythology; his eyesight was so keen he could see through the earth.

has all the vices without their being so fierce and inflamed as some are in some people. Every vice can be found in everyone, but not all vices stand out in particular individuals. One person may have a natural drive to avarice; others may be given to wine or lust or, if not yet given that way, so formed that their characters will take them in that direction.

(4) And so, to get back to the question, everyone is ungrateful, if he is bad, since he has in him every germ of evil. 'Ungrateful', however, is strictly the name for someone with a tendency to this vice; and this kind of person will not receive any favours from me. (5) You are not taking care of your daughter if you marry her to a brute with several divorces behind him. It is a poor head of a household who puts his inheritance in the care of a man condemned for mismanagement. It is sheer madness to make a will entrusting your son to the guardianship of one who despoils his charges. In the same way, it will rank as the worst sort of benefaction to select the ungrateful as recipients of favours which will then go to waste.

28 (1) 'Yet even the gods bestow much on the ungrateful.' But they designed it for the good. It just happened to fall to the bad as well, because they cannot be segregated. And it is better to help the bad too on account of the good than to fail the good on account of the bad. So the things to which you refer – the day, the sun, the cycle of winter and summer, the median temperature of spring and autumn, the showers and water filling the springs, the winds that blow regularly – were devised for the benefit of all. Individual exceptions were not possible. (2) A monarch gives honours to those who deserve them; he distributes his largesse even to those who do not. Grain from the state goes to thieves, perjurors, adulterers, indeed – without any moral discrimination – to anyone on the civic register; and anything else handed out on the basis of citizenship rather than virtue is shared alike by the good and the bad. (3) God, too, has given some things as a present to the entire human race, excluding no one. It would not be possible for the same wind to favour the good and go against the bad; it was for the common good that the sea was opened up for trade and the domain of the human race was widened; and there could hardly be a law forbidding the rain to fall on the fields of the bad and unprincipled. (4) Some things are on common ground. Cities are founded for the good and the bad alike; works of genius, even if they are going to meet with unworthy readers, are edited and published; medicine shows its power even on criminals; and no one has banned the mixing of wholesome drugs in case they should heal the unworthy. (5) Assessment and personal evaluation are needed for special gifts awarded on merit, not for those that are open without distinction to the crowd. There is a great difference between not excluding someone and actually choosing him. Even a thief has his rights; even murderers enjoy the blessings of peace; even those who plunder others can recover what is their own; assassins and those who use weapons on home territory still have the city wall to defend them from enemy forces. The laws extend their protection to those who break them the most. (6) Some things could not fall to particular people without being given to everyone. You cannot argue about things which are offered to us *en masse*. It is only where I can decide whether a thing should go to some particular person, that I shall refuse to give to one whom I know to be ungrateful.

29 (1) 'Does that mean that you will not give an ungrateful man advice if he consults you, or let him draw water and show him the way if he has lost it?[53] Or is it that you will do this, but will not make him a gift?' I shall draw a distinction here, or at least try to do so. (2) A favour is a useful service, but not every useful service is a favour. Some are too slight for the name. Two things must come together to make up a favour. Firstly, a certain importance, since there are things which do not measure up to the standards for this name. No one ever uses the word 'favour' to describe a slice of bread, or a copper coin tossed to a beggar, or permission to light a fire. And yet there are times when these are of more use than the greatest services. But their sheer triviality, even when circumstances make them necessary, lowers their value. (3) Secondly, and this is very important, I must further be acting for the sake of the person for whom the favour is destined, I must judge him worthy and be glad to bestow it, deriving joy from the gift that I make – none of which occurs in the cases under discussion. If we bestow anything, it is not as though they deserve

---

[53] In Stoic theory, these are examples of the minimum by way of altruism that one human being owes another on account of their 'common humanity'. Compare *Letters* 95. 51; Cicero, *On Duties* I 51–2, III 51–3.

it; we do it carelessly as though it did not matter – not a gift to the man, but to humanity.[54]

30 (1) At times, even the undeserving are going to be given things by me – I shall not deny it – as homage to others, in the same way that, in the pursuit of public honours, some highly infamous men thanks to noble birth take the lead over men of diligence but no birth at all. And not without reason. There is something holy about the memory of great excellence, and more people will delight in being good, if they know that the influence of good men outlives them. (2) What made Cicero's son a consul if not his father?[55] More recently, what took Cinna to the consulate from the enemy camp,[56] as well as Sextus Pompeius[57] and other Pompeians,[58] was simply the greatness of one man, a greatness formerly such that his very fall was enough to raise all his clan. What made Fabius Persicus, a man whose kiss the shameless themselves found offensive, a priest in more than one college? The Verrucosi and Allobrogici and that three hundred who for their country set their one household to stop the invading foe.[59] (3) We

---

[54] Having stated at 28. 6 that he will not on principle give to a known ingrate, Seneca asks at the beginning of this paragraph whether this means that he will do nothing at all to aid him, or only that he will not make him any actual gift. He begins his reply by explaining what is involved in real giving, that is, in really doing a favour (*beneficium dare*). Trivial acts of common decency to known ingrates (giving directions when asked, etc.) are not favours and so are not excluded by his principle. He will do those. Now, in 30. 1, he goes on to explain that in fact his principle has an exception, that in some cases he will go further, and 'make a gift' to an ingrate.

[55] Cicero's dissolute son, also named Marcus Tullius, was consul with Octavian (Augustus) in 30 BC, and in fact had a not undistinguished public career as military officer and senior administrator in the near east. See also *On Mercy* I 10. 1.

[56] On Gnaeus Cornelius Cinna Magnus, consul in AD 5 and a grandson of Pompey the Great (d. 48 BC), see *On Mercy* I 9.

[57] Probably Sextus Pompeius, consul in AD 14 (see Tacitus, *Annals* XVII 2), a friend of Ovid's (see *Epistles from Pontus* IV 5).

[58] These included Sextus Pompeius, consul in 35 B.C, nephew of Pompey the Great, a nonentity not to be confused with his cousin of the same name (see previous note).

[59] On Paullus Fabius Persicus, consul in AD 34, see also II 21. 5. He belonged to the famous family of Fabii, whose numbers had included Hannibal's great opponent Quintus Fabius Maximus Verrucosus (see II 7. 1 and IV 27. 2 above and *On Anger* I 11) and Quintus Fabius Maximus Allobrogicus, a name earned for subduing the Allobrogi, a tribe in Transalpine Gaul, in 121 BC. Legend had it that in 477 BC. the whole clan but one, 306 in number, had fallen in battle against the city of Veii. See Livy, II 46–50.

owe it to excellence that we cherish it, not only in its presence, but when it is taken from our sight. Just as it served to help us for more than one generation, leaving its benefactions to survive it, so too our gratitude should last more than one generation. One person may have fathered great men; he deserves our favours, whatever he may himself be like, having given us men that do. (4) Another has famous ancestors; whatever he is like himself, he can take cover under their shadow. Dingy places gleam in reflected sunlight. The useless can glitter in the light of their ancestors.

31 (1) At this point, dear Liberalis, I wish to offer you a defence of the gods. From time to time we are given to saying things like: 'What did providence mean by putting Arrhidaeus[60] on the throne?' So you think that *he* was given the throne? No. It was a gift for his father and for his brother. (2) 'Why did it put Gaius Caesar[61] in charge of the world, that greediest of men for human blood? He would order it to be shed in his sight as though he was going to swallow it!' So you think that he was given the empire? No. It was a gift for his father Germanicus, for his grandfather and great-grandfather,[62] and for men before them no less distinguished even if they led the life of a private citizen like any other.[63] (3) When you[64] made Mamercus Scaurus consul, did

---

[60] On the death of his half-brother Alexander the Great in 323 BC, Philip Arrhidaeus became king Philip III of Macedon (jointly with Alexander's posthumously born son, Alexander IV). Mentally defective, he was murdered in 317 BC by Alexander's mother, Olympias, who wanted her grandson to be sole king.

[61] I.e. Caligula.

[62] I.e. Drusus and Augustus. Caligula's father, Germanicus (15 BC–AD 19), a successful military commander popular with the people of Rome, had married Agrippina, Augustus' granddaughter. Germanicus' father, Nero Claudius Drusus (38–9 BC), himself a stepson of Augustus and brother of the emperor Tiberius, had been a distinguished general whose exploits in Germany had earned him and his descendants the surname of Germanicus.

[63] Tiberius and Drusus came from the distinguished patrician family of the Claudii, several of whom had been prominent in the history of the Roman Republic.

[64] Here and at the end of the paragraph, if the text is right, Seneca is addressing Providence itself, without making clear the change in addressee from Liberalis. Alternatively, as Lipsius suggests, one might read something like *'Quid?* Tum *cum Mamercum Scaurum consulem* faceret, ignorabat ... ', 'when *it* made Mamercus consul, did *it* not know ...?' Or perhaps the passage was never properly revised. As it stands, it suggests that, forty years earlier, Liberalis himself had played a part in Mamercus' election, whereas in fact the consuls were nominated by the emperor.

you not know that he used to catch the menstrual discharges of his maid-servants in his open mouth? Did he make any secret of it? Did he want even to seem decent? I can tell you a remark of his against himself – I remember its going the rounds and being cited in his presence. (4) To Annius Pollio[65] who was lying down, he had declared, in obscene language, his intention of doing something which he would rather have had done to himself. When he saw Pollio frown, he added, 'Have I said something bad? If I have, may it fall on my own head!' He used to recount this witticism himself. (5) Have you really admitted a man of such open obscenity to the fasces and the seat of justice? But of course . . . you must be thinking of grand old Scaurus, the leader of the Senate! You are outraged to see his descendant brought low.[66]

32 (1) It is probable that the gods do the same. They show a greater indulgence to some for the sake of their parents and grandparents, to others for qualities yet to come in their grandchildren, their great-grandchildren and the long succession of their descendants. For they know the chain of events, they know everything that is to pass through their hands; and the knowledge is clearly before them all the time, whereas it takes us by surprise. What we see as sudden comes to them foreseen and familiar.

(2) 'Let these men[67] be kings,' <they say,> 'since their forebears were not; putting justice and restraint on a par with supreme power, they gave themselves to the commonwealth, not the commonwealth to themselves. Let these men reign, since a good man was once their ancestor, a man with a soul superior to fortune, a man who at a time of civil strife, for the good of the commonwealth, preferred personal defeat to victory.[68] To repay him in person after this length of time has

65 Gaius Annius Pollio, consul AD 21/2, accused of *lèse majesté* in AD 32 (Tacitus, *Annals* VI 9. 3).
66 Mamercus Aemilius Scaurus, from the noble family of the Aemilii, was consul in AD 21, under the emperor Tiberius. An orator and poet of scandalous behaviour, he was indicted for *lèse majesté* and committed suicide in AD 34 (see Tacitus, *Annals* VI 29. 4). His ancestor, Marcus Aemilius Scaurus, mentioned by Seneca just below, consul in 115 BC, had been a vastly powerful leader of the Senate and established the family's reputation.
67 Probably Caligula and Claudius, unworthy members of the Claudian family.
68 Perhaps Tiberius Claudius Nero (father of the emperor Tiberius, grandfather of Claudius and great-grandfather of Caligula), who had fought on Antony's side but submitted to Augustus, even divorcing his wife, Livia, to let her marry him.

not proved possible. In his honour let this man here hold the presidency – not because he has the knowledge or ability to do so, but because another has earned it for him. (3) This person's body is misshapen, his appearance disgusting.[69] He will expose his regalia to ridicule, and people will blame me, calling me blind and rash, ignorant of where to allocate what is owed to the greatest and loftiest. But I know that it is someone else to whom I am granting it, someone else to whom I am repaying an old debt. (4) How could *they* know that man who once was keenest to flee the glory that followed him,[70] who went out to danger wearing the look that others wear when they come back from it, who identified his own with the public good? "And where is that man?" you ask, "And who is he?" How are you to know? The accounts are for me to check. I know what I owe to whom. Some I repay in the long term, some in advance, as the occasion and the resources of my commonwealth allow.'[71]

There are times, therefore, when I will give things to the ungrateful, but not for their sakes.

What do I do if I cannot be sure of the person?

33 (1) 'But tell me. If you do not know whether he is grateful or ungrateful, will you wait till you do know? Or will you just seize the chance to do a favour? The wait will be long (as Plato says, the human mind is a hard thing to guess),[72] but not to wait would be rash. (2) Our answer to this will be that we never wait for absolute certainty, since the truth is hard to ascertain. We just follow probability. That is how everything that has to be done gets

---

[69] The emperor Claudius.

[70] Perhaps Gaius Claudius Nero (consul 207 BC), who defeated and killed Hannibal's brother Hasdrubal at Metaurus in 207 BC but modestly allowed his colleague and former enemy Marcus Livius Salinator to celebrate the subsequent triumph. See Livy, XXVII 9, Valerius Maximus, IV 1.9.

[71] The last sentence of this speech alludes to the Stoic theory that each human being is primarily a citizen of the vast cosmic commonwealth constituted by god and all other rational beings. See *On the Private Life*, Chapter 4.

[72] Nothing in Plato's writings corresponds exactly to this rather trite maxim, though *Alcibiades* 133e and *Epistle* VII 342d–e, 343e and 344a have been suggested, implausibly, as its source.

done.[73] That is our principle in sowing, in sailing, in going to war, in marrying or having children. The outcome of all these is uncertain. We embark on projects where we believe our hopes to be good. No one will guarantee you a harvest if you are sowing, or a haven if you put out to sea, or victory in war; no one will guarantee that your wife will be chaste or your children dutiful. We go where reason, not truth, has drawn us. (3) Wait till you are absolutely sure of success, acknowledge nothing if its truth has not been ascertained, and all action will be abandoned, life will come to a standstill. Probability, not truth, is what drives me to this or that; and I shall do a person a favour if it is probable that he will be grateful.

34 (1) 'But so much can happen that allows a bad person to slip into favour in place of a good, and makes the good instead of the bad person seem objectionable. Appearances, which are what we put our trust in, are deceptive.' Yes, of course. But I can find no other guide for my thought. They are the traces for me to follow in search of truth; I have nothing more definite. I shall try to examine them as carefully as possible, and I shall not be quick to give them my assent. (2) The same thing can happen in battle. My weapon may be aimed at a fellow-soldier through some mistake, and the enemy may be spared as though he were on my side. But this happens seldom and is not my fault. My purpose was to strike the enemy and protect my fellow-citizen. So if I know a person to be ungrateful, I shall not do him a favour. But suppose he has crept in and insinuated himself. I am not to blame in bestowing it on him. I did it on the assumption that he would be grateful.

(3) 'Suppose that you have promised to do a favour and then come to know that the person is ungrateful, will you do it or not? To do it knowingly is wrong, since you are giving to one to whom you should not be giving. But not to do it is also wrong; you are failing to give what you promised him. At this point, your Stoic

---

[73] The Stoic philosopher Sphaerus once was tricked into taking a bite out of a waxen pomegranate – apparently with the false belief that it was real. No, he replied: I assented to the proposition, not that it was a pomegranate, but that it was probable that it was. And that was true (Diogenes Laertius, VII 177). On the standard Stoic definition, an 'appropriate' act (καθῆκον, *officium*) – the right thing to do at any given time – is 'that which, when done, has a "probable" defence' (Diogenes Laertius, VII 107; Cicero, *On Ends* III 58).

firmness[74] falters, along with its proud claim that the wise man never regrets an action, never corrects what he has done or changes him mind.' (4) No, the wise man does not change his mind, if all the circumstances remain the same as they were when he made it up. The reason why no regret ever comes over him is that nothing could have been done better at the time than in fact was done, no better decision reached than was reached. Besides, he approaches everything with a reservation: '. . . if nothing occurs to get in the way'. That is why we say that everything turns out successfully for him, that nothing happens contrary to his expectation. He has assumed in advance that something could occur to thwart his designs. (5) Only the thoughtless have this confidence that fortune has given them a guarantee. The wise man reflects on both its aspects. He knows the scope for error, the uncertainty of human afairs, the numerous obstacles in the way of any plans. He follows with detachment the unsure, slippery course of things. With a certainty of plan, he weighs up the uncertainty of events. The reservation which accompanies all his designs and undertakings protects him here as well.[75]

35 (1) I promised the favour – unless some good reason occurred to forbid my doing it. What if my country were to demand for itself what I had promised him? What if a law were passed forbidding anyone to do what I promised my friend to do? I may have promised you my daughter in marriage, only for it to turn out that you were a foreigner, while I am barred from intermarriage with aliens. The very prohibition is my defence. (2) I am breaching my trust and opening myself to the charge of fickleness, if and only if everything is the same as it was when I made the promise

---

[74] Reading, with Lipsius, *constantia*. The firmness of the Stoic wise man, in particular his indifference to injury or insult, is the theme of Seneca's *On the Wise Man's Constancy*.

[75] The wise man's constancy in the face of fortune is assisted by 'reservation' (*exceptio*, ὑπεξαίρεσις) towards it. By accepting and making allowance for the fact that circumstances (morally neutral, though some of them may be preferable to others) are not entirely in his control, he can at least control his (morally all-important) response to them. This was a doctrine of some prominence in later Stoicism, for example in Epictetus (*Manual* 2. 2) and Marcus Aurelius (IV 1. 2, V 20. 2, VIII 41. 4, XI 37). A psychological technique closely related to 'reservation' was the *praemeditatio*, the 'meditation in advance' of evils that may befall one, so as to prevent their catching one unawares and improperly affecting one's mind. *On Anger* II 10. 7 is an example of such a meditation.

and I still fail to keep it. Otherwise, any change gives me the freedom to make a fresh decision, freeing me from my obligation. Suppose that I promised my support in court, and it then turned out that the case was intended to set a precedent against my own father; or that I have promised to travel abroad with you, and reports arrive of brigands infesting the route; or that I was on the the point of coming to the scene of action, but was detained by my son's illness[76] or my wife's confinement. (3) Everything must be the same as it was when I made the promise, if you are to hold me to it. But what greater change could there be than discovering you to be a bad and ungrateful person? Whatever I gave on the assumption that you were worthy of it, I shall refuse you if you are not. What is more, I shall have reason to be angry at the deception.

36 (1) But I shall also examine the importance of the matter at issue. The amount of the sum promised will suggest what I should do. If it is small, I shall give it, not because you deserve it but because I promised;[77] nor shall I be making a gift of it, but paying the price of my own words. I shall be boxing my own ears; I shall castigate myself by the loss for my rashness in making the promise: 'Here you are! I hope it hurts you and teaches you to talk more carefully in future!' (2) As our phrase has it, I shall be paying for my language. If, however, the sum is greater, I shall not allow myself, as Maecenas[78] puts it, to be punished to the tune of ten million sesterces. I shall put the two things side by side. There is some value in holding fast to your promise. On the other hand, there is considerable value in not doing a favour to damage[79] yourself. But how serious is the damage? If it is slight, we can turn a blind eye to it. If, however, it is going to mean considerable loss or embarrassment to me, I would rather make my excuses once for refusing than forever after for having been generous. It

---

[76] Seneca is possibly recalling Cicero (*On Duties* I 32) who cites the same case as an example of when it would be right to go back on a promise.

[77] In which case, on the two principles put forward at 29. 2–3, I will not be doing you a favour at all.

[78] Gaius Maecenas (d. 8 BC), proverbial for his wealth and liberality, was a trusted friend and diplomatic representative of Octavian (Augustus). He was famous for his generous and influential patronage of literary figures, including Vergil, Horace and Propertius.

[79] Reading with Préchac, *ne* in te *beneficium des*.

all comes down to the value I put on the exact words of my promise. (3) Nor shall I merely hold back what I was rash to promise. If I gave anything I was wrong to give, I shall demand it back. It is crazy to treat a blunder as a solemn obligation.

37 (1) Philip, king of Macedonia, had a soldier who was brave in battle and had proved his worth in several actions.[80] More than once, he had granted the man some of the booty, thus inflaming his covetousness by repeated remunerations. The man found himself cast in a shipwreck on to land belonging to a certain Macedonian who, upon receiving the news, ran up to him, resuscitated him, transferred him to his house, relinquished his own bed to him, brought him round from a state of weakness and virtual death, looked after him for thirty days at his own expense, restored him to strength and provided him with journey-money, being told more than once: 'I will repay you, if only I manage to see my general.' (2) He did tell Philip about his shipwreck, but not about the help which he had been given; and he promptly asked to be granted a certain person's property. That person was his host, the very man who had taken him in and restored him to health. Monarchs from time to time, especially in war, make many grants with their eyes closed. 'A righteous man is no match for so many appetites in armour. No one can simultaneously act the good man and the good general. How are so many thousand insatiable men to be satisfied? What can they get, if each is to get what is his?' (3) That is what Philip told himself, as he ordered the man to be put in possession of the property he asked for. Its owner was driven off. But he did not bear the wrong in silence like a peasant happy not to be included himself in the grant. Instead, he wrote Philip a terse and frank letter, and Philip flared up with anger on reading it. He at once ordered Pausanias[81] to restore the property to its former owner and, further, to take that most rascally of soldiers, most ungrateful of guests, most rapacious of castaways, and brand him with a tattoo saying 'ingrate'. (4) Indeed, he deserved to have the letters not just branded but carved onto him, having driven his host like a naked castaway onto the very shore where he himself had lain shipwrecked. (5) But the proper limit of punishment in

---

[80] Seneca's source for this story is unknown; it appears in no other ancient author.
[81] Who later assassinated him. See Plutarch, *Life of Alexander* 10. 4.

his case is another question. At all events, he had to be deprived of what he had seized by unparalleled villainy. Yet who would be moved by his punishment? After such a crime, no one with any sense of pity could feel pity for him.

38 (1) Is Philip to give it, do you think, just because he promised? Even if he ought not to, even if it means doing a wrong and committing a crime, even if this one deed will serve to deny any castaway the shore? There is no fickleness about abandoning what you have recognized and condemned as a mistake. You have to be frank and admit, 'This was not what I thought. I was misled.' On the other hand, it is sheer obstinacy of arrogant folly to declare, 'What I have once said, whatever it is, stays fixed and authoritative.' (2) There is no disgrace in changing your mind when the facts change. Suppose that Philip had left the man in possession of the coast which he had gained by his shipwreck; that would have been to ban all human kindness to the unfortunate?[82] 'It would be better', he might say, 'within the boundaries of my kingdom for you to carry around with you on your shameless forehead these letters to be inscribed for the eyes of all. Go, display the sacredness of hospitality. Show this verdict on your face for all to read, so that shelter to the unfortunate may never prove fatal. In this way my enactment will be more authoritative than if I had engraved it on bronze.'

39 (1) 'Then why did your Zeno, having promised to lend a person five hundred denarii and having found him to be insolvent, despite the fact that his friends urged him not to make it, go through with the loan because he had promised it?'[83] (2) In the first place, a loan works differently from a favour. Even a bad loan can be called in. I can issue the debtor with a summons and, if he goes bankrupt, get my share. If a favour is lost, it goes altogether and at once.[84] Moreover, this loss is a moral failure, whereas a bad debt means simply a failure of management. Besides, not even

---

[82] The Latin says literally, 'would he not have banned all unfortunates from fire and water?' These represent the minimum of 'common humanity' that one human being can expect from another when in dire need (see 29. 1 above). By leaving the soldier in possession of the property, Seneca suggests, Philip would have given everyone reason to fear a similar loss, thus putting an end to such common decencies.

[83] Von Arnim prints this story as *SVF* 1 16.

[84] Compare IV 12.1, where a favour was described as 'a loan that cannot be repaid'.

Zeno, had the sum been larger, would have gone through with the loan. It was only five hundred denarii – a sum, as the common phrase has it, 'to be spent on a foible.'[85] It was worth that much not to go back on his promise. (3) I shall go out to dinner because I have promised, even if it is cold – but not if it is snowing. I shall get up to go to an engagement party because I have promised, though I may have indigestion – but not if I have a fever. I shall go down to act as guarantor because I have promised – but not if you are asking me to guarantee an unspecified sum or undertake a debt to the public account.[86] (4) Implicit, as I say, is the tacit reservation: 'if I can', 'if I ought to', 'if things remain as they are'. See that the situation is the same when you exact performance as it was when I made the promise. Default will then mean fickleness. But if anything new crops up, are you surprised that a change to the circumstances of my promise should lead me to change my mind? Make everything the same for me, and I will stay the same. We give bail, but not everyone who jumps his bail is liable to suit: defaulters can plead *force majeure*.

Should gratitude always be shown and favours always returned?

40 (1) You can expect the same answer to the further question of whether *gratitude* should be shown in every case and whether a favour should always be returned: I am obliged to be grateful in my mind, but there are times when repayment is prevented either by my own ill-fortune or by the good fortune of the person to who I am obliged. (2) What return can I make to a king or to a rich man, if I am poor, especially when there are some who think it an injury to be done a favour and are constantly piling one favour on top of another? What more can I do in their case than

---

[85] Seneca clearly moved in wealthy circles. In his day, 500 denarii (= 2,000 sesterces) would have been worth something like £2,000 sterling or US $3,000 in 1994. A legionary soldier was paid 250 denarii *per annum*, with deductions for clothing, fodder, etc.

[86] I.e. to be your surety in a public contract. All contractors with the state – e.g. for building works or military supplies – had to give guarantees for their contracts, pledging property themselves and getting others to do so (see Crook, p. 244). The huge security demanded for some public contracts would be way beyond the means of all but the wealthiest individuals.

just wish to make a return? Nor should I refuse a fresh favour simply because I have not yet returned its predecessor. I shall accept it as gladly as it is given and provide my friend with ample scope for exercising his kindness. Unwillingness to accept new favours implies discontent with those already accepted. (3) If I fail to show my gratitude, so what? The delay is not my fault, if I do not have the opportunity or the means. He bestowed it on me, you see, because he did have the opportunity and the means. Is he a good or a bad man? If he is good, my case will be accepted by him as good; if he is bad, I shall have nothing to do with him. (4) Nor, in my judgment, should we rush to show our gratitude, when it is against the wishes of those to whom we are showing it, or to press it upon them as they shrink back. You are not showing gratitude by giving back what you were glad to get, when he does not want it back. There are people who, when some tiny gift has been sent to them, promptly and inopportunely send something else back and thus demonstrate that they are under no obligation. But that is a kind of rejection – to send something at once in return and cancel out the one gift with another. (5) There are even times when I shall not return a favour though I could. When? If the loss to me outweighs the benefit to him, if he is not going to notice any gain on receiving what it has caused me great loss to give in return. Anyone in a hurry to repay at all costs has the attitude not of a grateful person but of a debtor. To put it briefly, anyone too keen to pay off is unwilling to be indebted; and anyone unwilling to be indebted is ungrateful.

Biographical Notes

Few of the people whom Seneca cites from recent or not so recent history make more than a single appearance in the essays of this volume. The following notes are confined to the more important of those who do. (The rest are identified in footnotes as they appear.) Their number is made up largely of emperors, other potentates and philosophers.

Seneca writes as moralist, not as biographer or historian, discussing figures from history purely as examples. But his references do indicate how these figures could be regarded in his time.

Alexander the Great (356–323 BC), king of Macedon, conqueror of the Persian empire and role-model for conquerors ever since, established the exalted, oriental style of monarchy in the Hellenistic world. He has a mixed press in Seneca. Commended for his steadfast loyalty towards one friend (*On Anger* II 23. 2), he is damned for his murderous rage towards others (III 17. I f., 23. I). Mocked for his megalomania (*On Favours* I 13, II 16), he stands contrasted with the true, selfless hero Hercules (*On Favours* I 13. I).

Aristotle (384–322 BC), the greatest of Plato's pupils, founded his own school, the Lyceum or Peripatos (after which his followers were called 'Peripatetics'). A tutor of Alexander's (*On Anger* III 17. I), he had to flee Athens on Alexander's death (*On the Private Life* 8. 2). While more or less accepting his definition of anger (*On Anger* I 3. 3), Seneca attacks him for approving of the emotion (*On Anger* I 9. 2, III 3. I).

Augustus (63 BC–AD 14), first emperor of Rome, began life as Gaius Octavius, the son of Gaius Octavius, a Roman knight, who died in 59 BC, and of Atia, niece of the dictator Julius Caesar, who adopted him and made him his chief heir. Recognized as Caesar's adopted son after Caesar's assassination in 44 BC, he took the name of Gaius Julius Caesar Octavianus. Over the following years, he gradually and ruthlessly assumed supreme military and civil power, receiving in 27 BC the title Augustus, a religious term meaning 'venerable'. His accession brought to an end a century of anarchy, civil wars and military tyranny at Rome. Already elevated in his lifetime by Vergil and Horace to superhuman standing as saviour of the city and sponsor of universal peace, he was proclaimed a god by the Senate after his death. Seneca follows in this tradition. Though candid about the bloodletting at the start of his career (*On Mercy* I 11. 1), he holds up 'our deified Augustus' as the model of what a prince ought to be – merciful (*On Mercy* I 9–11), mild (*On Anger* III 23. 4–8, *On Favours* II 25. 1, III 27) and unassuming (*On Mercy* I 15).

Caligula ('Baby Boots'), properly Gaius Julius Caesar Germanicus (AD 12–41), so nicknamed by legionnaires in Germany as an infant, succeeded his great-uncle Tiberius as Roman emperor from 37 to 41. After an autocratic, capricious and cruel reign of less than four years he was murdered with the connivance of his personal staff and palace guards. His bizarre behaviour led many (including Suetonius) to conclude that was mad. He serves for Seneca as a paradigm of all that a supreme ruler ought not to be; for examples of his arrogance and cruelty see *On Anger* I 20. 7–9, II 33. 2–6, III 18. 3–19. 5; and *On Favours* II 12, IV 31. 2.

Cato, Marcus Porcius Cato the Younger (94–46 BC), republican hero and implacable opponent of Julius Caesar, ranked as the nearest thing that Rome had produced to a Stoic wise man. Having made him the starting-point of his whole treatise *On the Wise Man's Constancy*, Seneca cites him in *On Anger* for his unruffled magnanimity (II 32. 2 f.) and imperturbable wit (III 38. 2).

Chrysippus of Soli in south-eastern Asia Minor (c. 280–207 BC), was the third and greatest head of the Stoa. A convert to Stoicism, he elaborated and defended the Stoic system, largely to meet the criticisms of the sceptic Arcesilaus, with unsurpassed energy and success. 'Orthodox' Stoic philosophy came to mean Stoicism in the form which he gave it. Chrysippus' voluminous writings have not survived, apart from fragments – reports, discussions and verbatim quotations in later authors – of varying trustworthiness. His treatise *On Emotions* was one of Seneca's models for *On Anger*. But Seneca shows his independence by citing and criticizing Chrysippus in *On the Private Life* (8) and *On Favours*, (I 3. 8–4. 6).

Claudius, properly Tiberius Claudius Nero Germanicus (10 BC–AD 54), reigned from AD 41 till his murder in 54. Seneca, who had spent eight years of that reign in exile, mentions or alludes to him, in essays written when he was safely dead, for his counter-productive cruelty (*On Mercy* I 23. 1), his dubious powers of judgment (*On Favours* I 15. 1) and a personal gaucheness enough to cast doubt on the wisdom of providence in placing him on the throne (IV 32. 3).

Epicurus (341–270 BC), born in the eastern Aegean island of Samos to Athenian parents, had espoused as a young man the 'atomist' theory of Democritus that matter can be entirely reduced to atoms and void. He became its best-known exponent, combining it with a thorough-going ethical hedonism. From about 307/6 he worked in Athens, competing with Zeno for pupils – the traditional rivalry between Epicureans and Stoics goes back to this time. Most of his writings have perished apart from fragments and three philosophical letters (preserved in Diogenes Laertius, Book X) summarizing his physics, meteorology and ethical theory. Seneca, while uncompromisingly critical of Epicurus' ethics and theology (notably in *On Favours* IV 1–25) and contemptuous of his school (see IV 2. 1, 13. 1, 16), is quite willing to draw on him (*On Favours* III 4. 1) for points useful to his own argument, or to claim that the Epicureans think the same as the Stoics, though on divergent grounds – for instance, on the eligibility of a private life (*On the Private Life* 3. 2) or the exellence of mercy (*On Mercy* I 3. 2).

Gaius Julius Caesar (100–44 BC) went down into history as the man who swept away the Roman republic and set up a monarchy in its place. In our texts, Seneca barely mentions this achievement (except perhaps at *On Mercy* I 1. 6). While condemning Caesar's assassination as a political misjudgment (*On Favours* II 20. 2 f.), he is more concerned with the personal motives – disappointed expectations – of the assassins (*On Anger* III 30. 4 f.), and pays tribute to Caesar's clemency to the defeated followers of Pompey (*On Anger* II 23. 4).

Plato (c. 428–348 BC), the great philosopher and founder of the Academy, is quoted by Seneca in these essays simply for his enlightened utterances on punishment (*On Anger* I 6. 5, 19. 7) and for a remark about the opacity of the human heart (*On Favours* IV 33. 1). A subject in anecdotes to do with freedom from anger (*On Anger* II 21. 10, III 12. 5), he is cited, along with Socrates and Xenophon, as an example of a son more famous than his father (*On Favours* III 32. 3).

Pompey the Great, Gaius Pompeius Magnus (106–48 BC), dynast and leader of the senatorial forces defeated by Caesar at Pharsalus in 48 BC, ranks no higher than his opponent in Seneca's judgment: he was not the champion of liberty – the question was simply 'to which of the two men the Romans were to be slaves' (*On Favours* II 20. 2). Elsewhere he appears, along with Cicero and Fabius Maximus, as a great man whose great name has profited his descendants (*On Mercy* I 9. 3; *On Favours* IV 30. 2), while his murder is one of those horrific events which arouse involuntarily a semblance of anger in those who read of them (*On Anger* II 2. 3).

Socrates (469–399 BC), the famous philosopher, known to us primarily through the dialogues of Plato and the Socratic writings of Xenophon – both of them had been among his young companions in philosophical discussion, mostly on ethics and politics – was condemned to death by an Athenian jury on charges of impiety. He left no writings. The Stoics, who saw their own ethical theory as a revival and continuation of his ideas, revered him as the paradigm of a 'wise man', perhaps the only one who ever lived; and it is as a model of temper under control (*On Anger* I 15. 3, III 13. 3), of imperviousness to provocation (III 11. 2) and calmly consistent deportment (II 7. 1) that Seneca brings him on stage. In *On Favours* his nobility is featured in an anecdote about generosity (I 8–9. 1) and he is cited, along with Plato and Xenophon, as an example of a son more famous than his father (III 32. 3).

Sulla, properly Lucius Cornelius Sulla Felix (138–78 BC), ruthless military commander and, for a time, elected dictator at Rome, is recalled by Seneca not for his political achievements in temporarily re-establishing the dominance of the Senate, but simply for a cruelty – shown in his proscriptions (*On Anger* II 2. 3), in his disenfranchising the children of the proscribed (II 34. 3), in the execution of Marcus Marius (III 18. 1) – which made him no better than a tyrant (*On Mercy* I 12. 1).

Tiberius, properly Tiberius Julius Caesar Augustus (42 BC–AD 37) succeeded Augustus in 14 AD. The early years of his principate were remembered as a time of good government (*On Mercy* I 1. 6). Later, it turned into a reign of terror with numerous trials for treason. These form the background to the story at *On Favours* III 26. Seneca also notes Tiberius' (calculated) ungraciousness in doing a favour (*On Favours* II 7. 2–3), but reserves his spleen for the next two emperors, Caligula and Claudius.

Zeno of Citium in Cyprus (335–263 BC) founded the Stoic school of philosophy. Having first come to Athens in 313 BC, he went on to lecture in a public portico there called the Painted Stoa – hence the school's name. None of his works survives. Seneca invokes Zeno in *On the Private Life* (1. 4, 3. 1 f., 6. 4) as the voice of Stoicism. Elsewhere in our texts, he tells one story about him (*On Favours* IV 39. 1) and cites one remark of his (*On Anger* I 16. 7).

Index

People and Places

With a few exceptions this Index is confined to people and places mentioned in the main text, not the footnotes, of our translations and introductions. Persons also in the Biographical Notes are indicated here by an *. Philosophers treated further in the Subject Index are marked with an †.

314

Index

315

Index

Subjects

See also Synopsis (pp. xxxiii–xxxviii)

Index

Epicurus (*see also* Epicureanism)
  calculation of pleasure and pain 179
  on public life 169, 173, 174
  gratitude to the past 244
  sees inactivity as the greatest
    happiness 275
  inconsistent piety of 288f.
equestrian status 249
examples
  of anger suppressed by fear 71f.,
    90–3
  of anger in potentates 93–8
  of anger well controlled 71f., 90–3,
    98–100
  of favours done by slaves to their
    masters 259–62
  of mercy 138–43
  of princely civility 147f.
  of savagery 45f.
  of surpassing filial devotion 271f.
externals, moral indifference of xxii,
  202, 290, 302

faith, good 189, 252f.
'Father of the Fatherland' 146
fathers. *See* parents, sons
favours
  'this most honourable of
    competitions' 200
  defined 202
  as against: acts of common
    humanity 185, 297; favourable
    judgments 211; investments 189f.,
    194, 217, 275; loans 196, 227,
    229, 239, 246, 282f., 306; duties
    and menial services 255; trivial
    kindnesses 185, 258, 297f.; their
    vehicle 184f., 201f., 239f.
  cannot be exactly evaluated 185,
    248f., 250
  immediate reward of 195, 238f.
  moral beauty of 285
  may sometimes be done to the
    undeserving 206, 297f.
  must be accepted cheerfully 231–3
  must be adapted to the recipient
    221f., 222f.; and to the capacities
    of the donor 222f., 230
  must be done: graciously 194, 214,
    215–17, 218; promptly 212–14;
    with thought and judgment 193,
    195, 208, 209f.; without thought

of the return 195, 275; for their
  own sake 191, 273–94; for the
  benefit of the recipient 221, 280,
  284, 297
must be returned voluntarily 185,
  246f.
should sometimes be concealed 217
the intention is all important 203,
  284
necessary, useful or agreeable 206f.
reminders of 196, 208
repayment of 236–41
role in ancient society 186f.
fear
  'let them hate, provided that they
    fear' 39, 144, 159
  'He needs must many fear whom
    many fear' 52, 151
  cure for anger 113
  motive for desperate courage 93,
    144
fellowship (*see also* human nature)
  source of all human strength 288
  what men were born for 70, 131f.
  depends on a feeling for gratitude
    288
fools 240 294 (*see also* Stoics,
  paradoxes)
force majeure 227, 307
forgetfulness 242–5
forgiveness 126, 162f.
formula 160 n.5, 247 n.10
Forum 47, 84
fortune 83, 102, 134, 204, 257, 280,
  303
freedmen 233, 245 n.5
friends
  choice of 84
  and benefactors 227

glory, Alexander's ignorant love of
  209
god, gods
  contemplation of 175
  concepts of, Epicurean 289; Stoic
    xviif., xviii n.14 (*see also* Zeus)
  defence of 299–301
  unceasing generosity of 194, 235f.,
    275–8
  honoured by uprightness of
    worshippers 202
  a model for the prince 135, 152

320

liberty (*cont.*)
 'wanting nothing save licence' 130
 the way to 92 (*see* suicide)
litigation 18, 47f., 252f., 283 (*see also*
 Forum, wickedness)
lives, choice of 178f.
loans. *See* favours
luxury. *See* self-indulgence

man (*see also* animals, nature)
 compared with animals 21
 human solidarity xxiv, 23, 69f., 131,
 288
 medical analogy (*see also* punishment)
 130
 mentality (*see also* intention, state of
 mind) cast of mind 281
mercy (*clementia*)
 Greek words for 120
 definitions 124, 151, 160
 distinct from pity and forgiveness
 125–7, 151–4
 the royal virtue 122, 131–7, 148–50
 shown by Augustus 138–42; Nero
 124, 126f., 129, 142f., 159
 to a conquered foe 105, 153
metaphor 18 n.3, 239, 282f.
mind (*see also* emotions, reason)
 capacities of 176f., 236
 master of the body 132
 physical constituents of 58
 source of freedom 257
 transformations of 126, 160
 Stoic view of 7f.
money 108

nature
 another name for god xviii n.14,
 278
 has designed man for contemplation
 175
 has given man a feeling for virtue
 288
 has made man sociable xxi, 23
 life according to nature 175, 292
 her way of revealing herself in
 small things 150f.

oral sex 49, 299f. (*see also* wickedness)
ordinary (not wise) people xvii, xxiv,
 168
otium 168

paradoxes. *See* Stoicism
pardon (*see also* mercy, remedies:
 'make allowances') 126, 163f.
parents, legal rights of 250
parricide, punishment for 34, 148,
 154
patronage. *See* favours
pity 125f., 161–3
Plato
 Phaaedrus 25 n.23
 Republic xxv
 Timaeus xvii
 remarks on punishment 24
 views on emotions 5–8
pleasure, Stoic and Epicurean
 attitudes towards 274
power, patterns of 148, 255f.
praefectus urbi 258, n.35
praetorship 106, 234
 praetor's list 248
prince (*see also* kingship, mercy, tyrant)
 his mirror 121, 128
 viceregent of the gods 128
 duties of
 above the law 124, 129
 'head' of the commonwealth 132f.,
 133, 159
 special position of 136f.
 constantly under observation 137
 virtues of 145 (affability, 147
 (civility)
 private life
 preferred by Stoics and Epicureans
 alike 174
 as valuable as public life to
 posterity 178
probability, a sufficient motive for
 action 302
proscriptions 43, 218 n.8
promises, may have to be broken 306
public life
 Epicurean attitudes towards 174
 Stoic attitudes towards 174, 179
public office 106f., 201, 234
punishment
 gradations of 23f., 33f., 38, 146
 principles of 38, 70, 152–5
 the medical analogy 23f., 34, cf. 51,
 130
 punishing in anger 33
 heavy use of only encourages crime
 154

Index

Authors cited by Seneca

Cambridge Texts in the History of Political Thought

Titles published in the series thus far

Aristotle *The Politics and The Constitution of Athens* (edited by Stephen Everson)
0 521 48400 6 paperback
Arnold *Culture and Anarchy and other writings* (edited by Stefan Collini)
0 521 37796 x paperback
Astell *Political Writings* (edited by Patricia Springborg)
0 521 42845 9 paperback
Augustine *The City of God against the Pagans* (edited by R.W. Dyson)
0 521 46843 4 paperback
Austin *The Province of Jurisprudence Determined* (edited by Wilfrid E. Rumble)
0 521 44756 9 paperback
Bacon *The History of the Reign of King Henry VII* (edited by Brian Vickers)
0 521 58663 1 paperback
Bakunin *Statism and Anarchy* (edited by Marshall Shatz)
0 521 36973 8 paperback
Baxter *Holy Commonwealth* (edited by William Lamont)
0 521 40580 7 paperback
Bayle *Political Writings* (edited by Sally L. Jenkinson)
0 521 47677 1 paperback
Beccaria *On Crimes and Punishments and other writings* (edited by Richard Bellamy)
0 521 47982 7 paperback
Bentham *Fragment on Government* (introduction by Ross Harrison)
0 521 35929 5 paperback
Bernstein *The Preconditions of Socialism* (edited by Henry Tudor)
0 521 39808 8 paperback
Bodin *On Sovereignty* (edited by Julian H. Franklin)
0 521 34992 3 paperback
Bolingbroke *Political Writings* (edited by David Armitage)
0 521 58697 6 paperback
Bossuet *Politics Drawn from the Very Words of Holy Scripture*
(edited by Patrick Riley)
0 521 36807 3 paperback
The British Idealists (edited by David Boucher)
0 521 45951 6 paperback
Burke *Pre-Revolutionary Writings* (edited by Ian Harris)
0 521 36800 6 paperback
Christine De Pizan *The Book of the Body Politic* (edited by Kate Langdon Forhan)
0 521 42259 0 paperback
Cicero *On Duties* (edited by M. T. Griffin and E. M. Atkins)
0 521 34835 8 paperback
Cicero *On the Commonwealth and On the Laws* (edited by James E. G. Zetzel)
0 521 45959 1 paperback
Comte *Early Political Writings* (edited by H. S. Jones)
0 521 46923 6 paperback
Conciliarism and Papalism (edited by J. H. Burns and Thomas M. Izbicki)
0 521 47674 7 paperback
Constant *Political Writings* (edited by Biancamaria Fontana)
0 521 31632 4 paperback
Dante *Monarchy* (edited by Prue Shaw)
0 521 56781 5 paperback
Diderot *Political Writings* (edited by John Hope Mason and Robert Wokler)
0 521 36911 8 paperback

The Dutch Revolt (edited by Martin van Gelderen)
  0 521 39809 6 paperback
Early Greek Political Thought from Homer to the Sophists
(edited by Michael Gagarin and Paul Woodruff)
  0 521 43768 7 paperback
The Early Political Writings of the German Romantics
(edited by Frederick C. Beiser)
  0 521 44951 0 paperback
The English Levellers (edited by Andrew Sharp)
  0 521 62511 4 paperback
Erasmus *The Education of a Christian Prince* (edited by Lisa Jardine)
  0 521 58811 1 paperback
Fenelon *Telemachus* (edited by Patrick Riley)
  0 521 45662 2 paperback
Ferguson *An Essay on the History of Civil Society* (edited by Fania Oz-Salzberger)
  0 521 44736 4 paperback
Filmer *Patriarcha and Other Writings* (edited by Johann P. Sommerville)
  0 521 39903 3 paperback
Fletcher *Political Works* (edited by John Robertson)
  0 521 43994 9 paperback
Sir John Fortescue *On the Laws and Governance of England*
(edited by Shelley Lockwood)
  0 521 58996 7 paperback
Fourier *The Theory of the Four Movements* (edited by Gareth Stedman Jones and
Ian Patterson)
  0 521 35693 8 paperback
Gramsci *Pre-Prison Writings* (edited by Richard Bellamy)
  0 521 42307 4 paperback
Guicciardini *Dialogue on the Government of Florence* (edited by Alison Brown)
  0 521 45623 1 paperback
Harrington *The Commonwealth of Oceana* and *A System of Politics*
(edited by J. G. A. Pocock)
  0 521 42329 5 paperback
Hegel *Elements of the Philosophy of Right* (edited by Allen W. Wood and
H. B. Nisbet)
  0 521 34888 9 paperback
Hegel *Political Writings* (edited by Laurence Dickey and H. B. Nisbet)
  0 521 45979 3 paperback
Hobbes *On the Citizen* (edited by Michael Silverthorne and Richard Tuck)
  0 521 43780 6 paperback
Hobbes *Leviathan* (edited by Richard Tuck)
  0 521 56797 1 paperback
Hobhouse *Liberalism and Other Writings* (edited by James Meadowcroft)
  0 521 43726 1 paperback
Hooker *Of the Laws of Ecclesiastical Polity* (edited by A. S. McGrade)
  0 521 37908 3 paperback
Hume *Political Essays* (edited by Knud Haakonssen)
  0 521 46639 3 paperback
King James VI and I *Political Writings* (edited by Johann P. Sommerville)
  0 521 44729 1 paperback
Jefferson *Political Writings* (edited by Joyce Appleby and Terence Ball)
  0 521 64841 6 paperback
John of Salisbury *Policraticus* (edited by Cary Nederman)
  0 521 36701 8 paperback

Kant *Political Writings* (edited by H. S. Reiss and H. B. Nisbet)
    0 521 39837 1 paperback
Knox *On Rebellion* (edited by Roger A. Mason)
    0 521 39988 2 paperback
Kropotkin *The Conquest of Bread and other writings* (edited by Marshall Shatz)
    0 521 45990 7 paperback
Lawson *Politica sacra et civilis* (edited by Conal Condren)
    0 521 39248 9 paperback
Leibniz *Political Writings* (edited by Patrick Riley)
    0 521 35899 X paperback
The Levellers (edited by Andrew Sharp)
    0 521 62511 4 paperback
Locke *Political Essays* (edited by Mark Goldie)
    0 521 47861 8 paperback
Locke *Two Treatises of Government* (edited by Peter Laslett)
    0 521 35730 6 paperback
Loyseau *A Treatise of Orders and Plain Dignities* (edited by Howell A. Lloyd)
    0 521 45624 X paperback
Luther and Calvin on Secular Authority (edited by Harro Höpfl)
    0 521 34986 9 paperback
Machiavelli *The Prince* (edited by Quentin Skinner and Russell Price)
    0 521 34993 1 paperback
de Maistre *Considerations on France* (edited by Isaiah Berlin and Richard Lebrun)
    0 521 46628 8 paperback
Malthus *An Essay on the Principle of Population* (edited by Donald Winch)
    0 521 42972 2 paperback
Marsiglio of Padua *Defensor minor* and *De translatione Imperii*
(edited by Cary Nederman)
    0 521 40846 6 paperback
Marx *Early Political Writings* (edited by Joseph O'Malley)
    0 521 34994 X paperback
Marx *Later Political Writings* (edited by Terrell Carver)
    0 521 36739 5 paperback
James Mill *Political Writings* (edited by Terence Ball)
    0 521 38748 5 paperback
J. S. Mill *On Liberty*, with *The Subjection of Women* and *Chapters on Socialism*
(edited by Stefan Collini)
    0 521 37917 2 paperback
Milton *Political Writings* (edited by Martin Dzelzainis)
    0 521 34866 8 paperback
Montesquieu *The Spirit of the Laws* (edited by Anne M. Cohler,
Basia Carolyn Miller and Harold Samuel Stone)
    0 521 36974 6 paperback
More *Utopia* (edited by George M. Logan and Robert M. Adams)
    0 521 40318 9 paperback
Morris *News from Nowhere* (edited by Krishan Kumar)
    0 521 42233 7 paperback
Nicholas of Cusa *The Catholic Concordance* (edited by Paul E. Sigmund)
    0 521 56773 4 paperback
Nietzsche *On the Genealogy of Morality* (edited by Keith Ansell-Pearson)
    0 521 40610 2 paperback
Paine *Political Writings* (edited by Bruce Kuklick)
    0 521 66799 2 paperback
Plato *The Republic* (edited by G. R. F. Ferrari and Tom Griffith)
    0 521 48443 X paperback

Plato *Statesman* (edited by Julia Annas and Robin Waterfield)
  0 521 44778 X paperback
Price *Political Writings* (edited by D. O. Thomas)
  0 521 40969 1 paperback
Priestley *Political Writings* (edited by Peter Miller)
  0 521 42561 1 paperback
Proudhon *What is Property?* (edited by Donald R. Kelley and
Bonnie G. Smith)
  0 521 40556 4 paperback
Pufendorf *On the Duty of Man and Citizen according to Natural Law*
(edited by James Tully)
  0 521 35980 5 paperback
The Radical Reformation (edited by Michael G. Baylor)
  0 521 37948 2 paperback
Rousseau *The Discourses and other early political writings*
(edited by Victor Gourevitch)
  0 521 42445 3 paperback
Rousseau *The Social Contract and other later political writings*
(edited by Victor Gourevitch)
  0 521 42446 1 paperback
Seneca *Moral and Political Essays* (edited by John Cooper and John Procope)
  0 521 34818 8 paperback
Sidney *Court Maxims* (edited by Hans W. Blom, Eco Haitsma Mulier and
Ronald Janse)
  0 521 46736 5 paperback
Sorel *Reflections on Violence* (edited by Jeremy Jennings)
  0 521 55910 3 paperback
Spencer *The Man versus the State* and *The Proper Sphere of Government* (edited by
John Offer)
  0 521 43740 7 paperback
Stirner *The Ego and Its Own* (edited by David Leopold)
  0 521 45647 9 paperback
Thoreau *Political Writings* (edited by Nancy Rosenblum)
  0 521 47675 5 paperback
Utopias of the British Enlightenment (edited by Gregory Claeys)
  0 521 45590 1 paperback
Vitoria *Political Writings* (edited by Anthony Pagden and Jeremy Lawrance)
  0 521 36714 X paperback
Voltaire *Political Writings* (edited by David Williams)
  0 521 43727 X paperback
Weber *Political Writings* (edited by Peter Lassman and Ronald Speirs)
  0 521 39719 7 paperback
William of Ockham *A Short Discourse on Tyrannical Government*
(edited by A. S. McGrade and John Kilcullen)
  0 521 35803 5 paperback
William of Ockham *A Letter to the Friars Minor and other writings*
(edited by A. S. McGrade and John Kilcullen)
  0 521 35804 3 paperback
Wollstonecraft *A Vindication of the Rights of Men* and *A Vindication of the Rights of
Woman* (edited by Sylvana Tomaselli)
  0 521 43633 8 paperback